The Fictive and
the Imaginary

The Fictive and the Imaginary

Charting Literary Anthropology

Wolfgang Iser

The Johns Hopkins University Press
Baltimore and London

The Johns Hopkins University Press
2715 North Charles Street
Baltimore, Maryland 21218-4319
The Johns Hopkins Press Ltd., London

This book was originally published as
Das Fiktive und das Imaginäre.
Perspektiven literarischer Anthropologie
© Suhrkamp Verlag Frankfurt am Main 1991

Library of Congress Cataloging-in-Publication Data
Iser, Wolfgang.
[Fiktive und das Imaginäre. English]
The fictive and the imaginary : charting literary anthropology /
Wolfgang Iser.
p.   cm.
Includes bibliographical references and index.
ISBN 0-8018-4498-3.— ISBN 0-8018-4499-1 (pbk.)
1. Fiction–History and criticism. 2. Fictions, Theory of.
3. Imagination in literature. 4. Imagination (Philosophy)
I. Title.
PN3347.I7413 1993
801'.953–dc20   92-25943

A catalog record for this book is available from the British Library.

To Lore, *non sequitur*

Contents

Preface

Literature stands in need of interpretation, for the fabrications that it verbalizes can be processed only by way of cognitive frames of reference. The techniques developed for such a purpose have now become so diversified that methods of interpretation and theories of textuality have themselves turned into objects for scrutiny. Strikingly, whatever method is in vogue seems to catch on at great speed, and then to fall with equal velocity out of favor. This is to be observed from the gamut of approaches ranging from New Criticism to Deconstruction. What they have in common is the variety of texts that are focused upon from different angles, and with different presuppositions.

The literary text has brought forth an increasingly elaborate network of hermeneutic systems to be distinguished from one another by the overriding concern that guides each approach. The literary text may be mediated through, applied to, or even appropriated by the present; or its meaning may be uncovered, its structure of communication disclosed, its values foregrounded, or even its semantic indeterminacy highlighted in order to illuminate its aesthetic potential. The variety of hermeneutic principles raises the question of whether literature as a medium can be anything other than the object of textual interpretation. This is especially the case since the discussion of methods shows clear signs of flagging, with some arguing for pluralism and others questioning the whole ethics of established literary criticism. Both tendencies reflect the increasing acceleration of methods and model-building coming into and going out of favor.

Literature has always been regarded as "evidence" of something, ranging from the exemplification of the poet's life to a mirror reflection of society. Such approaches involve just as many methodological implications as a text-oriented interpretation, with the implicit frameworks through which it orders its findings.

Two dominant trends have emerged from the focus on literature as evidence: the attempt to grasp what is literary about it—often using such unwieldy structuralist terminology as 'poeticity'—and the view of it as a representation of society. The first of these arouses the suspicion that perhaps literariness may simply be another name for what used to be called autonomous art; the second seeks to counter the fringe status of literature by making it into a divining rod for the hidden dimension of social organizations and relationships. In both cases, however, literature is seen as a medium. They do not confine themselves to the interpretation of texts, which had become the object of an increasingly sophisticated hermeneutics. There is, however, a twofold problem in viewing literature as a medium: first, the attempt to pinpoint its literariness hypostatizes it, albeit in the effort to salvage some of its erstwhile importance; and second, the attempt to conceive it as a means of promoting social enlightenment reduces it to the status of a document.

Furthermore, as a medium, literature is put on a par with other media, and the ever-increasing role that these play in our civilization shows the degree to which literature has lost its significance as the epitome of our culture. The more comprehensively a medium fulfills its sociocultural function, the more it is taken for granted, as literature once used to be. It did indeed fulfill several such functions, ranging from entertainment through information and documentation to pastime, but these have now been distributed among many independent institutions that not only compete fiercely with literature but also deprive it of its formerly all-encompassing function. Does literature—a medium whose ground, like that of all the other media, lies outside itself—have anything significant left to offer?

Since literature still exists, it would seem that meeting the pragmatic needs of social life is not everything, especially since even these needs point to something outside themselves. If we try to fathom the historical necessity of the literary medium—no longer monopolizing the field of entertainment and leisure and now dwarfed by the competition of visual media—we shall have to penetrate beyond its former, widely accepted forms of legitimation: its autonomy, its mimetic reflection of social conditions, and even its generative force in constituting reality, as enlightened Marxism (Kosík) would have it. What then comes into focus is the anthropological equipment of human beings, whose lives are sustained by their imagination.

Literature, then, also has a substratum, albeit one of a rather featureless plasticity that manifests itself in a continual repatterning of the culturally conditioned shapes human beings have assumed. As a medium of writing, literature gives presence to what otherwise would remain unavailable. It has gained prominence as a mirror of human plasticity at the moment when many of its former functions have been taken over by other media.

Such a process of specialization is reflected on a larger scale in anthropogenesis, as confirmed by anthropologists such as André Leroi-Gourhan and Paul Alsberg, who trace human evolution from the upright posture through the diversified utilization of the hand—no longer needed for walking—right up to the development of the arts as an ever-differentiating ramification of specializations. If literature permits limitless patternings of human plasticity, it indicates the inveterate urge of human beings to become present to themselves; this urge, however, will never issue into a definitive shape, because self-grasping arises out of overstepping limitations. Literature fans out human plasticity into a panoply of shapes, each of which is an enactment of self-confrontation. As a medium, it can only show all determinacy to be illusory. It even incorporates into itself the inauthenticity of all the human patternings it features, since this is the only way it can give presence to the protean character of what it is mediating. Perhaps this is the truth through which literature counters the awareness that it is an illusion, thereby resisting dismissal as mere deception.

If literature reveals that human plasticity is propelled by the drive to gain shape, without ever imprisoning itself in any of the shapes obtained, clearly it can bring to light a good deal of our anthropological makeup. The task, however, that confronts a literary anthropology is to devise an adequate heuristics for revealing that makeup. The frameworks so far developed by various branches of anthropology offer no adequate modes of access, for neither evolutionary nor teleological approaches will work here, as practiced by an ethnologically oriented cultural anthropology (Frank Robert Vivelo and Marvin Harris).

With regard to preconditions, assumptions such as those made by philosophical anthropology are equally ineffective. Arnold Gehlen, for example, axiomatically defines human beings as creatures of deficiency, exposed to an open-ended world within which they can consolidate themselves only by establishing institutions. His definition goes far beyond the scope of a presupposed human plasticity whose continual patterning and repatterning is borne out by historical experience.

Of greater relevance is the concept of roles (Helmuth Plessner) developed by social anthropology. In this view, the multiplicity of roles into which the human being expands appears to coincide with what that being is supposed to be. But if roles are the situational patternings of the human being, even the sum total of these roles cannot be identical to what precedes them.

Other presuppositions are offered by structural and generative anthropology; but these, too, pose problems for the task of opening up the anthropological dimensions of literature. Structural anthropology (Claude Lévi-Strauss) takes its premises from structural linguistics, with binarism as a descriptive mode that covers all human ties, from totemism through tribalism to the family. Structural anthropology is more concerned with grasping social regulators than with elaborating the consequences of a preconditioned view of humankind. The fact that it has taken its epistemological premises from another discipline may perhaps be partly explained by the sometimes open question of whether structure is merely a mode of description or an integral part of what is being described. Certainly an anthropological approach to literature should not borrow its descriptive framework elsewhere. If it does, it downgrades literature to an illustrative foil for the assumption chosen, as is so often the case when literature is used to exemplify psychoanalytical principles.

Generative anthropology constructs a hypothetical "originary scene" (Eric Gans). This scene must be minimalistically conceived so that instead of being loaded with all kinds of assumptions, it can be viewed as the mainspring of culture in all its diversifications and ramifications, from language through changing tribal organizations to the rich variations of art. This "originary scene" is a sort of retrospective projection of the productive process that is to be observed in culture and that unfolds human history as a rhythmic alternation between restriction and derestriction. Plausible as it appears to be, the scene nevertheless remains a construct that, in contrast to a constructivist view, aims to explain; it tends to become a transcendental stance for assessing the emergence of culture.

Finally, there is the less homogeneous historical anthropology, which focuses on human beings as agents interacting with the historical contexts in which they are embedded and from which they can never be separated. Such a view makes them historical beings to the core, whose permanence is change. Thus historicity becomes the hallmark of humankind (Oskar Köhler), although change requires something other than itself in order to become operative.

A common feature of the rapidly proliferating recent anthropological studies is the effort to round off a basically ethnological account of human evolution with an assessment of the arts. Art appears to be indispensable, because it is a means of human self-exegesis. If we see literature in these anthropological terms, then from the start we must dispense with all axiomatic definitions of humanity, such as those forming the preconditions for the different branches of anthropology— for example, creature of deficiency, role-player, or initiator of taboos. The heuristics of an originary scene and change as the epitome of humankind also offer inadequate parameters when applied to literature. Although they may explain functions, they cannot explain why literature seems to be necessary as a continual patterning of human plasticity.

This book seeks to develop a different form of heuristics for human self-interpretation through literature. There are two essential preconditions: (1) Such heuristics must not be taken from other disciplines and imposed on literature. (2) They should—even if they are constructs—be linked to those human dispositions that are also constituents of literature. These conditions are met by the fictive and the imaginary. Both exist as evidential experiences, whether these involve lies and deceptions that take us beyond the limits of what we are, or whether we live an imaginary life through our dreams, daydreams, and hallucinations. But these experiences certainly do not tell us in any direct way what the fictive and the imaginary are, and if we call the one intentional and the other spontaneous, we only pinpoint their forms of manifestation, which allow a rough distinction between them without providing an explanation of what they might be.

Since both the fictive and the imaginary feature anthropological dispositions, they are not confined to literature but also play a role in our everyday lives. The special character of literature is its production through a fusion of the two that marks off its parameters as a medium. The fictive and the imaginary are not in themselves conditions for literature, whose emergence from their interaction is due not least to the fact that neither the one nor the other can be definitively grounded. It is precisely because any assumed origin eludes cognition that they gain salience by becoming contexts for one another in ways that issue into differentiated manifestations. The proliferation results in an ever-expanding interaction, with play becoming a structure that regulates the interplay between the fictive and the imaginary. Such a play structure allows for a twofold operation. First, it enables the interplay to take on different forms, and since no one form can ever determine the fictive, the imaginary, or their interaction, every form bears the mark of historical conditioning. This means that the text as a space for play is always open to the imprint of history. Second, the special features of each of the forms reveal both a determinate patterning to which human plasticity has been restricted and the urge of human beings to become present to themselves. In consequence, the text as a space for play can provide answers to questions concerning the human need for fictions.

For the work at hand, it is necessary to devise a heuristics of a literary anthropology, which must simultaneously involve anthropological dispositions and try to trace the different historical manifestations and conceptualizations of the fictive and the imaginary. Since the fictive and the imaginary cannot be determined transcendentally, they can only be ascertained contextually. By contrast with the diverse application of the fictive and the imaginary in real life, literature is their paradigmatic interplay, the result of their being freed from immediate pragmatic needs. But delineating the salient features of such interplay requires an investigation of different discursive applications, including the thematizing of fiction in philosophical discourse and the attempt to conceive the imaginary in cognitive discourse. In such a process the fictive takes on a more pronounced profile, because it is primarily to be grasped in terms of use, whereas the imaginary is exposed to the power of cognitive discourse, which seeks to define what it ought to be. Use cannot be limited, but cognitive discourse ranges itself into typologies. One central goal of this study is to produce an alternative pattern that can do justice to literature, the fictive, and the imaginary by bringing their limitless aspects into focus.

In order to come to grips with this objective, I shall briefly trace the main currents of my argument. Instead of harking back to the old fiction/reality dichotomy, I propose at the outset to conceive of the fictive as an operational mode of consciousness that makes inroads into existing versions of world. In this way, the fictive becomes an act of boundary-crossing which, nonetheless, keeps in view what has been over-stepped. As a result, the fictive simultaneously disrupts and doubles the referential world. Chapter 1 details the diversifications of fictionalizing acts whose hallmark is such doubling. .

Because fictionalized doubling eludes our cognitive grasp and de-fies essentialization, I turn to the example of pastoralism to illustrate it. Pastoralism held sway in the West as a literary device for over fifteen hundred years. Its basic pattern features two worlds that are distinctly marked from one another by a boundary, the crossing of which can be effected only by donning a mask. The disguise allows those who have veiled their identity to act out either what they are denied in the socio-historical world out of which they have come, or what seems impos-sible even in the pastoral realm of artifice that they have penetrated. Thus duality is maintained, unfolding the distinguished positions into a changing multiplicity of their possible relationships, which issue into proliferating iterations between the two worlds as well as between the character and its disguises.

The upshot of such a boundary-crossing is the generation of double meaning, with the manifest meaning not supposed to mean what it says in order to make the disguise reveal what it hides. Such a form of dou-bling emblematizes the fictive as the coexistence of what is mutually exclusive, and at the same time points to a "family resemblance" between the fictive and the dream, whose disclosure through disguise corre-sponds to a basic desire to overstep boundaries. Chapter 2 describes the multifariousness into which doubling explodes and ponders the reasons why human beings are driven by the need to have access to the condition achieved in fictionalizing and dreaming, a condition in which they can simultaneously step out of and be with themselves.

Pastoralism provides a vivid perception of what fictionalizing acts potentially entail and, equally, to what extent boundary-crossing as the hallmark of fictionality is dependent on a context within which an over-stepping is taking place. Context-bound, fictions in general elude clear-cut definitions, let alone ontological grounding. Instead, they can be grasped only in terms of use. As their use is potentially manifold, fiction-alizing manifests itself in constantly shifting modes of operation in accordance with the changing boundaries to be overcome.

If, as I argue, particular use determines the operational nature of fictions, I feel it important to consider the need for fictions in a type of discourse different from that of literature in order to contrast fictionality in literature with its changing functions and forms in other realms of human activity. The use of fictions in philosophical discourse provides such a contrast, especially because philosophers' increased awareness of the indispensability of fictions has resulted in a radical reversal in their attitude toward the fictional.

In philosophy fictions have advanced from a form of deception to a basic constituent of cognition. This turnabout occurred to a large extent in the empiricist tradition, whose important junctures provide the guideline in chapter 3 for charting the rise of fiction's philosophical status. In the process of that rise, fiction, once the object of critique, becomes the basis for a totalizing omnifictionalization. So long as fiction was subjected to criticism, it was defined—despite the many variations on the theme of unmasking—with relative consistency as an aberration of the human mind. Only when it was seen affirmatively did a shift begin in the view of what it might actually be. Since its use kept changing, and it was identified with its use, it could have no permanent identity, for the use testifies to the function and not to the foundation.

Although fictions thematized in philosophical discourse will serve here only as a foil to the fictive in literature, chapters 2 and 3 taken together highlight an important historic sequence. In Renaissance pastoralism, literary fictionality budded into full-fledged self-exhibition, which displays the workings of doublings that arise out of the coexistence of the mutually exclusive. Concurrently, in Renaissance philosophy fiction appeared as a target to be battled because it deluded the human mind at a time when self-preservation became an overriding issue. The growing necessity of philosophers to rely on fictions in considerations of cognition, action, and worldmaking corresponded to a paling of fictionality's self-image, no longer needed for delineating the doubling of decomposition and recomposition exercised by fictionalizing.

As literature is assumed to arise out of the interplay between the fictive and the imaginary, chapter 4 moves the imaginary into a systematic perspective. In the course of history three different types of cognitive discourse have tried to determine the imaginary: it was conceived as a human faculty, as an act, and as Ur-fantasy. These historic classifications tend to gloss over certain important features of the imaginary which are responsible for the production of the aesthetic dimension that inhabits not only works of art but also other basic human activities. The operations of the imaginary as a faculty, a creative act, or

Ur-fantasy must be differentiated if we are to pinpoint its variegated manifestations. This is especially the case because the imaginary shares with the fictive its resistance to essentialization, a resistance borne out by the fact that it has a history. Over that history the imaginary has been labeled fancy, fantasy, and imagination. All of these, however, are specific, context-bound demarcations of the imaginary whose potential eludes cognition and takes on a shape only in response to historically conditioned needs for understanding and deployment.

The imaginary is basically a featureless and inactive potential, which accounts for the failed attempts to grasp it cognitively. In spite of the different conceptualizations to which the imaginary has been subjected as faculty, act, or Ur-fantasy, there are certain features that all three have in common. A large part of chapter 4 details how the imaginary is not a self-activating potential but has to be brought into play from outside itself by the subject (Coleridge), by consciousness (Sartre), or by the psyche or the sociohistorical (Castoriadis), a list that by no means exhausts the stimulants. It follows that the imaginary has no intentionality of its own but has intentions imposed on it by the demands of its activator. Thus it can never be identical to its intention-led mobilization; instead, it discloses itself in an interplay with its different activators. Play, as a result, is both a product of activation and the condition for the productivity brought about by the interaction it stimulates. It is this dual process that gives rise to the imaginary and its presence, and it is to the topic of play that I turn in chapter 5.

While the paradigms discussed reveal how the activating agent uses the basic play movement of back and forth for its own purposes, the potential of play's transitory character is given freer rein when pragmatic purposes are less in evidence. In this respect the fictive component of literature is bound to mobilize the imaginary in a different manner, for it has far less of the pragmatic orientation required by the subject, by the consciousness, or by the sociohistorical, all of which channel the imaginary in quite specific directions.

By opening up spaces of play, the fictive compels the imaginary to take on a form at the same time that it acts as a medium for its manifestation. What the fictive targets is as yet empty and thus requires filling; and what is characteristic of the imaginary is its featurelessness, which thus requires form for its unfolding. Consequently, play arises out of the co-existence of the fictive and the imaginary.

If such an interpretation issues into play, the basic oscillation of back and forth through which the fictive and the imaginary become contexts for one another is acted out in the literary text on various levels: (1) the floating signifier; (2) the games played (*agōn, mimicry, alea, ilinx*); (3) the unforeseeable combinations of the four basic games; (4) the modes of gaming: free play as undoing the possible results of gaming, and instrumental play as a recuperation of what free play disperses; (5) the various combinations of different rules according to which the text game can be played; and (6) the extent to which the reader is played by the text.

These interlocking operations unfold the clearly distinguishable positions of the text into a changing multiplicity of their various possible relationships. Consequently, the positions are no longer present exclusively as representatives of their respective referential systems, but also are changing aspects and relations, by means of which the game once again forces difference into the positions themselves. During this process the text game brings to the fore what has been obscured by the representative character of the various positions, and what emerges will in turn have retroactive effect on representation. Play becomes a mode of discovery but is also itself changed by what it has set in motion; as a result, in the text game the play-forms themselves switch kaleidoscopically between what they are and what is eclipsed by their being. Representation, then, brings about the reciprocal permeation of what is separated by such doublings, and since these doublings are brought about by play, it is play that forms the infrastructure of representation.

In the Epilogue, a few conclusions are drawn as to the apparent necessity of what an institution like literature may indicate by allowing the staging of the human condition in a welter of unforeseeable patterns. Staging in literature makes conceivable the extraordinary plasticity of human beings who, precisely because they do not seem to have a determinable nature, can expand into an almost unlimited range of culture-bound patternings. The impossibility of being present to ourselves becomes our possibility to play ourselves out to the fullness that knows no bounds, because no matter how vast the range, none of the possibilities will "make us tick." This impossibility suggests a purpose for literary staging. If the plasticity of human nature allows, through its multiple culture-bound patternings, limitless human self-cultivation, literature becomes a panorama of what is possible, because it is not hedged in by either the limitations or the considerations that determine

the institutionalized organizations within which human life otherwise takes its course. Monitoring the changing manifestations of self-
fashioning, and yet not coinciding with any of them, literature makes
the interminable staging of ourselves appear as the postponement of
the end.

Acknowledgments

I am indebted to David Henry Wilson for providing a translation of the German original *Das Fiktive und das Imaginäre. Perspektiven literarischer Anthropologie,* on which I was able to work so that the English version is the result of a collaborative effort.

I received further assistance from Professor John Paul Riquelme, Boston University, who carefully read the manuscript and made many valuable suggestions as to the phrasing of certain issues and, above all, the critical terminology. I am very grateful to him. Professor Emily Miller Budick, Hebrew University, Jerusalem, was kind enough to go over the manuscript, trying to weed out a few of my German abstractions that David Wilson was prepared to condone. I greatly value her helping hand as an act of friendship. Angela Lippus-Broll deserves my gratitude for preparing the final manuscript.

Last, but not least, I am deeply obliged to the Rockefeller Foundation for a stipend that allowed me to put the finishing touches to the manuscript in the land of Cockaigne, the Villa Serbelloni in Bellagio, Italy. It was a special privilege for me that my sojourn coincided with the temporary directorship of Francis X. Sutton, an outstanding American intellectual who, along with his wife, Jackie, earned my greatest admiration.

The Fictive and
the Imaginary

Chapter One

Fictionalizing Acts

Tacit Knowledge of Fiction and Reality

It has long been a commonplace that literary texts are by definition fictional. Such a classification of the literary text clearly distinguishes it from those texts that, according to current terminology, are expository, meaning that they have a referent outside themselves. This opposition between reality and fiction is an elementary item in what the sociology of knowledge has come to call tacit knowledge—a term used to designate that storehouse of beliefs that seem so soundly based that their truth may be taken for granted. Convenient though this distinction may be, is it in fact as cut and dried as it seems? Are fictional texts truly fictions, and are nonfiction texts truly without fictions? The implications and ramifications of this question are such that it is doubtful whether our tacit knowledge can help us overcome the difficulties.

It is perhaps to state another commonplace to point out that a piece of fiction devoid of any connection with known reality would be incomprehensible. Consequently, if we are to attempt a description of what is fictive in fiction, there is little point in clinging to the old distinction between fiction and reality as a frame of reference. The literary text is a mixture of reality and fictions, and as such it brings about an interaction between the given and the imagined. Because this interaction produces far more than just a contrast between the two, we might do better to discard the old opposition of fiction and reality altogether, and to replace this duality with a triad: the real, the fictive, and what we shall henceforth call the imaginary. It is out of this triad that the text arises: Just as the text cannot be confined to those of its elements which are taken from referential reality, so it cannot be pinned down to its fictional features. For these fictional features do not constitute an end or an entity unto themselves. Rather, they provide the medium through which a third element emerges. This is the element I have called the imaginary, whose salient features will evolve as we proceed.

In this triadic relationship of the real, the fictive, and the imaginary lies not only the justification for our study of the fictive but also our best means of approaching such a study. The old opposition between fiction and reality presupposed a tacit knowledge of what constituted each of them, with the fiction being basically characterized by the absence of those attributes that defined the real. Such a questionable "certainty" obscured a central problem that has bedeviled modern epistemology. This is the problem bequeathed to the modern world by Cartesian thinking: How can something exist that, although actual and present, does not partake of the character of reality?[1]

The Triad: The Real, the Fictive, and the Imaginary

This dilemma provides the heuristic justification for replacing the customary antithesis of the fictional and the real with the triad of the real, the fictive, and the imaginary, which will provide us with the background against which we may grasp the specifically fictive element of the literary text. The fiction-reality dichotomy necessarily foreshortens a vital dimension of the text. Undoubtedly, the text is permeated by a vast range of identifiable items, selected from social and other extratextual realities. The mere importation into the text, however, of such realities—even though they are not being represented in the text for their own sake—does not ipso facto make them fictive. Instead, the text's apparent reproduction of items within the fictional text brings to light purposes, attitudes, and experiences that are decidedly *not* part of the reality reproduced. Hence they appear in the text as products of a fictionalizing act. Because this act of fictionalizing cannot be deduced from the reality repeated in the text, it clearly brings into play an imaginary quality that does not belong to the reality reproduced in the text but that cannot be disentangled from it. Thus the fictionalizing act converts the reality reproduced into a sign, simultaneously casting the imaginary as a form that allows us to conceive what it is toward which the sign points.

The triadic relationship among the real,[2] the fictive,[3] and the imaginary[4] is basic to the literary text, and from it we can extrapolate the special nature of the fictionalizing act. Whenever realities are transposed into the text, they turn into signs for something else. Thus they are made to outstrip their original determinacy. As this transformation of the determinate into the indeterminate is brought about by the fictionalizing act, the basic quality of this act begins to emerge: the act of fictionalizing is a crossing of boundaries. It amounts to nothing short of an act of transgression. This transgressive function of the fictionalizing act links it to the imaginary. In our ordinary experience, the imaginary tends to manifest itself in a somewhat diffuse manner, in fleeting impressions that defy our attempts to pin it down in a concrete and stabilized form. The imaginary may suddenly flash before our mind's eye, almost as an arbitrary apparition, only to disappear again or to dissolve into quite another form. "The peculiar quality of fantasy," says Husserl, "is its self-will. And so ideally it distinguishes itself by its absolute arbitrariness."[5] The act of fictionalizing is therefore not identical to the imaginary with its protean potential. For the fictionalizing act is a guided act. It aims at something that in turn endows the imaginary with an articulate gestalt—a gestalt that differs from the fantasies, projections, daydreams, and other reveries that ordinarily give the imaginary expression in our day-to-day experience. Here, too, we have an overstepping of limits, as we pass from the diffuse to the precise. Just as the fictionalizing act outstrips the determinacy of the real, so it provides the imaginary with the determinacy that it would not otherwise possess. In so doing, it enables the imaginary to take on an essential quality of the real, for determinacy is a minimal definition of reality. This is not, of course, to say that the imaginary *is* real, although it certainly assumes an appearance of reality in the way it intrudes into and acts upon the given world.

We can now see two distinct processes, which are set in motion by the act of fictionalizing. Reproduced reality is made to point to a 'reality' beyond itself, while the imaginary is lured into form. In each case there is a crossing of boundaries: the determinacy of reality is exceeded at the same time that the diffuseness of the imaginary is controlled and called into form. Consequently, extratextual reality merges into the imaginary, and the imaginary merges into reality.

The text, then, functions to bring into view the interplay among the fictive, the real, and the imaginary. Although each component of the triad fulfills a significant function, the act of fictionalizing is of paramount importance: it crosses the boundaries both of what it organizes (external reality) and of what it converts into a gestalt (the diffuseness of the imaginary). It leads the real to the imaginary and the imaginary to the real, and it thus conditions the extent to which a given world is to be transcoded, a nongiven world is to be conceived, and the reshuffled worlds are to be made accessible to the reader's experience.

Given this reformulation of the situation, then, the old antithesis between fiction and reality is revealed as inadequate and even misleading. Tacit knowledge implies a transcendental vantage point that can no longer be upheld in view of the transgressing operations of the fictionalizing act. Hence, our task now is to elucidate relations, not to define positions; there is no longer any need to assume the transcendental stance that was necessary whenever the opposition between fiction and reality had to be explained. The triad rids us of such a burden. We are well rid of it, especially if we consider the latter-day fate of epistemology, which, in its struggle to grasp the nature of fictionality, has ended up having to recognize its own premises as fictions and, in the face of its ever-increasing implication in the fictiveness it is attempting to define, has had to forfeit its claims to being a foundational discipline.

Functional Differentiation of Fictionalizing Acts: Selection, Combination, Self-Disclosure

On the basis of this triadic relationship, we may now focus on the act of fictionalizing, which upon closer inspection appears to comprise three separate acts. These can be distinguished according to the functions each is meant to perform, so that there are several interacting functions that bring about the merger between the real and the imaginary. It is, however, a basic characteristic of each act that it crosses a boundary of some kind.

As the product of an author, the literary text evidences a particular attitude by which the author directs himself or herself to the world. As this attitude does not exist in the given world to which the author refers, it can take on a form only by being literally inserted into the real world. The insertion takes place not by plain mimesis of existing structures but by a process of restructuring them. Every literary text inevitably contains a selection from a variety of social, historical, cultural, and literary systems that exist as referential fields outside the text. This selection is itself a stepping beyond boundaries, in that the elements selected are lifted out of the systems in which they fulfill their specific function. This applies both to cultural norms and to literary allusions, which are incorporated into every new literary text in such a way that the structure and semantics of the systems concerned are decomposed.

This fact has several consequences. Owing to the inroads made into the various systems, the systems themselves move into focus and can be discerned as the referential fields of the text. So long as they are organizational units of the given world, fulfilling their regulative function, they are taken for reality itself and thus remain unobserved. The act of selection, however, disassembles their given order, thereby turning them into objects for observation. Observability is *not* a component of the systems concerned. It is brought about by the act of selection. Thus the referential fields of the text are thrown into relief, and this happens precisely through specific elements of the system being dislocated and transposed into the literary text. Systems as referential fields of the text are highlighted by the subversion of their patterning. The elements that are now incorporated into the text are not in themselves fictive, but their selection is an act of fictionalizing through which existing systems, as fields of reference, can—paradoxically—be separated precisely because their boundaries are transgressed.

The observability of the referential fields is given its perspectival slant by each of the fields being split into elements that either are actualized by the text or remain dormant within it. While the chosen elements initially spotlight a field of reference, opening it up for perception, they also permit the perception of all those elements that the selection has excluded. These, then, form a background against which the observation is to take place. It is as if what is present in the text must be judged in the light of what is absent.

Because it defies referentiality, this process has the character of an event. There are no preconceived rules governing selection. The author's choice, therefore, can be described only in terms of the selections made. These selections in turn reveal the attitude adopted by the author to the given world. If an act of selection were governed by a set of rules given prior to the act, then the act itself would not transgress existing boundaries but would simply be one form of actualizing a possibility within the framework of a prevailing convention. The specific form of the 'event' created by the act of selection exists, however, only in and through that which it produces. It marks off the referential fields from each other and turns them into clearly distinguishable systems whose existing relations are wiped out, and whose chosen elements are extended into new patterns, as the boundaries between them are crossed. The elements are therefore differently weighted than they were when they had their places in their respective systems. Deletion, extension, weighting—these are all basic "ways of worldmaking,"[6] as outlined by Nelson Goodman.

These operations point to a purpose, although this purpose is not verbalized in the fictional text itself. Thus selection as a fictionalizing act reveals the intentionality of the text. It encapsulates extratextual realities into the text, turns the elements chosen into contexts for each other, and sets them up for observation against those elements it has excluded, thus bringing about a two-way process of mutual review: the present is viewed through what is absent, the absent through what is present. This provides an angle from which the interrelationships are to be perceived. The whole process brings to the fore the intentionality of the text, whose reality comes about through the loss of reality suffered by those empirical elements that have been torn away from their original function by being transposed into the text.

If we confine our discussion in this way to what the text *does,* rather than what the text is meant to mean, we relieve ourselves of one of the perennial bugbears of critical analysis, the attempt to identify the author's actual intention. The desire to penetrate authorial intention has led to countless investigations of the author's mind, with results that can, at very best, be only speculative. If we are to uncover the intention of a text, our best chance lies not in the study of the author's life, dreams, and beliefs but in those manifestations of intentionality expressed in the fictional text itself through its selection of and from extratextual systems. The intentionality of the text thus consists in the way it breaks down and distances itself from those systems to which it has linked itself. The intention, therefore, is not to be found in the world to which the text refers, nor is it simply something imaginary; it is the preparation of an imaginary quality for use—a use that remains dependent on the given situation within which it is to be applied.

Selection, then, is an act of fictionalizing, insofar as it marks off from each other the referential fields of the text both by spotlighting and by overstepping their respective limits. Out of this operation arises the intentionality of the text, which is to be identified neither with the system in question nor with the imaginary as such (for its conditioning depends largely on those extratextual systems to which reference is made). It is, rather, a "transitional object"⁷ between the real and the imaginary, and it has the all-important quality of actuality. Actuality is the basic constitutive feature of an event, and the intentionality of the text is an event in the sense that it does not end with the delineation of referential fields but breaks these down in order to transmute their elements into the material of its self-presentation. The actuality lies in the way the imaginary takes effect on the real.

A complement to the act of selection, which is an act of fictionalizing, is the act of combination. The different elements that are combined within the text range from words and their meanings through encapsulated extratextual items to the patterns in which characters and actions, for example, are organized. Combination, too, is an act of fictionalizing, with the same basic mode of operation: the crossing of boundaries.

On the lexical level this is to be seen, for instance, with neologisms such as Joyce's coining of the term *benefiction,* which combines the words *benefaction, benediction,* and *fiction.* Here lexical meanings are used to derestrict semantic limitations. The lexical meaning of a particular word is faded out and a new meaning faded in, without the loss of the original meaning. This establishes a figure-and-ground relationship that allows both the separation of the individual elements and a continuous switching of the perspective between them. In accordance with whichever reference forms the foreground or background, the semantic weighting will be shifted. Indeed, it is the instability of the references that produces the oscillating semantic spectrum, which cannot then be identified absolutely with any of its lexical components, though it cannot exist without the stability of each of them.

A similar derestrictive effect can be seen in rhyming strategies such as those employed by T. S. Eliot in *Prufrock:*

> Should I, after teas and cakes and ices,
> Have the strength to force the moment to its crisis?⁸

Through their consonance, the rhymes lay stress on the semantic divergence. With similarities signaling their nonequivalence, the combination here functions as a means of revealing what is different in what is similar. Again we have a figure-and-ground relationship: the crisis may appear as trivialized, and the ices may take on a hitherto unsuspected significance. The end effect of this, and many similar strategies, is a heightening of the semantic potential; the combination is so structured that the foreground-background balance can be tilted virtually at will.

What applies on the lexical level holds equally true on the levels of the extratextual and intratextual items that in narrative literature organize the constellations of characters and their actions. Semantic enclosures within the text are built up from selected outside items and are delineated by the schematic presentation of characters and actions. But here, too, we have a basic foreground-background relationship, because as a rule the hero will step beyond the restrictions of the semantic enclosures.[9] Thus the relevance of the respective field of reference will fade in and out of focus, unfolding a whole network of possible combinations that are not to be found in the specific, articulated patterns of the text.

Consequently, the fictionalizing act of combination, like the fictionalizing act of selection, produces relationships within the text. And just as in the process of selection these relationships yield the intentionality of the text, so in the process of combination they lead to the emergence of the 'factualness' of the text, of what Goodman has called "fact from fiction."[10] This 'factualness' of the text is created by the relational process through the determinacy of the elements it combines, and through the reciprocal interaction of those elements in combination. The factualness of the text is not, therefore, a quality of the elements the text puts into combination. Rather, it is constituted by what the text produces. Whenever a relationship within the text is realized, the elements connected with one another are bound to change, as certain aspects of them are privileged at the expense of others. Consequently, while each relation achieves stability through what it excludes, it creates its own background of unchosen qualities. These are, as it were, the shadow cast by the realized combination, and they help to give it its shape. Thus what is absent is made present. But while the realized combination draws its life from what it has excluded, the fictionalizing act of relating clearly brings about a copresence of the realized and the absent. This in turn causes the realized relations to be undermined. It makes them sink back into the shadows of background existence, so that new relations can come to the fore, gaining stability against this background. Thus the relational process oversteps the inherent limits of each figuration, links them together, but then—in accordance with the intentionality of each particular text—causes the realized link itself to be overstepped by those possibilities that it has excluded.

It goes without saying that the relational process functions in many different ways. However, if we are to grasp the peculiar nature of this fictionalizing act, there are certain categories of relationality that require special attention. In particular, there are three levels of derestriction or boundary-crossing that must be discerned in the fictional text.

First, there is the relational process that arranges the selected extratextual conventions, values, allusions, quotations, and the like within the text. As Jonathan Culler puts it, "Fiction can hold together within a single space a variety of languages, levels of focus, points of view, which would be contradictory in other kinds of discourse organized towards a particular empirical end."[11] The mutually contradictory elements of the text are enabled to coexist through the relations that are established among them. It is difficult to describe these relations systematically because the relational process does not follow any predictable rules. On the contrary, in Culler's words, "The force, the power of any text, even the most unabashedly mimetic, lies in those moments which exceed our ability to categorize, which collide with our interpretive codes but nevertheless seem right."[12] The fact that such connections appear to be convincing without being guided by any code-governed rules is due mainly to the manner in which the linked elements are made to extend beyond the borders of their previous validity. The revaluation becomes plausible, not least because it is continually fed by relating norms and conventions that are lifted out of their original context and thus recoded. This process is most evident in narrative literature, where the characters represent different norms, the validity of which is disclosed by the relational process only in order that the inevitable limitations of these norms should serve as the starting point for their being transgressed.

A second level of relating is to be seen in the organization of specific semantic enclosures within the text. These give rise to intratextual fields of reference, themselves brought about by the relationship between and among external items encapsulated in the text. Generally, these fields of reference provide the occasion for the hero to step over their boundaries. Such boundary-crossing is, in Lotman's terms, a subject-creating event. It is a "revolutionary element" because it breaks down "accepted classification."[13]

This structure applies just as much to poetry as to narrative fiction. For example, the lyrical self is the point of intersection among the schemata that are drawn into the poem from various forms of extratextual discourse, but they must then be exceeded if the lyrical self—as their point of intersection—is to assume its individual delineation.[14] Like the hero of the novel, the lyrical self can emerge only by breaking out of and thereby moving beyond the semantic topography established in the poem. Such encroachment on the semantic system built up in the text has the character of an event, for the 'reference' of the ensuing semantic phase is the derestriction of that determinacy initially produced by selection and combination. The "actions of fictional characters," suggests Johannes Anderegg, "interest us to the extent that they represent possibilities of relation. Fiction, in this case, is not just the *accomplishment* of relating things, but it is also a *representation* of possible relations or a communication concerning possible relations."[15] The capacity of the relational process actually to go so far as self-presentation is an indication of the vast range of relations possible between elements, and also of the extent to which elements, set up in different networks of relationships, may be transformed.

The third level of relating is the lexical one already discussed. This consists of the derestriction of lexical meanings through their reciprocal influence on one another: "[M]eanings vanish in favor of certain relationships."[16] On this level, the fictionalizing act of combination has a special consequence for language. The literal meaning of words is faded out in the same way as their denotative function. The relational process manifests itself in the derestriction of lexical meanings, the encroachment on semantic enclosures, and, ultimately, the recodings and transcodings that ensue. It is not, however, itself explicitly verbalized. Consequently, relating—as the product of an act of fictionalizing—is manifested by way of the effects it conveys through language, although these effects are not themselves articulated.

Language's function of denotation is transformed by the relational process into a function of figuration. But even if the denotative character of language is suspended in this figurative use, such language is still not devoid of references. These references, however, are no longer to be equated with existing systems; their target is expression and representation. If we follow Goodman's suggestion,[17] and take expression and representation as the consequences of figurative language, we can draw two conclusions:

1. The reference is not itself of a linguistic nature; nor does it exist as given data that would merely require denotative language to designate it. Therefore this form of language outstrips the denotative

function of language in order to indicate, through its figurations, the linguistic untranslatability of its references.

2. At the same time—owing to its figurations—figurative language makes its references conceivable. Such language dwindles to an analogue that merely contains the conditions that will allow a reference to be conceived, but it cannot be identical to that reference. We may therefore discern a strange ambiguity in the function of this figurative language: as an analogue it permits and conditions conceivability, and as a sign it denotes the linguistic untranslatability of what it refers to.

The fictive quality manifested in the relational process can now be pinpointed. Combination as a fictionalizing act endows the imaginary[18] with a specific form according to the relations to be established. This form of the imaginary eludes verbalization. At the same time, however, it can never dispense with language, for language points to what is to be concretized. It also enables the concretization to be shaped and thus fed back into existing realities.

We have so far noted two fictionalizing acts pertaining to the fictional text: those of selection and combination, each of which entailed the boundary-crossing of literary and sociocultural systems on the one hand, and of intratextual fields of reference on the other. As the focus shifted from selection to combination, an increasing complexity became all too evident. Combination occurred on two levels at once. Through the relational process, fields of reference had to be produced from the material selected, and these fields, in turn, had to be linked with each other, thereby becoming subjected to a reciprocal transformation. This sufficiently complex differentiation is complicated still further by yet another fictionalizing act. This is the fictional text's disclosure of its own fictionality.

Literary texts contain a range of signals to denote that they are fictive. It would be tedious to run through the whole repertoire of these signals. More important than the repertoire is the fact that these signals are not to be equated exclusively with linguistic signs in the text. All attempts to treat them as linguistic have proved unsuccessful. For these signals can become significant only through particular, historically varying conventions shared by author and public. Thus the signals do not invoke fictionality as such but conventions, which form the basis of a kind of contract between author and reader, the terms of which identify the text not as discourse but as "enacted discourse."[19] Among the most obvious and most durable of such signals are literary genres, which have permitted a wide variety of contractual terms between author and reader. Even such recent inventions as the nonfiction novel reveal the same contractual function, since they must invoke the convention before renouncing it.

The implications of fictionality's self-disclosure are far-reaching. It is a commonplace that the fictive is not confined to the literary text. Fictions also play vital roles in the activities of cognition and behavior, as in the founding of institutions, societies, and world pictures.[20] Unlike such nonliterary fictions, the literary text reveals its own fictionality. Because of this, its function must be radically different from that of related activities that mask their fictional nature. The masking, of course, need not necessarily occur with the intention to deceive; it occurs because the fiction is meant to provide an explanation, or even a foundation, and would not do so if its fictive nature were to be exposed. The concealment of fictionality endows an explanation with an *appearance* of reality, which is vital, because fiction—as explanation—functions as the constitutive basis of this reality.

By contrast, the self-disclosing fictional text signals to the reader that a change of attitude is required. If the reader fails to recognize the contractual sign, an inappropriate reaction will ensue, as is frequently thematized by literature. In Fielding's *Tom Jones,* for instance, Partridge takes a performance of *Hamlet* for reality and not a play, and in view of the dreadful goings-on he finds it necessary to intervene.[21] Similarly, in *A Midsummer Night's Dream* Shakespeare provides a perfect example when the artisans, acting their play, remind their audience that they need not be afraid of the lion, which is not a real lion but one being played by Snug the joiner. The unmasking going on here does not simply concern the fictionality of the text, which is clear to everyone, but the naïveté of an attitude that fails to register the signals of the fictional convention. When a fiction signals its own fictionality, it necessitates an attitude different from that adopted toward fictions that hide their fictionality.

Besides requiring a changed attitude, the fictional text contains a large number of identifiable items from the outside world as well as from previous literature. These recognizable 'realities', however, are now marked as being fictionalized. Thus the incorporated 'real' world is, so to speak, placed in brackets to indicate that it is not something given but is merely to be understood *as if* it were given. In the self-disclosure of its fictionality, an important feature of the fictional text comes to the fore: it turns the whole of the world organized in the text into an 'as-if' construction. In light of this qualification (implicitly accepted the moment we embark on our reading), it is clear that we must and do suspend all natural attitudes adopted toward the 'real' world once we are confronted with the represented world. This is not present in the text for its own sake, nor is its function exhausted merely by its denoting a reality. Just as the incorporated 'real' world is bracketed off, so too are our natural attitudes.

Here we can see a first vital difference between the literary fiction and the fiction that masks its fictionality: in the latter, our natural attitudes continue unchanged. Indeed, it may even be a purpose of the masking to leave natural attitudes intact in order that the fiction may be construed as a reality capable of explaining realities. But where the world and our attitudes are separated, that world cannot remain an object in itself; it must be the object of whatever kind of study or manipulation toward which the text is geared. Reality, then, may be reproduced in a fictional text, but it is there in order to be outstripped, as is indicated by its being bracketed. Whenever bracketing occurs, a purpose makes itself felt that can never be a property of the world represented, not least because the represented world is built up out of a selection of items from the world outside. In this overarching purpose the pragmatic function of the fictional work is adumbrated—for fictions are inextricably tied to their use. The reality represented in the text is not meant to represent reality; it is a pointer to something that it is not, although its function is to make that something conceivable.

In order to understand this more fully, we might take a closer look at the 'as-if' construction mentioned above. As Vaihinger points out, the conjunction signifies "that the condition is an unreal or impossible one."[22] The world occurring in the fictional text is judged as if it were a reality, but the comparison is only implicit—what is in the text is linked with something it is not. Therefore "the equation of a thing with the necessary consequences of an impossible or unreal case, is expressed as a thing demanded ... Thus an impossible case is here imagined, the necessary consequences are drawn from it and, with these consequences, which must also be impossible, demands are equated that do not follow from existing reality" (p. 259). The 'as-if' construction serves as "the equation of something (with the necessary consequences flowing from the impossible case)" (p. 259). If the fictional text combines the represented 'real' world with an 'impossible' one, the resultant representation leads to the determinacy of something that by nature must be indeterminate. This, then, is the imaginary that the acts of fictionalizing mediate through the world represented in the text. In Vaihinger's words:

> [W]herever an imaginative comparison or a comparison with something imaginative takes place, and this comparison is not merely an empty game of ideas but has a practical purpose through which the comparison may lead to consequences, the conjunction 'as-if' takes its rightful place, because ... it compares an existing something with the necessary consequences of an imaginary case. Here it must be emphasized that this imaginative activity must have some practical use, some purpose: only if this is so will the consequences emerge from that imaginative function; it is not a question of aimlessly accepting reality as real.[23]

If the "imaginative" attains its gestalt in the purpose, clearly the represented world cannot constitute that purpose but is, rather, the point of comparison which enables the adumbrated dimension of the text to become conceivable.

This function is fulfilled by the represented world insofar as representation itself is of a dual nature: it may have a denotative or a figurative reference. The concreteness of the represented world appears to denote a given world. But since the represented world, as we have seen from our study of the fictionalizing acts of selection and combination, has arisen out of a prevailing intentionality and a relational process, it cannot, in fact, be identical to any given world. Consequently, the world represented in the text is neither totally denotative nor totally representative of anything. Taking into account that the world represented is in itself the product of fictionalizing acts, the 'as-if' in once overstepping this emergent world highlights the transgressing of boundaries as the basic quality of fictionalizing. The acts of selection and combination, and the 'as-if' construction described so far, are geared to each other. They allow for a graded transcoding of given realities, thereby enabling us to grasp both these realities and the processes of their transcoding.

The importance of the distinction between a denotative and a figurative reference in representation is strikingly illustrated by Dürrenmatt's criticism of Giorgio Strehler's production of his play *Der Besuch der alten Dame*. Dürrenmatt claimed that Strehler had blundered by presenting the scene in the station as realistically as possible.

He complained that Strehler's striving after realism could only destroy the play. In other words, Dürrenmatt's play was, in his view, permeated by fictional signals which indicated that the world represented was to appear in the mode of an 'as-if' construction. The moment the director eliminated these signals, and hence the 'as-if' construction, he shifted the emphasis of presentation to that of a specific reality that the theatergoer could verify in the empirical world.

By striving to denote reality, such a production could only fail to fulfill its figurative role, which, however vital for its author, is thus left empty. By increasing an illusion of reality through an exclusive foregrounding of the denotative function, the production was bound to raise the question of what its representations were meant to achieve. For when we are confronted with something with which we are familiar, the representation—unless it offers some sophisticated technique—will strike us as redundant. Only when redundancy is made a mode of representation does the figurative function make its presence felt. In this case the redundancy is not present for its own sake but refers to something else. This is a mode used nowadays by documentary fiction, though it was clearly not the mode intended by Dürrenmatt.

It is evident from Dürrenmatt's remarks that the attempt to translate fiction back into reality involves the undoing of the 'as-if' dimension. The represented world then ceases to be an analogue for what is to be conceived. If that leads to the undoing of the world represented, then second thoughts begin to arise as to whether representation can really be equated with mimesis. Since the world represented is bracketed, it cannot take on a determinate form of its own but must find it through its relatedness to something else. Strehler's "blunder" vividly illustrates the duality of the represented world, which in an accurate production would have retained only enough of its denotative function to provide a basis for its figurative one (i.e., to enable the world to be experienced *as if* it were real). Denotation, then, has to be divested of its original function if the world designated is to be taken *as if* it were real. It is through this change into 'as-if' that the represented world fulfills the purpose foreshadowed by its figurative use. If the denotative function is made subservient to the figurative one, the dual nature of the represented world moves into focus: it is concrete enough to be perceived as a world and, simultaneously, figures as an analogue exemplifying, through a concrete specimen, what is to be conceived.

As the world of the text is to be taken only *as if* it were real, it becomes part of a comparison that—according to the 'as-if' construction—has to be related to something 'impossible' or 'unreal' (i.e., in either case to something other than itself). To be viewed 'as' appears to be the purpose of the relationship to be established, and this implies creating a position from which the represented world becomes observable.

Since it is not a characteristic of the world that it should possess the quality of its own observability, the 'as-if' employs the represented world to stimulate affective reactions in the reader. Attitudes will be produced through which the represented world will be surpassed, while at the same time the 'impossible' or 'unreal' will take on a conceivable contour. As the represented world is not a world, but the reader imagines *as if* it were one, clearly the reader's reaction must be guided by that representation. Thus the 'as-if' triggers acts of ideation in the recipient, causing him or her to conceive what the world of the text is meant to bring about. This activity eludes qualification as either subjective or objective, for the stimulated conceivability is patterned by the world represented, the surpassing of which opens up a dimension to be imaginatively concretized. In this very process of ideation, once again boundaries are overstepped: the world of the text is exceeded and the diffuseness of the imaginary assumes form. Triggering an imaginative reaction to the world represented in the text proves to be the function of the 'as-if' construction, which comes to fruition through the attitudes the reader is induced to adopt to the world exemplified by the text.

Let us briefly summarize what the fictionalizing act of the 'as-if' is able to accomplish. Self-disclosure of fictionality puts the world represented in brackets, thereby indicating the presence of a purpose that proves to be the observability of the world represented. Observability requires a stance, the necessity of which causes attitudes to be adopted by the recipient, who is made to react to what he or she is given to observe. Thus the purpose of the self-disclosing fiction comes to light.

Furthermore, if the world represented is not meant to denote a given world, and hence is turned into an analogue, it might serve two different purposes at once. The reaction provoked by the represented world could be directed toward conceiving what it is meant to "figure forth." The analogue, however, could simultaneously direct the reaction to the empirical world from which the textual world has been drawn, allowing this very world to be perceived from a vantage point that has never been part of it. In this case the reverse side of things will come into view. The duality of the analogue will never exclude either of the two possibilities; in fact, they appear to interpenetrate, making conceivable what would otherwise remain hidden.

Now the question arises as to whether these ideational activities released by the textual world have repercussions on the reader. In other words, does the 'as-if' not only cause an overstepping of the bracketed world but also instigate the reader to extend beyond habitual dispositions? To help us answer this question, let us consider the concrete example of an actor playing the role of Hamlet. The actor cannot identify himself totally with Hamlet, not least because even he does not know precisely who Hamlet is. He must always remain partly himself, which means that his body, his feelings, and his mind function as an analogue, enabling him to represent what he is not. This duality makes it possible for him to offer a particular embodiment of what Hamlet might be. In order to produce the determinate form of an unreal character, the actor must fade out his own reality.[24] Similarly with each of us as readers: to imagine what has been stimulated by the 'as-if' entails placing our faculties at the disposal of an unreality and bestowing on it a semblance of reality in proportion to a reduction of our own reality.

If the fictional 'as-if' is able to cause such a turnabout, then structurally at least this process endows our reaction to the textual world with the quality of an event. This event arises out of a crossing of boundaries, and can no longer be equated with given frameworks. Our subsequent journey to new horizons translates the imaginary into an experience—an experience that is shaped by the degree of determinacy given to the imaginary by the fictional 'as-if.' The event, as we experience it, is open-ended, giving rise to a tension that demands to be resolved, but resolution can take place only if what has manifested itself in the event can be made to mean something. We know from Gestalt psychology that the grouping activity involved in both mental and physical perception always tends toward closing off gestalts. Indeed, it is only when a gestalt is closed that the object perceived or imagined can make its presence felt in our conscious minds. For this reason, we continually try new arrangements of data until we can pattern them in such a way that the tension is resolved and a degree of determinacy by which the gestalt may be closed is achieved. In the same way, the fictive in the text sets and then transgresses boundaries in order to endow the imaginary with that degree of concreteness necessary for it to be effective; the effect is to trigger the reader's need to close the event and thus to master the experience of the imaginary.

At this juncture it is worth considering one of the important findings of psycholinguistics, the fact that all linguistic utterances are
accompanied by the "expectation of meaningfulness."[25] For every utterance arouses the feeling that it must have a specific meaning, although
at the same time it should be remembered that whoever wants to understand language must understand more than just language.[26] It is therefore only natural that the experience of the imaginary should set off in
the reader the urge to make it meaningful, so that he or she may bring
the experience back to the level of what is familiar; this, however, runs
contrary to the character of the experience itself, insofar as it can
become an experience only by exceeding the borders of what is familiar. But even if the reader is aware of this fact, the awareness will not
prevent the attempt to sound out the possible meaningfulness of the
event. This drive is both natural and unavoidable. The expectancy of
meaningfulness and the activities resulting from it have their origin in
the tension brought about by the open-endedness of the event indicating the presence of the imaginary, and so any meaning imposed must
be in the nature of a pragmatization of the imaginary. Consequently,
meaning is not inscribed in the text as a solid be-all and end-all. Rather,
it is the result of an inevitable operation of transmutation triggered and
sustained by the necessity to cope with the experience of the imaginary.
Should we, however, be inclined to consider meaning as the generative
matrix of the text, the suspicion will mount that we interpolate our
need for semantic closure as the basis of the text. Psychologically, such
an interpolation would be thoroughly understandable, for it not only
would relieve the tension of the open-ended event but also would meet
our expectations of meaningfulness accompanying utterance. However,
it also suppresses the vital fact that if we are to understand language, we
must understand more than language, and this understanding is not
confined to our tacit knowledge; it also applies to the ways and means
by which we extend ourselves beyond what we are.

By moving these semantic operations into perspective, we are not
trying to say that they have to be dispensed with. On the contrary, they
are important because they reveal the inescapable necessity of prag-
matizing the imaginary. They embody the whole process of transmutation by which we can assimilate an experience that arises out of our
stepping beyond ourselves. If the fictional 'as-if' is considered to be a
medium for molding the appearance of the imaginary, the semantic
operations conducted by the recipient translate this appearance into an

understanding of what has happened. Thus the imaginary is both shaped and transmuted in these two interlocking phases; it proves to be the constitutive basis of the text. If instead we were to interpolate meaning as the text's source, which we are so prone to do, we would eclipse the very dimension out of which meaning arises.

The existence of this meaning-making dimension is abundantly clear already from the history of interpretation, which shows how the same text can be understood in many different ways, according to the prevailing codes that have been brought to bear on it. If the generative multiplicity of meaning—though enclosed within the literary horizon of the text—is not due to the inadequacies of the thousands of readers who, like Sisyphus, are trundling in vain toward the hidden meaning, then polysemy sets limits on semantics itself. Furthermore, it adumbrates a dimension accessible to experience without ever being pinned down, let alone exhausted, by a semantic definition. Semantics can no longer be conceived as the principal referent when the constitutive matrix of the text comes under consideration. It is precisely for this reason that the same text can make "sense" in a variety of historical situations. As the sense itself is capable of many variations, it follows that any one meaning is merely a limited, pragmatic construction, not an exhaustive and objective datum. Instead of seeking to pin down a single meaning, we may be better advised to recognize the multiplicity of possible interpretations as a sign of the multiplicitous availability of the imaginary.

All the acts of fictionalizing that we have distinguished within the fictional text have in common the fact that they are acts of boundary-crossing. Selection transgresses the limits of extratextual systems as well as the boundaries of the text itself by pointing to the referential fields that link the text to what is beyond the page. Combination transgresses the semantic enclosures established by the text, ranging from the derestriction of lexical meanings to the buildup of the event through the hero's infringement of strictly enforced borderlines. Finally, the 'as-if' construction discloses the fictionality of fiction, thus transgressing the represented world set up by the acts of selection and combination. It brackets off this world and thereby indicates that it is to be used for an as yet hidden, though overarching, purpose. The self-disclosure has a twofold significance. First, it shows that fiction can be known as fiction. Second, it shows that the represented world is only to be conceived *as if* it were a world in order that it should be taken to figure something other

than itself. Ultimately, the text brings about one more boundary-crossing that occurs within the reader's experience: it stimulates attitudes
toward an unreal world, the unfolding of which leads to the temporary
displacement of the reader's own reality. As the acts of fictionalizing are
geared to each other and have a clearly punctuated sequence, their
differing types of boundary-crossing ensure assimilation of a transformed world that issues forth from them.

The acts of fictionalizing to be discerned in the fictional text can
be clearly distinguished by the different gestalt each of them brings
about: selection results in intentionality; combination results in relatedness; and self-disclosure leads to what we have called bracketing. In
all cases they might be described by the phrase already quoted from
Goodman: "fact from fiction."[27] They are, as we have seen, neither
inherent in what they refer to nor identical to the imaginary. They are
the nongiven in relation to the given, and they are the determinate in
relation to the imaginary. The fictive, then, might be called a "transitional object,"[28] always hovering between the real and the imaginary,
linking the two together. As such it exists, for it houses all the processes
of interchange. Yet, in another sense, it does not exist as a discrete
entity, for it consists of nothing but these transformational processes.

Like meaning, the fictive element of fiction cannot be the basic
constituent of the text. Meaning is primarily the semantic operation
that takes place between the given text, as a fictional gestalt of the
imaginary, and the reader; hence it is a pragmatization of the imaginary.
The fictive, in turn, brings about a transformation of the realities incorporated in the text by overstepping them; hence it is a medium for the
imaginary. While the imaginary attains its concreteness and its effectiveness by way of the fictive, its appearance is inevitably conditioned
by language. Since it has to have a linguistic structure, the imaginary
inscribes itself into this structure by making it open-ended. This openness applies to all the gestalts we have mentioned, from intentionality
through relatedness to bracketing.

There is no verbalization of the reason why certain choices
through which intentionality manifests itself have been made from
extratextual realities. There is no verbalization of the relatedness of
semantic enclosures, let alone of the revolutionary event of their transgression, and there is no verbalization of the purpose underlying the
bracketing of worlds and of our natural attitudes toward them. Thus the
cardinal points of the text defy verbalization, and it is only through

these open structures within the linguistic patterning of the text that the imaginary can manifest its presence. From this fact we can deduce one last achievement of the fictive in the fictional text: It brings about the presence of the imaginary by transgressing language itself. In outstripping what conditions it, the imaginary reveals itself as the generative matrix of the text.

Chapter Two

Renaissance Pastoralism as a Paradigm of Literary Fictionality

As an act of boundary-crossing, fictionalizing is a mode of operation that produces a result. Is this result a fiction? Or is it a "fact from fiction"? The first would be a tautology, and the second would no longer be fictive. But if fictionalizing neither facilitates itself nor constitutes its own product, what is it? The very question opens up a trap set by language that has already claimed many victims in the struggle to define fiction. For the question of what fiction is, automatically implies that it can be ontologically grounded, whereas it constantly changes in relation to the frames of reference set up for its definition.

This is obvious from current discussions concerning the status of fiction, particularly in those types of discourse which borrow their criteria from analytic language philosophy. The prime focus of these attempts at defining fiction is the propositional mode of fictive speech that aims to relieve fiction from the burden of substantiating any "truth claim."[1] This release, however, implies a subjection of fictive speech either to criteria of truthfulness (according to propositional logic) or to conditions of sincerity (according to speech act theory) that would turn fictive speech into either 'quasi-judgment' or 'pseudo statement'. Such definitions qualify fictive speech as parasitic, since it lives on what is not,[2] and they deprive it of any claim to truth, since it does not correspond to the references that both propositional logic and speech-act theory provide.[3]

It is, however, characteristic of literary fictionalizing to disregard such referential hierarchies. Instead of defining fiction by way of the references proposed, the process of boundary-crossing puts these very references in brackets, so that they tend to become objects of observation *through* fiction, instead of providing conditions for its definition.

Quite different conclusions about fiction can be drawn when attention is focused not on its status but on its use. When it is conceived primarily in terms of communication,[4] it is gauged according to its success in opening up to its potential recipient a world to which it is a response. But even if this approach bypasses the problems arising out of a referential definition, its equation of fictionality with the literary text as a whole leads to a new problem. Understood as a means of communicating reality to a reader, fiction cannot be identical to what is communicated. All the same, the concept of fiction as communication has clear advantages over ontological definitions, and the approach is limited only insofar as it cannot bring to light the conditions that facilitate this use.

Current theories of fiction are beset by problems arising from their own premises. The question concerning the status of fiction leads to negative definitions, because fiction does not correspond to the criteria posited. The question of communication leaves out what it is that makes fiction into a communicator. What the two different approaches, then, have in common is a conspicuous, even if clearly distinguishable, deficiency. In the one instance, fiction appears to be grounded in an unplumbable base. In the other, the generative matrix that brings about communication eludes our grasp. This may be largely due to the fact that in each case fiction is subjected to references taken either from analytic language philosophy and speech-act theory or from information theory and communication theory. The lack of convincing results suggests that fiction will differ according to the categories chosen for defining it. It would be advisable, then, to take literary discourse itself as a context for exploring fictionality. Such a context will bring to light the historical shifts of fictionality's manifestations and may in the end change the manner in which these manifestations are to be viewed. Perhaps the most far-reaching problem posed by fiction is neither its status nor its communicative function but, rather, the question of why it exists at all.

Following the historical thread of literary fictionality will also shed new light on another aspect relevant to present-day discussions. Setting fiction against the background of language philosophy or communication theory means relating it to ruling concepts of late twentieth-century intellectual preoccupations. This, in turn, may imply that fiction has become important, a force to be reckoned with. It may also imply lifting some of the pressure regarding its legitimation by linking it to the prevailing cultural codes in order to give it an authenticity of its own. Whatever the individual aim may be, such approaches seek epistemological legitimation for fiction, whereas legitimation of that sort is not directly relevant to its character as an anthropological phenomenon.

By taking literary discourse as a reference for fictionality, we can avoid giving precedence either to the status or to the use of fiction, and instead focus attention on the conditions that are antecedent to both of them. By emphasizing literary discourse we need not determine the status of fiction nor define it in terms of use. We can instead fill the spaces left empty by other theories.

If there is one form of discourse in literature that demonstrates the operations of fictionalizing, it is Renaissance pastoralism. This extraordinary phenomenon was to permeate the literature of the whole era. The shepherds—originally restricted to the lowly genre of the eclogue—pushed their way into virtually every genre of Renaissance literature, even creating a new one, the pastoral romance, which actually thematizes the crossing of boundaries. As Renaissance genres were still geared to the social pyramid, the breaking of these bounds endowed pastoralism with an extraterritorial status. Thus it became a literary system of its own. Such systems are rare in literature, and no other has lasted as long as that of the pastoral.

Last vestiges of it may be spotted in Marie Antoinette's espousal of pastoralism, which she and her ladies acted out in the gardens of Trianon as a reality when the gathering storm of the Revolution was about to break. This late echo shows how the whole social order could in fact be translated into pastoral life. It also shows the pastoral world as a kind of counterimage, permitting what was excluded by reality. And finally, it shows that a mirror image does not exist on its own account but requires a reality that it is to reflect. Marie Antoinette's actions are symbolic insofar as at the very moment when the pastoral world merged with reality, the difference that had been eliminated was again thrown wide open by the Revolution.

What perhaps makes pastoral poetry unique in literary history is the fact that it thematizes the act of fictionalizing, thereby enabling literary fictionality to be vividly perceived. This perception forms the basis of pastoralism as a literary system no longer bounded by genres, and thus it seems plausible that pastoral poetry lost its place of importance at the moment when the function of literary fictionality no longer needed to be exhibited.

Scenarios of Pastoral Poetry in Antiquity

According to established tradition, pastoralism originated in the poetry of Theocritus, although he did not designate his work as such. Only posterity gave preference to those portions of his poetry in which herdsmen figured prominently. This is borne out by the fact that the adjective *pastoral* established itself as a noun "between Theocritus and Virgil—as indicating a type of poem and a title (for anthologies of such poems); we may conclude from this that pastoral poetry progressively made itself independent, freeing itself from other minor forms of Hellenistic poetry in its own right or at least in the minds of the existing literary public."[5] Thus it was the "product of a selective reception."[6] Is this a matter of historical chance, or did this preference spring from the pastoral's own special qualities? The very tradition it inaugurated through Virgil and whose almost unbroken vitality was sustained for over seventeen hundred years suggests that it must have fulfilled certain basic human needs. These were certainly not always the same needs, and so despite its high degree of continuity, pastoral poetry had to adapt to changing situations. This required schemata incorporating both the variable and the invariable; as a result of this dual structure, pastoral poetry unfolds itself as a process of reception which gains its own history from its continual reworking of the pastoral world.

Even Theocritus's poetry contains constants as well as conditions for change, and from these one can draw up a blueprint for pastoral poetry. In the *Fifth Idyll,* for instance, a topic is to be found that remains a basic constituent of the genre right through to the Renaissance: the herdsmen's singing contest. What was to establish itself as a topos actually sprang from the imitation of a real-life situation, since the singing contest was—and, as Merkelbach has shown, still is, in a ritualized form—a widespread social custom.[7] It was particularly popular among herdsmen, because their work "is boring, and such a contest is an enjoyable pastime" (p. 114). What takes place in Theocritus's *Fifth Idyll* is therefore the "reproduction of a real and existing custom" (p. 115). It may be an entertainment, and it is most certainly playful in character, as the competition in the *Fifth Idyll* is agonistic.

Thus, in Theocritus, the ritualized game of real life became the subject matter of poetry. This development marks the change from an oral tradition to a written one, but the permanent record is far from being its only consequence. The written word creates possibilities that were not available to the games borne by memory. These games had been fixed as ritualized schemata that enabled them to be retrieved at will. As the written word relieves the memory, it allows for a diversification of playing, in the course of which an ever-increasing multifariousness of gaming strategies begins to emerge. Ritualized games provide relief from the monotonous hardships of the herdsmen's ordinary life; the poetic imitation of games, however, opens up an exploration of playing itself. Agon thus turns out to be the invariable, while the procedure of the contest is the variable that poetry explores. It is the writing down of this variable that determines precisely the patterning of the agon.

In Theocritus's *Fifth Idyll* there are two discernible features of play that were to become pastoral archetypes: the mirror and the outplaying of the partner. The contest is a mirror insofar as each partner has to latch onto whatever his counterpart has said. Consequently, the theme is always mirrored in the encounter, though with the proviso that it is, so to speak, refracted by the repetition. The resultant procedure is one that turns the subject inside out, because whenever the mirror reflects what has been said, it brings out (as part of the outplaying) aspects that will top the opponent's utterance. Thus the contest demands the invention of new ways of extending the game by giving it unforeseeable turns. Overturning and outplaying become paradigmatic strategies, because they always supply something unpremeditated and additional to what is or will be said. This something cannot, however, be deduced from what is said, because it is intended to obliterate the previous statement. This is what leads to the improvised richness of the game, for in the written contest the formulaic patterns of oral poetry can be relinquished, giving free rein to new and unexpected structures that can be held fast by the written word. The written word then becomes the precondition for activating fantasy.

The fact that the contest was regarded as a game is borne out by the presence of a referee who must render a final decision. The referee represents the public before whom the contest takes place and who expect a definite outcome. He also represents the reader, who is likewise confronted by the game's agonistic reversals and successes, and who must ultimately resolve the clashes between all the different possibilities. The referee—like the reader—will not be able to take into consideration all the shifts and turns of the game but is bound to base the decision on a selection. The decision will depend on certain rules. When, for instance, Comatas wins the contest in the *Fifth Idyll*, it is not because he outperforms his rival but because he obeys the rules that Lakon violates. If one takes seriously the "understanding formulated by Lakon at the beginning of the idyll, that he will 'outsing' Comatas so that the latter will not know what to say next . . . one must conclude that this in fact is what actually happens to Lakon. He 'runs out of steam.' He can no longer vary what Comatas has sung, and so he loses . . . These rules are clear to both contestants from the start and need no discussion."[8] This is the criterion for the referee's decision, and since he judges by the rule that has been violated, he does not need to accommodate all the variations of the game within his decision. Comatas therefore stresses toward the end the incomparability of the positions represented in the game,[9] which, however, cannot remain unreconciled but must be resolved by a final judgment.

Since each player's move entails blocking the opponent, both the mirroring and the outplaying give rise to the semantic potential that, though infinite in itself, must remain within limits if the game is to be kept comprehensible. The meaning of the text therefore comes into being by way of a decision that, inevitably, involves a selection from the possibilities presented, since not all of them can be geared to the chosen frame of reference. So the reader's role is adumbrated by the referee, while at the same time the game shows the extent to which comprehension restricts meaning.

What we have seen so far is the herdsmen's game as the invariable of pastoral literature, while the need for every different form of gaming brings about its variability. Consequently, each variation decides what the game is to be, though each variation also depends on what it varies. In this respect, one cannot talk of pastoral literature as a generically defined entity—after all, the pastoral transcends generic boundaries— but is, rather, a process of reception; and this process, in turn, would scarcely have survived as long as it did if, from the very beginning, it had had a clear-cut identity.

The reasons why pastoral poetry should be regarded primarily as a process of reception are not yet fully apparent in Theocritus, but one can find substantial hints. The singing contest in the *Fifth Idyll*, for example, is a poetic form derived from the herdsmen's everyday lives, and it allows them to stage themselves. Through the game, they can become something other than herdsmen. Later, in Virgil, they stage themselves as poets or, as we shall see, poets even stage themselves as herdsmen. In no case, however, is this self-enacting to be equated with their own nature, or Nature itself, let alone with an Aristotelian *morphē*. Theocritus's imitation of real-life situations modifies the concept of mimesis insofar as the object imitated is not natural but man-made—actually, a departure from Nature. The game as enactment permits repetition of whatever becomes part of it, which in principle might extend to everything, including Nature—already cast in the *locus amoenus* as man's pleasant environment. By initially repeating a game played in a real-life situation, pastoral poetry becomes an epitome of gaming which, in the final analysis, enables it to repeat the world itself. The implications of this become apparent in Virgil's *Eclogues*. While Theocritus imitates the herdsmen's ritualized games, Virgil highlights the artificiality of these man-made pastimes by inventing Arcadia as the realm of poetry in which poetry becomes its own concern.

Classical scholars vary in their views of this artificial world. Much controversy surrounds Snell's pronouncement that Arcadia is a "spiritual landscape," that is, "a land of the soul yearning for its distant home in the past."[10] The objection to this interpretation is that it reveals merely an "expression of a longing of the Philhellenist after the presence of Greek Antiquity has faded away," and thus ultimately it has little to do with Virgil, whose poetry "springs not from . . . escapism and the longed-for dream, but from the experienced reality and presence of poesy."[11] But the critics are all agreed that in Virgil's *Eclogues* poetry itself has become a subject matter of poetry, epitomized by the invention of Arcadia as presented most vividly in the *Fourth* and *Tenth Eclogues*.

If Arcadia is not to be regarded as a "spiritual landscape," "a faraway land overlaid with the golden haze of unreality,"[12] but as the self-presentation of poetry, what are its chief characteristics? Snell's answer remains unchallenged: "In his [i.e., Virgil's] mind, political matters are closely connected with mythical concepts; and here the combining and blending of myth and reality, which is so characteristic of the Arcadian temper, achieves a singularly impressive result. . . . His Arcadia is set half-way between myth and reality; it is also a no-man's land between two ages."[13] This means, however, that Arcadia is always linked to a historical realm outside the bounds of its own artificiality: "In Virgil, politics is the ever-present condition without which the pastoral fiction could not last."[14] What, then, are the constituents of this "no-man's land"? The *Fifth* and *First Eclogues* show an almost mirror-image reversal of the relations between historical and artificial worlds.

In the introductory stanzas of the *Fifth Eclogue,* the shepherds discuss what sort of song should be sung, and the first suggestion of something erotic is rejected; instead, there follows the Daphnis song. The rejection of the erotic goes against expectations, since the shepherds' songs were almost always erotic.[15] Something new is to take the place of the old, but this novelty is the old myth of Daphnis that already formed part of the Theocritean poetic repertoire. Expectations are therefore shattered not in order to introduce a new theme but in order to offer a new treatment of the most traditional of all bucolic myths.

Mopsus begins with a song that mourns Daphnis, whose death has brought disaster to the world. As long as he lived, he "adorned us all." This concept is different from that of Theocritus, whose Daphnis in no way symbolized such a division. Menalcas sings the second part of the song, praising Daphnis as the resurrected god, thereby restoring harmony. Thus the Daphnis song is divided into two contrasting halves, which in turn are doubled by their respective coupling of poetry and world. The eclogue embraces all these contrasts, and thereby shows that pastoral poetry not only mirrors the world but also incorporates the world into poetry. If the poet's death indicates disaster in the world, and if his return means the world's restoration to harmony, then the relation between poetry and world is moved into focus through the removal of the boundary between the two.

Though the boundary itself is not thematized, the invocation of the Daphnis myth shows that only through myth can the difference between poetry and world be obliterated. If myth, however, proves to be the last resort for overcoming what is otherwise different, one might say that difference turns all forms of its elimination into myth. Therefore, if poetry is to resist becoming myth, it is bound to unfold the changing relations between what is different, and thus to uphold rather than to obliterate difference. Since the elimination of difference results in myth, myth can also be made to be seen as a pointer to what it conceals: the telescoping of poetry and world.

Paul Alpers has characterized the climaxes of the *Eclogues* as follows: "'Suspension' seems to me the best word to use for such moments, because it suggests a poised and secure contemplation of things disparate or ironically related, and yet at the same time does not imply that disparities or conflicts are fully resolved. This quality in the *Eclogues* is found not only in specific moments but in whole poems—and indeed . . . in the whole sequence . . . we see that Virgil is concerned to contemplate differences and their potential composition without losing sight of either."[16] This is borne out in the *First Eclogue,* where the two worlds are clearly interwoven. At the beginning, the *locus amoenus* becomes a mirror reflecting the calamity caused by politics, which threatens the peace of the blissful location. This situation unfolds as a game that, unlike Theocritus's song contest, has no particular form but takes place in a kind of pendulum movement. The world of the poetic shepherds is constantly penetrated by another world, and the consequences of such an interpenetration are to be acted out. The shepherds are therefore not just shepherds but also husbandmen and poets, and sometimes impersonate Virgil himself. The *juvenis* is not just a youth but also a god and Augustus.

What the *Fifth Eclogue* resolves through myth is in the *First Eclogue* fanned out into a variety of possible relations. The characters are multirepresentative, thereby giving rise to a multiplicity of potential combinations. The game takes on additional complexity as the different meanings of the characters alternately take the foreground or fade into the background. This makes reading itself into a game, in which particular constellations establish themselves at the expense of others. But these in turn are changed by the continued presence of the other facets of the characters, and in this way the agonistic character of the game forces its way into the reading process as well. If the interweaving of worlds were intended to eliminate their difference, the irritation caused by the continued presence of other possible relations serves to bring out not only the interweaving but also the encounter of opposite worlds.

As a result, the shepherds represent a world that is very difficult to locate. Nevertheless, representation presupposes 'realities' to which the poem will always be related. In the *First Eclogue,* the relations and the realities are multiplied, so that the link between signifier and signified is no longer nearly as rigid as it was in the Platonic concept of mimesis. And even where the link does appear to be firm, as in the *Fifth Eclogue,* the correspondence between poetry and world reveals itself to be a myth that, through the interplay between poetry and politics prevalent in the rest of the *Eclogues,* highlights a past relationship. Thus pastoral poetry presents itself as a sphere between then and now, indicating that the received notion of mimesis—in either the Platonic or the Aristotelian sense—can result only in myth. This is so because the relation between the poetic and the political worlds is no longer pregiven, and hence cannot be imitated, but must be constituted in order to bring out its potentially unbounded multifariousness.

This departure from the traditional concept of mimesis ends up as mimesis of poetry itself, which now for the first time reveals what it is or, rather, what it has been taken to be. For this reason it is hard to trust any reading of pastoralism that, deliberately or otherwise, hinges on the traditional concept of mimesis. This applies to Snell's description of Arcadia as "a spiritual landscape"[17] as well as to Alpers's "representative anecdote"[18] for the description of human life in general. These are both Platonically inspired readings of a form of poetry that, though mimetic of itself, breaks away from the traditional poetry imitating nature or any other pregiven. Being self-imitative, poetry has to establish a view of what it is; it must use familiar sign relationships to make itself concrete. In order to establish a view of something unfamiliar, however, signs must be stripped of their familiar designations. Virgil achieves this through the world of the shepherds. As Schmidt has stressed, it is "an incontrovertible fact that there is no external reality linked to or corresponding to the shepherd poets. This means that the world they live in . . . the 'shepherds' world,' is not a given reality either but—just like themselves, created by their poet—is a poetic world."[19]

What makes this world "poetic" is its liberation from what it originally relates to—the daily routine of country life. The signifier (the shepherds' world) is dislocated from what it conventionally signifies (the rustic world) in order that it may bring about something unfamiliar, which is the imaginability of poetry. Departure from traditional mimesis goes hand in hand with departure from the convention-governed relationship between signifier and signified by letting the signifier float, so that it may serve to produce hitherto unforeseeable significations, resulting ultimately in a fictionalization of established connections. The signs now have to be read differently. They no longer denote given positions or substances; instead, they insinuate links, unfold directions, and adumbrate realizations in order to reveal what cannot be denoted. Thus Virgil's pastoral poetry imitates a nonmimetic state of affairs, which is not a given but something that had first to be produced. This change imparts a new objective to poetry. Virgil's pastoralism constitutes poetry written by poets about poets, though these poets enact themselves as shepherds so that, in the guise of simple people, they can explore the imaginative possibilities of poetry's acting upon the ordinary sociopolitical world. Traditional mimesis fades into the wings, for the shepherds are mere trappings for the poets, and poetry becomes nonmimetic (in the conventional sense) because, in exploring its own possibilities, it confronts a world that is no longer to be imitated but is to be intruded upon.

Why were shepherds chosen to be the instruments for poetry's self-imitation? Why not huntsmen, husbandmen, or—as sometimes in the Renaissance—fishermen? All of these stand in a special relationship to Nature. Assuming that the choice was not arbitrary, what particular relationship to Nature is enjoyed by the shepherds, whose rustic life is not to be portrayed, let alone imitated, but rather serves as a medium for the portrayal of something other than itself?[20] There is already the germ of an answer in Theocritus that assumes the status of a topos in Virgil; this is the link between the shepherds' singing contest and the consequent competition over the animals that the victor is to claim as his prize. Here is a typical example from the *Third Eclogue*:

> Menalcas: What can lords do, when thieves so greatly dare?
>   Did I not see you, scum, sneak up to catch
>   Damon's best goat, while Lowder barked his head off?
>   And when I shouted, "Where's he dashing off?
>   Tityrus, gather the flock!" you skulked in the reeds.
>
> Damoetas: Oughtn't he, bested in song, have handed over
>   The goat, which my melodious pipe had won?
>   In case you don't know, that goat was mine, and Damon
>   Admitted it, but said he couldn't pay.
>
> Menalcas: You beat him singing? Whenever did panpipers
>   Belong to you?—street-corner bard, whose skill's to
>   Murder on scrannel straw a wretched song.
>
> Damoetas: Then how about trying what we two can do
>   Singing by turns? This heifer, with udder full
>   Enough for double milkings plus two calves,
>   Is my stake. What will you put on the line?[21]

So long as the shepherds are slaves, they possess nothing but their art.[22] Only eventually, through their animals, do they possess a piece of Nature. Songs and animals, therefore, are equivalents, so that shepherds may lose their animals because of imperfect art, a situation which may in turn be corrected by stealing back the stake that has been lost.

If we set this situation against its ethnological background, the equivalence of songs and animals takes on still another perspective. Unlike huntsmen, shepherds do not kill to live. Instead, they domesticate their animals and tend their piece of Nature. Unlike husbandmen, they do not settle on the land in order to wrest their living from the soil. Rather, they roam the countryside with their flocks and have leisure time. Here, then, we have a varied "economy of tropes," each based on a different ethnographic relation to Nature. Since huntsmen had to kill animals in order to possess them, their link with Nature was manifested pictographically: the uncontrollability of Nature was averted by pictures, but this picture writing meant death. "Writing would indeed be the pictorial representation of the hunted beast: magical capture and murder ... The hunter paints beings, the shepherd already incribes languages." This results in a "total revolution in the structure of representation."23 Writing is now able to represent Nature. In Derrida's terms it becomes an "ideo-phonogram," differing from the huntsmen's pictography in that it is already "a mixture of signifier and signified"24 before the phonetism of the alphabet gains the upper hand.

If Nature can be represented through writing, then it can be made to speak through its representation. This, however, entails representation's proclaiming what Nature is. Thus writing makes Nature available and simultaneously turns Nature into a picture of writing. Consequently, Nature achieves its ideality in the written picture as exemplified by the *locus amoenus,* with the signifier and the signified substituting for one another. What becomes an ideogram in the *locus amoenus* has its parallel in the interchangeability of songs and animals, which shows even more clearly than the purely literary topos the ethnological trace that permeates pastoral poetry: writing as a displacement of or supplement for Nature.

Both the *locus amoenus,* however, and the possession of Nature in the form of the flock remain vulnerable—they can both be put in jeopardy. The idealized landscape is a representation of Nature that conceals the very character of representation (which is to stand for something else). The signifier and the signified can therefore be separated again, indicating the distance between them. The possession of the flock depends on the justice of civil institutions that initially safeguard both the possession and the resultant welfare, and this is why Virgil's *Eclogues* turn political. The *Eclogues* do not describe the shepherd's life, they represent it, and that means they make the possession of Nature (in the form of domesticated animals and the writing of poetry) into an inverted mirror image of the political world. This structure brings out the artificiality of the shepherd-poets, who no longer serve to designate what they are but, through what they are, serve to indicate another meaning. In Virgil's *Eclogues* politics stands side by side with Nature, the latter being mastered by poetry while the former— man-made—at times appears to be uncontrollable. Consequently, the self-imitation of poetry is not an autonomous art[25] but rather the means of righting something that threatens to go wrong.

Once again this entails a change in the concept of mimesis. Poetry does not imitate politics. Rather, politics inscribes itself into the artificiality of poetry, so that the eclogue represents both the separation and the pictorial blending of politics and poetry. This double character of representation indicates something that is very difficult to pinpoint, because it is not in the nature of a tangible object. Whatever state of affairs might be conveyed by each individual representation, it is, despite its multiformity, the product of the poem and cannot be traced back either to the forms of Nature or to the ideality presumed to underlie them.

If we set Virgil's shepherds against their ethnological background (in which domestication and writing signify mastery of Nature), we can see why the poet used them to reflect the world of politics. There are two remarks of Dr. Johnson's that will help us to understand Virgil's reasons. In pastoral poetry's waning phase during the eighteenth century, Dr. Johnson criticized Sannazaro for making fishermen the protagonists of his *Eclogues*. The sea, according to Dr. Johnson, "will be sooner exhausted by a descriptive writer [than the land]"; furthermore, the sea is an obstacle to the reception of such poetry because of the "ignorance of maritime pleasures, in which the greater part of mankind must always live."[26] Moreover, the sea features at best an aspect of Nature that lacks the multifariousness necessary for turning Nature— made available through writing—into a mirror to reflect the disfigurement caused by the incursion of the political world.

The Eclogue and Its Referential Reality

Arcadia is Virgil's invented world of poetry—a work of art that thematizes art itself. It does so by withdrawing from another world, although this other world continues to impinge on that of poetry. The nature of the relationship between these two worlds is never verbalized in the *Eclogues*. This could mean that Virgil's reading public was more homogeneous than in succeeding centuries—and especially in the Renaissance—so that it was possible to present telescoped worlds without specifying how they were to be interlinked, but there can be no doubt that this linking of worlds became a problem in the centuries to come. This is evident from the allegorical reading prevalent in the Middle Ages, which was by no means restricted to the prophetically understood annunciation of Christ in the *Fourth Eclogue*. The very need for such an allegorical reading indicates that the *Eclogues* must contain two different spheres whose relationship requires some form of exegesis. Virgil's poet-shepherds are not meant to represent the daily routine of rustic toil; they embody the meaning of poetry and song in human culture. Even Theocritus, whose *Idylls* come closest to presenting scenes of country life, sees his shepherds as tropes, and his poetry "does not describe a life in the country, but arranges elements taken from the country in such a manner as to permit the full flowering of another order: the life of the soul, the *otium* of the free."[27] Pastoral poetry is therefore a trope that comes to full fruition in its figurations. It provided a schema that laid itself open to allegorization, for against the background of a substantialist concept of the world only allegory could embrace what appeared to be a split between image and reference by pinning down the latter while at the same time preserving the pastoral nature of the former.

In the Renaissance, too, the allegorical reading of the *Eclogues* remained a commonplace, as shown by Puttenham in his *Arte of English Poesie*:

> [T]he Poet deuised the Eglogue ... not of purpose to counterfait or represent the rusticall manner of loues and communication: but vnder the vaile of homely persons, and in rude speeches to insinuate and glaunce at greater matters, and such as perchance had not bene safe to haue beene disclosed in any other sort, which may be perceived by the Eglogues of Virgill, in which are treated by figure matters of greater importance then the loues of Titirus and Corydon. These Eglogues came after to containe and enforme morall discipline, for the amendment of mans behauiour, as be those of Mantuan and other modern Poets.[28]

In Spenser's eclogues the rigid structure of allegory is on the wane. Even though the allegorical *modus dicendi* still has a role to play, it has been marginalized, giving way to an increasing complexity of the inter-relationship between what is said and what is meant. The introductory section of the *Shepheardes Calender* already makes it clear that the pastoral world means something other than itself. The author—according to Spenser's presumably feigned commentator—has chosen the shepherds only in order "to vnfold great matter of argument couertly, then professing it . . . Now as touching the generell dryft and purpose of his Aeglogues, I mind not to say much, him selfe labouring to conceale it,"[29] so that the commentator can finally claim: "I was made priuie to his counsell and secret meaning in them."[30] Clearly, then, the shepherds' world shades off into the figuration of another world.

In this respect, Spenser is still following the pattern of Virgil's *Eclogues* by invoking the contract established by Virgil, and subsequently turned into a convention, between author and public that the shepherds mean something other than themselves. But the commentator now goes one step further than Virgil insofar as what is said, instead of merely meaning something else, actually serves to conceal what is meant. This must inevitably affect the nature of the allegory. Of course, allegory always depends on the space between signifier and signified, but the exegetical procedure, as developed by biblical hermeneutics, was designed to bring out the inherent polysemy of the divine word. Such procedures began to assume an ever-increasing importance for the allegorical mode in medieval secular literature, since here, too, the space between the letter and the spirit had to be bridged. Two different types of bridging ensued: the figural schema and that of *personificatio* and *significatio*. According to the figural schema, the spirit antedates the letter through which it attains its manifestation. According to the relationship of *personificatio* and *significatio*, the letter is absorbed by the spirit in order either to picture the invisible or to prove the spirit's effectiveness in concrete situations. Thus both schemata, though different in character, regulate the sign relationships in order to bring about clearly distinguishable significations by means of which the inherent polysemy of the linguistic medium is channeled in such a way that tangible solutions may arise. Letter and spirit have always been overarched by a third dimension, and this hierarchical stratification has its foundation in the medieval world picture, which foregrounded itself in the relationships it imposed on letter and spirit. This sign relationship is ternary by nature; it emerged in late antiquity and was persistent until it began to become problematical in the Renaissance. Foucault has provided a pertinent outline for this impending reshuffle of an inherited tradition:

> Ever since the Stoics, the system of signs in the Western world had been a ternary one, for it was recognized as containing the significant, the signified and the 'conjuncture'. . . . From the seventeenth century, on the other hand, the arrangement of sign was to become binary, since it was to be defined, with Port-Royal, as the connection of a significant and a signified. At the Renaissance, the organization is different, and much more complex: it is ternary, since it requires the formal domain of marks, the content indicated by them, and the similitudes that link the marks to the things designated by them; but since resemblance is the form of the signs as well as their content, the three distinct elements of this articulation are resolved into a single form.[31]

In Spenser's eclogues the ternary sign system becomes severely strained, resulting in an increasingly complicated linkup no longer to be conceived as the preestablished "conjuncture" that had once stood for the all-encompassing medieval cosmic order. Instead, sign relationships now have to be devised, and this need makes it clear why Spenser published his eclogues with a commentary that mapped out the changing fields of reference reflected by the pastoral world. In all probability he wrote the commentary himself and attributed it to a fictitious character.[32] In any event, to publish secular poetry with a commentary was still something extraordinary in the Renaissance. Even more extraordinary is the fact that the commentary formed an integral component of the poem—and this from a young poet who was making his debut with the *Shepheardes Calendar!* Though Petrarch had earlier added explanations to his *Bucolicum carmen* that proved to be a vital key to the understanding of his eclogues, they served first and foremost to stimulate "commentary by professors of rhetoric and poetry,"[33] especially since Petrarch regarded the coding of his eclogues as a kind of camouflage. In Spenser, however, the commentary signalizes the "similitudes," so that the reader may focus on the other world that is adumbrated in the pastoral.

Thus it is the commentaries at the end of each eclogue which tell us that the shepherd Colin Clout is sometimes a poet, sometimes Spenser himself, sometimes just a shepherd, and sometimes the English people as a whole. The same is true of the shepherdess Eliza, who at different times embodies the beloved, Queen Elizabeth, and the grieving Dido. The figure of Pan undergoes curious variations: god of the shepherds, Jesus, Henry VIII, and even Satan. Such ad hoc "similitudes" no longer arise out of the allegorical structure, even though they still serve to make the pastoral world imaginable as the figuration of another world. While the allegorical mode imposed a predetermined semantic relationship on what the personification was meant to signify, these ad hoc "similitudes" actually release a welter of potential correlations. The shepherds take on multiple meanings, which may be literary, personal, romantic, moral, religious, or political. Often the meanings are so interwoven that, despite the temporary dominance of one of them, the others shade into the one actually present. If Colin Clout is shepherd, poet, Spenser, and the English people, and if Eliza is shepherdess, Dido, and Queen Elizabeth, the preordained interdependence of the two levels, otherwise fixed by the allegorical mode, begins to fade, and we obtain a host of semantic adumbrations that impinge on every meaning of every situation in every eclogue. Consequently, when the shepherds foreshadow certain political figures, the "resemblances" become increasingly complex and begin to proliferate.

The *April Eclogue* is a case in point. Here the whole Arcadian repertoire is offered up as a eulogy of Queen Elizabeth. Strikingly, the ternary system makes its reappearance, and the queen is linked typologically to the ancient gods, to Arcadian personae, to the chain of being, and to the political situation. But she is at one and the same time *figura* and *complementum*, so that the figural schema becomes a metaphorical expression of transfiguration. However, the hymn of praise which Colin Clout—is he now a shepherd, Spenser himself, or the English people?—has composed for Elizabeth is overshadowed by the shepherdess's rejection of him. We learn, however, of this unavailing courtship—acted out on multiple levels—from another shepherd, who recites the hymn in order to highlight both Colin's poetic talent and his alienation from it, caused by the futility of his efforts that has plunged him into melancholy. Thus the hymn is staged in the eclogue merely to light up semantic dimensions for the purpose of their subsequent erasure. Finally, the commentator remarks that Colin Clout's typological correspondences display the "hugenesse of his imagination."[34] This means that the whole network of correlations is nothing but an offshoot of the imagination with hardly any bearing on the reality meant to be acted upon.

This can be gauged from the wide range of changing sign relationships to be observed among the different levels. First there is the political link between Eliza and Elizabeth as well as between Pan and Henry VIII, though this level signalizes a rejection of Colin Clout's courtship (he may be the poet or the English people). Then there are the typological links, though these ideal correspondences are locked in the poet's imagination. And finally there is the level on which the shepherds conjecture about Colin Clout's melancholy—conjectures that must all be abandoned. Although there is a common objective underlying each of the individual levels, their differences shade equally into one another, setting free what remains concealed in the manifest correspondence. In consequence, a potentially unrestrained interplay between signs replaces the old "conjuncture" and transforms the substantialist-oriented ternary system into a semiotic game.

The variety of possible connections engendered by the interaction of the different levels leads to a suspension of the hierarchical principle that had always governed medieval allegorization. On the other hand, by tending to favor certain connections at the expense of others, the commentator gives the impression that the connections are more rigidly controlled than in medieval allegory. For this reason, however, the reader is compelled to bear in mind all the changing patterns of interconnections, as is clearly to be seen from the sequence of the eclogues. *The Shepheardes Calendar* is obviously meant to be read cumulatively, for only in this way can the eclogues unfold a succession of favored connections set out by the commentator, pushing previously established connections into the background. From there they overshadow what moves into focus and exercise control over a developing semantic multifariousness. Even if the basic pattern of the ternary system still prevails, the range of possible connections opened up by the commentator demands a cumulative reading, if there is to be any understanding. Such a mode of reading takes the place once held by the medieval world order that decreed what the correspondences had to be. This change is due not least to the fact that, unlike the traditional allegory, the pastoral realm—as an artificial world—does not relate to the invisible or other world but to an empirical, political, and historical one. In medieval allegory, the hierarchical order of things was regulated by the predominance of a substantialist worldview. The "conjuncture" could become an issue only at the moment when the pastoral world, distinguished by its artificiality, was meant to designate a world other than itself, although the world in question lacked all the attributes presupposed by the cosmic order of the chain of being. But could something, while not denoting itself, be linked to something else that, in Platonic and medieval terms, was basically insubstantial?

In Spenser's eclogues medieval allegory remains present only as a schematic skeleton that is deprived both of its original function and of its original significance. The structure of correspondences is still unimpaired, yet the manifold correlations of these correspondences fan out into ranges of ever-changing significations. The effect is to enhance conceivability of what are to be regarded as central issues of the sociohistorical world. Their very variety eludes allegorization, and therefore access to them requires schemata of conceivability that will identify the problems and simultaneously prevent identification of themselves with what they are designed to make available. Providing multiple connections inevitably complicates the "conjuncture," as is all too obvious from the increasing complexity of the commentary that combines a variety of genres such as the epistle, the argument, the gloss, and the emblem. Such differentiation endows the correlation of levels—according to the significance of the genre chosen—with a specific importance out of which arises a fine-tuning of the "conjuncture"; this is necessary for the establishment of a graded network of relationships, if a hitherto insubstantial world is to be made available.

Spenser leaves no room for doubt that the shepherds' names conceal other names, which need not necessarily be historical persons but—as in the *May Eclogue*—may represent Catholicism or Protestantism. Even when precise identification is impossible, the commentator hints that the shepherd's name is a made-up one meant to conceal that of another person. Thus Spenser's characters are never simply shepherds, historical persons, or types but are all these simultaneously. When real people are mirrored in the shepherds, this mirroring endows them with possibilities not available to them in the sociohistorical world.

This basic structure also underlies the tropes and literary genres that recur throughout the eclogues. In the *January Eclogue,* for instance, we learn of Colin Clout:

> Thou barrein ground, whome winters wrath hath wasted,
> Art made a myrrhour, to behold my plight.[35]

The commentator declares unequivocally that Colin Clout is the poet: "Vnder which name this Poete secretly shadoweth himself."[36] And as the barren winter mirrors the lovesick shepherd, so later his plight is mirrored by the wasting herd. Mirror and correspondence are basic tropes of the period, with correspondence being the more important of the two, since it provides the indispensable coherence for cosmic stability by linking the different degrees in the chain of being. The concept of correspondence figured, therefore, in the syncretistic Platonic and Christian world order as the mainspring of harmony. But now correspondences feature increasing disorder, and this is represented by a trope that had originally guaranteed cosmic concordance. If "similitudes"—as Foucault conceived them—served as substitutes for the "conjuncture" in a now waning ternary system, Spenser casts them as indicators of a shattered harmony; instead of perfection, they spell disaster. This view is further endorsed by the fact that the concept of correspondences also invokes the old pastoral cliché of paradisiacal concord between shepherd and Nature. Thus, the negative slant imparted to the cosmological notion of correspondence reverberates in the destruction of the otherwise blissful harmony of man and nature.

This recasting of pastoral clichés and contemporary tropes is a distinctive mark of *The Shepheardes Calendar*. It reaches a peak in the *June Eclogue,* where the correspondence serves only to illustrate its own devaluation. In the middle of the year, with the sun at its zenith, Colin Clout's deep despair cancels out the harmony that the received notion of correspondence was meant to convey. In order to spotlight this reversal, Colin's plight is set as a backdrop for Colin's friend, Hobbinol. Hobbinol has regained the very paradise from which Adam had been driven, thus enjoying once again the accord with Nature that even Colin's art is unable to recapture. Traditional tropes and pastoral clichés have to split into countervailing references, as only their duplicity can mark the difference between sign and world. The conventional signification of "similitude" is now employed to point out an emergent unlikeness.

What is to be observed within the recurrent repertoire of tropes and clichés spills over into a growing tendency to incorporate other genres into the sequence of Spenser's eclogues. Because the traditional form of the eclogue appears no longer to be adequate to the expanding demands of its representational function, the eclogues begin to include other genres. This is already discernible in their external organization. Each eclogue is headed by a woodcut exhibiting the appropriate image of the zodiac, which is in itself a visual presentation of what the text seems to be concerned with. Then comes the Argument, followed by the eclogue itself, which concludes with an Emblem. Eclogue and Emblem lead to a commentary that to a degree opens up the territory that has been hidden in the eclogue. In this respect one might say that the eclogues are multimedia, and indeed they need both pictorial and literary forms to bring out the various facets of their signification. The ensuing perspectivization indicates that representation is no longer exclusively conceived as mimesis but unfolds as a dynamic process. Whatever representation is meant to picture is now imbued with a sense of motion in order to capture what had hitherto appeared to be unrepresentable.

For this procedure the *February Eclogue* is a case in point. Various literary genres are telescoped together: the *altercatio* provides the frame for the eclogue, the fable for the *altercatio,* and the forensic plea for the fable. The eclogue begins with the typical song contest between two shepherds. This, however, is reduced to a mere outline, because instead of being presented as trying to outdo each other in praise of the adored shepherdess, the two shepherds enter into an altercation on youth and old age. In this way, the pastoral theme is replaced by the "debate" that was a much-favored form in medieval literature and became widespread in vernacular versions, reaching a peak with Abelard's *Sic et non.* The confrontation between youth and age demands a decision, but instead of the judge one might have expected, there is a fable that constitutes a *genus mixtum* insofar as it is cast in the form of a forensic plea. In the fable, the oak and the brier quarrel over their importance and over the disturbance they cause each other. They take their case to man—representing humankind—who, called upon to pass judgment, makes a wrong decision that destroys both oak and brier. A moral conclusion would now appear to be pertinent. Here, as elsewhere, however, the expectations aroused by the genre itself are not fulfilled: the eclogue ends with a dual emblem that, instead of a single moral, draws different conclusions from the case presented. In this instance, as in all those that have preceded it, the constitutive component of the genre is eliminated and replaced by another, though different, genre. This decomposing of genres robs them of their original function that was geared to the various levels of the social hierarchy as well as to the ramifications of social anthropology inherited from the ancient and medieval worlds. Now the genres are representative only to the degree in which they invoke and run counter to established expectations.

Once a genre can no longer be identified with the state of affairs it is supposed to represent, it becomes a mere schema of representation that—in contrast to its traditional functions—highlights the space between itself and the object represented. Thus the individual genres within the Spenserian eclogue turn into frames for the staging of other genres. This nesting of genres divests them of their inherited representational function and transforms them into a sequence of schemata that outstrip one another. The ensuing dynamism, then, points to the conceivability of what eludes representation by each of the genres assembled.

What this process entails becomes tangible in the *February Eclogue* as well. In the altercation between youth and age the respective values represented by the two clash: Youth represents spring, rebellion, and pleasure of the moment; age stands for winter, experience, and resignation. But the content of the dispute does not consist in these well-known medieval categories; instead it pivots on what each representational instance conceals: to the old man, youth is just a flickering light, helpless and exposed to temptation, while the young contestant sees the old as ossified, envious, and destructive. Viewed from the standpoint of the disputants, the traditional topoi of youth and age take on special meaning, with each believing that the other's traditional argument conceals a form of behavior which is not meant to come out into the open. This delving below the surface of conventional clichés reveals the topos itself to be a mask, for the authority of the commonplace serves only to conceal. With the quarrel now stripping this mask away, the topoi and their presentation become duplicitous, because they no longer represent but instead serve to signalize what is not covered by them. The consequences of these apparent limitations are different from those produced by the split driven into traditional tropes and pastoral clichés: the split inverts traditional usage, whereas representation as a mask releases a whole range of new possibilities.

There is an echo of this in the fable as well. Man, whose gift of reason has given him a high-ranking position in the chain of being, is called upon to settle the dispute between oak and brier. But he falls prey to the rhetoric of the rose that stirs his passions. He cuts down the oak, and destroys the balance of Nature so that the rose also perishes, having lost the protection of the oak. Reason was supposed to triumph in the judgment, but the fable leaves no doubt that a different motivation underlay that judgment. Once again, a traditional attribute of man serves to bring out whatever else man is. In this case, the power of reason that man is supposed to represent is reduced to a mask concealing a hidden duality within himself. The split emblem, which one might have expected to resolve this duality, then provides an emphatic confirmation of it, while the commentary adds that the attitudes depicted may be seen from different standpoints and hence might give rise to different conclusions.

The nesting of literary genres epitomizes a departure from the received notion of representation, whose patterns were meant to give presence to the represented and not to be strategies of concealment. The telescoped genres serve to indicate both the limitations of representation and the necessity of conceiving what cannot be grasped. This two-tiered arrangement is in itself a form of representation, though it is no longer geared to the stratification of the social pyramid. Instead, the disrupted correspondence between the genres and the social hierarchy points to the growing expansion of the sociopolitical world. The nesting indicates that very expansion by making the genres encroach upon one another, reducing them to a mere schema. The upshot of this recasting of the traditional notion of representation is the emergence of two worlds: one that can be represented and another that cannot, and that therefore is only to be impinged upon.

Spenser's whole cycle of eclogues is permeated by this doubleness. At the very beginning, the commentator claims that what is said is not what is meant, and more often than not conceals the meaning. Such a duplicity exposes the pastoral world as one of semblance or—to cite a popular view of pastoral poetry in its time—highlights it as a shadow of the reality intended. This shadow is fashioned by traditional patterns of representation that function as analogues for conceiving what is to be imagined. The shepherds are only 'shadows' of real people, the tropes and clichés are just reversals of their traditional indication, and the genres only frames of enactments. The pastoral world is clearly always doubled by another world.

Doubling, then, is a basic structural feature of the eclogues, and it brings to light fundamental conditions of literary fictionality. It establishes a frame that allows the continued presence of what has been exceeded. Spenser's shepherds have been exceeded because they stand for historical figures, and historical figures have been exceeded because their reality appears in a different light when transplanted into a pastoral world. The tropes and clichés have been exceeded because their traditional correspondences are reversed, and the reversal is utilized for establishing ad hoc "similarities." And the literary genres have been exceeded because their nesting shows representation to be a form of masking, and masking points up the limits of representation. The retention of what has been exceeded brings about this doubling structure through which the pastoral world always remains present in another world and vice versa. But if the vividness of the pastoral world is merely a shadow, and if the world adumbrated by this shadow remains abstract, then the concreteness of the former reveals its own illusoriness in order to endow the latter with the status of reality.

It is important to note that the other world adumbrated by the pastoral world is not simply that of political and historical reality. If it were, then the pastoral world would serve only as the camouflage initially expected. The commentator, however, discounts this by referring to a "secret meaning," and this points to the fact that the guises under which the referential world recurs in the pastoral realm impose changes on the very world repeated. Thus there is reciprocal doubling.

Since the pastoral world is linked to another world that, in turn, is cast in terms of pastoral imagery, their relationship is no longer to be conceived as allegorical. Simultaneously it is understandable that the Virgilian *Eclogues* in particular were read allegorically throughout the Middle Ages. The guise of the shepherds suggests that there are relationships to be established, though they are no longer governed by an overarching world order. It is not surprising, then, that the Renaissance should have regarded the pastoral world as a shadow, since the world it incorporates does indeed cast its shadow. But if the real world is abstract, and the unreal is concrete, the former needs the illusion of the latter in order to come into view; it is shaped by something which it is not. In consequence, it appears not as reality but as potential reality.

Ever since Virgil, the pastoral world had been regarded as designating something other than itself, and as the other world had to be found by way of interpretation, the eclogue was read allegorically. But why does this allegorical *modus dicendi* no longer apply to a reading of *The Shepheardes Calendar*? First and foremost, because the pastoral world no longer personifies preestablished significations. Instead, the incorporation of a referential world into the pastoral world signifies the intended transmutation of this referential reality into a potential one. By marking off the areas in which connections may take place, the doubling of worlds replaces the "conjuncture" of the ternary system and simultaneously risks a loss of control over the multiple linkups. Control, however, is maintained through the pastoral imagery that provides the necessary guidelines according to which the referential world is meant to change. In superimposing itself on a referential reality the pastoral world determines the signification of what it refers to, and ceases to personify what is pregiven. For transformation to occur, options have to be opened up. In this case, the options arise when the doubling of worlds blocks an allegorical reading and at the same time sets off a semiotic game of signifiers designed to bring about a signified.

The Two Worlds of the Pastoral Romance

With Spenser, the eclogue reached the limits of its capacity. The problem it had as a genre was that it could not delineate its referential reality in detail; it could only invoke it. This is all too obvious from the elaborate and often cumbersome techniques Spenser had to employ.[37] The sociohistorical world assumes shape only through various transcodings of the pastoral repertoire that stimulate the reader to imagine this other reality. Without the commentary that functions as the "conjuncture" of the now rather more complex ternary sign system, even this other world threatened to remain quite vague.

The eclogue could indicate the presence of another world only by inscribing it into pastoral clichés, traditional tropes, and literary genres, whereas a basic constituent of the pastoral romance is the actual representation of two worlds. Instead of being joined by a "conjuncture," the pastoral and sociohistorical worlds in the pastoral romance are separated by a boundary that poses the problem of their correlation. They are presented through two different sign systems, and—unlike the eclogue—the pastoral romance does not set the pastoral world against another that lies outside itself. Instead, it depicts the sociohistorical world and focuses on the crossing of the borderline between the sign systems, so that it is only the resultant connection that conveys the romance's reaction to an empirical world outside itself.

It would appear that here the ternary system has been supplanted by a binary one. If this were so, the two worlds would have to be conceived in terms of opposition, turning the boundary into a difference that would guarantee the stability of such a pairing. The protagonists of the pastoral romance, however, cross the boundary between the worlds, and since they maintain the presence of the first in the second, a network of possible connections arises. The difference does not, therefore, stabilize opposition but allows for the readability of two mutually exclusive semiotic systems as their interconnections evolve from and intend to bridge that difference, which—having no content of its own—cannot indicate any particular way of reading, as do the "similarities" of the ternary sign system.

In its heyday, the pastoral romance was read as a binary sign system. It was taken primarily as an image of the Golden Age, sometimes even of Utopia.[38] But the eclogue had already revealed that the singing shepherds were not meant to be the opposite of reality so much as its mirror image, and it is this feature that the pastoral romance now develops to the full. Certainly the artificial worlds of the shepherds have escapist tendencies that might induce readers into conceiving the pastoral world as the Golden Age. Yet the apparent escape does not so much indicate a flight from a deteriorating reality as it provides a chance of stepping back out of what one is involved in. This enables the protagonists to obtain an increased awareness that they can finally take back with them into the ways of life they have temporarily left behind. This leads not to the restoration of the Golden Age but to a revolution within the existing historical world, as evinced by Lodge and Shakespeare at the end of the century.[39] The fact that the pastoral romance was indeed read as an image of the Golden Age may in part be due to the convention, accepted since Virgil, that the shepherds meant something other than themselves. But identifying this meaning with the Golden Age would merely prove to be a historically conditioned form of reception, and not yet the basic pattern of the pastoral romance itself. The difference between the two worlds permits several ways of reading that are interpretations which replace the earlier preordained sign relationship. Therefore, if the pastoral world was subject to the same conflicts as the sociohistorical world—for instance, as a realm of lost happiness—this indicated the mounting pressure of coping with problems that must have prevailed in the sixteenth century; for the only distinction between the conflicts of the pastoral world and those of the empirical world were that the former turned out to be without consequences. Similarly, if the pastoral world was taken as the image of the Golden Age, it would be the contemporary code that governed the way in which the difference was spelled out. Again this shows the extent to which difference demands interpretation as a replacement of what had once been guaranteed connections.

Difference, then, marks the boundary between the two worlds, and at the same time it is again inscribed into each of them. In this way both worlds have dual references. The artificial pastoral world relates simultaneously to an ideal state and to a historical world, but always in such a way that the latter is refracted as the reorganization of the former. The historical world also appears both as what it is and as what it ought to be. The one world gains its significance only by functioning as a mirror, and the other by being refracted in the reflected image. Neither is fulfilled simply by what it denotes, for only their interaction can unfold the implications of their references. It is here that the crossing of the boundary is so vital, since this is what establishes the correlation between the two interacting worlds. In crossing the border between a historical and an artificial world, the pastoral romance provides a vivid portrayal of literary fictionality that is lodged neither in the artificial nor in the historical world. Rather, it embodies an act that allows for worlds to be surpassed within the world.

INTERPLAY BETWEEN REPETITION AND MEMORY IN SANNAZARO'S *ARCADIA*

The thematization of boundary-crossing figures prominently in Sannazaro's *Arcadia,* the first important pastoral romance. The author himself—though disguised as a shepherd and simultaneously revealing his true identity[40]—leaves his native Naples for a Virgilian Arcadia because he cannot reveal his passion to his beloved. He therefore longs to link his personal grief to the collective unhappiness of Arcadian shepherds in love.[41]

This correlation has the character of a typological correspondence.

> One and a half thousand years after Virgil, the poet sets out once more for the same Arcadia—in order, he says, to escape from the memory of an unhappy love, though in fact it is because there he can abandon himself all the more readily to his grief. Although, in contrast to Virgil, the hills and forests remain silent in the face of laments, they are the same hills and trees that have already heard the laments of Gallus's unhappy love. Since the Arcadians are the only true experts in song, they alone are able to understand his sorrow properly, and they console him with the tales of their own experiences of love.[42]

The typological correspondence linking the poet's fate with the collective sorrows of the Arcadians reveals a striking inversion of its traditional form: instead of pointing forward, it turns back. The same applies to the shepherds whom Sannazaro meets. Although they remind him of

Virgil's, they themselves remember a past Golden Age.[43] The typology becomes a symbol of longing and ceases to be one of fulfillment. The fact that the shepherds reverse the order of *figura* and *complementum* reflects the irretrievability of what the poet is seeking.

With the figural schema reduced to a mere token of sentimentality, the ternary sign relationship that linked the different semiotic systems is abandoned, and so the last substantialist guarantee of connection disappears. The reversal of the figural schema spotlights instead the misapprehension that Arcadia might bring relief of suffering. Arcadia is not a land into which one can emigrate, and those who feel compelled to go there will find that they cannot free themselves from the world they have left, let alone from what they themselves are. The world they have passed from has always been present in Arcadia.

This continued presence makes its mark on Sannazaro's narrative mode. In the prose passages that lead to the shepherds' eclogues, the first-person narrator articulates his perceptions that force an external perspective onto the shepherds' world because Sannazaro is striving to register everything that might relate him, the Neapolitan nobleman, to the shepherds' sufferings. This very intent, however, inscribes salient features of another world into the pastoral realm, thus highlighting a distance he was anxious to overcome. On certain occasions this difference is given an almost emblematic illustration. As he penetrates Arcadia, for example, the disguised Neapolitan sees a flock of sheep grazing on a slope; they are reflected in the crystal-clear water of the stream from which they are drinking, and they clearly take pleasure in their own reflections, whereas to the distant observer it seems as if they were hanging headfirst from the banks.[44] The pastoral cliché of animal and Nature in perfect accord appears to the outsider to be an unlikely perception, indicating that the pastoral world is structured in terms of correspondence, whereas the empirical world is slanted according to the dominance of a central perspective. Just as the apparent inversion of the figural schema converts the typological concordance, shrinking it to a mere frame for the portrayal of sentimental longing, so the superimposition, one on the other, of correspondence and central perspective reveals the lack of any overarching link between the two worlds. This points up their separateness by means of figures and tropes that had once organized tightly knit interrelationships.

The difference now opened up triggers multifarious attempts at overcoming the duality of the two worlds; the welter of possibilities produced in this pursuit does not eliminate that difference but reveals what it entails. By identifying with the sufferings of the Virgilian shepherds in Arcadia, the Neapolitan nobleman is trying to get over his unhappy love, but the temporary relief that he thus gains occasions the new and even more profound grief of being cut off from his homeland. What had remained hidden in Naples is brought out by Arcadia; each world exposes the other. If the poet had hoped to forget his world by leaving it, now in Arcadia he is afraid of leaving his memories behind, and his growing desolation finds its correspondence in the loneliness he feels as an exile in Arcadia.[45] Originally viewed typologically, Arcadia suddenly turns into a perspective for viewing the poet's real world, the concealed aspects of which take on concrete form as Arcadia dwindles to a correspondence of eclipsed memories.

Initially, the poet had wanted to forget his painful memories by joining the Virgilian shepherds, but lovesickness brings back memories of his beloved homeland, which he comes to realize he had all too hastily left. Back in Naples, however, he remembers what he has experienced in Arcadia, and the pastoral world rebounds in his own world.[46] "Repetition and recollection," Kierkegaard contends, "are the same movement, except in opposite directions, for what is recollected has been, is repeated backward, whereas genuine repetition is recollected forward."[47] But only if difference is maintained in this "same movement"—as shown by the narrator's crossing the borders of the two worlds—will displaced memories have a chance to resurface in the other realm. Thus, while suffering in Naples, the poet's memory of Arcadia repeats the peaceful contentedness of the Virgilian shepherds. Repetition facilitates the return of what has been displaced, and memory causes the transformation of what actually exists.

In *Arcadia*, however, the two movements are distinguished less by direction—in the sense in which Kierkegaard emphasized it—than by the exchange of predicates: repetition bends backward in order to uncover lost memories, and memory strains forward in order to bring out hidden desires. These countervailing movements disclose each other's reverse sides.

Sannazaro's *Arcadia*, then, represents neither the one world nor the other but the simultaneity of two mutually exclusive semiotic systems. *Simultaneity,* here as elsewhere, should be taken not as a temporal category but as the copresence of fundamentally different spheres in a manner that exceeds, in equal measure, both time and space. The copresence brings out the difference, and this in turn sets in motion a game of combinations between the coexisting worlds. In the ternary sign system, this game was always predetermined by the "conjuncture," but now the difference creates an empty space that Sannazaro virtually allegorizes when, in the transition from Arcadia to Naples, he speaks of the great emptiness[48] stretching between the two worlds that he can bridge only through dreamlike sleepwalking.[49]

The reference to dreams raises a new aspect of the overlapping of repetition and memory: this is not a matter of two worlds confronting each other but of a telescoping that conditions the uncovering of what is suppressed in each of them. Like the crossing of thresholds in dreams, repetition brings back the 'forgotten' aspects of what it repeats.

ENACTMENTS IN MONTEMAYOR'S *DIANA*

Sannazaro's *Arcadia* has always been considered the first pastoral romance, in the wake of which a new pastoral genre came into being.[50] This is due in part to its elaborate—though very schematic—fashioning of the artificial world, but even more to its explicitly linking two separate worlds. It must be said, however, that Sannazaro's indication in his epilogue that he wished to reawaken the shepherds in the "slumbering woods"[51] shows a longing for Virgil's *Arcadia* rather than the desire to pave the way for a new genre.

Nevertheless, *Arcadia* has been afforded the status of a trendsetter in literary tradition, and Montemayor's *Diana* represents the first fully developed stage of this burgeoning genre. Traditions are formed by recasting significant features of preceding works as well as by supplementing what are taken to be omissions whose salience is brought out only by the subsequent filling. Sannazaro demarcated the two separate worlds by a boundary in order to make them recur in one another through the interplay of repetition and memory; Montemayor—though maintaining a boundary—inscribes the sociohistorical world into the pastoral world of his disguised shepherds. The keynote of the genre— the simultaneity of the mutually exclusive—is preserved but the boundary is shifted, allowing Montemayor to utilize the divisions of worlds for hitherto unforeseeable purposes.

Right from the start, the pastoral world is permeated by another, and so boundaries must be marked off within the artificial world itself, as opposed to boundaries between the sociohistorical and the artificial. This shifting of boundaries results in different modes of presentation:

"Involvements in the contemporary real world are narrated in novella form, and are incorporated into the Arcadian framework as *historias intercaladas*."[52]

If *Diana* continually encompasses two different texts (pastoral and real world), its main focus is the interweaving of one with the other, for the protagonists have long since crossed the old borderlines and now reproduce their real world in their guise as shepherds. This leads to a proliferation of inlaid stories that enhance the role of the real world to a degree that anticipates the massive reduction the pastoral world is to undergo in Sidney's *Arcadia*.

In Sannazaro, the boundary between Naples and Arcadia still seemed almost geographical, whereas in Montemayor it turns into an abstract marker, differentiating two separate worlds that are constantly merging. As such, the boundary unfolds a wide range of different possibilities arising from an interaction between distinguishable semiotic systems that takes the basic pattern of nascent intertextuality. The interlacing of different types of text shows up their ineradicable differences, which generates multiple meanings by making each text exceed the other. This basic structure of intertextuality is vividly present in *Diana,* whose stories-within-a-story illuminate the way in which the two worlds overlap and interlink. Cervantes then provided a frame for this constitutive overlap of intertextuality by the inlaid story in *Don Quixote* that punctured and punctuated the main plot line; this mode of narration was to dominate narrative literature for more than two hundred years until the pictorial presentation of intertextuality disappeared in an almost explosive diversification of the texts stored within a single text.

Montemayor does not confine himself to merely repeating the historical-political world in the pastoral world. Instead, he thematizes their intertwining by showing up their multiple connections and differences that now become the subject matter of the repetition. Sannazaro drew just one boundary between Naples and Arcadia, whereas Montemayor establishes two: one between the historical-political world and the pastoral, and the other inside the pastoral realm itself. This doubling of boundaries is the first step toward a proliferation that characterizes later examples of the genre and indeed the literary text in general.

The difference that is repeated in the pastoral life is manifested formally by the alternation between verse and prose. In Sannazaro this alternation was still in compliance with a convention flourishing in the late medieval humanistic tradition that favored the genre of *prosimetrum*. But in *Diana* this alternation assumes a particular function: the song repeats what the prose presented as the shepherd's situation. *Diana* is therefore no longer just a *prosimetrum*. At critical moments the shepherds double themselves, as is manifested by the repetition of their "reality" in verse. When Syrenus, the shepherd first loved but then rejected by Diana, tells of his pain, which is then repeated in a lament,[53] the doubling—especially dense in Book I—shows that repetition is an enactment through which experiences may be transposed into another medium.

The inlaid stories also take on new significance insofar as they not only denote the presence of a different world in the pastoral world but also present vivid images of the real world, thereby staging it. This is entirely in keeping with the pastoral tradition that always regarded the shepherd-poets as signifying an artificial world existing not for its own sake but as a medium for the recurrence of a referential reality. The latter need not be another world; it can be another situation, such as we see in the pastoral poetry of *Diana*, which repeats the sometimes very detailed grief of the lovesick protagonists, thereby embodying duplication within the pastoral world itself. Presenting the artificial world as a duplication means thematizing the actual process of staging, and to ensure that this intention is absolutely clear, Montemayor encapsulates it in an emblematic scene: Syrenus joins Sylvanus and Selvagia, who are also lovesick, and unexpectedly the three of them witness the river nymphs enjoying themselves as they perform Syrenus's farewell to Diana. Syrenus thus experiences his former 'reality' as a piece of 'theater'. The shepherds continually practice transposing their own situations into poetry, and in this scene the transposition is acted out in front of them (see pp. 58–75).

If we are to evaluate the consequences and implications of this process, we must bear in mind the pastoral convention that the shepherds are not shepherds but masks. When Syrenus sees his own situation being enacted, the thing enacted is itself already a role, so that the nymphs are actually staging the imitation of a staging. As a rule, enactment is always dependent on something that is to be staged, whereas here staging turns into the subject matter of its own enactment. This self-representation of staging becomes feasible because the nymphs enacting it do not know love and are therefore isolated from the experience that underlies the scene they are playing. Having no direct experience of love, the nymphs can only act out what they have witnessed, that is, the curious behavior of the lovesick shepherds, which to them remains an empty role whose staging, however, provides a vivid impression of what the artifice of pastoralism is meant to be: a stage on which all kinds of referential reality may be enacted.

By repeating the historical-political world of the now disguised shepherds, the inlaid stories shift a real world into a horizon alien to it; by featuring a self-enactment of the shepherds, the poetry highlights staging as a mode of repetition; by performing a play, the nymphs exhibit the artifice of fictionality. In each of these instances doubling appears as the hallmark of fictionalizing acts that put in brackets whatever is, in order to allow a repetition under different circumstances and conditions. In *Diana* this self-fictionalizing arises out of the lovesickness suffered by the shepherds and shepherdesses, and since their desires cannot be fulfilled, they are driven to distance themselves from what they are inextricably engaged in. By repeating their sorrows in their songs (which is tantamount to staging themselves), they open up ways of exceeding the limits of circumstances that oppress them.

There is also an archaic strand discernible in the attempts to cope with one's own afflictions. Singing of one's own sorrow, or even discussing one's own fate, grants only temporary relief. The transmuting of pain into poetry often involves an attempt to understand the nature of the affliction; in this respect poetry is not an escape from suffering but a means of exorcising anxieties. Thus Syrenus says to Sylvanus, as once more he begins to translate his misery into verse: "But now good Shepherd, said *Syrénus*, take out thy Kit, and I will take my Bagpipe, for there is no greefe that is not with musicke relented and passed away, and no sorrow, which is not with the same againe increased. And so both the Shepherdes tuning, and playing on their instruments with great grace and sweetnesse began to sing that which followeth" (p. 25).

Poetry simultaneously increases and moderates pain, but it does not elimitate it; instead it allows the shepherd to step out of what has entangled him. Poetry makes his plight unreal in order to make his longing available as an experience of reality. This interchange is basic to duplication, which underlies all forms of enactment: it provides two different modes of manifestation for events or states of affairs, which in themselves are only a single occurrence.[54]

The staging, then, is not a compensation but a doubling that enables the hidden aspects of a situation to assume a form. The shepherds' poetry gives them a chance to gain access to their own condition. Because self-staging is meant to find out what is inaccessible to the shepherds, their reality has to be bracketed off, though kept in view, in order to bring out the cause of their plight. Staging their affliction, then, entails reaching behind whatever has afflicted them. Such a staging may well result in an illusion, yet it testifies to the fact that reality in the final analysis is not to be defined as a restriction on what is possible.

The importance of staging as a means of making available what is unavailable can be gauged from the casuistic love debates in *Diana*. Since all the shepherds labor under the same incomprehensible passion, they look for what might be identical in their individual experience of lovesickness. Syrenus and Felicia discuss mythological and casuistic explanations;[55] others describe their feelings to the river nymphs in order to convey an idea of love to those who have no experience of it.[56] In the course of these various endeavors to identify or specify the supposedly identical features of love, which everybody is striving to ascertain, the experience of love bursts into a multifariousness of individual sufferings that defy explanation, let alone generalization. Resorting to mythology and the casuistry of love proves to be just as futile as the attempt to derive identical features from individual experiences. Staging, however, allows revelation of what is common to all the shepherds' afflictions, because what is withheld in each and every individual case has to be translated into poetry, which makes accessible what is otherwise sealed off.

Staging, then, is a further manifestation of a basic structure of the pastoral romance: the simultaneity of the mutually exclusive. In Sannazaro this consists in the interplay between repetition and memory, while in Montemayor it gives shape to unavailability. The development of these games goes hand in hand with the disappearance of ternary sign connections; instead of a "conjuncture," we now have differentiated modes that link separate worlds. Contrast and opposition are replaced by boundary-crossing, which is a basic characteristic of fictionalizing that makes it resemble the dream in some ways. For in the dream, too, there are mutually exclusive worlds that are intertwined, separated by the "censor," and able to appear simultaneously only by way of overlapping, telescoping, mirroring, and staging. Against this backdrop Sannazaro's interplay of repetition and memory takes on its full significance: It aims to reveal the reverse side of different worlds.

The same is true of Montemayor's staging, which presents as tangible what is unavailable.

Contemporaries must already have been aware of this resemblance to dreams. Cervantes, who also wrote a pastoral romance, called such works "cosas soñadas,"[57] because he regarded their artificiality as a departure from the truth of life. Certainly true life is not the same as the simultaneity of the mutually exclusive, but it may well be precisely this truth that compels us to try to 'have' ourselves under conditions different from those in which we are caught up in real life.

Whatever else Cervantes's remark may mean, it clearly shows an awareness that the doubling structure of the pastoral romance repeats patterns of the dream. In both we have the copresence of two opposed realms, giving rise to a network of complex potential relations in which the difference always remains inscribed. This difference can never be eliminated in the dream or in the pastoral romance, and for this very reason it offers a matrix for limitless variations.

DOUBLE MEANING IN SIDNEY'S *ARCADIA*

Montemayor took over Sannazaro's schema of doubled worlds, and made *Arcadia*—conceived by Sannazaro as being linked to the humanistic tradition—appear retrospectively as the first pastoral romance of the Renaissance. Sannazaro had recast the Virgilian difference between pastoral and political worlds by sentimentalizing the typology of *figura* and *complementum,* and by inscribing the central perspective into the prevailing concept of correspondences. Subsequently it is this recasting of difference that leads to the growing complexity of the genre. Virgil had already separated two worlds from each other, and the resultant doubling led to the search within pastoral romance to find out what was taking place between those worlds. Since neither world disappeared in the other, the playing out of their potential connections was virtually endless, as is borne out by the historic sequence of the genre in which the play movements take on an ever greater sophistication. For this reason there is no such thing as *the* pastoral romance in which the genre reaches its apogee; there are only continual reorganizations of the basic difference that is common to all instances of the genre. This leads to a constant expansion of the range of doublings, giving dynamic life to the interplay between different semiotic systems. In Sidney's *Arcadia* the interplay reaches what for the Renaissance was a critical level that illuminates the very origins of such doubling.

The pastoral romance is, then, an autopoetic system, in which the original duality spawns more and more doublings indicative of what Gregory Bateson calls "a difference which makes a difference."[58] Progressively the genre differentiates the basic difference, so that each new stage proves to be the product of a reception, in that it not only reshuffles the nature of the boundary between the two worlds but also endows their interplay with an ever-increasing complexity. In Sidney's *Arcadia* the doubling proliferates to an unprecedented degree. The original pattern of the genre was discernible in the division between Arcadia and the political world of Greece and Asia Minor. Then Arcadia itself was doubled. The Arcadian ruler withdrew to the innermost region of Arcadia, so that the Arcadia outside that retreat appeared to be a political world cast as a feudal society. As a result of these proliferating doublings, the shepherds were relegated to the fringes not only of Arcadia but even of the retreat, where their marginal existence merely served to denote that the retreat was a pastoral realm as well.

Just eighty years after the publication of Sannazaro's *Arcadia,* Sidney's *Arcadia* reverses the proportions of the two worlds: The originally almost all-embracing pastoral world gives way to the expanding representation of the historical-political world. This shift lays far greater emphasis on the function that Arcadia was, from the beginning, meant to fulfill in the pastoral tradition: to provide the setting for another world, not so much in order to depict it as to refract whatever it conceals. In Sidney the pastoral world is present only as an indicator of artificiality. Its sign function is by now so well established that it no longer needs any detailed presentation. The shepherds therefore shrink to a cipher serving merely to set the stage for the multifarious enactments of doublings.

Since Arcadia is now no more than a setting for a ramified sociohistorical world, a lavish description of pastoral life would obscure the function that the artificial world is meant to fulfill. But in order to prevent this function from disappearing altogether through the marginalization of the shepherds, Sidney emblematizes it at the beginning, when the princes, stranded in Arcadia, enter Kalander's house:

> The backside of the house was neither field, garden nor orchard, or rather it was both field, garden and orchard; for as soon as the descending of the stairs had delivered them down, they came into a place cunningly set with trees of the most taste-pleasing fruits; but scarcely they had taken that into their consideration but that they were suddenly stept into a delicate green; of each side of the green a

thicket, and behind the thickets again new beds of flowers, which being under the trees, the trees were to them a pavilion and they to the trees a mosaical floor, so that it seemed that Art therein would needs be delightful by counterfeiting his enemy Error and making order in confusion.

In the midst of all the place was a fair pond whose shaking crystal was a perfect mirror to all the other beauties, so that it bare show of two gardens; one in deed, the other in shadows. And in one of the thickets was a fine fountain made thus: a naked Venus of white marble, wherein the graver had used such cunning, that the natural blue veins of the marble were framed in fit places to set forth the beautiful veins of her body. At her breast she had her babe Aeneas, who seemed, having begun to suck, to leave that to look upon her fair eyes which smiled at the babe's folly, meanwhile the breast running.[59]

Arcadia as a garden evokes both the *locus amoenus* and the Garden of Eden. Art and Nature appear interchangeable, and each seems to be a product of the other. However, the difference between them, as the one appears to collapse into the other, is sustained solely by the way in which the princes look at the scenery. The emerging mythological and biblical references are not responsible for the apparent identity of what is different. Instead, the interchangeability springs from the refinement of a rather sophisticated deception. Art, so it appears, does not have its roots in Nature but in "cunning" and "counterfeiting," out of which arise perfect objects. Art makes Nature seem as if it were ordered, whereas this order is in fact a pattern feigned by Art. If the trees turn into a "pavilion" for the beds of flowers, and these turn into a "mosaical floor," then Art is feigning the subject matter of a picture while simultaneously pretending that the content exists independently of Art, though its very existence is brought about by the ruse employed.

The metaphor of the pond as a mirror is a vivid example of the intended deceit through which Art and Nature are made to seem interchangeable: this indeed shows the extent to which mimesis as the imitation of Nature has changed to mastery of Nature through Art. The object of this is not, however, to eliminate the difference—as it was, for instance, in the legendary painting by Zeuxis, who was said to have imitated Nature so accurately that birds pecked at his painted grapes; here the deceit varies between mirror and shadow, signifying that such artifice does not exist through itself but only as shadow gives shape to its source, and as mirror makes vivid the object it reflects. When the marble statue of Venus seems like flesh and blood, and beds of flowers are like mosaics, this triumph of feigning is no longer to be equated with lying; instead, it provides a sense of what eludes depiction. At the beginning of *Arcadia,* when Sidney uses Kalander's artificial garden to endow the intangible character of fictionalizing itself with a visible form, it becomes perfectly clear that fictionalizing is an act of doubling.

Just how this fictionalizing—featured as mirror and shadow—functions is evident from the plot of *Arcadia,* through which various referential realities are linked to the pastoral realm. The more elaborately the sociohistorical world recurs within the pastoral realm, the more intricate becomes the interlocking network of the two worlds. Since referential realities can no longer be alluded to, but have to be depicted, Sidney had recourse to contemporary thought systems as an organizing code for representing the sociohistorical world. In *Arcadia* attention is focused mainly on three spheres: the heroic world of adventure, the feudal world of chivalry, and the world of myth (the Arcadian ruler consulting the Delphic oracle). The heroic and feudal worlds are given most space (Books II and III). They also incorporate the main bulk of the revisions to which the *Old Arcadia* was subjected and which Sidney left behind in the large fragment of the *New Arcadia.* This massive extension applied to two prevailing thought systems, the diversification of which enhanced the complexity of links with the pastoral realm proportionately. What this amounts to can best be exemplified by the interlinkage with the heroic world out of which the protagonists were driven to Arcadia.

A detailed description of referential reality, however, presented the pastoral romance with a problem, as pastoralism had hardly had any schemata at its disposal for portraying a sociohistorical world. The referential reality of the eclogue remained elusive, and even Sannazaro confined himself to mere references to his native Naples. Montemayor was the first to reach beyond the pastoral tradition into other spheres in order to illuminate the world that underlay the stories of the disguised shepherds. But the formulaic genres that he used (fairy tale, exemplum, myth) proved inadequate when it came to the more detailed depiction of reality. And so Sidney amalgamated the Greek adventure tale of Heliodorus[60] with pastoral tradition, and he did so in such a way that the outline of the pastoral realm faded to a bare hint.

It was necessary for Sidney to dip into the repertoire of Heliodorus in order to represent the referential realities of Arcadia, for representation requires existing or inherited schemata that will give form to what is to be represented. The aspect concerned will depend for its representation on those traditions that have already proved successful. Because the pastoral tradition lacked the range necessary for Sidney's purposes, he had to look elsewhere. Consequently, the pastoral romance became permeated by epic features—a development already foreshadowed in pastoral prose when Longus, for instance, and also Sannazaro (though with different motives), began to break open the constricting framework of the eclogue in their partly voyeuristic, partly sentimental portrayals of pastoral life.[61] With Sidney this tendency toward epic form shifts to a more explicit representation of referential realities, which are so densely packed that they almost obliterate the pastoral world. The shift is due not least to the fact that the artificiality no longer has to be focused upon, as its mirroring function has long since become an established convention. Of prime interest now is what is refracted and revealed by the mirror. The marginalized shepherds merely signal fictionality, and the vividness of these signals—here still preserved—gradually fades in the course of history until, finally, genres and the typographical layout of the text suffice to invoke the contract between author and reader, the latter being reminded that the text provides not documentation but a staged version of it.

What do we learn from the depiction of a heroic world that is given shape by the patterns of the Greek tale of adventure? First of all, this dependence leads most strikingly to an endless sequence of adventures, even though each individual adventure is meant to demonstrate the system of moral virtues. Epic achievement, however, cannot be made real merely by a succession of adventures that—as here—drift off into aimlessness. The protagonists themselves seem to be aware of this movement away from epic perfection, for after the princes have survived another of their adventures and been heaped with honors, we read:

> But as high honour is not only gotten and born by pain and danger, but must be nursed by the like or else vanisheth as soon as it appears to the world, so the natural hunger thereof which was in Pyrocles suffered him not to account a resting seat of that which ever either riseth or falleth, but still to make one occasion beget another, whereby his doings might send his praise to others' mouths to rebound again true contentment to his spirit. And therefore having well established those kingdoms under good governors, and rid them by their [i.e.,

Pyrocles's and Musidorus's] valour of such giants and monsters as before-time armies were not able to subdue, they determined in unknown order to see more of the world, and to employ those gifts, esteemed rare in them, to the good of mankind; and therefore would themselves . . . go privately to seek exercises of their virtue, thinking it not so worthy to be brought to heroical effects by fortune or necessity, like Ulysses and Aeneas, as by one's own choice and working.[62]

Evidently the quest for honor requires the continual proof of courage and virtue. But while the epic heroes of yore set out on their course with a particular aim, Sidney's heroes are motivated solely by private impulses. These are demarcated simultaneously both from the exemplarity of epic heroes and from any predetermined goal for their adventures, which unfold in a random sequence. Sidney's heroes save one kingdom after another, they re-establish endangered order, they resolve personal conflicts, and they display such fearless virtue that their fame echoes through the Orient, so that finally all the rulers of Asia gather to do homage to them. But all these glorious deeds remain inconsequential, because the exercise of courage and virtue does not in itself change anything. It is fitting, therefore, that the princes meet their end in a shipwreck.

If the exemplarity of Ulysses and Aeneas gives way to private goals ("go privately"); if, as the princes explicitly state, the epic queste is replaced by an "unknown order"; and if the epic norms of fortune and necessity are replaced by personal decision, then all of these heroic adventures assume a "minus function." They invoke epic ideals only to draw attention to their absence. Instead of reintegrating the world into a social unity, the princes leave it in a state of uncontrollable instability, characterized by the emptying out of all epic schemata.[63]

The princes, however, narrate their adventures to the princesses with whom they are in love but to whom they cannot reveal their identity, as their boundary-crossing requires masking themselves. When they tell Basilius's daughters of their deeds, the epic queste is unexpectedly restored, for now, through their disguises, the princes must use their tales in order to convey their true selves to the princesses without having to remove their masks. The aim of their queste is not to reproduce what they have achieved in the world but to endow their adventures with a meaning that is not inherent in them. This meaning does not consist in the demonstration of virtue or courage, the rescue of the oppressed, the overthrow of tyrants, or the punishment of envy and vindictiveness; it is, rather, the desire to impress the princesses with the suggestion that the Amazon and the shepherd are in fact the heroes of these adventures.

Thus the manifest meaning of the heroic adventures has to be understood simultaneously as a different meaning in order to make the mask transparent without lifting it. As the princes want to mean something other than what they say, the tales of heroic deeds are turned into carriers for a latent meaning without ever ceasing to mean what they say in the first place, since the princesses have to be impressed by what the princes did. Consequently, the special use that is made of the tales begins to fictionalize them; they are turned into signs for spelling out a hidden reality, as only the fictionalized meaning of the tale can bring to light what is to remain elusive. However, if the one meaning (that of the heroic deeds) serves as a sign for another meaning (the protagonists' desire to be taken for what they are), a mutual displacement is out of the question, and this inseparable duality presents itself as the structure of double meaning. The latter entails that there is always a manifest meaning adumbrating a latent one, which obtains its salience through what the manifest says.

Arcadia itself even contains an explicit reference to the nature of double meaning, though it stems not from Sidney but from Sir William Alexander, who combined the fragmentary version of *New Arcadia* with the necessary books of *Old Arcadia* to form the *Complete Arcadia* (1621). At the end of his insertion, Sir William writes: "As for Pamela she kept her accustomed majesty, being absent where she was, and present where she was not. Then, the supper being ended, after some ambiguous speeches which might, for fear of being mistaken, be taken in two senses or else were altogether estranged from the speaker's mind (speaking, as in a dream, not what they thought, but what they would be thought to think) everyone retired to the lodge where they had used afore to lie."[64] This explicit characterization of double meaning by means of the dream structure is all the more revealing, since contemporary readers would not only have noticed double meaning but also would have referred it back to its anthropological reference. The significance of this reference will be discussed later.

The structure of double meaning is the ultimate flowering of the schema that had always underlain pastoral poetry. In the eclogues, the shepherds had been signs for something other than themselves. Now in *Arcadia* this pattern comes to fruition: The sociohistorical world of the protagonists shrinks to an image that serves to illuminate what eludes perception. As a metaphor, the sociohistorical world shapes what has to remain hidden, and in so doing it inscribes double meaning into what it brings to light. In this respect *Arcadia* exemplifies the basic structure of literary fictionality: it translates the real world into a language through which the unspeakable is spoken, or in this case expresses what must not be spoken. If such a demonstration comes uppermost, it is all the more pertinent that a depiction of the pastoral realm should become marginal, since now attention is to be focused on what is being staged within that world.

What distinguishes *Arcadia* from other examples of the pastoral romance is its attempt to elucidate the nature of the relationship among the signs that bind the different levels of meaning into the unified duality of double meaning. The princes' love scenes offer particularly striking examples of this. Disguised as a shepherd, Musidorus certainly cannot woo the princess, and yet at the same time he could never have approached the princess without this disguise. Therefore, he must somehow reveal his nature through his disguise. The task of preserving the mask and yet revealing the true identity entails the simultaneity of the mutually exclusive, and demands increasing fictionalization.

> But love (which one time layeth burdens, another time giveth wings) when I was at the lowest of my downward thoughts, pulled up my heart to remember that nothing is achieved before it be throughly [sic] attempted, and that lying still doth never go forward; and that therefore it was time, now or never, to sharpen my invention to pierce through the hardness of this enterprise, never ceasing to assemble all my conceits one after the other how to manifest both my mind and estate. Till at last I lighted and resolved on this way, which yet perchance you will think was a way rather to hide it. (p. 222)

For the shepherd to manifest himself as prince means that Musidorus can be neither exclusively shepherd nor exclusively prince. He can neither cast off his disguise nor remain hidden by it. Hitherto the mask has taken precedence over his princehood (though of course the latter has continued to direct the former's behavior), but now the prince-hood must override the mask, although he must not reveal himself openly and so can be present only under the conditions imposed by the mask. Musidorus must therefore stage his disguise as an unveiling, his unveiling as a disguise. His method and its consequences for double meaning can be gauged from the following scene:

I began to counterfeit the extremest love towards Mopsa that might be; and as for the love, so lively it was indeed within me (although to another subject) that little I needed to counterfeit any notable demonstrations of it: and so making a contrariety the place of my memory, in her foulness I beheld Pamela's fairness, still looking on Mopsa but thinking on Pamela, as if I saw my sun shine in a puddled water. I cried out of nothing but Mopsa: to Mopsa my attendance was directed: to Mopsa the best fruits I could gather were brought: to Mopsa it seemed still that mine eye conveyed my tongue. So that Mopsa was my saying; Mopsa was my singing; . . . she was the lodestar of my life, she the blessing of mine eyes, she the overthrow of my desires, and yet the recompense of my overthrow; she the sweetness of my heart, even sweetening the death which her sweetness drew upon me. In sum, whatsoever I thought of Pamela, that I said of Mopsa; whereby as I gat my master's goodwill (who before spited me, fearing lest I should win the princess' favour from him) so did the same make the princess the better content to allow me her presence—whether indeed it were that a certain spark of noble indignation did rise in her not to suffer such a baggage to win away anything of hers, how meanly soever she reputed of it, or rather (as I think) my words being so passionate and shooting so quite contrary from the marks of Mopsa's worthiness, she perceived well enough whither they were directed; and therefore being so masked, she was contented as a sport of wit to attend them. (pp. 222f.)

Within the triangular relationship among the shepherd Dametas, his daughter Mopsa, and Princess Pamela, Musidorus stages his disguise with the aim of conveying his love to Pamela. The disguise must completely fictionalize all its utterances so that it can be understood as the image of a hidden reality. What is said is not what is meant, and the manifest meaning must give way to the latent. At the same time, the latent needs the manifest, for only through the overdeterminacy of the latter can the former gain salience. The disguise allows for the enactment within limits of the hidden self. When the manifest is fictionalized as an image, it is released from what it says and becomes free for other uses. Thus once again we have a basic pattern of literary fictionality, in which the world represented (Dorus's [that is, the mask of Musidorus] declarations of love for Mopsa) does not designate itself but serves as a metonymy that fictionalizes itself, releasing what it says for other uses. Musidorus achieves several things at once: he deceives Dametas, who takes what is said for what is meant; he makes Mopsa curious, thus diverting her—at least temporarily—from her duty to supervise Pamela; and he is able to insinuate to Pamela that he is in love with her. These multifarious references would not materialize if Musidorus's speech were confined to what it designates; only the fictionalization of what is said allows for the simultaneity of mutually exclusive meanings. These graded effects are not necessarily intended by Musidorus, whose contrivance is meant to convey his love of Pamela, but clearly the fictionalization of utterances can lead to certain advantages, whether intended or not; it can also run out of control, since it opens up new possibilities of usage that cannot be calculated in advance.

Musidorus is lucky insofar as Dametas takes the words at face value and accedes to the deceptive component of fictionality. Deceit, however, cannot be an end in itself, for if Pamela were to stick to the common view that fiction is a lie, Musidorus's plan would fail. Deceit, therefore, is simply a strategy of fictionality that, however, lacks adequate powers of control to guarantee its success. This is shown by Mopsa, who, despite her naïveté, is not deceived by Musidorus. Although she is not averse to flattery, she finds Dorus's (the mask of Musidorus) declarations of love comic precisely because they are so exaggerated (see p. 224), for lovesick shepherds simply do not use such bombastic language. Through this same exaggeration of a love addressed to the less than lovable Mopsa, Pamela is meant to recognize herself as the true addressee. In fact, she simply enjoys the wit of the shepherd's inventions, and so engages him in a casuistic exchange (see pp. 225ff.). Scarcely any of these consequences were intended by Musidorus. His self-staging was not meant to deceive but to reveal by means of deception. It was not intended to be comic but to distract attention, not to show off his wit but to arouse awareness. This ramification of staged speech comes about because the spoken word is to be taken as if it meant what it says only in order to spotlight hidden realities. If what is said is only the metaphor for what is not said, then fictionalized speech creates an area of indeterminacy between manifest and latent meanings, and the interplay between the two allows the production of a 'reality' that can become concrete only by means of individual appropriation. This is evident from the different reactions of Dametas, Mopsa, and Pamela.

In Sidney's pastoral romance, the area of indeterminacy as a play space is no longer organized in accordance with a given set of rules, as was the case in allegory, typology, and the system of correspondences.

Instead, it takes shape according to the viewpoints of those concerned. Indeterminacy thus acts as a kind of generator for a semantics whose chief characteristic is that its signifiers—no longer geared to an existing convention—must seek a signified. Historically the old unifying frame of the ternary sign relationship has been split wide open and is replaced by a play space that—though it may be said to have superseded the ternary sign system—is not yet a fully-fledged binary sign system. For manifest and latent meanings are not set up as opposites. Rather, latent meanings are inscribed into manifest ones, so that what is said serves to initiate the search for how the sign brings about what it signifies.

In the scene we have described, Sidney stages double meaning for the reader, who alone is aware of all the different levels of meaning unfolded by Musidorus's fictionalized speech. Depending on the location of the semantic focus, double meaning resolves itself into a particular meaning that will be different from the manifest one, and also different in each individual resolution. The shepherds will not grasp the latent meaning because they live in only one world. Pamela suspects it, because she lives in two worlds. The reader, however, living in language, understands it out of an awareness that meaning arises from what is excluded by the utterance. Able to operate the play of double meaning whose instability turns into a source of semantic productivity, the reader may experience an alignment with Dametas or Mopsa or Pamela, according to the link between the different levels of meaning.

While the play space gives full scope to double meaning, adequate comprehension of this meaning can be brought about only through its counterimage, which here consists in the mirror technique typical of the pastoral romance. The Basilius plot appears to eliminate the double meaning dramatized in the princes' plot in *Arcadia*. This elimination of double meaning leads, however, to a complete debacle. The mirror image in fact cleanses double meaning from that stain of duplicity which is prone to sully its application.

Basilius does not relate Arcadia to a sociohistorical world beyond; he splits it in order to withdraw into an inner Arcadia. The doubling of the world as a stereotype of the genre is preserved, but instead of linking the pastoral realm to a world outside, the splitting of Arcadia leads to a withdrawal from the world of politics. This pattern of inversion continues with Basilius's decision to relinquish governance of Arcadia— at least temporarily—since he believes that his flight is necessary because of a prophecy made by the Delphic oracle. By reducing the double meaning of the prophecy to a single meaning, he removes the area of indeterminacy and makes the oracle into a meaning that is unequivocal. While double meaning in fictionalized utterances gives voice to the unspoken, the double meaning of the oracle is presented as an alternative decision: the one meaning obliterates the other and leads to the fatality already highlighted by myth. This is in complete contrast, of course, to the unresolved double meaning of fiction that opens up a whole network of possible connections, allowing new ways of testing and investigating reality.

The oracle functions as a reversal of double meaning, whose elimination by Basilius leads in turn to the splitting of the pastoral world. The fact that the latter is now seen as a place of refuge does not, however, cancel out its mirroring function. It exhibits instead the fatal nature of the oracle. Rather than resolving conflicts, the divided Arcadia becomes the scene of catastrophe. This takes the form of the political upheaval resulting from the ruler's departure and finally leading to the supposed murder of Basilius by the queen. The shepherds can no longer understand the world in which they had hitherto lived unquestioningly (see pp. 773, 780). Basilius had been driven to his resignation out of fear that his happy reign might come to an end—even though it had lasted some thirty years. In the light of this stability his decision seems like madness—a view confirmed by Philanax, the governor appointed by the king: "Why should you deprive yourself of government for fear of losing your government, like one that should kill himself for fear of death? Nay, rather, if this oracle be to be accounted of, arm up your courage the more against it, for who will stick to him that abandons himself?" (p. 81).

Evidently Arcadian happiness has corrupted the mind of the Arcadian ruler, thereby indicating that the artificial world of the shepherds is not a permanent dwelling place. Basilius, however, wanted to make it one, and by dividing off a retreat inside Arcadia itself, he thinks he can compress pastoral artificiality into its essence. But what is the essence of something that does not have any existence of its own? Basilius misunderstands the nature of Arcadia, because he wants to turn what Snell called Virgil's "no-man's-land between the ages" into one that is firmly and autonomously based, so that he can escape from all threats to his happiness. Arcadian happiness had traditionally had its roots in detachment from those realities in which people were entangled. Consequently, it constituted a kind of break between two situations, but by hypostatizing this break, the king robs Arcadia of its very function.

Nonetheless, despite his intentions, Basilius cannot dislocate the pastoral world from its surroundings. The very fact that he has referred to the Delphic oracle as a mythical reality shows that the artificial world must be linked to others. Making myth into a referential reality means removing the relevance of the pastoral world, for this product of Virgilian art became significant precisely when myth began to lose its reality.

When Basilius renounces his responsibilities, he takes with him twenty selected shepherds, who are well versed in games and in poetry, and a priest, "who being excellent in poetry, he makes him write out such things as he best likes" (pp. 82f.). Basilius hopes that the priest will confirm him in his decision to withdraw into the realm of poetry. The priest as an intermediary is to function as an exegete, though the king wants the interpretation to fit in with his own requirements. It would appear, then, that Arcadia is acknowledged implicitly as a stage, though Basilius does not intend to produce himself as something he is not but simply wants to escape from an imaginary threat. He delegates the task of interpretation in order to close it off once and for all. But having dislocated the artificial pastoral world from all outside realities, he has himself become the referential reality and must involuntarily experience a staging of himself that brings out what he himself cannot admit. This is especially true of his fantasy,[65] which now gives free play to hidden desires, so that the man emerges from the king, vanity from government, fear from happiness, disorder from power, and self-centeredness from considerateness.

After having moved to the retreat inside Arcadia, Basilius experiences a doubling of himself, and it is clear that the pastoral world is to remain the theatrical stage it has always been. While the princes transform their adventures into metaphors in order to stage their reality through their disguises, the unmasked Basilius is split into something other than what he thought himself to be. The princes thus make use of the stage, whereas Basilius becomes its victim. The structure of double meaning opens up areas of play, but the involuntary double role of the king reveals what his fantasies hide. Basilius is so dominated by the omnipotence of his imaginings that finally the only way out of this constriction appears to be a faked death.

The Basilius plot makes it clear that fantasy must be tamed if one is to regain control over one's desires and to free oneself from the dominance of one's imaginings. When the direct intrusion of fantasy into an existing world manifests itself as hallucination, fantasies of this kind must be manipulated so that they can take effect in a manner suited to the situation. This demands a degree of consciousness that will make the hallucination—which has no function of its own and only indicates the presence of pure fantasy—strategically usable.

The Basilius story reflects back on that of the princes, in which there was still control over the images through which the princesses were to glimpse the reality behind the masks. The princes' speech became ambiguous because of the interplay between consciousness and fantasy. Fantasy, then, stood in the service of a hidden reality (the identity of the princes) that was to find expression through language. Thus double meaning can be neither consciousness nor imagination, but consists in the copresence of both that would remain formless if fictionality did not initiate a process of reciprocal boundary-crossings. Fictionality thus becomes a medium for the manifestation of double meaning. If the conventional pastoral romance could hitherto be characterized as the coexistence of two mutually exclusive semiotic systems, there now emerges from the two different sets of signs a very clear dimension of reference: the copresence of the conscious and the imaginary as a means of testing reality.

Literary Fictionality as Staging, Ecstasy, and Transforming Process

As the hallmark of the pastoral romance, doubling signals the fading of the ternary sign system, which was an expression of a substantialist world order. "Conjuncture" is supplanted by the play space, which in turn prevents the two worlds from establishing themselves as the binary opposition of a logocentric order; instead the two worlds interact.

In Sannazaro two different worlds are telescoped by way of the interrelationship between repetition and memory. For him the difference between the two worlds was so vivid that he could grasp the transition from one to the other only as a dream.[66] Although this process may still reflect the medieval journey to the other world—that is, to one radically different from the known world—here, by indicating boundary-crossings within this world, dream brings to light the hidden dimensions of two inner-worldly realities. Thus the first pastoral romance of the Renaissance suggests a correlation between separate worlds whose difference can only be acted out.

In Montemayor the shepherds are disguised historical characters who stage their own world in the pastoral milieu. Instead of acting out their memories, they confront themselves with themselves. Such a viewing of the self aims at penetrating behind one's own reality, the staging of which evinces the desire to take possession of what has been blocked off by that reality. This desire is like the dream situation that Cervantes—though with a critical intent—had established as an overriding characteristic of the pastoral romance.

For Montemayor repetition became simply a means of thematizing staging itself, while for Sidney enactment was a basic condition that enabled him to compress the two worlds into the structure of double meaning. Repetition and enactment, which govern the relation, allow the concealed to emerge through what is said.

The more closely the two worlds merge, the more relevant is the dream analogy, as was noted by Sir William Alexander, editor of the *Complete Arcadia* (1621), who actually referred to double meaning as a dream structure. In its own time the pastoral romance was coupled with the dream, albeit for varying reasons, and this gives rise to three questions: (1) What does the apparent similarity consist of? (2) Are the two structures indeed identical, or do they simply have elements in common that are differently expressed? (3) To what extent does overstepping as a feature of fictionality open up possibilities that, in turn, allow an overstepping of what is made possible by the dream?

It is the coexistence of mutually exclusive semiotic systems and of primary and secondary processes that constitutes the similarity between pastoral romance and dream. In both cases different spheres are interwoven through overlapping, staging, reflection, and condensation, all of which signal both the existence and the crossing of boundaries and barriers. This basic structure, which dream and fictionality have in common, seems capable of different manifestations that turn fictionality into a revealing index of the human makeup.

The doubling of worlds, repeated by the splitting of characters, denotes more than just a semiotic difference. What initially seems a geographical division (Sannazaro) shows that the bisection is not restricted to different sign systems but is also—as in the dream—indicative of the presence of a dual unity. In the first Renaissance pastoral romance, it was Sannazaro the author who presented himself as the doubling of mask and character, while in Montemayor anonymous historical personages staged their conflicts in the guise of shepherds.[67] Finally, with Sidney, the disguised author stands on the fringes, while the protagonists are invented figures.[68] Whereas initially the masks served to disguise historical characters, the balance shifts increasingly from the presentation of real people to that of the relationship between mask and person. There is a correspondingly more abstract division between the two worlds—geographical in Sannazaro, largely imaginary in Montemayor, and multifarious in Sidney. This trend has its parallel in what the characters represent: disguise simply becomes a means of showing the interplay between mask and character.

For this once again we may take Sidney's *Arcadia* as an example. Because the protagonists come from outside, they reverse the old form of the pastoral mask—still to be seen in the eclogue—that served to reflect the historical world. For the princes, gaining access means overcoming a barrier, and for this they need their disguises. The barrier is like the dream threshold, which is watched over by the censor. Dream thoughts also require fashioning; this has to be done by dream work, which cloaks them in disguises in order to make them cross the poorly guarded threshold in sleep and so penetrate into consciousness. In both cases the disguise is a process of channeling, whereby the forbidden may be bypassed: the dream thoughts and the princes seeking to enter the retreat inside Arcadia can achieve their ends only by seeming to be something they are not. Crossing the threshold thus entails doubling. While fictionality incorporates the double meaning of the dream, the dream needs fictionality in order to veil its thoughts. Arcadian disguise, however, unlike the dream, does not end with the bypassing of the forbidden. The topography of *Arcadia* and the assumed patterning of the psyche are not, despite all their similarities, identical, for the pastoral disguise extends into an anatomy of disguise itself.

The masks bring out something that also plays a part in dreams but has generally been left in the margins of dream analysis: the *form* of the disguises in which dream thoughts are wrapped. Ricoeur contends: "All question [sic] of schools aside, dreams attest that we constantly mean something other than what we say; in dreams the manifest meaning endlessly refers to hidden meaning; that is what makes every dreamer a poet."[69] If this is indeed so, the forms of dream thoughts cannot be exclusively the private archaeological deposits of the sleeper, since strangeness of the disguises is not enough to make them poetic. Freud, who was always careful to avoid interpreting dream symbols in the traditional, and for him discredited, mode of representation, frequently referred to myths, legends, and fairy tales when attempting to classify such symbols. He was concerned with what was encoded in the dream. But if the private archaeology overlaps the collective, the myth and the dream—for all their contact—cannot be one and the same. Mythology simply embodies a means of explanation, denoting that dream thoughts have form, but such a form cannot be a product of fantasy, since it imposes a consistent pattern that is clearly not inherent in fantasy itself. Nor can the disguises of dream thoughts stem purely from consciousness, for according to Freud, consciousness has no other role than *"that of a sense-organ for the perception of psychical qualities."*[70] Thus the forms in which consciousness is outwitted cannot spring from consciousness itself. If the poetry of the dream lies in the forms of its disguises, then neither the private nor the collective repertoire will suffice; the depths of the sleeper's psyche are not poetry any more than fantasy and consciousness are in themselves sources of forms. Fantasy and consciousness have to work together, and so dream symbols stem from the structure of double meaning in which fantasy and consciousness, private and collective archaeology, merge. Form comes into being because what has been suppressed must be channeled into consciousness, which means that separate spheres must be made translatable into each other's terms.

The therapeutic orientation of dream analysis has paid little attention to the aesthetic element of such forms, even though there is a striking contrast between the comparatively limited contents of dreams and the extraordinary multiplicity of forms through which these contents find expression: "[T]he same subject matter can be symbolized by almost anything."[71] Ricoeur concludes from this observation that the dream does not symbolize anything. "Hence the elaboration of a dream does not involve any work of symbolization comparable to what was described as the work of condensation, displacement, and pictorial representation."[72] But if, as Freud maintains, the symbols derive from fairy tales, myths, jokes, folklore, and such, then they are not products of "dream work" at all but of "culture work." Both may have a common root, but they grow in different directions; therefore cultural objects are not products of dreams, and dream thoughts are not myths.

In Sidney's *Arcadia* the division of the protagonists into mask and person resembles the dream structure insofar as the disguise conceals what the princes are in order to bring about access to a world that is barred to them. In both cases deception is necessary if forbidden thresholds are to be crossed. But it is the princes' desire, once they are in the forbidden zone, to be perceived as what they really are. This leads inevitably to a game within a game, as they play with their own disguises. It is here that the masquerade begins to diverge from that of the dream, for in the dream, it is the mask that dominates and has to be maintained if the displaced is to recur. The princes, on the other hand, would like to lift their masks in order to reveal their true identity.

So long as the princes are in disguise, they represent neither aristocrats nor shepherds, let alone Amazons. Not only do they overstep their origins but they also overstep their disguises. This gives rise to a certain unease, as Musidorus shows when commenting on his friend's change of sex, to which Pyrocles replies: "Neither doubt you because I wear a woman's apparel I will be the more womanish, since I assure you, for all my apparel, there is nothing I desire more than fully to prove myself a man in this enterprise."[73] If Pyrocles, disguised as a woman, wishes to prove himself a man, then he is clearly aware that mask and princehood do not represent one another. The prince here makes himself unreal in order to lend reality to the fictionalizing mask, but at the same time he wishes to shine through the mask in order to unveil both it and himself. This manifest abandonment of all representation sets in motion a game that goes far beyond the dream analogy we have been tracing. In the dream, the disguise of the suppressed desire dominates, aiming at bringing a buried past back into the present; in *Arcadia,* the protagonists desire the love of their princesses, which means gaining a future. They have to combine the regressive element of concealment with the progressive one of unveiling, which does not mean throwing off the masks, for they have to overcome serious obstacles and must cross closely guarded borders. Their goal forces them to reveal themselves *through* their disguises, and this duality of veiling and unveiling has to be practiced simultaneously. As Pyrocles says at the end of *Arcadia:* "[W]e disguised ourselves in such forms as might soonest bring us to the revealing of our affections."[74] A veiling that unveils itself cannot represent anything except the process itself—and this had been the feature peculiar to the pastoral tradition ever since the self-imitation of poetry in Virgil's *Eclogues.* The dual unity of simultaneous veiling and unveiling is thus an illustration of fictionality that allows the hidden to be revealed through deception.

This veiled unveiling drives the protagonists into a startlingly revealing relationship with themselves. While in disguise they have to stage their real selves in order to achieve something that does not yet exist. Thus the person in the mask is not left, as it were, behind himself, but "has" himself as something that the person himself cannot be. In contrast to the dream, in which the sleeper is imprisoned in his or her images, the person now unfolds himself, through the images of his disguise, into a multiplicity of possibilities. In his staging, he steps out of himself, and yet he remains present as himself, because otherwise nothing could be enacted. The result is an ecstatic condition: the person has himself by standing outside himself. At this point, fictionality goes far beyond the dream analogy. Ricoeur, who still tends to bracket dream and poetry together, calls special attention to this veiled unveiling: "To overcome what remains abstract in the opposition between regression and progression [i.e., in the dream] would require a study of these concrete relations, shifts of emphasis, and inversion of roles between the functions of disguise and disclosure."[75]

In literature, the form of this veiled unveiling can become concrete, for literature (unlike dreams) does not have to solve the archaic conflicts of the psyche. The veiled unveiling corresponds to a basic desire to overstep our own boundaries, and in this respect there is a similarity to Derrida's observation about the form of wish fulfillment, which is distinct from dream analysis:

> As in the dream, as Freud analyzes it, incompatibles are simultaneously admitted as soon as it is a matter of satisfying a desire, in spite of the principle of identity, or of the excluded third party—the logical time of consciousness. Using a word other than dream, inaugurating a conceptuality which would no longer belong to the metaphysics of presence or consciousness (opposing wakefulness and dream even within Freud's discourse), it would be necessary to define a space in which this regulated 'contradiction' has been possible and can be described.[76]

As a supplement that entails its own cancellation, literary fictionality offers just such a space in which the "regulated 'contradiction'" would manifest itself as ecstasy. The ecstatic state of being simultaneously in and out of oneself needs form to become tangible, although this form cannot represent it and must not ossify it if it is to remain a "regulated 'contradiction.'"

The necessary form can be observed in Sidney's *Arcadia* through the interweaving of presence and absence in the double roles of the protagonists, who are simultaneously themselves and not themselves. Right from the start, even before the princes enter the retreat inside

Arcadia, this relationship is strikingly illustrated. Musidorus is looking for his friend Pyrocles after the shipwreck: "So directed he his course to Laconia, as well among the Helots as Spartans. There indeed he found his fame flourishing, his monuments engraved in marble, and yet more durably in men's memories; but the universal lamenting his absented presence assured him of his present absence."[77] The theme announced here indicates how the protagonists are to be understood. When they act in their disguises, their royalty is made absent, even if this absence remains present in its guidance of the actions of the mask. The reverse applies when Pyrocles becomes present to his beloved as himself, thereby making the mask absent. In this case the absent mask becomes present partly through reflections on its possible strategic uses and partly through the doubts it casts on the credibility of the prince himself.[78] What is present remains in close relationship to what it has made absent.

The absent has to condition the present because the protagonists have to master unfamiliar situations. There are times when their own attitudes, abilities, norms, and values must be relegated to the background, simply because they do not meet the demands of the situation. Consequently the relationship between the person and the mask is continually changing in accordance with a shift in demands. The prince, then, is merely the reference point for the shepherd or Amazon, whose success or failure depends on behavioral adjustment dictated by the prince. If the mask were to take over completely, it would be without guidance, and if the protagonist's own code of behavior were totally to take command, he would be unable to cope with the changing demands of the situation and would fail—as is evident from the actions of those characters who are not doubled (Basilius, Gynecia, Amphialus). The code of the disguise is formed by the absent person who guides the operations of the mask and takes on presence through his guidance, his testing, and his choice as to whether he or his disguise is to predominate. Consequently, neither mask nor person is ever totally present, and the continual alternation between presence and absence indicates that the person always extends beyond what, at any moment, he is.

The disguise plays a vital role in this respect: it imposes an image on the person that will conform to the needs of the situation, thereby enabling him to expand into a multiplicity of possibilities that are essential as the person has to adapt to a welter of changing situations. The difference between mask and person is carried through into the person himself, who at every given moment is a determinate aspect of himself that extinguishes other aspects. Simultaneously, the mask itself is permeated by difference, for it is at once concealment (hiding the person) and discovery (revealing the person as a multiplicity of his aspects). Because it facilitates an ecstatic condition of being himself and standing outside himself, the mask is a paradigm of fictionality which discloses itself as a deception in order to show that such deceptions are always modes of revelation.

In *Arcadia* deception as disclosure involves not only the princes but also those characters they are pitted against: above all, the rulers of Arcadia. The deception of the disguises brings out the secret desires of both Basilius and Gynecia. Pyrocles confronts them as an Amazon, and they believe what they see. As in all perception, the imagination supplies what is not seen. Since Pyrocles has crossed a forbidden frontier, he has to strengthen the illusion, so that the Amazon's contact with Basilius brings to light the latter's hidden adulterous desires, while Gynecia is consumed by an unbridled longing for the youth she imagines she sees, whose love she feels should be for her and not for her daughter. The deep-seated affinity between semblance and fantasy emerges: semblance, which here constitutes deception, rouses the imagination, and the emptiness of its form provokes the imagination to fill it. Through this process, semblance becomes a divining rod for what has hitherto remained hidden and now reveals itself in undisguised form. This is the negative counterpart of the ecstatic state; at one and the same time we have both adherence to and stepping out of the self. What is to be learned from this?

We have seen from the relationship between the present and the absent that the disguise brings out particular aspects of the person, who is fragmented in accordance with the needs of the situation. The person directing the masking suffers a constant self-division that turns into a dynamic process in which any particular operation of the mask may be canceled, but only by adopting another disguise. The protagonists are therefore present neither as mask nor as person, but as interplay between the two that resembles what in psychoanalytical aesthetics has been called "creative ego rhythm," which Anton Ehrenzweig describes as a swing "between focused gestalt and oceanic undifferentiation."[79] Following the views of Winnicott and Milner, Ehrenzweig explains that the

> creative ego [must] be able to suspend the boundaries between self
> and not-self in order to become more at home in the world of reality

where the objects and self are clearly held apart. The ego rhythm of differentiation and dedifferentiation constantly swings between these two poles and between the inside and outside world ... Temporary dedifferentiation if it is extreme, as in oceanic states, implies a paralysis of surface functions and so can act very disruptively. But the ego could not function at all without its rhythm oscillating between its different levels.[80]

Ehrenzweig's concepts of structured focusing and oceanic dedifferentiation describe two movements that branch out and then fold back on themselves in their conditioning of self. The structuring operation reaches out into a world that is independent of the self. It brings about fragmentation insofar as the ego must split off from itself in order to master what it is not. Such separations, however, remain linked to the self of which they are a fragment, and this gives rise to the tension between differentiation and dedifferentiation that characterizes the ego rhythm.

   The basic form of the ego rhythm seems to have found its paradigmatic illustration in the interplay between mask and man; the person can efface what the mask had imposed on him, but here, too, modification is a crucial term. Just as the protagonist's boundary-crossing is no imitation of the dream, so this counterplay is no imitation of the ego rhythm. The parallels concern only the anthropological roots of literary fictionality. The person may be trapped in the disguise, but he will free himself again because his imprisonment is conditioned only by the requirements of the situation. This rhythm of trapping and liberating permeates not only the relationship between person and mask but also that between person and person, and that between mask and mask. The mask is, of course, a restriction of the person, but it is also his extension, for the person must fictionalize himself as something else in order to reach beyond himself. The mask, then, reflects the double movement of restriction and derestriction in a process of reciprocal decomposition. The same applies to the person: he may withdraw his disguise, but only in order to reprogram it. The person becomes present through the effacement of the mask, but he must also force himself back into it in order to be able to act. There is, then, a continuing switch between constructing and deconstructing impulses that springs from neither mask nor person but from the play of difference. The effect of this is that the constructing tendency—as a precondition for mastery—always leads to a deconstructing tendency as a precondition for liberation. The constant switching from one to the other is potentially endless, and herein lies a minimal condition for the creative act.

Since this countermovement prevents both person and mask from ever taking on pure presence—the present constantly being doubled by the absent—and since the actual is always linked with the nonactual in order to produce something, it follows that there can never be pure presence in the creative act itself, which therefore cannot be taken as being a representation. Indeed, the creative act can take place only if it is *not* representative. The person and the mask have no representative value in the mimetic sense, and if they are to represent anything at all, it can only be the absence they bring about, and this absence removes any representative function they may have had. For representing the absent through the present can occur only through the deauthentication of whatever does the representing.

Thus fictionality is an ideal reflection of the creative act. Its self-revelation as fiction withdraws authenticity from whatever form it may take, and the resultant inauthentic state—facilitated by the disguise—allows the self to be simultaneously inside and outside itself, making it possible for the self to create itself. Such "ecstasy" is a paradigm of production in general, whether of the self or of the world. With Sidney's disguised princes, self and world are still geared together, thereby typifying the historical situation on the threshold of the modern era, when the making of the world coincided with human self-preservation. Being outside oneself does not, however, mean transcending oneself; it means staging oneself. Overstepping oneself by means of the mask allows the self always to be with itself in a different manner. "Man can exist only by defining himself," writes Cornelius Castoriadis, "but he always outstrips these definitions—and, if he outstrips them . . . this is because they spring out of him, because he invents them . . . and hence because he *makes* them by making things and making *himself*, and because no rational, natural or historical definition allows us to establish them once and for all. 'Man is that which is not what it is and is what it is not,' as Hegel has already said."[81]

Fictionality offers an essential anthropological pattern for this overstepping; its doubling nature generates the condition of ecstasy. In order for this to be made conceivable, fictionality must disclose itself as semblance, because only through such seeming can the mutually exclusive be made to coexist. As a paradigm of self-fashioning and worldmaking, it illustrates the creative process whose minimal condition is the ego rhythm. As Ehrenzweig observes, the "minimum content of art, then, may be the representation of the creative process in the ego."[82] What is represented, then, is not something given but the attainment of something that does not yet exist. And so fictionality has not a determinate but a dynamic form that presents the ecstatic state only as a matrix from which determinacy can emerge. Rather than a state of permanence or of relief, ecstasy involves a staging of what is that, through repetition, realizes the possibility of becoming other.

Anthropological Implications: On Doubling and Totality

The anthropological implications of literary fictionality have hitherto received little attention. Thomas J. Roberts writes:

> So far as I have been able to determine, the concept of fiction by intention as a thing that was invented by one culture and then borrowed by other cultures does not appear in the writing of anthropologists and sociologists ... the question of invention and borrowing is not an idle one, for its answers might suggest answers to more important questions: What are the uses to which a culture puts fiction by intention? Which kinds of cultures need a device of this kind and thus exploit it to the full when they discover it? Which cultures have no use for it and remain indifferent?[83]

If fictions do have any significance for cultural anthropology, how far can this significance be gauged through the structural formula that we have extrapolated from literary fictionality: the coexistence of the mutually exclusive? We may tackle this question on two levels: that of representation and ecstasy. Any description will therefore have to be twofold, since there can be no overarching explanation of the doubling phenomenon that can be identified only in the interaction of different levels of its manifestation.[84]

The doubling of fictionality may be conceived as a place of manifold mirrorings, in which everything is reflected, refracted, fragmented, telescoped, perspectivized, exposed, or revealed. In Nietzsche's terms: "If we try to observe the mirror in itself, we finally discover nothing but things on it. If we want to grasp the things, we ultimately come upon nothing other than the mirror."[85] The mirror cannot be grasped in transcendental terms any more than it can be pinned to a dialectic that would eliminate interplay. The structural formula entails not a synthesis but an endless unfolding of interwoven and interacting positions. The lack of any transcendental reference and the impossibility of any overarching third dimension show literary fictionality to be marked by an ineradicable duality, and indeed this is the source of its operational power. Since the duality cannot be unified, the origin of the split eludes capture, and yet it remains present as the driving force that constantly seeks to bring separated entities together.

Literary fictionality thus realizes a fundamental anthropological pattern that manifests itself at times as the doppelgänger, and at times as an intramundane totality. The doppelgänger informs the structural formula, while marks of totality indicate fictionality's ecstatic condition. In both cases duality turns out to be the underlying category.

According to Plessner, division is characteristic of human beings:

> Our rational self-understanding can be formalized thanks to the idea of the human being as a being that is generally related to its social role but cannot be defined by a particular role. The role-player or bearer of the social figure is not the same as that figure, and yet cannot be thought of separately from it without being deprived of its humanity . . . Only by means of the other of itself does it have—itself. With this doppelgänger structure in which role-bearer and role-figure are bound together, we believe we have found a constant which is open to every type of human socialization and forms one of humanity's basic preconditions. The doppelgänger always has the possibility of forgetting itself as such or of not actually being aware of its duality, and thus losing itself in its social figure, or . . . establishing and maintaining a balance—between the private and the public half of itself . . . Given the disposition of being a doppelgänger—a structure which allows the human being any kind of self-understanding, does by no means imply that the one half of the other is to be seen as 'by nature' the better. The doppelgänger merely has the possibility of making it so.[86]

A vital feature of Plessner's observation is his rejection of any ontologically based structure of the self that might—to use idealist terminology—contrast the *homo nuomenon* with a *homo phaenomenon*, a contrast that has remained equally virulent in Marxism and in psychoanalysis. Marxist self-alienation presupposes an idealist base in human beings, through which a true self can be distinguished from the forms of its debasement. Psychoanalysis speaks of a core self that can view itself in the mirror self. As their own doppelgängers, however, human beings are at best differential, traveling between their various roles that supplant and modify one another. Roles are not disguises with which to fulfill pragmatic ends; they are means of enabling the self to be other than each individual role. Being oneself therefore means being able to double oneself.

Of course the individual role will be determined by the social situation, but while this adaptability of individual roles conditions the form of the roles, it does not condition humankind's doppelgänger status. By putting its stamp on the division without binding or eliminating it, the social situation unfolds humanity's duality into a multiplicity of roles. This duality itself arises out of our decentered position—our existence is incontestable, but at the same time is inaccessible to us. Plessner does not conceive this fundamental disposition of the human being in Lacan's psychoanalytical terms of decentered subjectivity, not least because he cannot subscribe to the view that an originary core self perceives itself as divided in the mirror image of itself, for he does not accept the idea of the self as a coming to itself. The decentered position of human beings also excludes the accessibility of the self to itself that emerges from the continual boundary-drawing and boundary-lifting of the self's own self-fashioning.[87]

Plessner's central paradigm for this doubling is the actor. If the actor identifies with the character that does not exist—Hamlet, for instance—this identification will be preceded by "a particular image with which he will align himself in his personification. His acting is based on the requisite splitting of a self that he has to be in the role—a splitting which ... is possible for him in very different ways." For Plessner the question then arises:

> ... would it be possible for a human being to recognize in a feigned character a side, a possibility of himself or herself, a human being in the light of an idea, and would it be possible for him or her to set such a character up if he or she did not already, by nature, have 'something of' the actor in him or her? ... Does not the actor, if his or her sphere of representation is potentially unlimited, reveal at least in one particular respect the human configuration?[88]

Identifying oneself with a phantom in order to bring it to life entails no longer being what one was, even if the new shape is partially conditioned by what one was before. Although this process of identification adumbrates the human configuration, it does not and cannot mean that an accumulation of roles will lead ultimately to the presence of the whole being, let alone the knowledge of what one is. Roles are not a form of self-availability; they merely indicate what one is in the particular gestalt of the particular role, without allowing one to "have" oneself. Desirable though it may be to "have" oneself as what one is, it would be fatal to be compressed into a single role, both because of the narrowness of any role and because any change of role would be precluded. We ourselves are separated from ourselves by the very fact that we exist but cannot know what existence is. The phantom images that we as actors make of ourselves lack authenticity insofar as we believe we have ourselves through them. The fact that we cannot capture ourselves in any absolute role lifts all limits on the number of roles that can be played.

The doppelgänger status of human nature can be understood in different ways. The current philosophy of subjectivity contends that the self is present to itself only insofar as it is aware that its ground is withheld from it, and therefore, in each of its manifestations, consciousness of this inaccessibility has to be inscribed. The subject becomes a subject by maintaining a balance on this vertex as the only way in which it can achieve conscious life.[89] Diametrically opposed to this view is the androgynous myth of the divided being, whose longing for integration is in many ways mirrored by the doppelgänger.[90] While the philosophy of subjectivity speaks of the unfathomable ground, the anthropogenic myth deals with a ground that is always occupied. Social anthropology, by contrast, does not reach behind the unfolding of the different roles but has recourse to the human being's decentered position as the core of its changing shapes. The doubling structure of literary fictionality does not deal exclusively with the unfathomable ground, role-playing, or the attempt to integrate the irreconcilable divisions, although every one of these may constitute individual manifestations of the structure. The structure is, rather, an abstraction from the various results of doubling, which the philosophy of subjectivity would see as conscious life, the anthropogenic myth as longed-for unity, and social anthropology as changing roles.

The advantage of literary fictionality over all these is the simultaneous presence of doubled positions, which makes it representative of the nature of doubling itself. Since doubling is an intangible state of affairs, representation cannot be mimesis—not least because representation as standing for something pregiven would limit in advance what is to be set free. Therefore literary fictionality is marked by a negativity that facilitates the copresence of mutually exclusive positions by undoing structure, function, ordering, significance, and meaning pertaining to the referential fields from which the items assembled in the text have been lifted. This cancellation creates an in-between state in which the apparent decomposition adumbrates its own concealed motivation. A no-longer and a not-yet come together, and the differential between them, to use Franz Rosenzweig's words, "combines in itself the characteristics of the Nought and the Aught. It is a Nought which points to an Aught, its Aught; at the same time it is an Aught that still slumbers in the lap of the Nought."[91]

Representing such doubling entails making conceivable the genesis of possible worlds—indeed, the whole process of generation itself. This kind of representation differs markedly from representation as conventionally conceived. Like Freud's idea of "representation of drives" that was meant to designate something inaccessible to cognition, representation of doubling points to an anthropological disposition that eludes grasping and that manifests itself only by way of its kaleidoscopically changing effects. Literary fictionality as a representation of doubling discloses itself as pure semblance; in other words, inscribed into the modes of representation is the denial of any correspondence to anything existing. By revealing itself as semblance, literary fictionality distances itself from all the specific manifestations of doubling—such as those set out by the philosophy of subjectivity, by anthropogenic myth, and by social anthropology. In so doing, it deprives them of the authenticity necessary for them to be representative. It is this unauthenticated representation that enables us to conceive of doubling in all its limitless variety.

In overstepping all boundaries, fictionality becomes the epitome of inner-worldly totality, since it provides the paradoxical (and perhaps, for this very reason, desirable) opportunity for human beings simultaneously to be in the midst of life and to overstep it. This simultaneity of two mutually exclusive conditions—achieved by literary fictionality—enables human beings to experience their inherent split. By also issuing into ephemeral images, it prevents this experience of doubleness from disappearing into the product of a bridged division. Consequently, the totality evoked remains a finite one, and this may be a more deep-seated reason why fictionality discloses itself as semblance. As a pattern of inner-worldly totality, it does not compensate for existing deficiencies, because it does not embody an ideal. Instead, it presents the constitutive dividedness of human beings as the source of possible worlds within the world. What does this state of affairs indicate? Literary fictionality embraces a vast range of contrary movements in a kind of *jeu sans frontières*. But it is true of all fictions that they are put to work for a particular use; they are meant to effect something, and so they may be said to represent the need that they are designed to meet. What is this need?

Literary fictionality, as we have seen, bears a family resemblance to the dream and the ego rhythm, although it represents neither of these. It merely shares their doubling nature, which in the dream manifests itself as the interpenetration of primary and secondary processes, and in the ego rhythm as the interplay of structured focusing and oceanic dedifferentiation. Now if boundary-crossing grants a state of "finding oneself outside oneself"—to use a Bakhtinian concept[92]—this stepping out of oneself is not to be seen as transcending oneself, as is the case in collective ecstasies or in Plato, where the body must be left in order to permit the contemplation of ideas. Instead, the fictional ecstasy permits us to step outside the contexts that normally define what we are. Such a state is like one particular form of dream: "lucid dreaming," during which "we become and remain fully conscious of the fact that we are dreaming—and therefore that we are asleep. Thus we are, in a sense, simultaneously both 'awake' and 'asleep.'"[93]

However, even this dawning consciousness of being "awake" and "asleep" at the same time in lucid dreaming does not enable the dreamer to move beyond the dream horizon. "So the lucid dreamer does not sustain the horizon for phenomenological reflection, but is 'at the mercy' of whatever the dream horizon happens to be and in terms of which the dreamer operates lucidly."[94] Retaining the state that one has overstepped entails more than detachment from the dream horizon in the course of "lucid dreaming," for the exceeded condition now is integrated into "finding oneself outside oneself" to such an extent that the resultant doubling is transformed into a continual state of being above and outside oneself. Such an in-between position would not be possible if boundary-crossing functioned only as a change in circumstances. The state of being above and outside oneself is not merely a transitory phase but is a fundamental characteristic of humanity.

Hans-Georg Gadamer considers this state to be a major achievement of humankind. "In the *Phaedrus* Plato already described the blunder of those who take the viewpoint of rational reasonableness and tend to misinterpret the ecstatic condition of being outside oneself, seeing it as a mere negation of being composed within oneself and hence as a kind of madness. In fact, being outside oneself is the positive possibility of being wholly with something else."[95] Once again the dream analogy offers itself, albeit from a point of view unlike that of Freud and subsequent psychoanalysis. According to Gordon Globus, the dream is not a syntactically organized pattern of mnemic copies, nor is it the mere recurrence of the suppressed. Rather, it is a creative process that "creates the dream world *de novo*."[96] Globus continues:

> This extraordinary creativity has two distinct levels. There is first creativity in the sheer variety of unique life-worlds that dreaming constitutes *de novo*. The meanings co-operative in dreaming are typically a novel set, never before associated, and accordingly result in *creative variety*. Given the right meanings, any world from the set of all possible worlds might be produced. But there is an even deeper level of creativity I shall call 'formative' that should not be confused with creative variety. The point about the product of formative creativity is not its variety but its facticity, that there is any world at all, that our thought might produce its own fulfillment stretching there concretely before us ... Dreaming is in this regard sharply distinguished from waking according to convention. We don't form the life-world of waking; this is just common sense. That world is already there, awaiting us, affording our unveilings of it ... In dreaming, however, we formatively create (generate, constitute) the very world and our life in it. Once we reject the compositional theories of the dreaming life-world, formative creativity comes into focus.[97]

Dreams constantly produce alternative worlds that are in no way imitative of dismembered memories. Night after night our duality creates something new, whose bizarre character is conditioned by the interruption of sensory input during sleep, though this interruption in no way impedes the creative process. The dreamer as active creator is always in the midst of his or her own creations. Consequently, no matter what intention may underlie the newly created worlds, it is not possible for the dreamer to stand at a horizon that enables a perspective for seeing what has been produced and what it may all mean. Other than the awareness that one is dreaming, "lucid dreaming" grants no further detachment.

In this creation of new worlds, literary fictionality and the dream resemble each other, even though their expressions of this anthropological disposition differ. With literary fictionality, the process of stepping out of and above oneself always retains what has been overstepped, and in this form of doubling we are present to ourselves as our own differential. But as the juncture of multiple roles, human beings would remain abstract to themselves, and so literary fictionality presents them as something in relation to what they "make and understand"[98] themselves to be. Because human beings must step out of themselves in order to penetrate beyond their own boundaries, literary fictionality modifies consciousness by making accessible what merely happens to human beings in the dream. It forms the horizon that is not present to the dreamer in the midst of the world he or she has created. It reveals itself to be pure semblance as regards whatever gestalt human beings make themselves into, and by so doing shows that whatever enables human beings to take on such forms can never be reified. But at the same time, semblance itself is the propellant for a variegated and limitless self-invention of what human beings are like. Finally, it shows that there is no absolute frame of reference for the results of self-fashioning, even if fictionality, as an extension of ourselves, functions as if it did represent just such a frame. Because it indicates that human beings cannot be present to themselves, literary fictionality involves the condition of being creative right through to our dreams without ever allowing us to coincide with ourselves through what we create. What we do create is the conceivability of this basic disposition, and as this eludes our grasp, fictionality turns also into a judgment that human beings make about themselves.

_____

Chapter Three

Fiction Thematized in
Philosophical Discourse

Introduction: Beyond Empiricism

Boundary-crossing as the hallmark of fictionality makes fictionalizing dependent on the context within which the overstepping takes place. Being context-bound implies that fictions elude clear-cut definitions, let alone ontological grounding, and can be grasped only in terms of use. Because their use is potentially manifold, fictionalizing manifests itself in constantly shifting modes of operation in accordance with the changing boundaries to be overcome. Literary fictionality is no doubt a prominent paradigm of what fictionalizing is able to bring about, though it is by no means the overriding pattern of all fictions. If the particular use determines the operational nature of fictions, it appears pertinent to consider the need for fictions in a type of discourse different from that of literature: in philosophy. Fictions as conceived in philosophical discourse, however, will serve here only as a foil to the fictive in literature to allow us to observe how changing uses issue into a recasting of fictions. Equally important for our purposes is the growing indispensability of fictions in philosophy, which indicates a reversal in the attitude adopted toward fictions: from a form of deception they advance to a basic constituent of cognition. This radical reversal occurred to a large extent in the empiricist tradition, whose important junctures will provide the guideline for charting the rise of fiction's status in philosophy. In the process of that rise, fiction, once the object of critique, becomes the basis for an omnifictionalization.

The unfolding of the argument is not altogether independent of what had happened before the thematizing of fiction became an issue in philosophy, not least since roots of fiction-making can be discerned from antiquity through the Middle Ages. As Frank Kermode reminds us in *The Sense of an Ending,* the Greek physician Alcmaeon is said to have earned Aristotle's approval with his remark that men must die because they are not in a position to link beginning and end.[1] If death proves to be the result of this impossibility, it may equally well be the inspiration for ideas seeking to eliminate it. This elimination would involve an imaginative fashioning of beginning and end in order to provide the unavailable connection that would alter life itself. Such imaginative fashionings swiftly proliferate, because the linking of unavailabilities carries not even the smallest guarantee of authenticity; instead, it is historically conditioned needs that are decisive in the formation of such links.

The counter to the unfathomableness of beginning and end develops as a process of completion, in the course of which concocted patterns are superimposed on and identified with the impermeable. "One of the ways in which they [i.e., these patterns] do this is to make objects in which everything is that exists in concord with everything else, and nothing else is, implying that this arrangement mirrors the dispositions of a creator, actual or possible."[2] Kermode calls these objects "concord-fictions" (pp. 62–64), because in establishing links between the given and the unfathomable, they endow the given with meaning by incorporating it into a totality of their own making. The "concord-fictions" aim at this totality by supplying ideas of what beginning and end are like, thus swallowing them up in the overall context that they provide.

Kermode sees the *apocalypse* as the first great paradigm of concord-fictions. It brings together a time characterized by its end with another that grows out of the end. Other examples are the *millennium,* which links the unfathomableness of the beginning with the certainty of fulfillment; the *transition,* which connects collapse with renewal; *decadence,* which combines decay with hope; and finally *aevum,* which is manifested in various forms: St. Augustine saw it in the angels as intermediaries between God and matter, while Thomas Aquinas regarded it as duration through which time and eternity, but also *nunc movens* and *nunc stans,* merge into one another (pp. 8–17, 67–82).

What permeates all these concord-fictions is their almost limitless adaptability to changing circumstances. They all stand under the compulsion of having to fulfill their promises, and when—as frequently happens—they unexpectedly fail to do so, they are not discredited but merely forced to reshuffle the connections they have established.[3] What enables them to maneuver in this way is the fact that in their capacity as the imaginative removers of unavailabilities, they seem to know no bounds. This, however, delivers the coup de grâce to the old and discredited argument that fiction is the opposite of reality. Concord-fictions, in fact, spring into being because of the inaccessibilities of life. They seek to endow reality with meaning that, ultimately, makes reality into what we think it is. Otherwise, it would be nothing but pure contingency.

To call the above-mentioned paradigms *concord-fictions* is, however, a modern assessment resulting from the devaluation that they have suffered in the course of history. Since originally they embodied collective certainties, they could hardly be viewed as fictions. They came to seem fictive only when the solutions they offered were no longer acceptable. But this does not mean that we can now do without fictions; on the contrary, a gap created by a discredited fiction will have to be filled by another fiction that seems more trustworthy.

Furthermore, concord-fictions turn into forms of make-believe only when our attitudes toward them change. Rather than bearing their own foundations within themselves, their status depends upon those attitudes. The discrediting of such a fiction indicates that an erstwhile collective experience is no longer shared. The resultant loss of their truth-claim exposes them as fictions in a process experienced continually by every individual, since one person's conviction will be for the other only a fiction. Once again this does not mean that we can do without convictions; we simply do not realize that they may be fictions, because they provide the conditions under which we establish meaning and orient actions.

Since fictions are so closely intertwined with, and indeed dependent on, our attitudes, their pragmatic nature is obvious. This becomes all the more apparent through the fact that fictions cannot be removed by means of falsification. If they prove to be inadequate, the substitution of others for them testifies to their indispensability. What counts is success, and not truth, and the former will always be endowed with the latter when it has been telling.

This may also be said of Kermode's concord-fictions, whose changing forms do not reflect incontrovertible truths so much as anthropological and also historical needs. The range of these concord-fictions denotes the need for repairs to be constantly carried out on human life, which requires continual interpretation. What the concord-fictions have in common is "that concordance of beginning, middle, and end which is the essence of our explanatory fictions."[4] Even though the aim of this concordance may be explanatory, and even if the removal of unavailabilities can only be imaginative, the achievements of concord-fictions are always marked by contradictions. It is true that by linking the two impenetrable poles of life, they endow our halfway position with meaning. Nonetheless, the totality that they make conceivable can only be an image; otherwise, the totality would elude human grasp. In his book *Krisis,* Husserl explains that totalities can be present only through the mode of *epochē,* because without such modifications the totality would move beyond reach. The bracketing imposes an 'as-if' that creates the all-important condition for the totality to be conceived. Once "concordance" has made totality conceivable as an image—for instance, the beast of the apocalypse or St. Augustine's angels—that image is identical to the whole, regardless of the fact that it can be so only under human conditions and in ways that seem to eliminate the distress caused by the basic inaccessibilities of human life.

In contrast to Husserl's notion of bracketing, the image is never to be taken as if it were something different from what it exhibits. The image can function as an explanation only if it has this 'as-if' character, whereas in picturing something, the image participates in what it makes present. Thus the meaning established by the concord-fictions is one of participation, and not of explanation. The image cannot explain because, being identical to what it presents, it cannot be a sign pointing beyond itself. Explanation is generally not pictorial, and whenever it does assume pictorial traits, these require a reference that always lies beyond what is to be evinced by the explanation. But the image as a self-presentation of a totality knows no "beyond" outside what it seeks to make present. The concord-fictions, however, are driven to explain, because it is essential to find out what beginning and end and being-in-the-middle actually are.[5] The need for explanation makes them contradictory because the whole that is being represented in the image cannot also be a sign for something else without losing its status of totality.

Therefore, the difference between meaning as participation and meaning as explanation cannot be bridged in the concord-fictions. This is possible only if fiction changes from being an image of totality to being an 'as-if' construction. Whenever this happens, it is no longer a matter of removing only unavailabilities but also differences, in spite of the awareness that these cannot finally be glossed over. If concord-fictions, however, did bear the inscription that differences can never be bridged, thereby exposing their images as either make-believe or 'as-if' constructions, they would undermine their own status as ostensible remedies for the constitutive inaccessibilities of life.

The inherent contradiction of concord-fictions is particularly relevant to the discussion of literary fictionality, since the paradoxical idea of using an image to picture the whole and thereby explain something is structurally akin to the doubling structure of literary fictionality. In the case of concord-fictions the doubling is contradictory, because the concord-fictions have to meet a challenge different from that of literary fictionality. If contradiction epitomizes the nature of concord-fictions, it is not so much the result of a structural fault in them as it is an indication of human necessities that demand to be met. As a pictorial presentation of totality, striving to provide an equal measure of participation and explanation, concord-fictions satisfy an urge for both certainty and knowledge. Participation entails an imaginative transposal of the self, and explanation a cognitive distancing from what is to be grasped. Both modes of understanding—so it seems—have to be brought to bear, if beginning and end are to be fathomed. If concord-fictions are meant to humanize the whole without letting it disappear through this process of humanization, the unbridgeable difference inscribes itself into them as an irremediable contradiction.

Since the roots of concord-fictions are the fundamental unavailabilities that must be removed, solutions can only be pragmatic, in spite of the desire to resolve unavailabilities once and for all. If they were really successful in this respect, concord-fictions would be cut off from their own roots and, in eliminating the problem, would also eliminate themselves. It is the ineradicable presence of unavailabilities that lends puissance to the concord-fictions and endows their response to the challenge with authority.

A concord-fiction that does not continually keep in view the cause of its necessity would be prone to ossify into a myth. Myth, too, lays claim to certainty, but its enigmatic character calls out for interpretation.[6] On the other hand, one should not expect concord-fictions to proclaim their own status (for an answer to death cannot reveal itself as a mere attempt, if this attempt is meant to provide a solution), and the presence of a purpose in concord-fictions does prevent them from petrifaction as myth. Thus in history it is not only the individual concord-fiction that changes; each one can be supplanted by others in ways that show how the original solution may be hewn out of the old stone and activated in a new setting. Such changes of form indicate that concord-fictions have no ontological foundation but are pragmatic in origin, dealing with the differences, gaps, and uncertainties that fragment and restrict human life.

Fictions become determinate by way of their aims but, as we have seen, these aims are not determinate in themselves. Consequently, fiction is a multifariously variable entity that would lose its own nature if it were defined in terms other than those of its usage. This usage, however, defies categorization; it remains as incalculable as the unavailabilities that are to be overcome. Pragmatics overwhelm all onotological definitions that in the light of this all-consuming usage appear to be nothing more than mythical ossification.

It will be necessary for us to glance at the different uses of fiction, for fiction—since the advent of the modern age—has itself become an object of scrutiny. It has taken on a dimension that concord-fictions could not possess because they responded to a different context. Fiction became fictive, though this most certainly does not mean that it is the opposite of reality. This latter misunderstanding of the term is deeply ingrained, yet it also reveals reality as something suddenly divided off from something else which—even if not 'real'—is nevertheless there. Such an existent 'nonreality' would clearly have repercussions on one's understanding of what is 'real' or indeed of what constitutes 'reality'.

The scrutiny of fiction entails uncovering its possible applications, and through these we may be able to spot specific needs prevailing in historical situations. Moreover, different needs will result in different manifestations, and hence in different forms of fiction. These may be *idol, modality,* a *posit,* or *worldmaking*—to name only the main paradigms that we shall consider.

Our investigation should not, however, be regarded as an end in itself. The objective is to obtain a backdrop for understanding literary fictionality that crosses boundaries and opens up a network of connections, unlike other types of fiction that are geared to the demand of a particular situation. Different forms of fiction correspond to different conditions of usage, and some may even take on the status of an ontologically grounded entity (when the situation demands it), although they are always only indicators of particular anthropological needs.

Fiction as Idol: Francis Bacon and Criticism

The title page of Bacon's *Instauratio magna* (1620) shows Ulysses's ship behind the pillars of Hercules that had once formed the boundary of the ancient world but now offer no further barrier to progress. In this symbolic gesture, Tasso's allusion to Canto 26 of Dante's *Inferno* shimmers through like a palimpsest: "'Hercules didn't dare to cross the high seas. He set up a sign and confined the courage of the human spirit in an all-too-narrow cell. But Odysseus paid little heed to the established signs, in this craving to see and to know. He went beyond the Pillars and extended his audacious flight (*il volo audace*) over the open sea.'"[7]

This daring enterprise of boundary-crossing required preparation—an undertaking that Bacon, in order to indicate the need for change, entitled *New Organon*. In the introductory "Proem" he says "FRANCIS OF VERULAM reasoned thus with himself": "Being convinced that the human intellect makes its own difficulties, not using the true helps which are at man's disposal ... he thought all trial should be made, whether that commerce between the mind of man and the nature of things, which is more precious than anything on earth, or at least than anything that is of the earth, might by any means be restored to its perfect and original condition, or if that may not be, yet reduced to a better condition than that in which it now is."[8] Just as the sea stretches beyond the Pillars of Hercules, so Nature stretches beyond the human mind that is its own obstacle. Instead of the necessary exchange, a gulf has now opened up, and this has to be bridged. Mind and Nature are no longer geared to one another, let alone in unison, as evinced by the Greek conception of *theoria,* which entailed the contemplation of the cosmos that presented itself to view.

Consequently, what is now to be seen or what appears to the mind's eye can no longer be equated straightforwardly with reality: "the universe to the eye of the human understanding is framed like a labyrinth; presenting as it does on every side so many ambiguities of way, such deceitful resemblances of objects and signs, natures so irregular in their lines, and so knotted and entangled. ... but before we can reach the remoter and more hidden parts of nature, it is necessary that a more

perfect use and application of the human mind and intellect be introduced."[9] The universe as a labyrinthine maze and Nature eclipsed from
visibility[10] suggest the gap between the human mind and Nature rather
than the actual character of Nature. The dislocation between thinking
and being is given expression through this gap, not least because there
is now an awareness that Nature was not made for humankind and pays
no attention to its needs. No longer able to act merely as *contemplator
coeli,* the human mind finds itself before an abyss that must be bridged
if human self-preservation is to be successful.

What makes the task especially difficult is that the human senses—
no longer conceived as organs for contemplating the orderliness of the
cosmos—are unable to gain access to what is in view. According to
Bacon:

> The sense fails in two ways. Sometimes it gives no information, some-
> times it gives false information. For first, there are very many things
> which escape the sense, even when best disposed and no way ob-
> structed; by reason either of the subtlety of the whole body, or the
> minuteness of the parts, or distance of place, or slowness or else
> swiftness of motion, or familiarity of the object, or other causes. And
> again when the sense does apprehend a thing its apprehension is not
> much to be relied upon. For the testimony and information of the
> sense has reference always to man, not to the universe; and it is a great
> error to assert that the sense is the measure of things.[11]

Bacon here disputes the anthropomorphic finality of the cosmos,
which would no longer be itself if the senses could condition its
conceivability.

> [D]arkness ... as an index of natural concealment ... is no longer
> respected as something intended by nature; and elemental difference
> in kind such as was ascribed to the stars by the traditional cos-
> mology—these remain for the sixteenth century the basic forms of the
> limit set for theory, whose transgression constituted the nature and
> the problematic of theoretical curiosity. What still scarcely enters the
> horizon of possibility is a limitation on the range of theory as a con-
> tingent result of the limits of the human organ of vision—the thresh-
> old of visibility in both the macrocosm and the earthly micro-
> nature.... As long as the universe was represented as limited and
> closed by the outermost sphere of the fixed stars, the totality of the
> stars appearing above the horizon was considered to be surveyable
> with a single glance and exhausted by the stock already catalogued by

Hipparchus. The geocentric system favored the unquestioned validity of this assumption by granting man visual conditions that were the same in all directions and constant. The supplementary teleological assumption that invisible things in nature would contradict the meaning of creation was current at least in the humanistic tradition and gave astronomy's postulate of visibility a more than methodical/economic foundation, namely, a metaphysical one. That the world could contain things withdrawn and inaccessible to man's natural optical capacity, not only at times and provisionally but definitively, was an idea unknown to the ancient world and the Middle Ages and also, by their philosophical assumptions, an impossible one.[12]

Because the "postulate of visibility" has become a dangerous error in Bacon's eyes, he praises Galileo—even if he does not altogether understand him—for inventing the telescope,

by the aid of which [the telescope], as by boats or vessels, a nearer intercourse with the heavenly bodies can be opened and carried on. For these [the telescopes] show us that the milky way is a group of clusters of small stars entirely separate and distinct; of which fact there was but a bare suspicion among the ancients. They seem also to point out that the spaces of the planetary orbits, as they are called, are not altogether destitute of other stars, but that the heaven begins to be marked with stars before we come to the starry sphere itself; although with stars too small to be seen without these glasses.[13]

If Nature eludes perception—and the experimental enhancement of the senses shows that this is the case—then amendments are required in order to remove human inadequacies. Nature no longer reveals itself directly to the senses, and indeed withholds itself from them, but only because they are still regarded as the yardstick of observation and even of cognition. They not only help to create the gulf between thought and being but also make it dangerous by concealing it.[14]

In the light of ancient and medieval cosmology, the ruptured correspondence between mind and Nature turns the anthropocentric finality of Nature into just as threatening a deception as does the inherited idea that thinking and being mirror each other. Human faculties now find themselves thrown back on their limitations, beyond which stretches a vast terra incognita. Ruptures of this sort are fertile soil for fictions, as we have already seen with concord-fictions, but what distinguishes the latter from modern fictions is their complementary character: they eliminated basic inaccessibilities such as the beginning and the end in order to close the gaps in a world order beyond which there was nothing. They dealt with gaps, whereas modern fictions deal with splits, that is, differences which divide an existing world at least into two, with one part known and the other unknown.

Such differences can no longer be resolved through complements. Indeed, it even seems impossible to build bridges, since bridges require grounding on two sides and cannot be suspended in midair. Beginning and end, time and eternity, were reconciled through concord-fictions, so that the state in between could gain significance; but now humanity has to reach beyond this in-between state since it is forced to attain self-preservation that appears—at least in contemporary thought—to be more basic and empirically more urgent than the umbrella concepts offered by concord-fictions. Complements can no longer assist in this venture into unknown territory; what is now needed is reflection on the means that are to be used in opening it up. In their time, concord-fictions had been taken as truths to which the character of reality was indisputably accorded, but now the instruments of exploration are mere assumptions whose serviceability has first to be ascertained.

In ancient tradition there is, to my knowledge, only one instance of anything comparable with fiction in its modern usage; this is in Roman law.

> And so the national Roman charge of theft was extended to foreigners and here the stratagem of fiction was employed: one pretended that the foreigner concerned was a Roman. It was not the legislator (people's assembly) but the magistrate (praetor)—who did not actually have the authority in this case—that constituted the main instance of further legal extension in Rome; Roman law was therefore, in many areas, adapted to the various requirements not through general norms (laws) but through the appropriate handling of individual cases (casuistry). This procedure suggests a method that carefully sought to model the new on the tried and trusted old; a favored means of establishing patterns was fiction: this extended legal definitions to related situations for which these definitions had not originally been created.[15]

Quintilian refers to this situation in his *Institutio* when dealing with the usefulness of fictional hypotheses in the analysis of legal matters:

> I think I should also add that arguments are drawn not merely from admitted facts, but from fictitious suppositions, which the Greeks

style [*cat' hypothesin*], and that this latter type of argument falls into all the same divisions as those which I have mentioned above, since there may be as many species of fictitious arguments as there are of true arguments. When I speak of fictitious arguments I mean the proposition of something which, if true, would either solve a problem or contribute to its solution, and secondly the demonstration of the similarity of our hypothesis to the case under consideration.[16]

Fiction becomes fictitious through its as-if character, but this must always be indicated or known, for fictions are means of solving problems—for the Romans to extend their laws, and for modern times to extend the human mind.

These extensions, however, initially required that the human mind should become aware of its habitual limitations, for as long as these are not apparent, there can be no starting point for such extensions. In order to clear the ground for what is now necessary, Bacon embarks on a critique of the idols that—owing to their structural similarity to concord-fictions—could just as well be understood as a form of unmasking in order to discard the inherited array of complementarities.

Now the idols, or phantoms, by which the mind is occupied are either adventitious or innate. The adventitious come into the mind from without; namely, either from the doctrines and sects of philosophers, or from perverse rules of demonstration. But the innate are inherent in the very nature of the intellect, which is far more prone to error than the sense is. For let men please themselves as they will in admiring and almost adoring the human mind, this is certain: that as an uneven mirror distorts the rays of objects according to its own figure and section, so the mind, when it receives impressions of objects through the sense, cannot be trusted to report them truly, but in forming its notions mixes up its own nature with the nature of things.[17]

Idols, then, are signs of an inadequate distinction between mind and Nature; they occur when the mind mingles itself with Nature—a Nature that has become eclipsed from visibility and is in no way geared to the mind. Idols are like the debris of the old cosmology, and they suggest fatal connections in a world where self-preservation must be achieved through one's own efforts. The unmasking of idols is thus a vital precondition in Bacon's "workshop philosophy"[18] for what is now considered to be a life-supporting discovery.

Bacon distinguishes four types of idols: Idols of the Tribe, Idols of the Cave, Idols of the Marketplace, and Idols of the Theater.[19] Underlying this listing is a Scholastic principle of classification highlighting the universal character of the idols. The Idols of the Tribe are innate in human nature, or at least are acquired by the human race; they embody the universal features of humankind. For this reason the Idols of the Tribe are of prime significance for Bacon's critique because they represent, according to Scholastic classification, the substance.

> The human understanding is moved by those things most which strike and enter the mind simultaneously and suddenly, and so fill the imagination; and then it feigns and supposes all other things to be somehow, though it cannot see how, similar to those few things by which it is surrounded. . . . But by far the greatest hindrance and aberration of the human understanding proceeds from the dulness, incompetency, and deceptions of the senses; in that things which strike the sense outweigh things which do not immediately strike it, though they be more important. Hence it is that speculation commonly ceases where sight ceases; insomuch that of things invisible there is little or no observation. Hence all the working of the spirits inclosed in tangible bodies lies hid and unobserved of man. So all the more subtle changes of form in the parts of coarser substances (which they commonly call alteration, though it is in truth local motion through exceedingly small spaces) is in like manner unobserved. (pp. 56–58)

Idols of the Tribe have a psychological root that grows from the need to extract the most far-reaching generalizations from a comparatively slender set of data. It follows that the human mind bases itself less on cognition than on a massive readjustment of given data. If one also takes account of the fallibility of the senses that filter these data, then the hidden areas will grow in proportion to the certainty with which the mind cuts itself off from what it is seeking to comprehend. The less transparent this process is, the more evident it will be that understanding remains trapped in the "figments of the human mind" (p. 58).

While the Idols of the Tribe feature the substance in Scholastic terms, the Idols of the Cave "take their rise in the peculiar constitution, mental or bodily, of each individual" (p. 59). In the individual case—highlighting a singular manifestation of the substance—a socially conditioned component comes to the fore, fanning out the nature of the idol into its possibilities. The allusion to the Platonic cave shows clearly that—for all the variety of individual differentiation—men remain chained to the floor of their own cave, with the shadows of their ideas passing by on the edges, lit by no sun but lost in the darkness of

Nature. For the idol adjusts Nature to its own conditions, and this characteristic becomes all the more marked when the individual is accomplishing self-deception. In Platonic terms, the individual's distance from Nature is still further increased by the fact that the Idols of the Cave "grow for the most part either out of the predominance of a favourite subject, or out of an excessive tendency to compare or to distinguish, or of partiality for particular ages, or out of the largeness or minuteness of the objects contemplated" (p. 60). In other words, the individual continually brings into play familiar frames of reference in order to master new and incalculable situations. One result of that process, however, is an unrecognized widening of the very gap that, by using these old and trusted measures, the individual had been hoping to bridge. While the tribe continually succumbs to the temptation of unsubstantiated generalization, the individual yields to misplaced trust in analogy.

Idols of the Marketplace undermine the very heart of Scholasticism, which is the realism of language. For Bacon these idols are "the most troublesome of all" (pp. 60f.), because they block access to Nature. "For men believe that their reason governs words; but it is also true that words react on the understanding . . . Whence it comes to pass that the high and formal discussions of learned men end oftentimes in disputes about words and names; with which . . . it would be more prudent to begin, and so by means of definition reduce them to order. Yet even definitions cannot cure this evil in dealing with natural and material things; since the definitions themselves consist of words, and those words beget others" (p. 61).

Bacon's objections are propped by circumstances both historical and psychological. According to the Scholastic understanding of language, the word is an action that takes what is given *in potentia* and transfers it into *actualitas*. In Thomas Aquinas's words: "Verbum autem in mente conceptum, est repraesentativum omnis eius quod actu intelligitur."[20] If the word conceived in the mind is representative of everything that is grasped through the act, then knowledge of the true nature of words must also be knowledge of the true nature of things. Since for Aquinas naming entails a change of status for things, he did not speak of the meaning of things; rather, in making reference to meaning, Aquinas calls it *participatio*. Consequently, word usage involves participation in reality. But Bacon regarded this as dangerous insofar as participation leads to self-delusion, because one's own ideas make it impossible to gain access to a Nature that lies beyond the human mind. This fact is concealed by the prevailing belief that "reason governs words,"[21] and since this is a collectively shared assumption, the Idols of the Marketplace effect a mutual confirmation of various cherished views. Psychologically, these collectively shared concepts correspond to a need for security that will be all the more lastingly satisfied when the views appear to be validated, mutually and publicly.

Idols of the Theater "are not innate, nor do they steal into the understanding secretly, but are plainly impressed and received into the mind from the play-books of philosophical systems and the perverted rules of demonstration" (p. 62). Philosophical systems incorporate the stores that supply the material for idol-building. The theater image reveals their illusory nature. There is, however, a certain ambiguity about these idols, even though Bacon's primary intention is to denounce them. It is the dogmatic character of the philosophical system that, in Bacon's view, shows them to be only a stage play: "And in the plays of this philosophical theatre you may observe the same thing which is found in the theatre of the poets, that stories invented for the stage are more compact and elegant, and more as one would wish them to be, than true stories out of history" (p. 63). The theater metaphor is meant as a condemnation of philosophy, which bars the way to an appropriate investigation of Nature, but at the same time the philosophers criticized would have to be seen as Bacon's allies if they understood that their solutions were merely a stage play. It would have taken Aristotle to be a Kantian in order to be accepted, for Bacon admits that "there is frequent dealing with experiments," so that his objection now weighs all the more heavily: "For he [Aristotle] had come to his conclusion before; he did not consult experience, as he should have done, in order to the framing of his decisions and axioms" (p. 65).

The appropriate method would not have been to twist experience to suit the axiom but to make experience accessible through constructs. In principle, all that would have been needed to achieve this is not a different system but a different attitude toward the axioms of the system. It follows that the idols are not inborn or socially acquired self-deceptions of the human mind, but forms of access to Nature that can function properly only through a change of attitude. Bacon uses the illusoriness of philosophical solutions as an argument to discredit the traditional inheritance. But this illusion arises out of a misconception of the idols, which at best are constructs, and one only needs to gain awareness of this in order to turn them experimentally in other directions and to other uses.

It is revealing that Bacon ends his description of the idols with those of the theater. Their nature as a stage play—even if it was misunderstood by the philosophers—makes them pale into insignificance in view of the Scholastic frame of reference brought to bear by Bacon in order to communicate his critique in terms familiar to contemporary thought. The Idols of the Tribe are the universals of the human race, the Idols of the Cave are the individual manifestation of the latter, and the Idols of the Marketplace are the 'accidence' of the 'substance'. Historically, the Scholastic procedure could be viewed as an attack on the prevailing world order: The Idols of the Tribe display the fatality of the mirror concept by which microcosm and macrocosm were related to each other; the Idols of the Cave show the fatality of analogical thinking through which the unknown is opened up by way of recourse to the known; the Idols of the Marketplace show the fatality of correspondences through which the world is seen as a grammatical model; and the Idols of the Theater denote the fatality of "similarities" (Foucault) through which reason and Nature were thought to be synchronized. Bacon's Scholastic approach serves the purpose of using a familiar style of argumentation to reveal what was hidden by the idols as manifestations of the inherited world order: the gulf between mind and Nature.

As the physical state of Nature is not related to the human mind, it can no longer be given presence through representation, which as substitution cannot body forth what is inaccessible. Covering the intangible by projections, however, and equating these with Nature, which basically eludes representation, is bound to have threatening repercussions on a situation in which human self-preservation has become a burning issue. Bacon therefore goes to great lengths to clarify the situation, sometimes using vivid images to do so:

> The human understanding when it has once adopted an opinion (either as being the received opinion or as being agreeable to itself) draws all things else to support and agree with it. And though there be a greater number and weight of instances to be found on the other side, yet these it either neglects and despises, or else by some distinction sets aside and rejects; in order that by this great and pernicious predetermination the authority of its former conclusions may remain inviolate. And therefore it was a good answer that was made by one who when they showed him hanging in a temple a picture of those

who had paid their vows as having escaped shipwreck, and would have him say whether he did not now acknowledge the power of the gods,—'Aye,' asked he again, 'but where are they painted that were drowned after their vows?' (p. 56)

If there is something that defies representation, then representation itself becomes a sign of a divided world, for it has no existence of its own, no inner core, but needs something else that will enable it to take on an appearance. Whatever resists representation cannot be given presence by it, and whenever it seeks to capture the inaccessible by means of concepts, it is the content of the concepts that becomes the object of representation. This, however, is a reification of representation through which the gulf between mind and Nature is hidden by the erroneous belief that it has been bridged. Thus a Nature defying representation becomes totally unavailable when represented. "But a representation, which is collectively mistaken for an ultimate—ought not to be called a representation. It is an idol."[22]

Idols, then, are reified forms of representation that the human mind spins out of itself, thereby revealing—though involuntarily—the limits of representation. Concord-fictions were marked by a contradiction insofar as representation meant both participation and explanation; they implicitly referred to something outside themselves, although they claimed to be identical to what they pictured. But now—according to Bacon—representation shrinks into idols when the human mind, challenged by an impenetrable Nature, has to explore what is withheld from it. Concord-fictions had facilitated participation by combining beginning and end under conditions valid for a substantialist world order, but for Bacon participation is the fatal linkup between the mind and its own concepts in the false belief that such a linkup achieves representation of a Nature that has become eclipsed to the human mind. In Bacon's understanding all such representations are "fictions."[23] Yet the term *fiction* is not to be thought of as opposed to reality, but as opposed to the unmasking of a deception or a self-deception of the mind, not least because many of these "fictions" seem like incontrovertible realities that are ingrained in the human constitution. Bacon splits open the contradiction of concord-fictions by showing that representation seeks to provide a longed-for satisfaction, but it cannot explain anything because it deals with a Nature that for the most part remains inaccessible to the human mind and senses.

This leads to two problems: First, the mind must be freed from its inclination to make things available by means of representation. Second, the appropriate instruments must be found for this purpose, even though ultimately these, too, must be fashioned by the same mind that stands in need of cure. Bacon himself confirmed the nature of the problem through Solomon's aphorism: "The glory of God is to conceal a thing; the glory of the king to search it out," which he extended with his own postscript, "man is a god to man."[24] He took himself as an example of how this problem should be solved:

> For all those who before me have applied themselves to the invention of arts have but cast a glance or two upon facts and examples and experience, and straightway proceeded, as if invention were nothing more than an exercise of thought, to invoke their own spirits to give them oracles. I, on the contrary, dwelling purely and constantly among the facts of nature, withdraw my intellect from them no further than may suffice to let the images and rays of natural objects meet in a point, as they do in the sense of vision; whence it follows that the strength and excellency of the wit has but little to do in the matter. And the same humility which I use in inventing I employ likewise in teaching.[25]

In order to open up an otherwise eclipsed Nature, two parallel operations are indispensable: the disentangling of the intellect from its mingling with Nature, and the continual inventing of contrivances for questioning Nature. Phenomena must be cleansed from representation[26] so that the contrivance can take full effect. This is to be brought about by induction: "For I consider induction to be that form of demonstration which upholds the sense, and closes with nature, and comes to the very brink of operation, if it does not actually deal with it."[27] It is experiment that actually deals with Nature as an "artificially devised" (p. 26) construct, for "the nature of things betrays itself more readily under the vexations of art than in its natural freedom" (p. 29). The experiment as a contrived question depends on two basic operations of human understanding: "The conclusions of human reason as ordinarily applied in matters of nature, I call for the sake of distinction *Anticipations of Nature* (as a thing rash or premature). That reason which is elicited from facts by a just and methodical process, I call *Interpretation of Nature.*"[28]

Anticipation—necessary if the experiment is to be construed—is not knowledge but an act of exploration whose findings must be subjected to continual testing. A precondition of possible success lies in the mind neutralizing its projections by means of an inductive procedure of rejection and exclusion (see p. 145). Bacon stresses that "it is the peculiar and perpetual error of the human intellect to be more moved and excited by affirmatives than by negatives" (p. 56). Thus the experiment must be pervaded by the awareness that it can only prefigure a state of affairs, and therefore anticipation must never be taken for the object itself. Consequently, experiments can never have the character of idols; the awareness of mere anticipation that is inherent in them divides them from Nature, to which they are regarded solely as a means of access. When it is pertinent to penetrate a Nature closed off from representation, the human mind has to dissociate itself from all its socially and historically conditioned ideas[29] that inevitably assume the character of projections when meant to give presence to Nature. In their place, as a counter to the idol, Bacon sets experiment. For now another gulf has opened up to replace the unavailabilities that led to concord-fictions, and this is evident from the fact that Nature can be explored only by way of operations.

With experiment replacing idol, and operation replacing representation, the possibility arises that Bacon has discovered a much more genuine form of fiction than the one he had denounced as deception. Nowadays we view experiment as heuristic fiction that—just as Bacon had described it—constitutes a construct designed for the purpose of an anticipated discovery. This discovery relates to forms and axioms of Nature that not only defy representation but are actually concealed by it. And so Bacon outlines the orientation for his experimental procedure as follows:

> For a true and perfect rule of operation then the direction will be *that it be certain, free, and disposing or leading to action.* And this is the same thing with the discovery of the true Form. For the Form of a nature is such, that given the Form the nature infallibly follows. Therefore it is always present when the nature is present, and universally implies it, and is constantly inherent in it. Again, the Form is such, that if it be taken away the nature infallibly vanishes. Therefore it is always absent when the nature is absent, and implies its absence, and inheres in nothing else. Lastly, the true Form is such that it deduces the given nature from some source of being which is inherent in more natures, and which is better known in the natural order of things than the Form itself. For a true and perfect axiom of knowledge then the direction and precept will be, *that another nature be discovered which is convertible with the given nature, and yet is a limitation of a more general*

nature, as of a true and real genus. Now these two directions, the one active the other contemplative, are one and the same thing; and what in operation is most useful, that in knowledge is most true.[30]

If, as Bacon assumes, Nature consists of the order of its forms, and if lack of form means the absence of Nature, then experiment aims to discover these forms, and every discovery will open up new access to still further discoveries. Just how Nature is to be encompassed in a network of axioms to cover all its forms, Bacon demonstrated in his tables, catalogs, inventories, and histories that he intended to set up for all the facts of Nature. However, Bacon was unable to chart the multifariousness of axioms underlying Nature, and this may be the reason why he considered such a task as a communal duty of researchers (pp. 251f.). His listing of procedures necessary for the cognition of Nature petered out into an endless taxonomy. Taxonomies, though nourished by the belief that the relevant order will eventually be discovered, are always a sign that a visualized or anticipated totality can never be encompassed completely. The potentially endless list of procedures did not, however, resign Bacon to the impossibility of ever penetrating Nature. On the contrary, as we have seen from a passage quoted earlier, he had no doubts about the usefulness of this method, since what is useful for tracing the orderliness and patternings of Nature must also be true. Bacon was not interested merely in knowledge of Nature for its own sake; he was concerned with fundamental repairs to the human condition brought about by the Fall (pp. 247f.), and for this purpose he claimed that "I have provided the machine"[31] whose function, he says later, is "to command nature in action."[32]

That Bacon strives to make truth and usefulness interchangeable indicates why mastery of Nature through knowledge of its forms had become for him an indispensable necessity of human life. The experiment as a construct was considered to be the appropriate means of bringing to light the hidden forms of Nature. Why, then, did Bacon not see the experiment as fiction, even though he knew the term well and conceived of experimentation as a trial-and-error process, whose anticipations were potentially subject to falsification?

The experiment was intimately geared to the necessity of human self-preservation, and so its internal structure as heuristic fiction did not come to view, as Bacon believed that the as yet unexplored Nature—whose exploitation would in the end guarantee self-preservation—had its axioms prefigured in the experiment, which therefore could not be fiction.

Instead, the layout of the experiment anticipates the forms of Nature it is supposed to discover. Consequently, there must be forms that are real and forms that are fictitious—a distinction that Bacon had indeed drawn:

> The human understanding is of its own nature prone to abstractions and gives a substance and reality to things which are fleeting. But to resolve nature into abstractions is less to our purpose than to dissect her into parts; as did the school of Democritus, which went further into nature than the rest. Matter rather than forms should be the object of our attention, its configurations and changes of configuration, and simple action, and law of action or motion; for forms are figments of the human mind, unless you will call those laws of action forms.[33]

If fictions embody deceptions and laws embody the axiomatics of Nature, how can forms be fictions at one moment and laws at another? Form as fiction depends on discourse, while form as law depends on necessity. For Bacon, the idols as forms are fictions insofar as they organize the discourse of representation. This is the projection of a mind that believes it has made Nature totally available through the forms of its own intellect. But the same forms are laws when—liberated from the discourse of representation—they open up Nature by parceling it into the axioms discovered; instead of representing Nature, they anatomize its structure.

In both cases, the forms spring from the human mind, even if they evince different degrees of consciousness. But why is discourse-related fiction recognized as such, while necessary fiction is not? The discourse of representation, as organized by the idols, pretends to know the whole, even though the whole only reflects the dispositions of the mind and senses in relation to a world that, by Bacon's time, has long since grown far beyond such parameters. This self-deceiving confidence is dangerous. Now that the need for self-preservation by means of Nature has dwindled into imperceptibility, Bacon cannot conceive his own modes of exploration as fictions, if for no other reason than that the whole sphere in which the techniques of exploration operate has not yet been fully disclosed to consciousness. Therefore Bacon cannot afford to identify those forms as fiction which, unlike organizing discourse, have to meet the necessity of laying bare the axioms of Nature. He denounces the idols as fictions in part because self-preservation makes it imperative that the heuristic element of experimentation should not itself be suspected of being fictitious.

For Bacon there is a close connection between idol and experiment, and his differing perspectives on two basically similar phenomena indicate that fictions are intimately allied to the attitudes taken toward them. He did not take the heuristics of experimentation as fictitious, because the experimental construct has—by means of a *via negationis*—to undo the assumptions underlying representation if it is to succeed in opening up Nature. Since criticizing idols as fictions was meant to secure the validity of the experiment, Bacon was unable to see that all fictions are contrivances for multiple usage, determined by the context in which they become operative. The extent to which the context determines the form can be inferred both from idol and from experiment. The idol had glossed over the gulf between mind and Nature because it was conditioned by the discourse of representation inherited from a substantialist world order. The experiment had to make inroads into Nature in order to spotlight what was to be mastered, because it was conditioned by the need for self-preservation. Simultaneously, however, both idol and experiment impinge on the very context that has conditioned their form—the idol, by creating blindness through its projections; the experiment, by "commanding Nature into action."

From all this we may draw two conclusions that are important for the history of fiction thematized in philosophical discourse. First, fictions are either discourse-related or necessity-related, that is, they arise out of the discourse of representation or out of the need to make incursions into what appears impenetrable. Second, form and content of fiction are not to be derived from, let alone made transparent by, the contexts within which they become operative. Bacon could therefore only unmask the fictitiousness of idols because Nature was dissected under the auspices of a different order, which he deliberately termed a "logic of research" and not a philosophy.[34] Furthermore, fictions are less open to the charge of deceit when they arise out of necessity. Nevertheless, there can be no denying that the necessity Bacon speaks of is tinged with an element of fictiveness from which he tries to shelter experimentation by unmasking the discourse-related fiction. The axioms of Nature that are to be gleaned from experiments are based on the assumption that Nature is present only when it possesses form. This postulates an ideal of equivalence that is certainly essential for self-preservation; but as a 'model' it can only be something posited. This becomes evident, however, solely when Nature is seen in terms of other 'models'—indeed, when the models themselves are recognized as heuristic fictions and not as the realities Bacon took them to be.

Bacon criticized the idols as fictions because he rejected the increasing impracticality of a mind trapped by representation. The idols became fictitious for him as they bore witness to an equation of the human mind's habitual disposition with an otherwise nonhuman Nature that appeared to him totally contradictory. And yet, despite its changes of status, this very contradiction remained a constituent of fiction right through to Vaihinger. Fiction is contradictory insofar as it is always meant to cope with unavailabilities while being utterly dependent on discourse, which is as evident in concord-fictions as it is in the reified representations of the idols. As a means of providing solutions, fictions lose their function when the context for which they were created changes. But what turns out to be even more revealing and surprising is that the inherent contradictions appear to have vanished whenever fictions conform to epistemological standards and turn into premises for cognition. Thus idols are better solutions than concord-fictions, and Bacon's experimentation gives greater access to Nature than do the various reifications of the idols. This sequence suggests that fictions are meant to compensate for anthropological deficiencies, even if their reliability has to be tested by epistemological criteria. Consequently, fiction itself initiates a conflict between anthropology and epistemology, for what may be anthropologically useful fails to conform to the premises of epistemology, though these must be heeded if solutions are to be validated.

Since fictions become duplicitous in order to correspond in equal measure to different frames of reference, empiricism right up to Hume could never quite cope with them. This duplicity does not, however, arise exclusively from the divergent references; it is also the manifestation of a duality that permeates the very heart of fiction itself: it satisfies anthropological needs only to the degree that its efficacy can be rationalized. It does not deliberately set out to stage the conflict between anthropology and epistemology; the conflict is an indication that the anthropological need can be satisfactorily fulfilled only if it is ratified by reason. It is the contextual usage that makes the duality of fiction ambiguous, whereas in literature the duality is acted out in a way that is not harnessed to any definite practical purpose.

This ambiguous duality is what leads Bacon alternately to criticize and to affirm thematized fiction. Forms, as he said in his Aphorism LI, are fictions when they are representative and laws when they are active incursions. Therefore one thing can be two things, the same can be different, and denunciation of fiction can go hand in hand with its indispensability. This alternation continues up through Vaihinger, and is yet another aspect of fiction's duality. Indeed, it can never be eliminated even when fiction is unmasked as fiction, or when its fictitious character is not recognized. Bacon proves the point both unmistakably and involuntarily.

Exposure of the idols as fictions entails highlighting the unrepresentable that they have veiled. From a critical standpoint, the duality is viewed negatively. The assumption that through experiment forms of incursion and axioms of nature may be equated with each other entails a projection that need not be wrong, but that certainly cannot possess the reality attributed to it—not least because this reality cannot be known. In the context of the affirmative view, the duality is suppressed, for Bacon did not see experimentation as mere heuristic fiction. If the idols figure as unmasked concord-fictions, the incursive operation of the experiment depends nevertheless on assumptions that have to be posited. This does not mean, however, that the experiment has the same structural fault that Bacon finds in the idols, for representation and operation are different processes with different aims: instead of making Nature subordinate to the mind, the mind is now penetrating Nature. All the same, it is obvious that representation of Nature in terms of the human mind requires an operation of transference, just as an experimental incursion requires a Nature represented as axiomatics; the difference lies in the respective weighting of what has precedence: representation or operation. But since the experiment cannot do without representation, even though it aims to chart unknown (and therefore unrepresentable) territory, the contraflow of representation and operation brings forth the duality of fiction in yet another form. Now it is more than an anthropological or epistemological indicator, for it shows that representation necessitates operation, and operation reaches its goal through representation.

Bacon was not fully aware of this fact because his view of fiction was limited—he saw the operational incursion into Nature as the opposite of concealment brought about by fictions. Even Newton still contended: *hypotheses non fingo*. It required one further stage of awareness in order to broaden the scope for scrutinizing fictions, and it is at this point in the history of empiricism that Jeremy Bentham becomes of

importance. It is, however, worth remembering that, at the threshold of
the modern age, philosophers were already drawing attention to the
duality of fictions, although, depending on their contextual usage, this
duality could appear as a conflict between anthropological and epistemological perspectives, between conscious critique and unconscious
affirmation of fiction, or between representation and operation. Indeed,
it would seem that the duality of fictions is the prime condition for their
almost limitless application.

Fiction as Modality: Jeremy Bentham and Affirmation

Looking back on Bacon, Jeremy Bentham said, "In the time of the English Philosopher, the mind was annoyed and oppressed by terrors
which in the time of his French disciple [d'Alembert] had lost, though
not the whole, the greater part of their force. In Bacon's time—in the
early part of the seventeenth century—everything in nature that was, or
was supposed to be, *extraordinary,* was *alarming;* alarming, and in some
shape or other, if not *productive, predictive* at least of human misery."[35] It
was this threat that gave dual impetus to cognition: if self-preservation
was to be achieved, then incursions into Nature had to be accompanied
by the mind's liberation from its own deceptive projections. Bentham
could already look back on such an achievement, but until late in the
eighteenth century a critique of fiction remained an almost essential
defense mechanism for empirical epistemology.

Fiction always had to be unmasked, but its nature varied according
to the epistemological premises that determined the unmasking. Locke
maintained that "our simple *Ideas* are all real and true, because they
answer and agree to those Powers of Things, which produce them in
our Minds, that being all that is requisite to make them real, and not
fictions at Pleasure";[36] "a fiction of the Mind ... has no power to produce any simple *Idea*" (p. 375). "On the contrary, those are *fantastical,*
which are made up of such Collections of simple *Ideas,* as were really
never united, never were found together in any Substance; v.g. a rational
Creature, consisting of a Horse's Head, joined to a body of humane
shape, or such as the *Centaurs* are described" (p. 374). Locke regards
fiction as the principle of association gone mad (see pp. 161, 394f.). A
mind that combines data according to its own whims, and not according to the regulative principles of God, archetypes, and mixed modes,
has bewitched itself.

But fiction still seems to be necessary for the Lockean system, because—although he excludes it—this very exclusion is what lends stability to the kind of knowledge that for him was beyond doubt, for every system establishes its validity in proportion to the degree in which it concretizes what it rejects. Fiction as the association of ideas gone mad seems to be just as much a matter of experience as the idol-building that Bacon condemned. But in neither case is the negative view of fiction confined to the exposure of its deluding character. For Bacon the idols formed the contrast to experimentation, which as an anticipation of Nature's axiomatics could not be fictitious because only a time span separated the experimental construct from the forms of Nature, and in due course research would close the gap between the two. For Locke, fantastical ideas provide retrospective assurance that the regulative principles of association, as the natural premises of the mind, function in such a way that knowledge can be gained from experience. Thus pathology serves to solidify normality, which means that even when negated, fiction finds itself in a context of practical usage.

The more urgent this contextual usage becomes, the more obvious will be the duality of fictions, not least because no matter how negatively viewed, they remain indispensable. David Hume brought about a kind of truce in the war against fiction, because he came to regard laws of causality and principles of cognition—especially those that Locke had still taken for granted—and indeed all epistemological premises as "fictions of the mind."[37] By this, however, he did not mean the usual denunciation of fiction; he took these premises, rather, to be forms of cognition that could plausibly be postulated but not satisfactorily proven. As terms to be used in describing experience, they need not be jettisoned, as we can see from Hume's description of the causality principle; indeed, "fictions of the mind" became an essential critical concept in his downgrading of what he had come to consider epistemological postulates. Instead of criticizing fiction, he used it as an instrument of criticism, and he turned the traditional negative view of it against the supposed laws of cognition. This signals a new use of fiction, even if once more it exploits the negativity of past uses, and it shows a marked change in the direction of consciousness as well as the extent to which fiction is related to consciousness.

Bacon and Locke had unmasked fiction as deceit, self-deception, and madness, though they did not claim that idols or fantastical ideas were deliberate lies or perverse insanity. Their criticism was meant to create awareness of how fictions came about, and even if at times it seemed to be attacking hidden preconceptions, this was not because fictions were lies or perversities, but because their effects were to be countered by simply excluding them from the realm of reason and sanity. Just as Bacon and Locke had tried and condemned fiction in the name of ethics or reason, Hume used the tarnished concept of fiction to undermine the premises of empirical epistemology. The recurring need for this condemnation indicates the abiding power of fiction.

Jeremy Bentham stands for a paradigm switch regarding the understanding of fiction, and this is all the more remarkable for the fact that throughout his life he remained a positivist, committed to the basic premises of empiricism. For Bentham, however, experience was of a far more practical nature than Locke's vision of the tabula rasa being bombarded by data from the external world. Bentham's revaluation of fiction was inspired by his intimate acquaintance with the practice of law and by his self-experience.

If there is still a residual negative attitude toward fiction, it relates to the law, even though that, too, embodies an indispensable fiction in Bentham's eyes: "The word *right* is the name of a fictitious entity; one of those objects the existence of which is feigned for the purpose of discourse—by a fiction so necessary that without it human discourse could not be carried on."[38] He supplements this statement with another: "Though fictitious, the language cannot be termed *deceptious*—in intention at least, whatsoever in some cases may without intention be the result."[39] If fictitious concepts such as the law are indispensable for human discourse, then in equal measure they depend on discourse and also make it possible. But this duality gives rise to legal manipulation that for Bentham is already apparent in such basic fictions as the social contract, whereby the ruler must look after the welfare of his subjects and the subjects must obey the ruler:

> This proposition, then, 'that men are bound by *compacts*,' and this other, 'that, if one part performs not his part, the other is released from his,' being propositions which no man disputed, were propositions which no man had any call to prove. In theory they were assumed for axioms: and in practice they were observed as rules. If, on any occasion, it was thought proper to make a show of proving them, it was rather for form's sake than for any thing else; and that, rather in the way of memento or instruction to acquiescing auditors than in the way of proof against opponents. On such an occasion the common-

place retinue of phrases was at hand; *Justice, Right Reason* required it, the *Law of Nature* commanded it, and so forth: all which are but so many ways of intimating that a man is firmly persuaded of the truth of this or that moral proposition, though he either thinks he *need not,* or finds he *can't,* tell *why.* Men were too obviously and too generally interested in the observance of these rules to entertain doubts concerning the force of any arguments they saw employed in their support. It is an old observation, how Interest smooths the road to Faith. (pp. 122f.)

When the contract is violated, the legal instances invoked are themselves fictions. But because of prevailing interests, they are treated as if they were truths. Manipulation then becomes possible because such apparently self-evident truths do not allow any questioning of their basis. If a more detailed explanation of legal instances is required, the discourse-related legal concepts give precedence to the authority: in the case of the social contract, to the ruler, and in matters of law, to the lawyers (see pp. 123–25, 141–50).

Bentham's often vehement attacks on legal fictions ("licensed thieves use fictions" [p. 146]) are directed less against fiction itself than against the way it is used, for the revaluation of fiction requires a reminder of its misuse in order to bring out its multifarious applicabilities. This is all the more necessary as fictions cannot be justified for their own sake, which was borne out by Roman law. For Bentham it is not a matter of eliminating fiction but of eliminating particular uses of it. He shares the objection of the inherited criticism that legal fictions—like Bacon's idols—have nothing inside them.

A central example of this is the legal concept of ownership, which is treated "as if the value of it were intrinsic" (p. cxix), that is, as if the concept merely articulated an objectively existing set of values. But as there is no such objective reality, the concept itself assumes the status of one. If concepts become objects, then they begin to mislead; and such reifications of legal fictions are reprehensible, for unlike the self-deceptions of the senses and of reason through the idols, these reifications spring from fictions that are known to be such. Legal fictions take their existence from discourse, which sets out to process the assumed reality; their use can therefore never be the state of affairs itself, for as an instrument of mediation they cannot collapse into what is mediated. Bentham calls them "*encroachment* or *imposture*" (p. 122), because legal practice suppresses awareness of their fictitious character and takes them for realities. Fiction must always be known to be such if it is to be capable of manifold usage, for this would not be possible if fiction coincided with something that presupposes this usage.

Bentham attributes the reification of legal fictions to the craftiness of lawyers, but they could not maintain their authority for long if their suppressed understanding of what fiction is like did not have another, perhaps even more powerful, sustaining force: its success. This elevates fiction into a self-sustaining reality. Bentham developed his critique of fiction by way of law partly because of the certainty that this type of fiction was discourse-dependent, and partly because legal fiction, which was always known to be fictitious, embodies only one special instance of fiction. In his attempt to initiate a turnabout in the assessment of fiction, Bentham had to have recourse to the inherited denunciation of fictions as deceit, lies, and delusions in order to outline the indispensability of a construct that had no foundation in re and that could be legitimized only by what its application was meant to achieve—not an easy undertaking for a positivist. What the legal fictions had obscured, he wanted to lay bare: fiction's dependence on discourse and its resultant generalization.

This purpose goes hand in hand with Bentham's notion of experience, which is much more personally related than the umbrella concept of experience that dominated empiricism from Locke to Hume. Such a relatedness is also true of the impulses that led to a new view of fiction, as first formulated by Bentham's observations of himself: if knowledge is to be gained from experience, he argued, then experience of oneself is a prime source. As a child Bentham was often haunted by a "fictional horror": "The devil appeared to me in a dream; the imp in his company" (p. xiii).

> I had—which is not uncommon in dreams, at least with me—a sort of consciousness that it was a dream; with a hope that, with a little exertion, I might spring out of it: I fancied that I did so. Imagine my horror, when I still perceived devil and imp standing before me. It was out of the rain into the river. I made another desperate effort. I tried to be doubly awake; I succeeded. I was in a transport of delight when the illusion altogether vanished: but it was only a temporary relief; for the devil and the imp dwelled in my waking thoughts for many a year afterwards. (p. xiii)

Bentham records several experiences of this sort, and even reading books such as Bunyan's *Pilgrim's Progress* or Defoe's *Robinson Crusoe* would

frighten him so much that he could not go on. But after he had learned
to distinguish between imagination and judgment (p. xiii), he felt free
enough to talk about it, although he admits that signs and symbols—
which clearly function in accordance with the principle of the association of ideas—continued to play a powerful, if at times unconscious,
role in his life. They were even able to conjure up apparitions:

> To this case I feel a very conformable parallel may be seen in the case
> of ghosts and other fabulous maleficent beings, which the absence of
> light presents to my mind's eye. In no man's judgment can a stronger
> persuasion of the non-existence of these sources of terror have place
> than in mine; yet no sooner do I lay myself down to sleep in a dark
> room than, if no other person is in the room, and my eyes keep open,
> these instruments of terror obtrude themselves; and, to free myself of
> the annoyance, I feel myself under the necessity of substituting to
> those more or less pleasing ideas with which my mind would other-
> wise have been occupied, those reflections which are necessary to
> keep in my view the judgment by which the non-existence of these
> creatures of the imagination has so often been pronounced. (p. xvi)

What Locke called "fantastical ideas," which he attributed to madness, are facts of experience for Bentham, and even if reflection and
judgment can banish them temporarily, the next time he lies down,
they will be there again. The very fact that the imagination can produce
such ideas, which for all their nonexistence demand the most concen-
trated attention, shows its increased importance. It is no longer what
Locke saw as a pictorial imprint made on the tabula rasa by external
data. Rather, imagination has become, in Bentham's own words, "my
mind's eye," which is made active precisely because there is nothing
physical for the senses to perceive. Locke's theory of passive perception
is here at least augmented by an active form of ideation that inevitably
must result in an upgrading of the imagination.

In the empirical tradition, the imagination had always held an
inferior rank. Bacon had subsumed it under poetry, to show that it
embodied the very opposite of the process of induction, which he had
developed. He argued that it "commonly exceeds the measure of
nature, joining at pleasure things which in nature would have never
come together, and introducing things which in nature would have
never come to pass."[40] He excluded it from the field of knowledge in a
manner that was paralleled by Locke: "be that as it will, these *Ideas* of
Substances, being made conformable to no Pattern existing, that we

know; and consisting of such Collections of *Ideas,* as no Substance ever shewed us united together, they ought to pass with us for barely imaginary."[41] This analytical view of the imagination, which throughout the seventeenth century was generally equated with and restricted to the rhetorical *inventio,* takes the arbitrary separation and combination of ideas to be the inverted mirror image of empirical modes of cognition. The product is "unlawful matches and divorces of things,"[42] which are nothing but caricatures of a cognitive dissection of Nature or of a regulated combination of received data. Nevertheless, the structures of empirical cognition constantly recur in this faculty, even though, corresponding to no reality, they are of no use to cognition. Concepts of things that do not exist are phantasms that endanger the authority of rationalism rather than stabilizing it.

There is no doubt that for Bentham, too, these 'ideas' were of the imagination and had no correspondence to reality. But being vexed by them was no longer a matter of madness; on the contrary, thanks to reflection and judgment (as manifestations of rationality), he was perfectly capable of distinguishing between facts and imagination. In contrast to the empirical tradition, however, to which he undoubtedly knew himself to be indebted, Bentham was aware that not only facts but also ideas could have an effect. Consequently, they could not simply be rejected just because the empirical system demanded it. Clearly, because there are experiences that go beyond the established premises of cognition, one has to ask whether 'effect' is not also a form of reality, of which some account must be taken.

This self-experience springs from the insight that inherited premises of cognition can no longer cope with the multiplicity of phenomena, particularly as these princip'es have, since Hume, been emptied of their last substantialist remains. As "fictions of the mind" these premises can no longer explain anything; instead, they become forms of usage, and that means no less than the opening of a new gulf: that between cognition and usage. Wherever differences come into being, fictions conjoin. The difference here emerged out of experience itself. The more limited the chances of knowledge being obtained by cognition, the more Locke's principles slipped down to the level of assumptions for use, since the task now was to apperceive experience in the midst of experience. Whatever makes possible such apperception must have no substance of its own, because otherwise experience will merely be subsumed under categories of what is already known. Consequently, the focus must shift from *what* can be known to *how* things can be known, and this is virtually impossible to grasp by way of empirical principles.

Bentham adheres to empirical epistemology, but with his affirmation of fiction he eliminates the disparaging connotations that were still inherent in Hume's concept. Against this background, legal fictions change into warning signals that a fiction must always be known as such, and hence must never be reified; furthermore, Bentham's self-experience allows him to see the imagination as the source of fiction.

His starting point is the coexistence of "real entities" and "fictitious entities."

> A real entity is an entity to which, on the occasion and for the purpose of discourse, existence is really meant to be ascribed. Under the head of perceptible real entities may be placed, without difficulty, individual perceptions of all sorts: the impressions produced in groups by the application of sensible objects to the organs of sense: the ideas brought to view by the recollection of those same objects; the new ideas produced under the influence of the imagination, by the decomposition and recomposition of those groups:—to none of these can the character, the denomination, of real entities be refused.[43]

The empirical framework is thus maintained, but with considerable modifications. Entity is a form of discourse (p. 7) that is necessary to describe the process of perception, because it is no longer possible to penetrate behind what happens in the process, as Locke was able to do with full confidence through his "simple ideas" that preceded all perception. Discourse is a sign that there cannot possibly be any kind of knowledge prior to one's contact with what is. Such an attitude need not be tantamount to skepticism, and indeed Bentham is far from being a skeptic; his view of discourse is rather a consequence of pursuing empiricism to one logical end, for it cannot accept any kind of transcendental stance for cognition. Since Locke's regulators—God, archetypes, and mixed modes—do smack of such stances, Bentham replaces them with discourse. The replacement denotes an important shift in empirical thought: While Locke sought to gain knowledge from experience, now—with the fading certainty of knowledge—usage takes over, and since usefulness replaces knowledge as the criterion, fiction takes on new significance. This revaluation of fiction is already apparent with the upgrading of the imagination, which separates and combines data in equal measure, thereby regulating the association of ideas in a manner that, for Locke, represented one of the first stages of madness.

Bentham had no doubt about the existence of a reality that was pregiven to the senses but independent of them; this conviction gave rise to the problem of how such a reality might be experienced. There could be no 'real' references outside this reality, any more than there could be principles of order, since these would have to be structures of the reality itself. For the positivist, the one was not possible and the other not knowable, so reality could not be used in order to speak about reality. Since for Bentham discourse had replaced the vagrant transcendental elements of empiricism, some kind of bipartition was needed if the "real entities" were to be talked about at all. The other linguistic part of discourse must therefore also be an entity but must share no characteristics whatever with the real entities, and the latter, in turn, must not be subsumed under instances that would place them in an order alien to themselves. Bentham solves the problem with the "fictitious entity":

> A fictitious entity is an entity to which, though by the grammatical form of the discourse employed in speaking of it, existence be ascribed, yet in truth and reality existence is not meant to be ascribed. Every noun-substantive which is not the name of a real entity, perceptible or inferential, is the name of a fictitious entity. Every fictitious entity bears some relation to some real entity, and can no otherwise be understood than in so far as that relation is perceived—a conception of that relation is obtained. Reckoning from the real entity to which it bears relation, a fictitious entity may be styled a fictitious entity of the first remove, a fictitious entity of the second remove, and so on. A fictitious entity of the first remove is a fictitious entity, a conception of which may be obtained by the consideration of the relation borne by it to a real entity, without need of considering the relation borne by it to any other fictitious entity. A fictitious entity of the second remove is a fictitious entity, for obtaining a conception of which it is necessary to take into consideration some fictitious entity of the first remove. . . . (pp. 12f.)
>
> By a fictitious entity, understand an object, the existence of which is feigned by the imagination—feigned for the purpose of discourse—and which, when so formed, is spoken of as a real one. (p. 114)

Bentham's "fictitious entity" has a double root: first, everything that is brought to bear on reality must be unreal; second, this unreality must be "feigned" in order that discourse should be possible. This duality mirrors the traditional heritage as well as the function of fiction, but here they interact without any conflict. Whatever discourse deals with cannot condition its own organization; but at the same time it must not be subjected to any postulate. Therefore an agency has to be invented that will act as if it were real, although its fictitious character must never be suppressed (p. xliii). Its duality enables the fictitious entity to organize without defining what is organized and yet remain totally bound to it, for in themselves, fictitious entities are "mere chimeras, mere creatures of the imagination, mere non-entities."[44] But in view of the structural equality of two ultimately different 'entities', the difference between them lies in their suitability for use, as Bentham stresses elsewhere.[45] Without this practical context, fiction would be pure phantasm, of which one could not say with any certainty that it even existed.

How is it, then, with fictions such as poetry, whose use is beyond dispute, though this does not automatically make them into fictitious entities? This question enables Bentham to specify the use that makes fiction fictitious in the first place. Poetry for him consists in "fabulous entities," whose purpose is to "raise up in the mind any correspondent images" (p. xxxvi). Instead of being related to "real entities," these "fabulous entities" stimulate ideas to which generally there is no correspondence in re, so that Bentham prefers to see them confined to the context of amusement, but he does not deny that they are able "in some cases to excite to action" (p. 18). This ability is a positive quality, because it sets them on the way to becoming what he means by fiction, although they cannot ultimately reach that status because they remain tied to the "insincerity" of poetry (p. 18).

This state of affairs is the very reason why Bentham is forced to establish the 'as-if' character of the fictitious entity, whose special duality consists in the fact that fiction always pretends to be real, but at the same time must eliminate its own pretense in order that *strategic* deception should not become *real* deception. "From what there is of falsehood not only is pure good the result, but it is the work of invincible necessity; on no other terms can discourse be carried on" (p. 59). Whenever fiction is associated with necessity, anthropological considerations come into play, but these balk the epistemological argumentation that Bentham needed to legitimize his revaluation of fiction. His 'as-if' is a deception that has been seen through but, contrary to epistemological expectations, does not liquidate fiction; instead, it endows fiction with multiple usage. In other words, fiction becomes a contrivance enabling discourse to open up realities that are inaccessible to

cognition. Therefore, what is attributed through perception and inference to real entities turns out to be classifications by a feigning imagination, and these classifications exist solely by means of language. For
epistemology this has serious consequences as soon as there is no
longer a difference (still maintained by Bentham) between these classifications and the reality that is independent of discourse. Although
fiction depends on language for its existence, it also constitutes discourse to such a degree that the only reality one can talk about is that of
discourse-related real entities. But if an independent reality is enveloped by discourse, then the assumed presence of physical objects is on
the way to becoming a type of discourse itself, which comes close to
liquidating its factual independence.

It was Bentham who opened up this path, although he did so with
a conviction that he could thereby safeguard empirical premises. But
what exactly are the fictitious entities that he set out to define? They are
related to real entities, and initially can be characterized only through
them. For instance, every body must either be at rest or in motion:
"This, taken in the literal sense, is as much as to say—Here is a larger
body, called a motion; in this larger body, the other body, namely, the
really existing body, is contained. So in regard to rest. To say this body
is at rest is as much as to say—Here is a body, and it will naturally be
supposed a fixed body, and here is another body, meaning the real
existing body, which is *at* that first-mentioned body, *i.e.* attached to it,
as if the fictitious body were a stake, and the real body a beast tied to it"
(p. 13). Motion and rest are therefore forms in which real bodies are
enveloped; in the course of his argument Bentham introduces the term
"receptacle" (p. 25), which is a fictitious entity characterizing the condition in which real bodies exist. It is only natural that for Bentham
the form should also be a fictitious entity of the first order (pp. 23f.),
not least because every body, although a real entity, possesses surface,
depth, and boundaries that in different ways envelop it and give it
its own particular outline. This means that real bodies never present
themselves as raw data but are always in a state of conditionality.
The conditions are called fictitious entities, because rest and motion,
surface, depth, boundaries, and the like are designations that have
no existence of their own but can function only through being related to real bodies. If they had an existence of their own, they
would be chimeras of the imagination, or what Bentham rightly calls

"non-entities," whose unrelatedness would invoke no conditions, let alone effects.

Why are the conditions fictitious entities? Bentham would answer that this linguistic characterization provides no guarantee that the presentations of conditions are integral qualities of real bodies, and indeed, if one thinks of rest and motion, they cannot be integral since, if they were, real bodies would possess two totally conflicting and mutually exclusive qualities. Thus all such descriptions are fictitious entities, which means that as they exist only in language, they cannot claim to say anything about the nature of reality. To this extent the empirical argument, which also sees the redefined concept of fiction as the opposite of an autonomous reality, still holds. But fiction now has to be upgraded, because the conditional presentation of real bodies is evidential.

If real bodies can appear only under conditions that cannot be part of them (because the bodies must exist prior to the conditions under which they are presented), then there can be no particles of reality present as such. Real bodies, in other words, exist only through the mode of their presentation. They cannot appear of their own accord, and are present only modally, although the modes are not restricted to designating the presence of realities. What we have here are predications through which the real bodies take on their own specific identity. The mode thus overshoots the real body without being merely a projection, for the real body is merged with a predicate that would be a "non-entity" by itself but can qualify the real body and give it presence.

Presence, then, means being enveloped in something else, because real bodies evidently cannot specify themselves or give themselves presence. Thus realities are just as dependent on connections as predicates are, for without this interdependence the former would remain sealed off and the latter would be a phantasm. In consequence, it is only natural that the central paradigm of fictitious entities should be the relation. "Once introduced upon the carpet, the fictitious entity called relation swells into an extent such as to swallow up all the others. Every other fictitious entity is seen to be but a mode of this" (p. 29). Relation brings the real body into presence, just as it transforms the chimeras of the imagination—as fictitious entities—into modes of the body; it extends the real body beyond itself and incorporates the imagination, through its products, into the body.

Bentham maintains that "To language, then—to language alone—it is, that fictitious entities owe their existence; their impossible, yet indispensable, existence" (p. 15). And so for him relation has its roots in the predisposition, and indeed in the prepositions, of language. If, for instance, the earth is *in* motion, the preposition (which need not belong to the real body) indicates a condition in which the movement (a fictitious entity) is meant to be seen only as if it were an integral quality of the body (pp. xxxvif.). As a description of the condition, the motion is a predication; but if something unknowable is to be visualized as real, the fictitious entity must also be a representation, for real bodies cannot be present except in terms of the qualities attributed to them. While the predicate equips the real body with its various and changing modes of presentation that act as if they were integral to the body, representation is a means of visualization whereby the particularity of the body appears to manifest itself. If designations of objects normally seem to stem from the object, and visualizations from the subject, here the opposite seems to be true. Real bodies cannot develop their own modes of self-presentation, while representation cannot exist if there is not already something that is to be represented. Predication is therefore always the representation of real bodies in the mode of their presentation, just as representation always designates conditions by a mode that does not belong to the real entity.

This amalgamation draws the real bodies out of their cognitive obscurity, and at the same time prevents the imagination from losing itself in the production of chimeras. All this happens through the modality in which predication and representation double one another. As a doubling phenomenon, modality is a paradigm of fiction that structurally always embodies the overstepping of boundaries: Realities are overstepped by their conditionality, and the phantasms of imagination are overstepped by their relation to reality. It is therefore not surprising that Bentham should regard relation as absolute fiction that not only constitutes modality as the doubling of predication and representation but also organizes its schemata in terms of relationships. As a schema of specification, predication is as universal as it is individual. It is universal in that real bodies are present only through the mode of their presentation; it is individual in that the appearance of those bodies is always particular. The same applies to representation, which linguistically possesses the universal schema of conceivability but which will always be conceived individually. Bentham's schema is thoroughly Kantian, with specification and conceivability embodying the universal relations to reality, whose realization brings about individual relationships. Thus the schemata never coincide with the object, because relation as a constituent of the schema prevents it from being reified. And so relation is less a connection between given positions than a matrix that makes it possible for real bodies to be specified and visualized (in the case of the schema), and produces a mode (in the case of interacting predication and representation) whereby the presentation of real bodies becomes a condition of their comprehension.

This was how Bentham believed fiction had to be characterized, mainly because it was impossible to find any correspondence in re. But he could not identify with Hume's skepticism, which emptied out what once had been established principles to mere "fictions of the mind." It is true that Bentham, too, saw the human subject as being confronted by a reality that was largely inaccessible, but instead of causing resignation, this situation inspired him to seek solutions to the problem. The contrast between real and fictitious entities still bears a trace of epistemological premises, but for Bentham fiction now ceases to be the opposite of reality; instead, it is a mode of bridge-building, although it never lets one forget the abyss being bridged, which is why the mode as an "imaginary being" (p. xlii) must remain recognizable. Beside reality, fiction appears to be false, but this very lowering of its status is what Bentham sees as a means of production.

It is certainly no coincidence that Bentham develops his view of the productive character of fiction by way of the causality principle that had proved to be an embarrassment for empiricism. All motions, he argues, can be distinguished as to whether they are directed by the human will or not:

> In the case of a motion of the thelematic class, you have for the *cause* of the motion—meaning in the *prime* cause of whatsoever motion happens in consequence to take place—the psychical act, the act of the will of the person by whose will the motion is produced; you have that same person for the agent. Fruitful or unfruitful, or, say, *ergastic* or *unergastic*. To one or other of these denominations will all the motions of the thelematic class be found referable. *Ergastic* or fruitful, all those which have for their termination and result the production of a *work*. *Unergastic* or unfruitful, all those which are not attended with any such result. Between these two classes the line of separation, it will be manifest enough, cannot, in the nature of the case, be determinate. A

work has reference to human interests and exigencies. When, in consequence of a motion or set of motions of the thelematic kind, in the
body or among the bodies in which the motion has terminated or
those to which it has in the whole, or in any part, been communicated,
any such change of condition has place, by which, for any considerable portion of time, they are or are not regarded as being rendered, in
any fresh shape, subservient to human use, *a work* is spoken of as
having thereby been produced . . . To the case, and to that alone, in
which the motion or motions, being of the *thelematic,* and therein,
moreover, of the *ergastic* kind, have had for their prime mover or
principal agent concerned, a rational, or at least a sentient, being,
belong the words *ends, operation, means, design.*[46]

Despite the somewhat unwieldy vocabulary of empiricism, it is
evident that here the premises of cognition have undergone a radical
shift. Instead of Locke's tabula rasa we now have the will, which is no
longer geared to passive reception but, as subjective manifestation,
reaches actively outward. The will is guided by interest and exigencies,
related to specific goals that are to be reached by way of plans and
operations. Intentions, aims, operations, instruments, designs, and so
on are related, as in Bentham's example, to motion that, whatever may
be its cause, will lead to a result intended by the will. While the motion
is a "fictitious entity of the first remove," because it is a mode allowing
the specific presentation of real bodies, will-directed operations are all
"fictitious entities of the second etc. remove," because they are related
to those of the first remove, through the arrangement of which they can
produce a "work."[47] The operation may be a fictitious entity of the
second remove, and those that follow may be of the third, fourth, and so
on, according to the way the will links existing requirements to the
corresponding network of connections.

Since in the early nineteenth century it was the will that characterized the subject, it is not surprising that reality itself should be increasingly viewed from the subject's standpoint. If real bodies move into
presence by way of predication and representation, this dual mode signifies different designations that, though grounded in language, nevertheless require an agent for their activation. Furthermore, all modalities
are selective in relation to the various possibilities through which the
real bodies can gain presence. It follows, then, that their reality—which
is sealed off from cognition—comes to light through the limitless ways
in which they can be differentiated and specified. Every mode of pre-

sentation incorporates its own distinction from other modes, and this virtual multiplicity unfolding behind the manifested modes is the reality that underlies the restricted, situational modality of real bodies.

Several points emerge from this observation: (1) Historically this might be a refutation of epistemological skepticism. (2) Pragmatically it shows that for the will-centered subject there can be no reality that is not based on modality; for Bentham himself, existence is "a fictitious entity; it is in every real entity; every real entity is in it" (p. 50). (3) Epistemologically it shows that henceforth reality must be understood as a process of realization, whose products are not so much cognitive insights as the consequences of action. The upgrading of fiction downgrades cognition to a condition of action, just as an increasing need for action demands an increase in fictions.

How are we to understand the realization that leads to the work? The author of the work is the will of the subject, whose imagination spins out of itself those fictions that make the real entities into facts of life; for if the real bodies and will-centered subjects merely existed side by side, there would be a state of entropy, which would proportionally consolidate itself through the functionlessness of the will. But since needs and interests prevail, goals and plans are necessary, and they require operations; all of them are fictitious entities of the second remove, which modalize those of the first remove insofar as they open up access to a reality closed off from cognition. Because the work links real bodies and an interest-oriented will, the driving force is not knowledge but availability, by means of which pragmatic consequences are drawn from epistemological skepticism. The link formed by the work is not a phantasm, because it springs from the processing of something that is independent of the will. At the same time, however, the product is not identical to the reality that has been processed in accordance with needs and interest. What happens in the course of realization is that reality is gradually replaced by the world. Reality is given; the world is made. The world comes into being by way of works, in a coherent unit that envelops the physical reality of bodies.

For Bentham the polarity of human will and real bodies was a basic theorem, and even if both of these were nothing but posits, he considered them at least to be real entities—their being ensured by perception and inference. But this made it all the more essential to bridge the gulf between the two poles. Real bodies are present only in the form of their appearance, which as a fictitious entity is simply a mode of description, though this is what gives them their significance. This significance, however, cannot be integral to the object concerned, whose representation will be less related to it than to the subject perceiving it. Thanks to modality, qualities are ascribed to the object that will enable it to be conceived, so that by way of the interest-oriented will, the object may then become a component part of a work. There is no predominance of either predication or representation; predication professes to understand the qualities of real bodies as if they were integral to them, and representation acts as if such a reality were graspable by the subject. This 'as if' indicates the difference—now minimalized but nevertheless ineradicable—between the two poles of will and reality. Such a difference could be eradicated only through a synthetic judgment, but this would have to be based on a priori principles of cognition that, as far as Bentham is concerned, no longer exist. Modality is therefore a fiction that presents the established coherence as if it were a judgment into which, however, awareness of fictitiousness must always be inscribed (p. xliii).

While relation acts out the difference, the difference appears to be concealed by the modes of predication and representation. Just as relation lacks any defining reference, so modality lacks definitiveness of judgment for the coherence established. This lack gives rise to a double coding of fiction. Epistemologically, Bentham finds it deficient: "[A] fiction proves nothing; from that which is false you can only go on to that which is false" (p. 121). But pragmatically he sees it as an indispensable precondition for the work: "[I]n so far as performed by denomination, the subjects, the immediate subjects are *names* and nothing more. Things? Yes; but no otherwise than through the medium of their names. It is only by means of *names* . . . that things are susceptible of arrangement. Understand of arrangement in the *psychical* sense; in which sense, strictly speaking, it is only the ideas of the things in question that are the subjects of the arrangement, not the things themselves" (p. xxxiv).

If the modalities were more than just designations, that is, cognitive regulatory principles or even a priori laws, there would no longer be the vast variety of possible arrangements, but instead all appearances would have to be referred back to the cognitive conditions underlying the objects concerned. Cognition, however, is no longer of any concern when appearances have to be arranged; instead, the designations ascribed to real entities as if they were integral to them allow discourse to convey the kaleidoscopic changeability of things. This makes fiction into a pragmatic precondition that has absorbed as "blameless falsehood" (p. 60) the criticism leveled against it since the inception of the modern age, and thus prevents it from becoming reified. If fiction is to open up the complexities of action, it cannot have the nature of an object, because it is an imaginary construct that sets free possibilities inherent in situations and does not pin them down to any pregiven conditions. What used to be viewed negatively now becomes the basis of efficacy; and since this efficacy is undeniable, criticism of fiction gives way to affirmation.

But if fiction can no longer be grasped by way of denunciation, its definition emerges as a problem. Since it initiates a process of realization that leads to the work as a form of produced world, it is difficult, if not impossible, to set up any transcendental stance that would allow a definition distinguishing among fiction, reality, and world. The epistemological skepticism of empiricism knows no such stance, and so Bentham is left with only one escape route, which is to classify fictions as pseudo realities, whose 'as if' character does not claim to be reality but instead conditions production.

As a pseudo reality, the 'as if' is defined negatively as an "imaginary being" (p. xlii) that indicates a blank in epistemology. This is why Bentham argues that fiction can gain content only in discourse. In semiotic terms, it is the signifiers of language that form the storehouse of fictions. They do not designate any signified, whose nature is sealed off from knowledge anyway, but they do designate changing qualities that highlight the conditionality of things in order to make them conceivable to the subjects which are participating in the language game. For, as Bentham argues:

> Unclothed as yet in words, or stripped of them, thoughts are but dreams: like the shifting clouds of the sky, they float in the mind one moment, and vanish out of it in the next. But for these fixed and fixative signs, nothing that ever bore the name of *art* or *science* could ever have come into existence ... Without language, not only would men have been incapable of communicating each man his thoughts to other men, but, compared with what he actually possesses, the stock of his own ideas would in point of number have been as nothing; while each of them, taken by itself, would have been as flitting and indeterminate as those of the animals which he deals with at his pleasure. (p. lxxi)

Discourse mediates between the appearance of things and the thoughts of the subject by designating changing qualities and giving form to transient thoughts; out of this arises the coherent work that, as a world produced, also allows communication between the participants in the language game about this very world.

For Bentham, the fictitious entities owe their existence exclusively to discourse, and their dual nature—amalgamating the qualities of things with their conceivability—manifests itself in a double function of the discourse itself, which is "information for the purpose of excitation" (p. lxxi). If this is so, then discourse becomes a kind of operational handbook in which the diversity of fiction's multiple uses is programmed. This testifies to a vital function of fiction's duality: it has its foundation in what it produces. It needs the will in order to become operative, but without fictions the world as discourse could never come into being. If we take this world to be a variety of works in the sense outlined by Bentham, then clearly the world as discourse is no longer to be cognized but is to be perceived or changed in accordance with prevailing exigencies. Whatever results from this process will again be deposited as an additional designation in discourse, so that fictions can use the worlds produced in order to develop more and more distinctions. This leads to a continual fine-tuning of designations; the more complex worlds ensuing from it make the old empirical reality of raw data seem archaic, if not obsolete.

Even if Bentham cannot say what fiction is, the manner in which it is realized through discourse allows insight into the way it functions. Bentham knows full well that fiction evades logical definition: as every definition is "a *genus generalissimum*, the names are consequently incapable of receiving what is commonly understood by a definition, viz. a definition *per genus et differentiam*. But, from their not being susceptible of *this* species of exposition, they do not the less stand in need of *that* species of exposition of which they are susceptible" (p. lxiv). Fiction cannot be represented by definition, but still it is in need of exposition, and this must be gained through the representation of its procedure, through which Bentham tries to show *how* fiction organizes the discourse of which it is made. As a particular genus fiction cannot be understood, because—although it depends on discourse—it is also the main reason for the increasing complexity of discourse; this is why for Bentham it is also a *genus generalissimum*. Epistemologically fiction remains a blank; pragmatically, however, it shows up what is actually real: the world as discourse.

The conception of fiction as linguistic designation came to the fore because qualities and conceivability say nothing about the nature of things but shed light only on the manner in which they appear. Fictional designation doubles the partial presence of things with their absence, and as things are definitely not linguistic in nature, every designation also carries an implicit account of their unavailability. Were this not so, the kaleidoscopic range of designations would no longer be possible. Similarly with thoughts, which would remain as dreams if they were not given linguistic form; these forms reveal something of the intentions behind them but nothing of the thoughts themselves. Thus fictional designation always tells us of the absence of what it makes present as quality, conceivability, and intention. The fictitious entity interposes itself between thought and thing, which despite their polarity have one common feature: the certainty that they cannot be known. Such in-between areas are the setting for fiction, which unfolds a network of connections that compete with what is known for certain and seek constantly to reach beyond it.

This, however, is precisely where the type of fiction thematized by Bentham reaches its limits, for the network of differentiating connections is ultimately meant to eliminate difference. This elimination, however, out of which fiction arises without eliminating fiction itself, leads to definitions that pertain only to the prevailing use of fiction and not to fiction itself. Since the use is potentially multifarious, each definition of the function of fiction is at the same time a restriction imposed on it. It follows that as pragmatic requirements change, so, too, does the definition of fiction, since this must vary according to the different pragmatic contexts to which it is applied. While fiction shifts boundaries, it is also bounded by the pragmatic context that decides its use. Because of its dual character, fiction always takes a form that permits its practical application and—if we reverse the perspective—enables us to trace the changes in practical requirements.

This dual character may also be a reason why the thematizing of fiction in philosophical discourse has survived consciousness of its own fictitiousness without being finally condemned as delusion. Ever since Descartes, consciousness has been taken to be a guardian against intellectual self-deception, and even Descartes's empirical opponents never questioned this function. So long as consciousness embodied judgmental cognition that could banish "*Fantastical* Ideas"[48] from the human mind, fiction had no hope. Nevertheless, consciousness still had to cope with fictions, and because they could not be exorcised, their persistence could only be viewed as a kind of madness. But now, with fictions being affirmed precisely *because* they were invented, they prove to be far more than just an achievement that can stand up to the probings of consciousness. Now consciousness itself becomes a means of legitimizing fiction. Such an affirmation could not have been brought about through Cartesian consciousness. Consequently, we may say that it not only renders the negative view obsolete but also consigns a certain concept of consciousness to history. We cannot yet say that with Bentham the Cartesian consciousness is undermined by an unconscious; but fictions incorporate awareness that they are no more than "imaginary beings," and the fact that this knowledge does not discredit them indicates that the epistemological view of consciousness has been overlaid by an anthropological dimension. Instead of identifying itself or even disguising itself before consciousness in order not to appear deceitful, fiction now brings about a change in consciousness itself, which it sets about exploring by breaking down epistemological boundaries.

Fiction as a Transparent Posit: Hans Vaihinger and Neo-Kantian Schematism

Since Jeremy Bentham did not reflect on the link between fiction and consciousness, he could not explore the consequences of this link; there is, however, no doubt that his upgrading of fiction created the problem of its relationship to consciousness. Some sixty years after Bentham,[49] Hans Vaihinger introduced his *Philosophy of 'As if'* with the comment that he was taking over the "'ideas' arising from intellectual and ethical needs . . . as useful, valuable fictions of humanity, without the 'assumption' of which human thought, feeling and action must wither; in this sense it is a 'phenomenology' of the ideating, fictionalizing consciousness."[50] Consciousness is no longer an epistemological court of appeal but is itself the source of feigning. What in Bentham's case looked like a contrast is now seen as interlocking. Vaihinger's "phenomenology" is not the same as Husserl's, but they have one common feature: like Vaihinger, Husserl regards the intentionality of consciousness—insofar as this embodies a protentional act—as an empty projection whose fictitious elements are not to be denied. But since even empty projections must be directed toward something, consciousness is always consciousness of something that is directed somewhere through intentionality. Such a conception of consciousness, however, does not apply for Vaihinger, for whom consciousness is defined through its fictionalizing operations and through its simultaneous exposure of assumptions and ideas as fictions. Such a notion of consciousness is marked by a duality: it appears equally to be both the source and the yardstick of fictions. In historical terms, fiction has now conquered consciousness, its worst enemy, by imposing its own doubling structure upon it.

This duality also means that every fiction must incorporate awareness of its own fictitiousness. In this particular form it did not apply to the fictitious entities, whose fictitious nature for Bentham was identified by discourse. Why discourse had become the reservoir of fiction had remained unexplained, for if designations only aim at the presentation of things—even if they are to be understood as if they were real—their fictitious character derives more from epistemological skepticism than from the peculiarities of language. Bentham, however, maintained that discourse qualified designations as fictitious. This unquestioned assumption allowed him to see modality as fiction par excellence, because as language it had no counterpart in re and could therefore function equally as predication and as representation. For Bentham, discourse regulated the processing of a reality that did not depend on the subject, and as such it replaced Locke's principle of association; and since discourse-dependent designations are instruments, their status is different from that of their counterpart, which as reality proper makes the instruments of discourse into fictions. This view of fiction derives from the old polarity, and although Bentham's detailed usage can no longer be deduced from this opposition, it serves as a handy means of elucidating the achievements of a fiction that is viewed affirmatively.

With the affirmative view firmly established, modality branches out into all kinds of fiction once the latter is no longer tied to linguistic designation. C. K. Ogden, Bentham's editor, regarded this fact as a cause for regret: "Today a Philosophy of As-if dominates scientific thought—without the sound linguistic basis which Bentham gave it; and an ingenious Logic of 'incomplete symbols' has partly obscured the linguistic issues which he approached at the level of everyday practice."[51] Now symbolic logic and everyday practice are, for all their importance, nothing but particular fields of reference for a fiction viewed as a linguistic modality. In both cases it is usage that is of prime importance, whereas the philosophy of as-if promises to analyze this usage. As Vaihinger stresses, such analysis needs the "assistance of language,"[52] but since this is quite an exclusive frame of reference for the syndrome of conditions out of which fictions arise, it tends to limit rather than to expand the explanation of the nature of fiction.

How, then, can fictions be made knowable for what they are supposed to be? The mere assumption of a feigning consciousness will not do, since the latter also qualifies its own products that must be related to a differentiated frame of reference if they are not to be declared fictions just because they are posited as such by consciousness. Furthermore, an analysis of use must take in many examples, and these will leave the massive range of different types of fiction to form an open-ended taxonomy—a danger that Vaihinger does not always elude. In this respect, Bentham's linkup between fiction and language, or the identification of fictitious entities with designations, is significantly more manageable precisely because of its limitations. For fictions are thus preconditioned by lexical and linguistic structures, and these keep in check the meaningless and functionless invention of fictitious entities. Of course there will be neologisms—Bentham himself was at pains to introduce a number of his own coinages into the English language[53]—but as 'names' they must be precise, and invention must always serve a purpose.

Once language ceases to be the only reference for fiction, other frames of reference will be necessary in order to identify fictions. By maintaining that linguistic designations are fictions, Bentham bypassed the question of how fictions could actually be known as such. This may have been due to his affirmation of fiction, but to posit linguistic designations as fictitious entities, even if it meets a pragmatic purpose, seems much like an a priori definition. Vaihinger did not have to concern himself any longer with an affirmation of fiction, but he did have to find ways of asserting its significance. For this purpose he needed a complex set of conditions that would reach beyond language, although looking back to Bentham, one must say that the equation of fiction and names—in a rather skillful manipulation of a nominalistic heritage—represented an ingenious way of upgrading fiction, for it would have been difficult to discredit the designative function of language.

How can fictions be known, and if they are known, how can they be characterized? The status and the structure of fictions form the central preoccupations of Vaihinger's *Philosophy of 'As-if.'* His inquiry into the status rests on a minimalistic but oft-repeated claim: "only what is felt, what confronts us in the world of perception, whether it be internal or external, is real."[54] This basic assumption of a "Critical Positivism" (pp. 64, 77) means that the

> psyche works over the material presented to it by the sensations, i.e. elaborates the only available foundation with the help of the logical forms; it sifts the sensations, on the one hand cutting away definite portions of the given sensory material, in conformity with the logical functions, and on the other making subjective additions to what is immediately given . . . and it is all the while departing from reality as given to it. Indeed it is inherent in the very idea of working over, of elaborating, the data, that those data should change, that immediate reality should be altered. The sensations produce within the psyche itself purely subjective processes to which on the modern view nothing in reality . . . can correspond. (p. 157)

The traditional split between subject and object is still present in outline, but now so very differently balanced that the two poles are bound to be affected. The subject shrinks to the dimension of "sensations" that embody the last reality of which one can be certain, while what is "immediately given" has only one certainty left, which is that it is radically separate from sensations. Reality as the contraposition loses its difference and takes on a formlessness that Vaihinger does not yet recognize as contingency, even if its epistemologically conceived patterning has most certainly disappeared. Talk of bodies, things, real entities, or even data, conditions, and qualities could now be nothing more than dogmatism. Because human sensations and a featureless reality are now totally disjoined, thought can no longer direct itself toward knowledge of what has become impossible to grasp. Consequently, Vaihinger argues: "The desire to understand the world is therefore ridiculous, for all understanding consists in an actual or imaginary reduction to the known. But to what is this 'known' itself to be reduced, especially if in the end it turns out to be something 'unknown'"? (p. 171).

Sensations, which remain an ultimate, cannot affect themselves; they need a stimulant to awaken them. This is the function to which "immediate reality" has now shrunk, and it inevitably begins to direct the sensations it has awakened toward itself. As no epistemological framework applies any longer, it is unable to place any restriction on the welter of awakened sensations. These activated sensations now mark an ultimate, though still only selective, relation between psyche and reality. Indeed, this point of intersection throws into relief the vastness of the divergences between them. If reality is present only when sensations are awakened, then generally it must be unperceivable, since perception always presupposes the existence of a given object. Instead, the awakened sensation directs itself toward the exterior cause that has mobilized it, and since this is unperceivable and generally featureless, sensation can range over the formlessness only by means of ideas. Ideas are operations that use existing knowledge and stored experiences to give presence to things that cannot be perceived. The sensations now address themselves to the reality that has awakened them, and through ideas they try to chart it in such a way that they may exercise an impact on its impenetrable givenness. Ideas are the instruments of these activated sensations, by means of which they try to take a grip on the very reality that has affected them, as the actions of the psyche are aimed at eliminating the disjunction. This has two consequences: (1) The disjunction can never be eliminated completely, immediately, or definitively through ideas. (2) The challenge requires analysis of how the ideas are formed through which sensation reacts to the reality that has mobilized it.

These consequences issue into Vaihinger's "Law of Ideational Shifts," which entails "that a number of ideas pass through various stages of development, namely those of fiction, hypothesis and dogma; and conversely dogma, hypothesis and fiction" (p. 124). "The law of the 'transformation of ideas,' as this phenomenon may be called, covers three epochs, three stages in the life-history of an idea . . . These three stages are the *fictional,* the *hypothetical* and the *dogmatic*" (p. 128). If the transformation of ideas has a history—incidentally, like that of perception[55]—in the course of which a radical change in the contents of ideas occurs, then it is plausible to assume that the idea as fiction should represent a comparatively late stage of this development. For Vaihinger, this is a "Progress . . . in the logical conscience of mankind,"[56] though the history of the idea served him primarily to establish the causes of this change, which he saw in "the equilibratory tendency of the psyche" (p. 127).

On one side we have groups of ideas which are without hesitation regarded as the expression of reality; on the other, ideas as to whose objective validity there is doubt. The former are dogmas, the latter hypotheses ... The mind [in the original, psyche] has a tendency to bring all ideational contents into equilibrium and to establish an unbroken connection between them. An hypothesis is inimical to this tendency in so far as it involves the idea that it is not to be placed on an equality with the other objective ideas. It has been only provisionally accepted by the psyche and thus interferes with the general tendency to adjustment. An idea that has once been accepted as objective has a stable equilibrium, the hypothesis an unstable one. The psyche tends to make every psychical content more stable and to extend this stability. The condition of unstable equilibrium is as uncomfortable psychically as it is physically ... If fiction and hypothesis are compared, the condition of tension developing in the psyche due to the fiction is far more important than that resulting from the hypothesis ... We are asked to assume something that we are convinced is not the case at all; we are to regard it *as if* it were such and such ... And yet the psyche is expected during the very process of application to burden itself with the fact that this ideational form is only subjective. Indeed a form of this kind is a positive hindrance and definitely interferes with the tendency toward an equilibration of ideational constructs. The hypothesis only hampers this adjustment negatively and indirectly, but the fiction hampers it directly and positively (pp. 125f.).

The history of the idea is one of psychological conditions. In dogma, realities are identified with the idea; in hypothesis, the idea becomes an assumption that has to be verified; in fiction, the awareness prevails that the idea is the radical 'other' to which it relates.

The shift of ideas happens as a graduated recasting of the structure of the idea, whose content must be doubly coded because otherwise the removal of an "unstable equilibrium" would constantly push or freeze the idea into dogma. Evidently, it is only the supervising consciousness that can interfere with this tendency toward stabilization, and through fiction create a lasting and highly unpleasant state within the psyche. In this respect, the shift of ideas may be called the process of enlightenment that by intensifying an unstable equilibrium prevents "mental slumber" (p. 132). In the doubly coded idea the psyche takes care of content, and consciousness sees to the modification of status. Ideas cannot be empty, because otherwise they would not exist. In the search for homeostatic balance the psyche creates variable contents, while consciousness points up the idea as an empty form that must fill itself with what it relates to. As an empty form it can never be identical to its content but can only be the processing of what it is directed to. Consciousness drives the psyche away from its need for balance, because sensations—the ultimate reality—are constantly being roused by external 'forces' that must be processed.

Consequently, the idea becomes an overarching reference that loses its function as dogma but comes to full fruition in fiction. The idea in itself as an empty form is a fiction, but in view of the necessity to establish proper conditions for action, it turns into a seemingly transcendental stance for mapping out the actual forms of action. As a fiction it incorporates the ungraspability of what it now has to process. Vaihinger's analysis leaves open the question of the idea as a product of the psyche or of consciousness. It presumably initiates the relation between them, but at the same time it modifies them. If consciousness fades, then the psyche falls victim to self-deception, and if consciousness dominates, then the idea empties itself out. While the status of the idea emerges from the graduated shifting of psyche and consciousness, the status, in turn, determines what psyche and consciousness actually are. The idea is a differential that moves between its constituents, and its changing manifestations mold psyche and consciousness in turn.

This is demonstrated equally by the line from dogma to fiction, and by the reversal of this line. Through dogma, the psyche reaches a state of satisfaction in which the idea is taken for reality; the psychic dominance reifies sensations and leads to immobility. However, the fact that reality is ungraspable alters this state, and doubts about the seemingly achieved identity between psyche and reality lead to tension; the psyche begins to be overlapped by consciousness that questions a reification of sensations. The idea gains the status of a hypothesis that, despite its now conscious distance from reality, rests on the assumption that the postulated preconditions correspond to a reality. In this status, the idea gives the impetus for exploration, whose purpose is to verify anticipation—in other words, cognition is delayed but appears to be possible. Once this cognitive optimism has faded, the status of the idea shifts from hypothesis to fiction, which discards reified sensations and creates an unpleasant state of tension. Consciousness inscribes itself into the idea, for the now total disjunction between external reality and sensation requires that the latter be prepared to process the former. Cognition no longer concerns the underlying correspondence between sensation and external reality but is directed toward the appositeness with which sensation works on what confronts it. As a fiction, sensation finds itself in a state of increased tension, but this sharpens the vision for what has to be mastered in order for balance to be achieved. For consciousness, in turn, only sensations are given (see p. 167) that are feigned by it "as attributes of things. Thus the process of thought is initiated, and the scaffolding is erected" (p. 167). Through fiction, consciousness attributes sensations to reality as if they were the latter's property.

If the "scaffolding . . . erected" proves to be successful, this success triggers the process of reversal as a kind of back-formation, because it relaxes the tension, and that relaxation hypostatizes fiction to dogma. But this also means that, even in its hypostatized state, fiction retains a latent duality: the psyche may have momentarily regained its balance, but reifying a contrivance into a reality is bound to produce increasing resistance that will ultimately discredit a fiction elevated to dogma. For it is characteristic of fiction that it can adapt to "the unchangeable coexistence and sequence of phenomena," (p. 107), which is how Vaihinger sees reality. To attribute reality to fiction itself is to rob it of its adaptability, which is due not least to the state of tension it causes; this may demand resolution, but precisely for that reason it offers un-limited opportunities for conceptualizing those phenomena that must be dealt with if adequate actions are to be performed. Why, though, does the "line of enlightenment" from dogma to fiction change again into processes of back-formation?

Vaihinger gives no direct answer to this question, but it is clear from his argumentation that the "line of enlightenment" represents an epistemological insight, and the back-formation processes an anthro-pological one. The line of enlightenment tends to stop the psyche from locking itself within its own ideas, which would rob it of its ability to act; back-formation aims to safeguard what has already been achieved in order to neutralize the disturbing features of phenomena. Fiction has to turn into dogma. Thus the two trends dovetail into one another: while problem-solving turns fiction into dogma, dogmatized fiction meets the resistance of "the unchangeable co-existence and sequence of phenomena." These two countervailing processes are triggered by pragmatic necessities, and their structure is virtually cybernetic. Fic-tion constantly upholds the difference between phenomena and sensa-

tion, whereas dogma flattens it out. The one case adumbrates the boundaries of cognition; the other, those of homeostasis. This is why fiction,
because of its diversified deployment, is significant for Vaihinger.

This diversity, however, should not be underestimated; the "law of
ideational shift" comes closer to fulfilling the demand Vaihinger himself made: that fictions should be knowable (see p. 98). Bentham's
positive slant on fiction was meant simply to bridge the gulf that had
opened up as a result of inherited epistemological skepticism; for
Vaihinger, it indicates the radical separation of sensations from phenomena. Only fiction can highlight this separation. But if the gap is not
merely the result of skepticism, then possible links with phenomena
cannot be only a matter of bridge-building; instead, they are projected
supplements to get the processing of these phenomena under way. In
this context, fiction achieves two things: it accentuates the separation
as unbridgable; and in so doing, it develops the difference between
sensation and phenomena into a range of possible supplements to be
projected onto the phenomena. Searching for connections within a gap
means endlessly multiplying the possibilities of connection, but for this
to happen, the gap has to be maintained. Therefore, as the potential
eliminator of difference, fiction has to invalidate its own achievements;
and as difference is ineradicable, it articulates itself through the multiple connections supplied by the various types of fiction.

By shifting the status of the idea, Vaihinger attempts to draw a
chart of difference. With dogma, hypothesis, and fiction, a range of
difference is marked out between sensation and phenomena. This
range provides a crucial criterion for the knowability of fiction. For
knowability is meant to prove that fiction is not deceit and does not
function as such. This fact, however, as Bentham had already pointed
out, tells us nothing about *how* fiction is knowable. Even if there may be
consensus as to how fictions are to be recognized, thematized fiction
entails no contractual conditions such as pertain to literary fictionality
as staged discourse. For this reason, Bentham felt compelled to decide
that 'names' are fictitious entities, a decision that was best supported by
a nominalistic concept of language, although this could hardly lay
claim to universal validity.

From Vaihinger's suggested gradation of dogma, hypothesis, and
fiction, we can develop criteria of knowability that reflect the changing
status of idea, although this was not quite what Vaihinger had intended
to do. The mere naming of criteria, however, is still not enough to

permit knowability of fiction; for this we need the presence of that tacit knowledge which Polanyi described as the precondition of all knowledge: A mathematical theory, he argues, "can be constructed only by relying on *prior* tacit knowing and can function as a theory only *within* an act of tacit knowing, which consists in our attending *from* it to the previously established experience on which it bears. Thus the ideal of a comprehensive mathematical theory of experience which would eliminate all tacit knowing is proved to be self-contradictory and logically unsound."[57]

From this it follows that "in an act of tacit knowing we *attend from* something for attending *to* something else; namely, *from* the first term *to* the second term of the tacit relation. In many ways the first term of this relation will prove to be nearer to us, the second further away from us. Using the language of anatomy, we may call the first term *proximal,* and the second term *distal.* It is the proximal term, then, of which we have a knowledge that we may not be able to tell" (p. 10). Tacit knowledge cannot be articulated, because it is only when we attend to the phenomenon concerned that it emerges as a framework. It cannot speak of its own accord, since it can function only as a conditioning frame with no intention of its own, adjusting the act of comprehension as soon as something definite is to be grasped. As sedimented knowledge it is internalized (see p. 17), so that in the "law of ideational shifts" it is dogma and hypothesis that form the "tacit framework" (see p. 17), permitting access to something they do not enclose.

Dogma and hypothesis play their part in the knowing of fiction because they are ideas themselves, but also because differing intentions condition their character as ideas. An idea that has no correspondence with reality is the negation of dogma and hypothesis, which makes fiction both incompatible with and yet dependent on the background knowledge invoked to explain it. It lacks something that characterizes other ideas, but it also contains something that is alien to them. "While conceiving/perceiving-imagining fictions, we oscillate between one frame and the other, but, naturally unaware of this oscillation, we sense simultaneity where temporal seriality is actually the case, and, nonconsciously, we sense the necessary 'tension' between incompatibles. What is 'tension,' but the result of an imbalance? And what is imbalance, but the product of something at one pole of a system which is in part or in whole *not* at the other?"[58]

This oscillation between tacit knowledge and fiction stems from the inconsistency through which fiction as an idea stands apart from other ideas. The lack of correspondence with reality entails the idea being filled with all kinds of contents. Hypothesis already indicated that idea and reality did not coincide, so that the idea changed into a trial-and-error procedure, and now negated correspondence to reality results in a split between the ideating act and the multiplicity of possible contents. There is no such split in hypothesis, let alone in dogma. While a dividing line is drawn between idea and reality in the hypothesis, albeit with the aim of verifying the hypothesis as a true correspondence, in fiction that very separation splits the idea itself. It means that the ideating act is basically empty, but this actually reveals an aspect of the idea that is missing both from hypothesis and from dogma. The empty ideating act can be grasped as a projected supplement that cannot exist by itself, and so it can be linked to every possible content because it is not defined through correspondence to reality.

As the empty ideating act of a projected supplement, once more the doubling character of fiction comes to the fore in a manner not possible for hypothesis and dogma. The empty act requires a filling because only then can it operate, but it removes the limitations of all possible contents because there is no appropriate filling of the ideational act by what eludes both cognition and comprehension. Furthermore, the projected supplement indicates various nuances within this doubling: it marks in equal measure both the separation of the idea from all reality and the resultant processing of reality. As a projected supplement, fiction prevents "the unchangeable coexistence and sequence of phenomena" from lapsing into entropy.

By identifying fiction as the empty ideating act that is able to project all kinds of supplements, we are finally rid of the old opposition between fiction and reality in a way that offers more attractive solutions in comparison with those of similar contemporary approaches such as Gestalt psychology and phenomenology. Von Ehrenfels's "gestalt qualities" were regarded as a dynamic grouping of data through which perception could initially be built up.[59] Von Ehrenfels himself left no doubt as to the fact that this grouping effect proceeded from the perceiver, and so the question was where these gestalts were formed, a question pursued by Wolfgang Köhler in his experiments with chickens and monkeys designed to trace the location of such an activity.[60] But ever since von Senden's operations on people born blind,[61] it has been revealed that gestalt-forming vision does not take place immediately with eyesight restored. What has to be added to perceived data has no organic basis of its own and needs training through interaction with a perceivable outside world in order to assume its operational function.

Gestalts are therefore as much a "ghost in the machine"[62] as Husserl's "figural factors" that were an indispensable component of his transcendental phenomenology. Sounds, for instance, can be "awakened" into melodies only by means of figural factors, although these have no sound quality of their own and resist conceptualization when applied elsewhere.[63]

A similar problem occurs in different form with Cassirer's *Philosophy of Symbolic Forms*. What Cassirer calls symbols are traces of the nongiven in the given that would remain inaccessible to comprehension without such interpolated schemata.[64] Therefore even concepts have no real existence for him, but function as a means of enabling perception and cognition, that is, as constructs for organizational purposes. While this reflects a neo-Kantian schematism, it is Vaihinger who draws a more convincing consequence from the Kantian schema. Fiction as a projected supplement is free from the mystifications that begin to arise out of gestalts, figural factors, and symbols whenever a foundation is to be provided for them. In the last analysis, these defy qualification, whereas the projected supplement always presents itself as something feigned, through which "tacit knowledge" of fiction as deception is evoked as a backdrop that frees the projected supplement from any concern regarding its foundation. Consequently, deception becomes the hallmark of fiction only when one seeks to provide a foundation for it; this implies that the historically internalized criticism of fiction as practiced by epistemology now makes fiction critical of all ideas and assumptions that lay claim to being foundations.

This double-edged character of fiction has consequences for all such assumptions. They are posits, and a posit "means the *conscious selection, recording and naming of whatever experience one wishes as a 'something' expressly belonging to an order.*"[65] Posits are not to be trusted, because "this whole procedure of creating absolutes is a form of fiction,"[66] which "changes the indeterminate, ungraspable and flowing into a determinate, graspable and static."[67] If posit and fiction are so alike in structure and function that they may be confused, the question of the difference between them arises, for the posit produces its object just as fiction does. "The object becomes an object in and with the posit, but at no time must one lose sight of the fact that every posit qua posit is had by myself. I find signs of order in the object, the given . . . confronts me to a certain extent in ordered projections."[68] This definition of the posit applies equally well to fiction, which, as Vaihinger contends,[69] proceeds in accordance with pragmatic exigencies by "isolating," "abstracting," "summating," or "neglecting." But although their selective processes are the same, posit and fiction initiate different attitudes toward them, even if the requirements that give rise to them spring from an equally subjective need. With the posit there is no consciousness of difference between itself and the state of affairs it organizes, whereas with fiction consciousness of difference prevails.

This distinction is sharpened by Vaihinger's description of fictions as "consciously false ideas,"[70] because for the sake of processing, it overlays an inaccessible reality with assumptions that cannot correspond to that reality. If this were not the case, reality would have to be graspable. Therefore fictions are

> l o g i c a l   f a l s i f i c a t i o n s . . .
> by means of which a fruitful cognition of the external world and a
> productive handling of it can be achieved. T h i s   c o u n -
> t e r f e i t i n g ,   d r i v e n   b y   t h e
> l o g i c a l   f u n c t i o n , must presumably have
> its justification and, I would add, its official sanction, because otherwise it could not be carried out to such an extended degree and in such a fruitful manner. In relation to these thought patterns we assume the correct attitude only when we free ourselves from the common superstition that thought and being are identical, so that on the contrary we do not allow any thought pattern to pass for real that cannot provide special proof of this reality.[71]

This "superstition" makes fictions into posits that postulate an identity where difference prevails. Why does this occur? Because a posit seeks to explain the order it creates, whereas fiction seeks to produce something through the calculations that it initiates. Posits gain validity through assent; fictions gain theirs through success.

Locke had already taken "Assent"[72] to be the central authentication of assumptions; on that basis he rejected Descartes's innate ideas as being incapable of ensuring such consent.[73] But if a posit regards its own order as an explanation, then premises become identical to what they are meant to explain. When Hume and Kant disturbed this "dogmatic slumber" by scrutinizing the explanatory pretensions of the posits, their nature began to change. At the end of the eighteenth century, the posit was broken up into heuristic fiction and ideological postulate. In heuristic fiction, the claim to reality gave way to processing contingency, which now had to be mastered instead of explained. On the other hand, the ideological postulate hypostatized the explanatory pretensions of the posit. In the late eighteenth century the concept of *ideology* was formulated by Destutt de Tracy, who, in continuation of Locke's observation concerning the human mind, saw ideology as "Science des idées."[74] "It studies the origin and formative principle of ideas. Only if ideas are constantly traced back to the sensations that condition them is that security guaranteed which is indispensable to the formation of knowledge concerning Nature and man. Only when it succeeded in avoiding false ideas was the progress of the sciences ensured" (p. 14). The positing nature of ideology is directed by the optimistic view that its explanations "possess the same degree of certainty . . . as the findings of the physical and mathematical sciences. By reducing all ideas, ideologists promised themselves that they could build up a science of man which in its turn might provide the basis for all political and economic life" (p. 19).

This same trend has persisted up to the present and is still a major factor for the advocates of ideology. Enzensberger, for instance, writes: "But through the *positing* of necessity, meaning can evidently be *produced,* and from then on can be confused with objective meaning. With this ability to produce meaning through posits, we stand at the source of ideology as a means of making plausible how social deficiencies are to be dealt with through prevailing consciousness."[75]

Ideology and heuristic fiction are the two historically divergent developments entailed in the concept of positing, in consequence of which they assume different functions. Ideology makes deficiencies plausible in a manner resulting from the original "Science des idées." Heuristic fictions, for the purpose of a calculation, radicalize "the deviation from reality" in order to substitute "something absolutely unreal . . . for something real."[76] While ideology comes up with a claim to explanation, heuristic fiction proposes trial runs for approaches to what is. Through explanation, ideology endows its made-up world with validity, though it still requires collective assent, while heuristic fiction brackets off its assumptions, because tool and task must be kept strictly separate. What is posited is equally overstepped in heuristic fiction, but in contrast to ideology it does not collapse into what is to be processed.

Yet both spring from the same root: for Destutt de Tracy, "Ideology consisted . . , in tracing thought back to sensation,"[77] just as for Vaihinger "an addition [is] made by the psyche, which sets up the sensations as attributes of things."[78]

The historical split of posit into ideology and fiction reveals a change in attitude. The old explanatory claims of posits are preserved in ideology, but in fiction the necessary assumptions are transferred into an As-if. This not only maintains the difference that ideology, by reifying explanation, obliterates; it also guarantees continuous interaction between reality and sensation. Thus in fiction sensation is doubled by a particular assumption of what reality is supposed to be, and its contingency is doubled by way of a specific form assumed by the awakened sensation. In this doubling structure, neither reality nor sensation takes precedence; fiction proves to be a matrix for all kinds of processes, whereas ideology rejects anything that does not fit in with its own explanations. This change in attitude toward assumptions indicates the importance of difference that develops by fanning out multifarious types of fiction; their limitlessness ultimately reveals all posits to be fictions. In the case of ideology, the revelation would be an unmasking, leading to another, though somewhat different, form of doubling. The projected supplement stabilizes its own individual character through the fictionalizing of all posits, so that the affirmation of fiction turns into a critique of ideological premises, for fiction discloses itself as an inauthentic posit.

If the achievement of fiction leads ultimately to universal fictionalization, the mystery concerning the actual nature of this As-if construction still remains. Bentham had insisted that the fictitious entities be viewed as if they were real entities, but this merely left fiction resting on fiction. The reason was clearly that 'names' had no correspondence in re, because they could only name but could not be the thing itself. If he is to solve the problem, Vaihinger now has to address the nature of the As-if.

Although Ogden criticizes him for falling behind Bentham by failing to lay stress on fiction's dependence on language, Vaihinger actually begins his "'As-if approach' . . . by a grammatical analysis."[79] Bentham had said nothing about the particles, although the linguistic nature of the fictitious entities should have drawn his attention to them, especially since Locke had already focused on them in his philosophy of language. Vaihinger actually refers to Locke in his discussion of particles: "Thus Locke had correctly recognized that particles indicate the finest turns of thought and give expression as it were to the flowering of the logical functions—in short, that the particles are the linguistic means of combining thoughts."[80] Grammatically, the As-if denotes a conditional sentence, and the "form of this conditional statement affirms that the condition is an unreal or impossible one."[81] The assumption cannot be proved, and it does not correspond to any existing reality, which in any case could become present only through the release of sensations and so could not be identical to this activity. But for this very reason, the particle complex serves " t o e q u a t e   a n   e x i s t i n g   s o m e - t h i n g   w i t h   t h e   c o n s e q u e n c e s o f   a n   u n r e a l   o r   i m p o s s i b l e c a s e . "[82] The As-if brings about the identification of the nonidentical by means of a comparison whose structure Vaihinger describes as follows:

> ... 'As if' ... is a linking of particles that recurs in all highly developed languages. ... Evidently an ellipsis takes place in which after the comparative particle 'as' etc. a whole clause has been left out, which is to be completed in the mind and inferred from the context. This missing clause has a double function to fulfill: on the one hand it is the second component of the comparative interrelation, and on the other it is that of the hypothetical link; in the latter it represents or would have to represent the independent main clause. Even though it is related both backward and forward, it is generally omitted. 'The circle is to be viewed as if it were a polygon' means 'The circle is to be viewed as it would have to be viewed if it were a polygon.' The middle clause evidently plays the role just described. And so there is a complicated comparison being made here. A simple comparison puts one thing into a comparative relationship with one thing, one fact with one fact. Whether this comparison is based on a real relationship or owes its existence only to the subjective play of ideas, is initially not linguistically expressed.[83]

The linkup of the particles is marked by an empty space that lies between two references: On the one hand it is part of a comparison, and on the other hand it is the common ground between the very different elements of the given and the feigned. The empty space of the As-if brings together the existing reality and sensations that guide the approach to it. It proves to be a source from which imaginative intuitions may penetrate consciousness. The missing sentence can only mark the imaginative as a blank, because the comparison that takes place in the As-if "is not merely an empty game of ideas but has a practical purpose through which the comparison may lead to consequences."[84] Thus, with its many guises—as comparison, link, reference for reality, and sensation—the As-if indicates the presence of the imaginative under the conditions of a pragmatically oriented consciousness together with a possibility for this consciousness to feign sensations as if they were inherent in things. The As-if is the region within which imagination and consciousness work on each other, although the practical purpose requires that consciousness remains dominant, so that the imaginative is present in the structure of consciousness only as an empty space. This empty space marks the possible influence of the imagination on the activities of consciousness—an influence brought about by the need to compare the incomparable.

The As-if is a kind of relay, insofar as it forces the imaginative into a form in order to open up the full range of possibilities for the projected supplement. For, as Vaihinger emphasizes, "with 'fictive' . . . one must always keep in mind the feature . . . that fictions are expedient patterns of the imagination; to this extent 'fictive' is a different term from 'imaginative'; the latter only denotes the side of what is imagined; but the former, in our sense, still has the essential feature of expediency, the device used for a practical purpose."[85] Since the As-if doubles the difference between psyche and phenomena with the difference between the conscious and the imaginative, it would have to eliminate itself if the difference were to be definitively resolved. Therefore it is, and must remain, a fiction because existing reality cannot be organized through itself but only through a mode that is not to be found in reality. This is more than mere opposition to reality, for instead of opposing it, fiction actually interferes with reality in order to make it serve a purpose that, once again, is not part of reality.

As a structural formula, the As-if can take on various forms in fiction, according to the intention that has to be fulfilled. Vaihinger's main categories are *contradiction, analogy, intermediary, similarity-centre,* and *transit-point.* "It is a character of all true fictions that they contain contradictions."[86] The projected supplement is contradictory because sensations cannot be qualities of things. But whatever runs counter to reality provides a basis from which to calculate reality, and in this way fiction takes on a pragmatic gestalt, conditioned by the situation in which it is to become effective. The "contradiction," then, arises from the expectations for what each gestalt is meant to achieve, and ultimately it marks the latitude fiction possesses with regard to its possible uses. For different contradictions will arise in accordance with different deployments of fiction, so that contradiction denotes the adaptability of fiction whose variations know no limits.

The "analogy" differs from contradiction by offering a pattern of classification that enables the psyche to "deliver itself to the sweet madness of grasping and having grasped,"[87] even though being cannot be grasped, because " g r a s p i n g   means: t r a c i n g something   b a c k   to something else, which in regard to being can no longer be the case" (p. 94). Nevertheless, comprehension is guided by the effort to subsume the unknown under the known. It follows for Vaihinger that "the analogy itself stands there as the eternally ungrasped" (p. 315). Here the epistemological argument surrenders before an anthropological necessity, and as Vaihinger is outlining an epistemological approach to fiction, boundaries for cognition inevitably begin to emerge. For the psyche's reasons for devising categories in order to grasp what it is not can in turn be grasped only in anthropological terms. While the contradiction principally denotes the use of fiction, the analogy is the pure embodiment of the As-if, which as an experience is evident but epistemologically eludes comprehension. Analogy is a refusal to accept the ungraspable, even if its ungraspability is recognized to the extent that whatever comprehension has been imposed on it will turn out to be a semblance only. To understand by means of feigning something is, however, a pragmatic necessity that aims not at insight but at production.

For this process, the "intermediary" and "similarity-centre" are indispensable types of fiction. The "intermediary" is devised in order to reduce "the gap between the mass of apperception and that which is to be apperceived," as with the 'atom,' which presents "the empirical material in the posited form of calculable points of mass" (p. 157). Exactly how such a mediation is to be conceived is of no importance, in view of the expected gain that the idea is meant to achieve by processing the "mass of apperception." "Intermediaries" are justified by "the external, purely methodical usefulness" (p. 573), and as is evident from the example of the atom, they are only constructs that, unlike hypotheses, do not intend to square reality with preconceived assumptions. Instead, these constructs operate as "comparative apperception(s),"[88] which means that they are neither pure comparison nor proper analogy but something in between. The As-if modifies comparison and analogy in equal measure, and so the "intermediaries" present themselves as models that cannot, however, offer information about what they are modeling.[89] Therefore model-building is only a precondition for acts of comprehension and cannot explain what is to be comprehended.

The "intermediary" relates more to the "mass of apperception," and the "similarity-center" relates more to sensation. Since the psyche always strives for balance, fiction as "similarity-centre" serves "to facilitate and accelerate the comparison of particular sensations."[90] For the psyche is "a machine which is continually improving itself, and whose purpose is to perform as safely, expeditiously and with the minimum expenditure of energy, the movements necessary for the preservation of the organism."[91] This feigned equation of the psyche with what it cannot be leads to a differentiation of sensations which is necessary in order to process the state of suspense which prevails in the psyche. This brings sensations increasingly into consciousness, whereby data can be more swiftly calculated and the psyche thus relieved. For acceleration entails the abandonment of the "similarity-centres" whenever they have fulfilled their function. "Just as the lever is put aside when it has done its work ... e v e r y   m e a n s   o f   t h o u g h t   is put aside when it has done what it should."[92] Since "similarity-centres" facilitate this endeavor, their sequence has to be accelerated so that in the course of its self-fulfillment the psyche may be set free to embrace more and more new comparisons.

The result of all this is not only a high rate of wear and tear on fictions but also their manifestation as "transit-points." "The ultimate attitude of logic with regard to fictions is and must remain to regard them as points of transition for the mind. But we have treated thought as a whole, with all its auxiliary apparatus, its instruments and devices, in other words, the entire theoretical activity of man as a mere transit-point with practical utility as its ultimate goal, whether this be taken to mean ordinary action or ideally interpreted as ethical action."[93] As "transit-points" fictions are "hinges" between individual sensations and, once again, between sensations and phenomena. But once a connection is made, they must disappear in order that they remain fictions and do not become states of affairs or even objects themselves. Their productiveness is proportional to what they accomplish. It is as "transit-points" that they come closest to their nature as mere projected supplements. Their contents are minimalized, and this brings out their elemental functionality, which is fulfilled by their catalytic effect.

These different forms of the As-if reveal the unmistakable features of a structural model. The As-if is in fact the structure of the structures that vary according to prevailing pragmatic contexts. Regardless of Vaihinger's neo-Kantian terminology, this structural model issues forth into an open taxonomy. This can be seen from the fact that Vaihinger's voluminous study expands more and more into a veritable catalog of fictions, the sheer number of which swamps both the qualitative and the functional differences between them. One has the impression that the accumulation of examples serves to produce a critical mass meant to prove incontrovertibly that, apart from sensations and "the unalterable co-existence and sequence of phenomena," everything is fiction. This enables Vaihinger to unfold a broad spectrum of effects emanating from fiction, but the "historical confirmations" that he seeks in his conclusion, mainly with reference to Kant and Nietzsche, show that fiction is to be justified but not explained by its function. Vaihinger's use of the Kantian As-if misappropriates its essential duality. For Kant this duality could imply, in Henrich's words:

> What is assumed "as if" it were true has the same effect that an insight might have, based on the knowledge that it is not a matter of truth but solely of the way it is used. It can, however, also have a meaning that in the decisive point is precisely the opposite of this way of reading: what is impossible for us to ground, but what proceeds from the whole of our rational being as an indispensable thesis, is what we may orient our lives by as if it were established knowledge. We are justified in thinking that what we thus assume, and what is true, continue into each other ... The first way of resolving the ambiguity of Kant's formula leads directly to an attitude of consciousness explained by Nietzsche. Vaihinger has rightly named his fiction theory, which is closer to Nietzsche's thinking than to Kant's *The Philosophy of the As-if*.[94]

Like Nietzsche's concept of semblance as a foundational principle of the world, Vaihinger's As-if finds itself in the dilemma that, by fictionalizing all posits, it ends up being one itself. Vaihinger's only divergence from Nietzsche is that he takes sensations and "the unalterable co-existence and sequence of phenomena" as given, so that in relation to what is, fictions "from the theoretical standpoint are seen directly to be false, but are justified and so can be termed 'practically true' because they perform certain services for us."[95] Even if fictions still incorporate a consciousness of being false ideas, they are true, because they bear witness to their falsehood. At the same time, though, they are false by comparison with the reality of sensations and phenomena, but it is precisely this "falsehood" that gives them their practical truth insofar as they explain nothing. In this respect Vaihinger differs from Kant as well as from Nietzsche and from structuralism: from Kant because his As-if does not represent the necessary alternative to a limited cognitive faculty; from Nietzsche because fiction for him does not embody a foundational principle; and from structuralism because the function precedes the structure, so that the As-if manifests itself differently according to its pragmatically determined context.

What is more important for our present purposes than these historical considerations is the form now taken on by fiction thematized in philosophical discourse. If we regard the As-if as a matrix functioning through the various types of fiction (*contradiction, analogy, intermediary, similarity-centre, and transit-point*), we shall see that all of them are frames of reference for calculating and processing reality. The As-if produces referential conditions that allow approaches to an ungraspable reality, for, like explanation, usage lays down certain premises that from the point of view of exploration have to be considerably more flexible than the postulates of cognition. Instead of subsuming, fiction has to embrace both sensations and phenomena in order to develop whatever play of doubling is necessary for the pragmatic context. In the above-mentioned types of fiction, therefore, the difference between sensations and phenomena is glossed over, even if it is present in one concretization or other: In the contradiction, it is the latitude that allows adaptation to different situations; in the analogy it is delusory semblance; in the intermediary it is a construct; in the similarity-centre it is tension; and in the transit-point it is an interchange. Difference therefore permeates all types of fiction, shifting ground in accordance with the requirements of their usage, and its changing reifications form the records by which reality is calculated.

But even the individual reification still maintains the dual character of fiction, for a resolved difference makes fiction at one and the same time inauthentic and practical—inauthentic insofar as the resolved difference is still present in the denial of truth and validity; practical in that the inauthentic appearance becomes a variable frame of reference for multiple patterings according to which sensations can be projected as qualities of phenomena. What is not present, however, is reflection on the doubling of the As-if and its reification in the different types of fiction. The basis of thematized fiction defies reflection because the latter would entail an explanation of fiction. This would mean either postulating a transcendental stance in order to predicate fiction or having to take the explanation itself as fiction, which would be impossible because fictions do not explain. If the As-if is an ultimate, it escapes conceptualization. The difference between sensations and phenomena, as manifested through the As-if, remains inaccessible; this is what brings to the fore the anthropological foundation of cognition, inviting a vast range of possible resolutions that must prove their efficacy in accordance with the pragmatic demands of the situation.

The As-if reveals itself as a basically limitless catalog of types of fiction providing the basis for paradigms that can only be models because they can give no information about what they are modeling. The paradigms, therefore, always under pressure to prove successful, stand in need of legitimation, which depends to some extent on the degree of assent accorded to the particular model. Consequently fictions are "consumed" at a high rate, because their situational effectiveness can be stabilized only through collective acceptance. The fact that contextual usage and attitude adopted toward fiction are closely bound up with each other makes the thematizing of fiction into a triangular relationship of purpose, usage, and attitude. Purpose lays down the pragmatic requirements, usage establishes the efficacy of the ideas deployed, and attitude brings about the consent necessary for the success to be achieved.

The interaction of these three constituents shows above all that fiction cannot be ontologically based. Furthermore, it is clear that fictions, by making something possible, have a performative character. Finally, the combined operations reveal that any reification of the As-if is caused by the exigencies to be met, so that the As-if becomes the reference for usage. What is concealed by this dominance of the pragmatic, however, is the driving force of invention that is present in the doubling but cannot spring from the pragmatic context because this context is what it seeks to cope with. The As-if gives rise to an open-ended series of types of fictions, which in turn lead to an equally limitless number of models. All of them are manifestations of the projected supplement that can be grasped only by way of its function or, at best, through its necessity. The claim that it comes from a fictionalizing consciousness, or from the imagination, can, in this context, only be a matter of taking refuge in an *asylum ignorantiae.*

Vaihinger's theory of fiction does not provide a hermeneutics of invention, although in relation to Bentham it does give a more detailed account of the conditions enabling us to appraise the function of fiction. By pin-pointing this function, Vaihinger makes fiction itself the object of cognition, and it emerges as a peculiar hybrid. Its efficacy is closely bound up with its falsity. In this respect the old criticism of fiction lingers on, but only linguistically, not least in order to make the affirmation of fiction all the more striking. Using epistemological frameworks to discuss fiction means forcing the insight through the barriers of the old vocabulary. Thus Vaihinger follows the obligatory trend of definition in order to legitimize his discovery. The definitions, however, remain those of a particular usage of fiction, which is why Vaihinger—perhaps *malgré lui*—inflated them, because only by so doing could he use the inherited presuppositions in order to talk about fiction.

Fiction as Differential: Nelson Goodman and Constructivism

Vaihinger argued that he had thought Kant's insights through to their logical conclusion by justifying as heuristic fictions what he deemed to be the contradictory concepts of reason and understanding. This argument was still based on the epistemological subject/object split, which Vaihinger, in spite of the impenetrableness of the "unalterable co-existence and sequence of phenomena," did not discard. This split is discarded in Nelson Goodman's constructivist approach, as developed in his book *Ways of Worldmaking:*

> I think of this book as belonging in that mainstream of modern philosophy that began when Kant exchanged the structure of the world for the structure of the mind, continued when C. I. Lewis exchanged the structure of the mind for the structure of concepts, and that now proceeds to exchange the structure of concepts for the structure of the several symbol systems of the sciences, philosophy, the arts, perception, and everyday discourse. The movement is from unique truth and a world fixed and found to a diversity of right and even conflicting versions or worlds in the making.[96]

Since several versions of world exist at the same time, worldmaking tends to become the focus of this "constructionalist orientation" (p. 1). Thus the gulf that for both Bentham and Vaihinger necessitated the production of fictions dwindles to insignificance. When Bentham conceived fictitious entities as linguistic designations, he tried—in keeping with prevailing epistemological skepticism—to indicate that it was possible to deal only with the appearances of things, while Vaihinger, taking sensations as the final residue of a tangible reality, took fiction as a means of processing what is beyond grasping.

What, however, is the status of fiction if it is no longer necessitated by such a gulf? Right at the start, it is Goodman's concern "How to interpret such terms as 'real', 'unreal', 'fictive', and 'possible'" (p. 2). Worldmaking conflicts with the alternatives of 'real' and 'unreal', and indeed it must get rid of them, since worlds are not made out of an "unconceptualized reality."[97] The traditional contrast between reality and fiction had, paradoxically, been maintained by Vaihinger through his omnifictionalization, and it had remained dominant solely because it was assumed that there was such a thing as an objectively given reality. For Goodman, the "fictive" releases itself from even a correlation with the "real," and instead links itself to the "possible"—which, however, is no longer to be seen as the mere adumbration of reality. Hence the questions "In just what sense are there many worlds? What distinguishes genuine from spurious worlds? What are worlds made of? How are they made? What role do symbols play in the making? And how is worldmaking related to knowing?"[98] If these questions are to be answered, then a distinction has to be made between worldmaking and the concept of possible worlds, as developed by modal logic.

The generated versions of worlds are not possible alternatives to the *one* world; they all have the same status, and are neither possible nor impossible in relation to a presumed 'real' world. The theory of possible worlds is unacceptable to Goodman, mainly because it would make a physically real world the reference point for other worlds that would be physically possible or impossible.[99] Regardless of the fact that even a physically impossible world may have attributes that make it a world,[100] the very relation of the real to the possible also implies a normative judgment of worlds: "To demand full and sole reducibility to physics or any other one version is to forego nearly all other versions."[101] And so for Goodman there are *only* versions of worlds, without "something stolid underneath."[102] Worlds are made out of worlds: "[T]he making is a remaking" (p. 6).

Whatever version is made is both real and actual—and this is as true of scientific theories as it is of works of art. If 'unreal' and 'possible' as predicates of worlds are eliminated, we are left only with the initially listed pair of 'fictive' and 'actual'. How are these related to each other? The construction of one version of world depends on the destruction of others, and the duality of decomposition and composition has a status different from that of the resultant version: if the latter is 'actual', then permutation between versions might be termed 'fictive'. "With false hope of a firm foundation gone," argues Goodman, "with the world displaced by worlds that are but versions, with substance dissolved into function, and with the given acknowledged as taken, we face the questions how worlds are made, tested, and known" (p. 7). Instead of given facts, there are only versions made, and thus 'facticity' turns out to be "fact from fiction" (pp. 102–7). The concept of fiction changes again.

Fiction can no longer be a "fictitious entity" because, as a "Fabrication of Facts" (see chapter 6, pp. 91–107), it is neither an 'entity' nor materially bound to language. Bentham's concept of fiction was still in line with his inherent positivism insofar as it was based on its having to be just as materially graspable as the undisputed givenness of facts. As language, it had a determinate gestalt, but at the same time Bentham saw it as an 'entity' that had to shape other 'entities'. Little wonder, then, that he had difficulty explaining the concrete application of "fictitious entities."[103]

Vaihinger also held fast to the idea of fiction having a solid structure, although he no longer viewed it as being exclusively bound to language. Without a material basis, however, fiction was also unthinkable for Vaihinger, and so he located it in the realm of ideas. In doing so, he ignored the problem of whether the idea that he regarded as being rooted in sensation was not just as fictionalized by this grounding as was language, the bearer of Bentham's "fictitious entities." Such a consequence was neither in Bentham's nor in Vaihinger's orbit, since their epistemological approaches demanded a material basis for fiction. But even the critical positivism to which they were committed regarded language and idea as realities in which fiction could be anchored, and the question of what fiction might actually do with such anchorages simply was not asked.

For Goodman, then, fiction produces facts, as facts—and here he takes up an argument advanced by Norwood Hanson[104]—are always "theory-laden." This view dispenses not only with the material basis of

fiction but also with the function—emphasized by Vaihinger—of enabling us to process a reality otherwise inaccessible to cognition. Vaihinger's hybrid As-if construction simply dissolves.[105] "Fact from fiction," however, indicates not the calculating of something given, though
eclipsed, but the constitution of versions of world. Against this background, Vaihinger's basic terminology of calculating and processing by
way of fiction is revealed in its full and ineradicable ambiguity: Processing is a halfhearted constitution of world that remains deficient
because the "unalterable co-existence and sequence of phenomena"
are, for Vaihinger, matters that are given in advance.

If we take fiction to be a means of constituting various versions of
world, then clearly it cannot have a solid structure of its own, nor can it
be a contraposition to an already given reality; rather, it must take effect
within versions of worlds. How, then, can one conceive of fiction, when
it fabricates facts from world versions in order to make other world
versions? Such a constitutive process can scarcely be accomplished by
solid structures or materially based entities, since they would inevitably involve a transcendental stance from which to view all versions. For
Goodman, there is no point outside the versions, and this enables him
also to avoid the danger to which constructivists have sometimes fallen
prey—the temptation described by Jerome Bruner as follows:

> We create realities by warning, by encouraging, by dubbing with titles,
> by naming, and by the manner in which words invite us to create
> 'realities' in the world to correspond with them. Constitutiveness
> gives an externality and an apparent ontological status to the con-
> cepts words embody: for example, the law, gross national product,
> antimatter, the Renaissance. It is what makes us construct proscenia
> in our theater and still be tempted to stone the villain. At our most
> unguarded, we are all Naive Realists who believe not only that *we*
> know what is 'out there,' but also that it is out there for *others* as well.
> Carol Feldman calls it 'ontic dumping,' converting our mental pro-
> cesses into products and endowing them with a reality in some
> world.[106]

Fictions for Goodman are neither concepts nor structures nor
entities, but "ways" of making worlds out of worlds. These ways do not
run the risk of possible reification because they merely embody a
modus operandi.[107]As such, they cannot be solid or consciously perceivable. They do point a way, offering means of changing world versions into other world versions, but no matter what characteristics they

may have in common, they cannot be traced back to a substratum. To illustrate this, Goodman quotes and extends a comment by Woody Allen: "Can we actually 'know' the universe? My God, it's hard enough finding your way around in Chinatown. The point, however, is: Is there anything out there? And why? And must they be so noisy? Finally, there can be no doubt that the one characteristic of 'reality' is that it lacks essence. That is not to say it has no essence, but merely lacks it."[108]

Using as an example the pre-Socratics, Goodman demonstrates how each constructed world arises out of the inroads made into the system of its predecessors. The newly formed patterns become alternative systems, but they do not discredit those of their predecessors, for each system is simply another version. There is never anything but interpreted world to which one can refer, and so there is no alternative to the versions of world, other than what Goodman calls "blankness . . . and . . . complete elimination of the so-called artificial [that] would leave us empty-minded and empty-handed" (p. 100). If emptiness is to be the only thinkable alternative to worldmaking, the question arises as to where the ways of worldmaking—in principle, an unlimited and unending reformulation of versions—actually come from. Goodman's nominalist position barely allows for any explanation, although he does observe that "whatever else may be said of these modes of organization, they are not 'found in the world' but *built into a world*. Ordering, as well as composition and decomposition and weighting of wholes and kinds, participates in worldmaking" (p. 14). Since all versions entail modes of reaching out and into other versions, the 'way' may be seen as a difference. Owing to its lack of 'essence', the difference gives rise to a multiplicity of versions functioning as the driving force behind reformulation. Thus emptiness translates itself into the production of worlds.

Who actually "builds" these 'ways' into world versions? Goodman says comparatively little about this, although certain turns of phrase seem to indicate that the subject appears to be responsible: "We start, on any occasion, with some old version or world that we have on hand and that we are stuck with until we have the determination and skill to remake it into a new one" (p. 97). Ways of worldmaking would therefore seem to be extensions through which we reach beyond the limitations of the version in which we find ourselves. Since each version is a product of "ways of worldmaking," worlds are always fabricated factuality. If so, Goodman could not avoid describing the modes of operation that govern the process of worldmaking. Since these, however, cannot be identical to what they produce, he calls the results "fact from fiction" in order to distinguish the product from the process of production. It is this distinction that leads to the final collapse of another distinction, that between fiction and reality. For now there can no longer be any reality without fiction, which as a restructuring of world versions becomes the integral precondition for all factuality.

This view of fiction is very different from Vaihinger's processing of independent phenomena through projected supplements, the objective of which was to bring an unknowable external world within the bounds of conceivability. Vaihinger says very little about the modes of operation whereby projected supplements take effect. He thinks in terms of positions, whereas Goodman, thinking in terms of relations, focuses much more on the operative nature of fiction, which Vaihinger did not deny but which he could pay little attention to because, for him, fiction manifested itself in types and models. Goodman, on the contrary, argues that "as meanings vanish in favor of certain relationships among terms, so facts vanish in favor of certain relationships among versions" (p. 93).

The enhanced significance attached to relationships derives from the dual reference: they are at one and the same time the link and the distinction between world versions. The ways of worldmaking are therefore catalysts that bring about a continual shift from difference to relationship and vice versa, permeating the versions of world as a kind of differential. Facts, then, are merely the end products of a process. As the only alternative to such fabricated facts is "blankness," there cannot be any transcendental foundation to such a process. This is why Goodman points out: "My outline of the facts concerning the fabrication of facts is of course itself a fabrication" (p. 107). Since the constitutive principle underlying his theory is itself a construct, we may conceive of the production of world versions by means of the same constructs, which cannot be separated from what they have constructed and so can explain nothing, though they can produce a great deal. If the construct itself is to be explained, what will emerge is the standpoint from which it is described, but this, in turn, as something designed to make explanation possible, has the character of a construct. Here, with hindsight, we may locate the blind spots of both Bentham's and Vaihinger's theories of fiction.

Versions of world do not require explanation; they need to be recast in accordance with prevailing needs. Recastings, however, are possible only if the system of the particular version contains at least an empty space that can be occupied. This blank would then be a fiction, entirely in Goodman's understanding of the term: "strictly speaking, fiction cannot be about anything nonactual, since there is nothing non-actual, no merely-possible or impossible worlds; for saying that there is something fictive but not actual amounts to saying *that there is something such that there is no such thing* . . . Fiction, then, no matter how false or how far-out, is about what is actual when about anything at all."[109] Thus fiction cannot be separated from each actual version but instead becomes an integral part of every version through its dual operation of separating and linking, for it conditions both the decomposition and the composition of the individual versions. Does this make fiction into a substitute for the long-lost substratum, or even reveal it as the "blankness" beyond the plurality of worlds? For Goodman's nominalism, these are certainly impermissible questions. The modus operandi of his ways of worldmaking defies even negative reification, which would then turn into an embodiment of a transcendental postulate.

Nonetheless, world versions are not pure inventions. "Pure fiction and pure nonfiction are rare,"[110] Goodman concludes from his reflections on fiction. If world versions are made from other versions, references are indispensable that can be neither convention nor consensus, since they would then constitute a given that would considerably reduce the scope of the world-producing process. Instead, there are multiple references of a formal nature, such as *denotation, expression,* and *exemplification* (see p. 70), that—and this is the vital element—are capable of a vast range of interconnections through which they mold the shape of each particular version. This means that each version, as a system of symbols, simultaneously carries and produces its own system of references. These develop in the process of production, which is why Goodman speaks of the roots of reference (see pp. 55–70) that build up referential chains (see p. 62 passim). The basic types of reference take on changing functions: denotation can become expression, just as exemplification can turn into denotation. In all cases world versions are characterized by a referential complexity derived from the interaction among the three types of reference.

The interplay of references is triggered by the ways of worldmaking, whose character is determined only insofar as they represent modes, directions, means, and procedures. Worldmaking therefore entails taking existing versions apart and putting them together again in a different manner, subjecting elements, categories, qualities, and complexes to a process of weighting, deleting, supplementing, and ordering. These are the syntagmas that regulate the permutation from one world version to another. Weighting means reversing emphases, shifting accents, and redistributing relevance; deletion means eliminating patterns, plans, structures, and functions; supplementing entails telescoping different elements, substituting one existing structure or function for another, and making additions; ordering involves imposing different relationships on patterns and measurements, on proximity and distance, and on correlation and derivation. From all this evolve the referential chains that stabilize the new version to the extent that this now bears within itself a dismantled symbol system of other world versions.[111]

If we take worldmaking to be a mobile system of signs, with 'facts' always disappearing in relationships so that new 'facts' may be fabricated out of them, it may be said that this syntagmatic model is kept in motion by differences. Goodman's nominalism forbids us to ask who operates the modes of worldmaking, and he stresses that the many distinctions he has drawn are meant only to serve the "advancement of the understanding."[112] But difference in this mobile sign system does take on more than one salient feature: it varies not only in the individual syntagmas of permutation between versions but also in the chains of reference developing through difference that, in turn, is given its shifting salience through the interchange of reference types in the chain. This shifting salience shows first of all that difference is not something tangible but exists only in relation to the items it separates—from which, however, it cannot be detached even though it is not identical to them. At the same time the changing salience spotlights the differentiation between syntagmatic ways of worldmaking and between referential chains, thereby building up the complexity of references unique to the particular version of world. Being identical neither to the modes nor to the types of reference, even though these could not be unfolded without it, difference manifests itself as sliding. Since this sliding difference has no substratum and is inseparable from what it effects, it appears as the fictive that underlies the fabrication of symbol systems.

Such an assessment, however, would remain nothing but an unsubstantiated assertion if it could not be borne out through recourse to reference; for Goodman's syntactically conceived theory of worldmaking operates within and not beyond a system of references, by means of which the ways of worldmaking have to be validated. This means nothing less than that a reference has to be found for worldmaking itself if the latter process is to be opened up to comprehension. This is the point at which the work of art becomes of vital significance to Goodman. "The bearing that this inquiry into the nature of works of art has upon the overall undertaking of this book should by now have become quite clear. How an object or event functions as a work explains how, through certain modes of reference, what so functions may contribute to a vision of—and to the making of—a world."[113] It does not matter here whether Goodman has developed his theory of art out of aesthetic interest or out of the necessity to find a point of reference for his ways of worldmaking.[114] What does matter is that he raises the work of art to the same level as scientific theory and all other symbol systems through which world versions are produced: "for a major thesis of this book is that the arts must be taken no less seriously than the sciences as modes of discovery, creation, and enlargement of knowledge in the broad sense of advancement of the understanding."[115]

Indeed, one must even talk of the arts' greater significance insofar as they can exemplify worldmaking itself. "Exemplification, though one of the most frequent and important functions of works of art, is the least noted and understood."[116] For one may argue that semiotic theories have described works of art predominantly as self-referential signs, whose iconic character is unrelated to anything outside itself.[117] If, however, a work of art is only a version of world, what enables it to exemplify worldmaking? Does this not eliminate an ontological difference between art and non-art, only to restore the difference afterward? Goodman tackles this apparent problem by substituting the question of when art occurs for that of what it is, which suggests that a version of world may tend toward art in proportion to the enhanced complexity of its symbol system. This shift is relevant to our context only to the extent that it represents an exemplification of the fictive.

Goodman names five criteria that must be fulfilled if a fabricated version is to be viewed as art:

> (1) syntactic density, where the finest differences in certain respects constitute the difference between symbols ... (2) semantic density, where symbols are provided for things distinguished by the finest differences in certain respects ... (3) relative repleteness, where comparatively many aspects of a symbol are significant ... (4) exemplification, where a symbol, whether or not it denotes, symbolizes by

serving as a sample of properties it literally or metaphorically possesses; and finally (5) multiple and complex reference, where a symbol performs several integrated and interacting referential functions,
some direct and some mediated through other symbols.[118]

What characterizes this listing of features is the insistence on a ramified
difference that, on the one hand, leads to syntactic and semantic density and, on the other, fans out the symbols into the spectrum of their
aspects in such a way that they give rise to multiple referentiality. By
implication, art occurs where the sliding difference is optimized. This
difference is then no longer to be understood as the boundary between
the versions that must be overstepped; nor does it mark the alternative
by means of which the versions of world determine one another; nor,
indeed, does it limit itself to distinctions that set in motion the process
of weighting, supplementing, deleting, and ordering that brings about
the restructuring of versions. Relieved of all these pragmatically oriented restrictions, difference turns into a network of relations, and
these turn into a differentiated multiplicity of possible references. The
smaller the pragmatic pressure, the greater the freedom of differential
interplay between decomposition and composition; the version of world
becomes art when this interplay presents itself as such. It follows that
syntactic and semantic density, the increased range and utilization of
significant aspects of symbols, and the resultant multiplicity of references are but manifestations allowing the game of interaction to be
perceived. Where the interplay is acted out, art begins, or the version of
world takes on the character of art.

Thus the work of art exemplifies a system of references whereby
the process of worldmaking can be made conceivable. But like everything else, the work of art is only a version of world; what sets it apart is
that it does not aim at a precise practical target, even if this does not
make it any less pragmatic than other versions. Its pragmatics consists
in exemplifying the operations through which worlds are made: "Exemplification is never fictive—the features or labels exemplified cannot be
null or vacuous—for an exemplified feature is present in, and an exemplified label denotes, at least the sample itself."[119] For this very reason,
exemplification through an artwork cannot be confined to a feature, a
pattern, an aspect, or even the explicit label *work of art*, although exemplification must entail individual characteristics. Instead, "what is
exemplified may be sought rather than found,"[120] for the features, patterns, and so on of a work of art are, as isolated parts of a whole, largely

indeterminate, not least because exemplification always implies relations between those elements which have been made explicit. Exemplification is therefore not merely an uncovering but consists in "discovering and applying what is exemplified."[121] The key to this is the sliding difference that gives rise to "fact from fiction." "Fiction, then, whether written or painted or acted, applies truly neither to nothing nor to diaphanous possible worlds but, albeit metaphorically, to actual worlds. . . . Fiction operates in actual worlds in much the same way as nonfiction. Cervantes and Bosch and Goya, no less than Boswell and Newton and Darwin, take and unmake and remake and retake familiar worlds, recasting them in remarkable and sometimes recondite but eventually recognizable—i.e. *re-cognizable*—ways."[122]

Since all processes of worldmaking—at least structurally—are more or less identical, they can be distinguished only through their pragmatic aims. Exemplifying such a process entails multiplying references and complicating their referential networks,[123] thereby bringing into play a double coding of the sliding difference: it produces the chains of reference, and at the same time is differentiated by them. As this relationship is to be exemplified by the work of art, it reveals how versions of world are made.

Goodman's constructivist approach—and perhaps constructivism in general—presents a strikingly circular argument. If *a* world version becomes paradigmatic for worldmaking, this is mainly because one can only talk of what happens on this side of referentiality. But what the paradigm shows is a differentiation brought about between types of reference, the opening up of referential roots, and the multiplication of referential chains. This means that the work of art cannot be more than a complex system of syntactic relations or, at best, a continually expanding process of regulation, which frames a game whose rules have to be found. The multiplicity of references indicates that there is a constant need to contain the fictive within frames of reference, though the result is a mobile referential system rather than a referential definition of the fictive.

In this context, too, it seems that the fictive entails boundary-crossing, which here takes place between world versions. If the work of art does indeed exemplify this process, it does so by embodying a version that is relieved of all situational pragmatics, thereby gaining its own pragmatic purpose through an illumination of worldmaking. To this function, however, the work of art remains confined. "What a portrait or a novel exemplifies or expresses often reorganizes a world more drastically than does what the work literally or figuratively says or depicts; and sometimes the subject serves merely as a vehicle for what is exemplified or expressed."[124] If the artwork is basically relevant as an exemplification of worldmaking, it is identified with a syntagmatic network of its chains of reference, and this reduction is the price that must be paid if "fact from fiction" is to be exemplified. If the artwork is primarily to be viewed as a reference for worldmaking, important features of it will definitely be eclipsed. Goodman, for instance, rightly points out that his thesis will not allow any statement about good or bad art.[125] Yet constructivism needs art to endow its approach with plausibility. It is therefore only of secondary importance whether Goodman intended to develop a new orientation for the integration of art and science,[126] although this is undoubtedly what he has done.

Of far greater significance is the bringing out of the circularity of the constructivist concept "fact from fiction." The circularity indicates that fiction cannot be cognitively grasped, let alone ontologically grounded, so that of all versions of world, one must seek the one that can exemplify what happens when fact comes from fiction. Weighting, deleting, supplementing, and ordering are what must be exemplified, since these operations disappear once the version of world has been made. As themselves they can be pinpointed only through the differentiating intensity of their operations, but this presupposes that all world versions are organized syntagmatically. If the circularity does not become a vicious circle, this is mainly because the work of art "reorganizes" what otherwise would always be lost. Recapturing what happens in all processes of worldmaking is likewise, as a matter of repetition, "fact from fiction"; indeed, it makes the fictive into a condition for unstoppable repetition, but because this repetition defies all possible referentiality, Goodman has recourse to pluralism "about the *purposes* as well as about the content of cognition."[127]

The significance of art grows in proportion to the decline of the pre-given reality with which the epistemological subject was considered to be confronted. So long as epistemology was based on the subject/object division, science always took precedence over art, especially when skepticism acknowledged nothing but contact with or, at best, the processing of phenomena. Processing, however, is already latent constructivism, even if only in terms of mode and not of pragmatic targeting. For bringing phenomena within the reach of conception—by projecting sensations onto them as if these were inherent qualities—appears, from the constructivist point of view, as a kind of scaffolding with which to shore up epistemological premises. If one renounces the substantialist view of reality, or, in other words, "if reality is what one stipulates (rather than finds)," then "the range of stipulation is great, and what one makes of what one has stipulated is not something to be determined by quick intuition."[128] For now one needs to weigh the achievements of the constructs, and this requires a multiplicity of them in order to find out, by way of comparison, what parameters the constructs are able to cover. The result, however, will only be a taxonomic plurality, although this would have to remain accessible to cognition if pluralism were to have any sense. The necessary orientation for such a process is provided by the work of art, which advances to the status of a central paradigm when construction itself is to be exemplified.

The Chameleon of Cognition: Some Conclusions about Fiction

It is clear from our discussion of the paradigms of fiction as thematized in philosophical discourse that the same term was continually used to mean something different. So long as fiction was subjected to criticism, it was defined—despite the many variations on the theme of unmasking—with relative consistency as an aberration of the human mind. Only when it was seen affirmatively did a shift begin in the view of what it might actually be. Since its use kept changing, and it was identified with its use, it could have no permanent identity, for the use testifies to the function and not to the foundation.

From the eighteenth century onward, however, fiction was used for purposes of cognition that in turn was able to make such a function plausible but was not able to provide any ontological foundation. Fiction became the elusive target for conceptualization, and it owed its protean character to the variety of attempts that were made to grasp it. The criticism of fiction turned out to be an easier task, since it could take for granted the recognizability of what was to be unmasked. But even the negative slant on fiction already contained hints of the dichotomy through which the character of fiction rapidly began to change, once its necessity became firmly established. Thus for Bacon idol and hypothesis were both forms of representation, with the idol reifying the schema of conceivability, and the hypothesis taking this schema to be a testing ground for cognition of Nature's laws. So long as there were no boundaries to cognition, fictions were not necessary, so that Bacon's hypothesis did not represent a heuristic fiction. Structurally, however, a dichotomy is adumbrated here. It is not yet made explicit, because the idol relates exclusively to a totally convention-bound human subject, while the hypothesis relates to the certainty of existing natural laws. But once this certainty had disappeared, a gulf opened up between the subject and a cognitively inaccessible reality, a gulf that necessitated bringing together what Bacon regarded as two irreconcilable elements.

The affirmation of fiction therefore entails a mental amalgamation of things that are categorically different. As a result, from that time on, fiction was drawn into the epistemological subject/object division, its nature changing according to the current perception of cognition's boundaries. Its thematization is an epitome of epistemological deficiencies that, in view of epistemology's aspirations to universal validity, have to be compensated for. And so from Kant's As-if through Bentham's multiple uses of "fictitious entities" right up to Vaihinger's proliferating types and models, fiction assumes increasing importance. This development is proportionate to the degree to which reality is taken to elude cognition. But even relativism, nominalism and pluralism are unable to dispense with fiction that now becomes a differential, marking distinctions as a precondition for transformation.

If, in the course of its thematization, fiction can be so many different things, then clearly whatever it might be resists conceptualization. But this observation may also be turned the other way: since conceptualization keeps striving to define fiction, fiction becomes a reflection of the blindness inherent in conceptualization. This is paradoxical, insofar as fiction—whether in relation to epistemology, nominalism, or constructivism—is meant to compensate for or to achieve something that is not covered by the systems. Since the repairs will clearly be conditioned by the theories that need repair, those theories determine what is necessary to enable them to function properly. Thus fiction becomes the chameleon of cognition, which means that as a sort of repair kit for conceptualization, it must inevitably transcend the concepts it seeks to encompass. In compensating for the weaknesses of the concept, the thematization of fiction diagnoses the deficiencies that are basic to the respective theory, and in this way the indeterminableness of thematized fiction can claim its truth. This truth, however, appears to be inaccessible to cognition and, consequently, fiction was always identified with lying as long as knowledge remained an uncontested frame of reference.

As a lie, fiction was endowed with a predicate that simultaneously was regarded as its foundation. It has also carried a similar burden of attributes through the history of its affirmation, for the study of its functions has entailed speculation on its 'nature'. The thematization of fiction has therefore developed as a series of changing predications, all of which lead ultimately to providing fiction with some kind of substratum. These substrata change continually—they may be idols, linguistic signifiers, or ideas, though these by no means exhaust the list of predicates. It is only when fiction becomes the differential between decomposition and composition that it at last dispenses with the foundations imposed on it. These changing predicates arose, however, out of its different functions, and not out of the supposed nature of fiction; each function, therefore, was considered to have originated from the quality of the underlying character of fiction, so that the function could be made plausible by means of a supposed basis. All predications were matters of strategy, not of definition, for the overriding aim was to make comprehensible the workings of something that was functionally necessary but not knowable. The qualities ascribed to fiction were therefore expressions of the control needed to reduce the risks inherent in the indispensable use of fiction. As a consequence, fiction always appears *as* something determinate, whereby the substrata imputed reveal themselves to be a mode of ascription that can quite easily be replaced by other ascriptions of fiction *as* something else.

If a mode of ascription is taken for the 'nature' of fiction, the result is reification, and fiction begins to assume the character of the idol. This need not be an idol in Bacon's sense of the word, for fiction itself is not equated with those realities within which it functions; but as a tangible structure it is a product, whereas in fact it only functions as an operation. This applies from Kant through to Goodman. It is therefore logical that in postmodern discourse, reification has been totally expunged from fiction, so that the wiped-out traces of all imputed substrata expose fiction as a simulacrum.[129] If fiction is present as an empty form, the form can represent fictionalizing itself that—as feigning something—has, in the history of thematized fiction, either collapsed into or been equated with its own product.

If this history has proceeded as a progressive emptying out of all the predications, contents, and features ascribed to fiction, it nevertheless testifies to the urge to find out what fiction is. In the course of such investigations, fiction always appears to have both a function and a location. For Bentham it functions as a modality for representing otherwise impenetrable realities but is located in language, which as such he does not see as fiction. If fiction is identified with linguistic designation, such nominalism takes into account the insight that the appearance of things requires representation when they are to be used. The predominance of representation disappears with Vaihinger, although he, too, still distinguishes between function and location. Fiction makes it possible to project sensations as assumed qualities of things, but it is located in the idea. The latter is certainly more ephemeral and diaphanous than language, but it gains a tangible structure by switching its anchorage from linguistic designation to the realm of idea. Goodman appears generally to remove the distinction between function and location, so that only traces are left of this strange intent to provide a tangible base for the function of fiction. Indeed, it is only these traces that still permit a degree of insight into fiction, which otherwise remains ungraspable even though it continues to function prolifically. By specifying differences, fiction becomes relevant for versions of worldmaking, and the unfolding of mobile referential systems shows that it is not totally without location. The vestiges of these locations point to the fact that fiction always precedes the versions and at the same time outlines what they will become. This makes it the keystone of nominalist constructivism.

From all this we may draw certain conclusions about the thematizing of fiction. First, the distinction between function and location denotes that fiction must always be situated where there is certainty of a reality—however this may be constituted—which must be worked on because of deficiencies in our knowledge of it. In light of this function, continuing to situate fiction means continuing to cling to the basic conditions of epistemology, for to operate beyond the borders of cognition requires starting points whose reality appears to be uncontestable: language and idea. Only when these conditions no longer apply does fiction, ceasing to be something tangible, elude cognition and, at best, manifest itself as a differential that in turn is changed by what it has changed.

Second, the gradual disappearance of the distinction between function and location indicates the historically observable shift from fiction as representation to fiction as intervention. If fiction is nothing but representation, it turns, as the reification of itself, into an idol. Hence the split between different entities so evident in Bentham, for whom the appearances of things are represented for the purpose of being qualified. Vaihinger's concern is to use models and types in order to manipulate the unrepresentable reality to the extent that it may become open to intervention. Fiction thus turns into an instrument of processing. The decrease in fiction as representation corresponds to an increase in fiction as intervention, both of which are reflected in changes in the manifestation of its character in philosophical discourse. As pure intervention in a world version produced by preceding interventions, it loses even its instrumental character, which disappears in the vestiges of differential operational modes.

Third, in such a change, the pragmatic significance of fiction for action becomes unmistakable. Such a significance is no longer the object of cognition but is gauged in proportion to the success achieved, the measurement of which is set by the requirements of the contextual usage. What remains to be cognized under these conditions is subordinate to the changing practical aim pertinent to the situation, so that fiction can have neither an independent form nor a fixed location, let alone be a product. As an act of boundary-crossing, it can be adequately described only if worlds are to be constituted in which actions are to be performed. Instead of repairing epistemology, fiction—in the history of its affirmation—becomes a precondition for pragmatic action.

If we want to say something about fiction itself, the approach should not be through cognition but through art. If we look back over the paradigms discussed, art does not illuminate fiction whenever—notwithstanding the reservations of epistemological skepticism—the givenness of reality remains unquestioned. Bentham needed fiction because things were present only as appearances, and these required designation suitable to their status if they were not to be treated as 'things'. When 'fictitious entities' had to be exemplified, he always turned to legal fictions, which were well known to be firmly anchored in Roman law and thus could offer a clear-cut illustration of the function of fiction. The oldest acknowledged fiction was for Bentham a paradigm of his breakthrough to the affirmation of fiction.

Vaihinger speaks—even if only occasionally—of aesthetic fictions, but he mentions them mainly in order to ensure that his catalog of fictions is complete. For him, aesthetic fiction is only one among many, and in contrast to scientific fictions he does not seem quite to know what to do with it. Of course, like all other fictions, it is determined by its practical use, but the use in question appears to be nothing but a cliché of classical aesthetics: "The aesthetic fiction and its theoretical explanation are, in part, closely related to the scientific fiction; and this is quite natural when we remember that the same elementary psychical processes contributed to the construction of both. Aesthetic fictions serve the purpose of awakening within us certain uplifting or otherwise important feelings. Like the scientific, they are not an end in themselves but a means for the attainment of higher ends."[130] The aesthetic fiction, in this view, has no special function of its own; the question remains open as to whether these "higher ends" are anything more than the dying echoes of classical aesthetics.

For Goodman, on the other hand, the ways of worldmaking are bodied forth in art. This may ultimately be because a plurality of worlds can have no single transcendental vantage point. Consequently, basic operations of worldmaking, if they are to be grasped at all, can be exemplified only through paradigms. Largely relieved of the burden of answering pragmatic necessities, art becomes a reference for the process of worldmaking, which would otherwise elude referentiality altogether, because it is groundless.

Exemplification, however, means that the 'ways' can never be presented in their totality; there will always be selected samples, features, patterns, referential networks, interventions, and combinations, each of which will be singled out in the process of exemplification. This is also true when exemplification changes into denotation and the latter becomes expression, and when referential roots are opened up and ramify into referential chains. Even though exemplification does endow its examples with a generalizing tendency, it can in no way cover the complexity of phenomena. This is ultimately linked to the fact that, for all its many applications, exemplification is a reference that, in relation to fiction, indicates the limits of referentiality. In other words, exemplification splits fiction into what is still open to cognition and what can be supplied only by the imagination. Subjecting fiction to reference makes it double-edged: it exceeds knowability and simultaneously pricks imagination into action, making conceivable whatever stretches beyond the bounds of reference.

In philosophical discourse, thematized fiction is marked by a conspicuous ambivalence. This ambivalence permeates fiction thematized in philosophical discourse, whose attempt at grasping fiction reveals boundary-crossing as its hallmark. If that, in turn, has not been suffi-ciently thematized, it is due to the fact that in the history of affirmation of fiction, boundary-crossing has always been instrumentalized for the changing purposes to be tackled. As an extension of human beings, fiction makes it possible for them to operate beyond their limitations. This may entail bringing within the necessary pragmatic bounds states of affairs that transcend language (Bentham) or consciousness (Vaihin-ger) or existing world versions (Goodman), as well as enabling human beings to reach out into an otherwise inaccessible reality by way of readjusting it to prevailing exigencies. If the main concern is success—whether through action, processing, or rearranging—fiction does not mediate between reality and cognition but takes effect by boundary-crossing, that is, by bringing imagination into play in a process that cannot be captured by cognition and that, in the final analysis, defies referentiality. When cognition and referentiality find their boundaries in fiction, cognition begins to uncover anthropological necessities.

Chapter Four

The Imaginary

Historical Preliminaries

In spite of the common practice of calling novels "fiction," fictionality is not literature; it is what makes literature possible. The accepted definition of fiction as something invented tells us nothing about its effects, let alone its achievements. These can best be studied if we examine the interplay between the fictive and the other vital constituent of the literary text: the imaginary.

Before focusing on this interplay, we need to examine some basic conceptualizations of the imaginary, which largely resists definition. Despite this resistance the experience we have of the imaginary is self-evident and hence beyond doubt. The 'imaginary', a relatively modern term, has gained currency in the face of mounting skepticism concerning the 'true nature' of imagination and fantasy. Obviously this human potential manifests itself in different ways: With flights of fancy it can wander off into worlds of its own, or, as imagination, it can conjure up images, or, through the powers of the imagination, it can summon the absent into presence. Since such a multifaceted potential can be explored only in terms of its aspects, it is scarcely surprising that the history of imagination, or fantasy, frequently involves irreconcilable discourses, concerned sometimes with its grounding, sometimes with its status as an *ars combinatoria,* and sometimes with its status as a faculty.

A glance at foundational discourses reveals an unmistakable reduction, whereby fantasy is always subordinated to something else. Fantasy was regarded as perfection, in which art enabled human beings to participate[1]—an idea that held sway right through to Nietzsche, for whom art was to transform itself into perfection.[2] Yet it is here already that we are confronted by ambiguity: Is fantasy perfection, or simply the indispensable power that enables perfection to be achieved through art? Whichever it may be, the argument implies that perfection gains its character by running counter to existing realities; it takes on its form by means of something that has to be overcome.

There is a similar problem with concepts that take fantasy as otherness. The traditional invocation to the Muses equates this otherness with inspiration or invention, both of which entail bringing something into the world that was not there before. In this view, the appearance of fantasy creates an impact that cannot be deduced from anything that existed earlier. The otherness of inspiration was regarded as a kind of holy madness that impinged on the world and drove away those who were possessed by it.

A different approach is that of psychoanalysis. This links fantasy to the unconscious, subordinating it to "the laws of the primary process,"[3] although its vagrant "offsprings," which appear only before the conscious mind, require another reference if they are to be identified. And as desire, fantasy needs a "mirror stage" (Lacan's term) of the self in order to bring to light the reverse side of the ego.

All these definitions of fantasy—as perfection, otherness, part of the primary process, or desire—show that generally it can be grasped only within contexts, whether these be pedestrian realities, a world altered by inspiration, the mechanisms of the mind, or a deficiency that demands correction. No matter how different the contexts and related definitions may be, all reveal fantasy to be an event: It runs counter to imperfection, it changes the world it enters, it roams round the mind, or it offers the mirror image of frustrated desires. Repeatedly, fantasy appears not as a substance but as a function preceding what is, even though it can manifest itself only in what is.

The fact that foundational discourse brings out the eventful nature of fantasy reflects the uncontrollable character of the latter and hence the difficulty of definition. Confining it to its contexts—whatever may be their purpose—means using it, and often the purposes are confused with definition: as when, for instance, Adam Smith identifies imagination with sympathy because it enables one person to put himself in another's place.[4] Here the eventfulness is almost humanized in the sense that the process of imagining enables the difference between human beings to be bridged. But if fantasy is uncoupled from such contextual anchors, it may well run wild. Hume warned that in such cases "imagination is liable to become a cannibal and turn on itself"[5]— a view he shared with Goethe, who regarded imagination as a split faculty that was incomparable as a creative means of access to experience but became a source of terror once it was released from such tasks.[6]

If fantasy can become a source of terror or of self-destruction, its various definitions would seem to relate less to inherent qualities than to agents that govern its application. But then one must ask whether the context revealed by discourses is really a definition or in fact merely an attempt to channel the explosive powers of fantasy. If so, the history of fantasy is a history of attempts to control its arising from a doubleness that is inherent in fantasy itself. Its history, then, involves how it is made to serve purposes, so that it remains under control. It is only a change in emphasis to say that fantasy's ambiguous potential and its potential ambiguity are the source of its history.

In 1728 Zachary Mayne, in his *Two Dissertations Concerning Sense and the Imagination*, remarked that the imagination is "like the Chameleon, of which Creature it is reported, that it changes its Hue according to the Colour of the Place where it happens to be."[7] This was by no means the first attempt to gain a cognitive hold on fantasy. Already in the seventeenth century, increasing attention to it had once more focused on Aristotle's conception of fantasy as lying halfway between perception and thought. Hobbes takes up the distinction drawn between the Latin *imaginatio* and the Greek *phantasia*, with the former applied to the imagining of an object no longer present, and thus constituting a "decaying sense." But then Hobbes confuses the issue by calling this remembered perception *phantasia*: "This *decaying sense* ... I mean *fancy* itself, we call *imagination*."[8]

These recollected perceptions allow connections to be drawn that, in the eyes of the empiricists, give increasing importance to the imagination as an active means of combination. Locke, however, had little regard for it, although there can be no doubt that what he called "power of the mind"[9] is, in fact, that of the imagination. At the beginning of his *Essay*, in "The Epistle to the Reader," he writes: "*But every thing does not hit alike upon every Man's Imagination. We have our Understandings no less different than our Palates*" (p. 8). Later, however, he makes his views on the imagination abundantly clear: "Is there any thing so extravagant, as the Imaginations of Men's Brains? . . . But *of what use is all this fine Knowledge of Men's own Imaginations,* to a Man that enquires after the reality of Things?" (pp. 562f.). Despite its uncontrollable character, against which Locke warns all through the *Essay* (see pp. 104, 161, 698), the association of ideas ultimately needs the imagination if it is to function. This is evident from the locus classicus of Locke's philosophy: "As simple *Ideas* . . . exist in several Combinations united together; so the Mind has a power to consider several of them united together, as one *Idea*; and that not only as they are united in external Objects, but as it self [i.e., the mind] has join'd them. *Ideas* thus made up of several simple ones put together, I call *Complex*" (p. 164). Repeatedly, Locke circumscribes this power that unites ideas, but repeatedly his circumscriptions entail attributes traditionally applied to the imagination: "[The] faculty of repeating and joining together its *Ideas,* the Mind has great power in varying and multiplying the Objects of its Thoughts . . . The *Mind* often *exercises an active Power in the making these* several *Combinations.* For it being once furnished with simple *Ideas,* it can put them together in several Compositions, and so make variety of complex *Ideas,* without examining whether they exist so together in Nature" (pp. 164, 288). McFarland is therefore right to point out that "such concessions actually constitute a chink in the associationist armor for imagination as innate power to enter."[10] At the heart of empirical epistemology there is an empty space, and imagination is the "completing power," which even Hume recognized despite all his reservations as to its graspability.[11] As a means of combining, the imagination is identified with its function, but this results less from the imagination itself than from the need to give plausibility to the acquisition of knowledge from experience.

The fact that Locke ascribes this combining faculty to the mind while dismissing the imagination as, at best, a source of pleasure, is closely linked to the traditional hierarchy of the faculties, in which the imagination had always occupied a position inferior to that of reason. When Locke talks of the "power of the mind," this is less an explanation than an indication of how much the combination of ideas needs explaining. Hume then identifies the "completing power" with the imagination, and not with the mind. If we take the "power of the mind" to be the *asylum ignorantiae* of Locke's empiricism, we can trace the growing importance of the imagination as it first—almost illegally—occupies this empty space, and then rises in association psychology—which hailed from Locke—to become the recognized agent responsible for combining ideas.

The way had already been prepared by the poets and authors of the eighteenth century. According to Engell, Addison suggested that "the exercise or pleasure of the imagination depends on a full and directed interplay and integration of as many faculties and operations of the mind as possible."[12] Dr. Johnson—unlike Hobbes—considered imagination no longer a "decaying sense" but a central guide, linking past, present, and future together so as to enable us to hold a steady course in the midst of all the changes we undergo.[13]

So long as the eighteenth-century view of the imagination prevailed that it acted as a means of combining—and this applies particularly to the first generation of association psychologists—it was characterized mainly in accordance with the guidelines of empirical cognition; it was conceived of as a mechanistic operation linking together existing data. As such, it was used as a foundation for cognition without any satisfactory account of how it could achieve such a status. This lack, however, preoccupied the second generation of association psychologists, who revealed the imagination as a synthetic power by describing it as a process of dynamic flow that fuses heterogeneous elements into a unity.

The diverse descriptions of the imagination functioning as a combining agent all omit the objective that foundational discourse had sought to tackle: a definition of what imagination actually is. Hume used the terms "fancy" and "imagination" synonymously; he saw the imagination as "a kind of magical faculty in the soul, which, tho' it be always most perfect in the greatest geniuses, and is properly what we call a genius, is however inexplicable by the utmost efforts of human understanding."[14] He is far from being alone in this view. In the late 1780s Herder described the imagination as one of the least explored of all the human faculties, although in fact it represented the real link between body and mind.[15] Fichte, generally following Kant, took it to be the bridge between reason and the senses—a power "of which we are seldom or never conscious,"[16] although in his *Wissenschaftslehre* he stresses: "Here . . . it is taught that all reality is brought forth solely through the imagination."[17]

Thus in both idealist and empiricist philosophy the imagination was on its way to becoming the ground of all cognition. But while foundational discourse—regardless of the context used as reference— always set imagination/fantasy in relation to something else, the various functional descriptions led only to its unfathomableness. A function whose basis is inexplicable and a grounding that dwindles into a *regressus* only serve to bring out the ambiguity of imagination. Is it an evidential experience that defies conceptualization by discourse, or is it discourse that makes it ambiguous because imagination cannot be contained within its demarcations? What is obvious is that imagination changes according to the direction from which it is approached, and since no approach can ever encompass it in its entirety, it turns into a stimulant for an unceasing endeavor to define it. What, then, is it as itself?

The perennial answer to this question is "a faculty." And perennially, from Aristotle through the beginnings of the modern age, imagination has been regarded as an inferior faculty. Its original designations as either imagination or fantasy were often confused, and not until the end of the eighteenth century was greater care taken over the distinction.

Historically, association psychology was responsible for describing the work of this faculty in more detail. Imagination was seen as a form of explanation for the association of ideas, since received data could not of their own accord join together in more complex ideas. The problem was to explain how the combination was guided, and how it was possible to join disparate data. Attributing this function to the imagination meant equipping it with intentions, since the combination of data appears to originate in an intention. That writers and philosophers were already conscious of this, is evident in recurring discussions from Dryden through Hume concerning how one could distinguish the synthetic nature of imagination from that of judgment. This problem, however, arose only because the imagination was considered to be imbued with intentions that, being part of consciousness, could scarcely also be inherent in the imagination. But the more problematical these distinctions became, the more prominence was given to the facet of the imagination which Dr. Johnson defined in his *Dictionary* as "the power of forming ideal pictures; the power of representing things absent."[18] That such a definition should find its way into the dictionary is evidence of its currency at the time, as borne out again, and at rather greater length, by Lord Monboddo's *Origin and Progress of Language* (1773): "The imagination has . . . a creative power . . . is conversant with the future as well as the past, and paints . . . scenes that never did exist, and it is likely never will; for it may be said to create even the materials of those scenes . . . formed upon the model of objects that have been presented by the sense, and are, as it were, imitations of them."[19]

This view was to become a commonplace, rendering obsolete the concept developed by the association psychologists, a concept that had been based on the empirical theory of passive perception, which regarded everything in the mind as having been put there by the senses. According to this understanding, there was no way to explain how the imagination's productivity had come into the mind; and as the mind was nothing but a tabula rasa, imagination must be antecedent to the mind, not least because it could also produce pictures of things that did not exist as objects. Furthermore, the combinations that imagination brought about had no correspondence in reality.

What may well have been the most important eighteenth-century analysis of the imagination as a faculty was that of Johann Nicolas Tetens. His analysis adopted—even with its examples—essential points of the empiricists' association of ideas. While Locke took the centaur as an illustration of "fantastical ideas,"[20] Tetens takes Pegasus as an example of illuminating the faculty of *Dichtkraft* (poetic power). We receive, he says, as "sensations" both a picture of the horse and a picture of the wings;[21] linking them together is simply a mechanistic activity, although the image of Pegasus does entail more than the combination of two sets of data: "The wings of Pegasus may have been a pure phantasm in the head of the first poet to have brought forth this picture; and the idea of the horse as well. But there is a place in the picture at the shoulders of the horse, somewhat darker than the others, where the wings are attached to the body; there the pictures of the horse's shoulders and of the wings' roots merge into one another; there, then, is a self-made semblance that vanishes if the picture of the horse and the picture of the wings are again clearly separated from one another" (p. 118). What had been omitted by the empirical association of ideas now stands at the very center of Tetens's analysis. If "sensations" imprint themselves on the soul, the latter has the power to continue the sensations and to conceive what in the meantime has disappeared, so that ultimately it can "mix [such] phantasms . . . together and make the new ones out of them" (p. 122).

The variety of such activities splits the faculty into three separate ones: "Therefore we attribute to the soul not only the faculty of absorbing ideas into itself (*facultas percipiendi*), a power of comprehension, but also a faculty of bringing them forth again, a POWER OF RE-CONCEP-

TION, which we normally call FANTASY or IMAGINATION . . . insofar as it renews pictorial ideas of sensation" (p. 24). The FACULTY OF POETRY" (p. 24), however, is a "DEVELOPING, DISSOLVING and REUNITING . . . BRING-ING TOGETHER and MERGING" (p. 117).

"Faculty of perception" and "power of re-conception" reflect both the empirical and the Aristotelian traditions. What Locke had called "power of the mind" has here become "power of comprehension," making available the modifications of the soul wrought by sensations to be processed according to need. What Hobbes had called a "decaying sense" has now become "power of re-conception," enabling "recurring, weakened sensations" to be grasped through "imaginings" (p. 50). But the "power of poetry" is "independent fantasy; GENIUS according to Herrn GIRARD's description, and undoubtedly an essential ingredient of genius" (p. 107).

Tetens's division of one faculty into several is significant for the history of the concept of the imagination.[22] For him the division arises out of the different activities of perception, ideation, and production, and the peculiarities of the now divided faculty are to be defined according to the functions they are meant to perform. This does not, however, mean that the particular application constitutes the definition of the faculty, for clearly what enables the imagination to be deployed precedes the actual deployment. Thus neither the context in which the faculty works nor the faculty itself can determine what the imagination is. Traditional faculty psychology had no problem in this regard, because the imagination was simply assessed through its relation to other faculties, the link apparently solidifying the explanation. But the attempt to understand the imagination as itself meant splitting it into multiple faculties, each endowed with its salient feature, and each providing a backdrop for the other.

As a power of "perception and re-conception," the imagination in its different forms will be determined by the demands made on it. The question of how it works remains unanswered and becomes critical when one seeks to explain the production of new images fashioned out of "sensations." Tetens attributes this "power" to "independent fantasy" that evidently becomes active of its own accord and needs no further impetus. How is this to be understood? Tetens tries to explain this problem by linking all three faculties to the soul, which for the eighteenth century represented the whole. He asks the following rhetorical question: "Is the FACULTY to PERCEIVE, that is to absorb with sensation

conceptions of present objects, of a kind with the second faculty to
REPRODUCE these conceptions in the absence of the objects, and are both
of a kind with the third faculty, the power of poetry, and to what extent
are they all one and the same faculty?"[23] He answers thus:

> Every impression on it [i.e., the soul] is an impression on a perfectible,
> self-activating power ... that not only allows something to happen
> within itself, but also takes it up actively, holding and grasping it. No
> new, absolute quality is to be added, but only through an enlargement
> and reinforcement of the existing principle, and through a TRANSITION
> from IMPERCEPTIBLE TO PERCEPTIBLE self-activation, from DISPOSITION TO
> CAPABILITY and through an extension and development of its capacity
> to store within itself all the different impressions in adequately sepa-
> rated compartments, does the receptiveness of our soul turn into a
> perceiving, reproducing and poeticizing power. All the above-men-
> tioned effects reveal one and the same principle, the same basic
> power, the same modes of effect, and the same faculties. (p. 164)

Since the faculties are all of the soul, their activities spring from the
unity underlying them. But the difficulty of comprehending the soul as
the underlying totality is evident from the fact that at best the soul
manifests itself through the effectiveness of its faculties, though these
manifestations are bound to preconditions that are not part of the soul
itself. The poetic power is similarly restricted, for it "cannot create any
elements, any basic material, cannot create nothing out of nothing, and
to this extent is not a creative power. It can only separate, dissolve,
bind, blend, but for this very reason it cannot produce new images"
(p. 139).

This is a highly progressive insight. Everything in the imagination
has come from elsewhere, and ultimately this means that the imagination is not self-activating but needs activating stimuli from outside
itself. Though linking the multiple faculties to the soul, Tetens does not
quite follow his argument through to its logical conclusion; since even
the "poetic power" needs given circumstances to bring it into operation, the inescapable impression remains that the imagination as a
faculty is a blank which resists filling by whatever faculty psychology
has proposed.

This seems to have been sensed by several eighteenth-century
writers, such as Dugald Stewart and Thomas Brown. Their ideas were
certainly not put forward as responses to Tetens, but they, too, circle the
problem that he approached but ultimately left unanswered. Stewart

sees the imagination as a "complex power" that differs from all other faculties in that it

> includes Conception of simple Apprehension, which enables us to form a notion of those former objects of perception or of knowledge out of which we are to make a selection; Abstraction, which separates the selected materials from the qualities and circumstances which are connected with them in nature; and Judgment or Taste, which selects the materials, and directs their combination. To these powers, we may add that particular habit of association to which I formerly gave the name of Fancy; as it is this which presents to our choice all the different materials which are subservient to the efforts of imagination, and which may therefore be considered as forming the groundwork of poetical genius. (pp. 435f.)

Since the imagination itself produces an alliance of faculties that Tetens had seen as springing from the soul, it seems only natural that Stewart should describe it finally as "the great spring of human activity, and the principal source of human improvement."[24] By bringing different abilities to work on each other, the imagination reveals itself to be a power of fusion that extends human beings beyond themselves.

This coalescence has repercussions on the notion of imagination as a faculty; it now begins more and more to assume the character of a process, as can be seen from a phrase of Thomas Brown, who seeks to track down the imagination's "spontaneous chemistry of the mind." This is "not the exercise of a *single power,* but the development of various *susceptibilities,*—of *desire,*—of *simple suggestion,* by which conceptions rise after conceptions,—of judgment or relative *suggestion,* by which a feeling of relative fitness or unfitness arises, on the contemplation of the conceptions that have thus spontaneously presented themselves . . . We may term this complex state, or series of states, imagination, or fancy,—and the term may be convenient for its *brevity.*"[25] What Tetens had seen as three faculties separated from one another according to the task they were to perform, Brown dissolves some forty years later into interacting forces that gain salience by becoming the backdrop for one another; he highlights the imagination as a dynamic process.

As we have seen, imagination manifests itself only as an impact on relationships brought about by forces external to it, and, therefore, is to a large extent conditioned by them. This is evident from the three basic paradigms that permeate its history. *Foundational discourse* related fantasy/imagination to something else but could not decide whether it was the medium enabling this something to appear, or whether it needed the something in order to appear itself. The *combining activity* ascribed to imagination by empiricism served to overcome a deficiency in the concept of the association of ideas but gave rise to the question of whether the imagination was always invoked when reason had reached its limits, or whether imagination needed deficiencies in order to come into operation. Finally, as an independent *faculty* imagination became subject to internal distinctions: being split into several faculties, or combining all other faculties, or changing what it had itself produced. There is also the question of whether one faculty can be a plurality of faculties, or whether this plurality in fact shows that the imagination as such can never be objectified. The variety of paradigms reveals, then, that the indefinability of imagination does not spring solely from the inadequacy of discourse but, rather, has no identity of its own; as itself it appears to be indeterminate.

If discourse is to capture the actual character of fancy, or fantasy, or imagination, interventions from outside are necessary. Indeed, these concepts in themselves can be seen as interventions seeking to uncover an anthropological attribute of human beings that does not seem to have a foundation of its own. Adjusting the concept of imagination to preconceived notions, discourse becomes myth, epitomizing a cultural code rather than expressing a cognitive grasp of what stretches beyond grasping. Thus the history of conceptualizing fancy, fantasy, or imagination runs like a mythology of the imaginary which mirrors the historical requirements that have called upon this potential power. Initially the imagination had occupied a lower rank, not least because, through its link to the senses and memory, it was present as a latent subversion, if not an actual defiance, of a reason-dominated hierarchy.

But in the sixteenth century, imagination began its advance, and toward the end of the eighteenth, it gained prominence thanks to its multiple uses. When it became a matter of trying to take possession of the empirical world, knowledge had to be wrested from experience, which meant processing the data that found their way into the mind. From Hobbes to Hartley it was imagination/fantasy that took on this task. And when the task was accomplished, one could turn to the power itself in order to find out what made its achievements possible. So long as epistemological premises prevailed, philosophers such as Hume and Kant regarded this faculty as something mysterious and, in the final analysis, impenetrable. But when, in late classicism and early Romanticism, the subject and self-realization became the all-important issues, imagination was given such clear-cut definitions that it appeared to be knowable. That this knowability smacks of gnosticism indicates the extent to which discourse held sway over imagination. With the self-fashioning of the subject, the imagination advanced to the head of the faculty hierarchy, only to fall dramatically when the self became a matter of dispute.

But even the concept of imagination as a faculty shows up the limits of intervention by discourse. In the most determinate descriptions of this ever-expanding faculty, the conceptual definitions melt away into metaphors that unravel this "power" into a series of images for an activity that for the most part cannot be conceptualized. The abundance of metaphors also sheds light on the differentiation of the faculty, which proliferates into so many shapes because its preceding history must be incorporated and reworked into the new context. This reworking constitutes what Blumenberg calls "work on myth," which entails a constant reshuffling of what has been inherited. The reshuffling indicates that what is called fancy or fantasy or imagination cannot be objectified, for it is not an entity but an activity.

For all this, it must be conceded that without such changing conceptualizations, the imaginary would remain meaningless. What we know as perception and idea, dream and daydream, phantasm and hallucination bear witness to a multifarious manifestation of the imaginary. Of these, perception appears to be the activity least permeated by the imaginary, but there are countless instances that suggest otherwise. Hume, Kant, and Wittgenstein all showed, in their different ways, that perception could not come into being without the participation of this 'potential'. It functions neither as optical registration nor as pure imagining. Above all, the continuity and identity of the object perceived can be ascertained only with the aid of an imaginary component, which means that an impression can be formed only if actual perception is combined with nonactual perception. Referring to Kant, P. F. Strawson summed up the process as follows: "Insofar as we have supplied anything like an explanation or justification of Kant's apparently technical use of 'imagination,' we have done so by suggesting that the recognition of an enduring object of a certain kind *as* an object of that kind, or as a certain particular object of that kind, involves a certain sort of connection with other nonactual perceptions. It involves other past (and hence nonactual) perceptions, or the thought of other possible (and hence nonactual) perceptions, of the *same* object being somehow alive in the present perception."[26]

The same applies to Wittgenstein: If seeing functions principally as 'seeing as', then the object is identified with the aspect of it that is being perceived. Mary Warnock formulates it as follows:

> In concentrating on the particular kind of seeing which he [i.e., Wittgenstein] calls seeing an aspect he has done two things. First he has linked at least *this* kind of seeing (or hearing) with knowing or having concepts; and in some cases he has linked it as well with the use of the imagination. Secondly, he has connected the actual use of images with some cases of aspect-seeing and has strongly suggested their use in cases of recognition . . . We may therefore quite legitimately argue that he has raised again the question raised by Hume and Kant as to the role in *all* perceptions (not just aspect-seeing) of the imagination; and that the connexion between perception and imagination is through the image itself (for the notion of aspects and that of images are, as he says, akin). Wherever seeing and hearing seem to take us beyond the actual immediate object of the senses . . . there it looks as if Wittgenstein . . . has left room for the imagination.[27]

If, as Strawson suggests, a perceived object derives its stability from a backgrounded, nonactual perception "being somehow alive" and shaping the particular, actual perception, then there is more than just recourse to memory, for in the course of perception, details are not recalled; instead, what is present is the whole store of virtual perceptions committed to memory that give salience to the present one, thereby stabilizing the actual object to be perceived. If the imaginary conjures up a range of nonactual perceptions, it simultaneously moves as a differential between that range and the actual perception and, being indeterminate, allows for the determinacy of the actual perception that acquires its individual stability against the backdrop of the nonactual ones.

Wittgenstein's "aspect-seeing" has a similar structure. If the aspect is just the image of part of an object, the image clearly contains its own limitations that lure perception into reaching beyond the comprehending powers of the senses. Here the productivity of difference is not the same as that suggested by Strawson; by limiting the image to being an aspect, it turns into a possible producer of aspect images. But still this tells us nothing about the nature of the interaction, or why an imaginary component is needed to stabilize the perception of an individual object. In any event, however, it is clear that such nonactual aspect images must always precede objects in order to turn them into objects of perception.

If the imaginary plays a role even in perception—its conceptualization as difference or as differential merely indicating its intangibility—the imaginary component increases in ideas, dreams, daydreams, and hallucinations. They are all different manifestations through which the imaginary takes on an experiential existence. As an idea, the imaginary gives presence to what is absent, guided by knowledge and memory: as a dream, it is the confinement of the dreamer to his or her images; as a daydream, it is a fading of gestalts to featurelessness; and as hallucination, it is consciousness overwhelmed. Perhaps it is only in madness that the imaginary takes on a comparatively pure presence; but even madness has forms that might either ossify the imagination through vagrant consciousness or drive intentionality out of consciousness. For madness, like all other phenomena, has the nature of a product, and the imaginary always bears the imprint of its contextually conditioned result.

This fact, however, means: The imaginary does not produce its own salience, which comes about through interplay with the factors that have mobilized it. The factors that influence the manifestation of the imaginary will vary in their complexity. In perception, it is visual anticipation governed by intentional projections that release the imaginary. In the idea, the imaginary is directed by memory-laden, cognitive factors aiming at presenting the absent or the nongiven. The dream is dominated by consciousness that the imaginary is nothing but imagistic, although consciousness has no control over the images. In the daydream, the imaginary plays with our preoccupations, producing projected gestalts and then snuffing them out. In the hallucination, the imaginary triumphs over consciousness, which is present only as mutilated intentionality.

The above-mentioned factors all endow the imaginary with its shape, but they, in turn, also undergo changes when mobilizing the imagination. Consequently, a mutual transformation occurs, indicating that the imaginary becomes tangible only in terms of products—perception, idea, dream, and so on—that are not exclusively products of the imagination. If the imaginary is present only in such manifestations, any attempt at conceptualizing its origin or ground is bound to end in failure, as is borne out by the growing inflation of concepts that were meant to fathom it. Owing to the urge of getting to know what it is, the imaginary has continually been forced into pigeonholes that do not fit. The massive revaluation, however, that it has enjoyed since Romanticism has been more concerned with its operational nature, which involves the interplay with the factors that mobilize it. Although the Romantics saw the imagination as a faculty—albeit one that needed differentiation if justice was to be done to its importance—the subsequent substitution of the term *imaginary* for previous terminology shows clearly that it began to be viewed as a basic act of relating us to the world. As a result the imaginary finally advanced to the status of Ur-fantasy.

Faculty, act, and the *radical imaginary* will therefore be the guiding concepts in our attempt to pin down the manifestations of the imaginary as they emerge from the different activities. Discourse remains unavoidable, but this exploration will be aimed less at a definition of the imaginary than at a clarification of what happens during these activities. The nature of the event will vary according to the source that sets it in motion: the subject (faculty), consciousness (act), or social institutionalization (radical imaginary). As a historical sequence, this line of reconceptualization testifies to the growing importance of the imaginary, which changes from a power to an act that annihilates what is, and eventually to a kind of *materia prima.*

Similarly, the approaches vary in accordance with the premises that govern the assessment of the imaginary. Philosophical idealism conceives it in terms of faculty, phenomenological psychology in terms of act, and social theory in terms of radical imaginary. Since the imaginary is able to assume such variegated shapes, its protean character will again be differently delineated if, instead of subject (faculty), consciousness (act), or social institutionalization (radical imaginary), the fictive becomes the mobilizing agent in the literary text. In order to spotlight this particular interplay, it is necessary to have a backdrop against which the mutual interpenetration of the fictive and the imaginary in the literary text can be perceived. As the workings of the imaginary are conditioned by its stimulants, the fictive will imprint itself on the imaginary differently than do the stimulants that are meant to meet pragmatic ends by tapping the imaginary. And as there is no normative assessment of even the workings of the imaginary, the resultant interplay can only be analyzed comparatively.

The Imagination as Faculty (Coleridge)

The last significant attempt to grasp the imagination as a faculty was made by Coleridge, though he changed the inherited notion to such an extent that the time-honored faculty concept ceased to be the overarching view of the imagination. Although the much quoted tripartition into "fancy," "secondary imagination," and "primary imagination" was not Coleridge's own,[28] he emphasized that it was his "object to investigate the seminal principle, and then from the kind to deduce the degree."[29] "Repeated meditations led me first to suspect, (and a more intimate analysis of the human faculties, their appropriate marks, functions, and effects matured my conjecture into full conviction,) that fancy and imagination were two distinct and widely different faculties, instead of being, according to the general belief, either two names with one meaning, or, at furthest, the lower and higher degree of one and the same power" (pp. 60f.).

This statement is important insofar as Coleridge did not attempt to develop the principle of differentiation but instead ended the first volume of *Biographia Literaria* with a letter from a friend who, for all his good will toward Coleridge, clearly felt that the explanation of the differences given to him stood the world on its head: "*your opinions and method of argument were not only so new to me, but so directly the reverse of all I had ever been accustomed to consider as truth, that even if I had comprehended your premises sufficiently to have admitted them, and had seen the necessity of your conclusions, I should still have been in that state of mind, which . . . you have so ingeniously evolved, as the antithesis to that in which a man is, when he makes a* bull" (p. 199). Unfortunately, we do not know what these arguments were, but the reaction to them shows that Coleridge's division of the imagination into multiple faculties was regarded as a radical break with tradition.

This is consistent with Coleridge's concept of faculties in general, as can be seen from a remark made in 1818: "As every faculty, with every the minutest organ of our nature, owes its whole reality and comprehensibility to an existence incomprehensible and groundless, because the ground of all comprehension."[30] The groundlessness of every faculty echoes Schelling's statement that "the ground is, against that for which it is the ground, not existent."[31] For what is, cannot be of the same quality as the source from which it springs. But this does not mean that the inaccessible ground will be lost sight of or forgotten. For

Coleridge it is not even mysterious—as it was still for Hume—for that would mean giving precedence to the intellect as the ultimate referential authority. Furthermore, one can leave a mysterious origin to itself so long as the workings of the faculty can be grasped through experience. But evidently this was not enough for Coleridge. The above-quoted passage continues: "not without the union of all that is essential in all the functions of our spirit, not without an emotion tranquil from its very intensity, shall we worthily contemplate in the magnitude and integrity of the world that life-ebullient stream which breaks through every momentary embankment, again, indeed, and evermore to embank itself, but within no banks to stagnate or be imprisoned."[32]

The stream metaphor makes vivid the groundlessness of the faculties, although it has to be twisted if it is to show what Schelling called "not existent." For the stream, precisely because it can be understood only by way of its activity, constantly flows in a double movement: It floods its banks but always "embanks" itself again. Here we have a play of differences that inscribes the groundlessness of the faculties into their operations. Indeed, the differences are the conditions that enable the faculties to manifest themselves as activities. But since activity only embodies the function of the faculties that the play of difference unfolds, the ground of the faculties clearly lies in neither. This groundlessness is what, in fact, brings the faculties to life. It is therefore little wonder that Coleridge's friend was shocked by the new description of the imagination: *"In short, what I had supposed substances were thinned away into shadows, while everywhere shadows were deepened into substances"*;[33] for now, as we may deduce, the split faculty is no longer to be viewed as an alliance of faculties as it was by Tetens. Instead, a differentiated spiritual "basic power" (in Tetens's words) is replaced by difference, which as the indicator of groundlessness so alters the workings and the objectives of the imagination that the world seems to have turned topsy-turvy.

This is the backdrop against which one must see the distinctions that Coleridge does draw in the much-quoted passage dealing with the imagination:

The IMAGINATION then, I consider either as primary, or secondary. The primary IMAGINATION I hold to be the living Power and prime Agent of all human Perception, and as a repetition in the finite mind of the eternal act of creation in the infinite I AM. The secondary Imagination I consider as an echo of the former, co-existing with the conscious will, yet still as identical with the primary in the *kind* of its agency, and differing only in *degree,* and in the *mode* of its operation. It dissolves, diffuses, dissipates, in order to recreate; or where this process is rendered impossible, yet still at all events it struggles to idealize and to unify. It is essentially *vital,* even as all objects (*as* objects) are essentially fixed and dead.

FANCY, on the contrary, has no other counters to play with, but fixities and definites. The Fancy is indeed no other than a mode of Memory emancipated from the order of time and space; while it is blended with, and modified by that empirical phenomenon of the will, which we express by the word CHOICE. But equally with the ordinary memory the Fancy must receive all its materials ready made from the law of association.[34]

This graduated definition of the faculties shows their groundlessness as well as their unfolding by way of different functions. If a faculty originated from a knowable ground, then it would, first and foremost, represent that ground and could not, therefore, ramify into a plurality of activities. But a graduated definition can be made only via contexts whose basic limitlessness allows the multiple faculties to manifest themselves in a limitless number of nuances.

We may assume, then, that this new, graduated definition of the faculties—arising from their groundlessness—was what gave Coleridge's friend such a headache. For initially Coleridge's specific comments on "primary imagination," "secondary imagination," and "fancy" feed off traditions reaching back as far as the Aristotelian concept of *memoria;* indeed, he may well have used them in order to stress the consequences of this graduated definition of the imaginative faculties. If these have no fathomable ground, then their groundlessness cannot be equated with a hidden intentionality. Activities are powered not by the faculties themselves but by the subject in his different attempts to relate to himself and to the world in an equal manner. Within the finite mind the infinity of self-constitution is to be repeated; the conscious will guides the operations of undoing the world of objects in order to enable the subject to re-create it anew in such a way that he will become present to himself; and finally empirical choices—made by fancy—facilitate the combining of data to meet the needs of the situation.

This graduated definition of the imaginative faculties is geared to a theory of the subject that leans heavily on philosophical idealism. We need not concern ourselves here with the details, but the relation at least should be mentioned in view of the fact that the intentionality underlying the operations of the faculties derives not from them but from the subject.[35] Coleridge avoids a central dilemma of traditional faculty psychology that, in the final analysis, conceived of the imagination as a self-activating potential and hence endowed it with an intentionality it cannot have, because intentionality pertains to consciousness and not to imagination. It is therefore only logical that Coleridge's graduated definition corresponds to an equal differentiation of activating agents, which in their turn represent basic conditions for the constitution of the subject, a process for which the imaginative faculties appear to be indispensable. This close interplay suggests that Coleridge adhered to the concept of the faculties because they embodied man's natural equipment.

The graduated definition fans the imaginary out into a plurality of faculties that require an equally differentiated context in order to render their workings tangible. The "primary imagination" serves to bring out the contextuality needed to repeat the creative act in the finite mind. If the faculty bore its own ground within itself, then it would not be capable of such an application but would define the subject according to the terms of that ground. Similarly, if the faculty were self-activating, it would no longer lend itself to be channeled into the subject's self-constitution, and would thus remain unavailable to the subject's intentions. But what does it mean to conceive of the subject as the creator of itself by repeating the "eternal act of creation"? Coleridge says in his essay "On Poesy or Art":

> Believe me, you must master the essence, the *natura naturans*, which presupposes a bond between nature in the higher sense and the soul of man. The wisdom in nature is distinguished from that in man by the co-instantaneity of the plan and the execution; the thought and the product are one, or are given at once; but there is no reflex act, and hence there is no moral responsibility. In man there is reflexion, freedom, and choice; he is, therefore, the head of the visible creation. In the objects of nature are presented, as in a mirror, all the possible elements, steps, and processes of intellect antecedent to consciousness, and therefore to the full development of the intelligential act; and man's mind is the very focus of all the rays of intellect which are scattered throughout the images of nature. Now so to place these images, totalized, and fitted to the limits of the human mind, as to elicit from, and to superinduce upon, the forms themselves the moral

reflexions to which they approximate, to make the external internal, the internal external, to make nature thought, and thought nature,— this is the mystery of genius in the Fine Arts.[36]

The repetition of the "eternal act of creation" in the human mind is the main task of the "primary imagination," in the execution of which it gains its vivid expression. What is repeated changes in the repetition because the purpose for which it is repeated is not an inherent part of it. Consequently, between mind and nature there lies difference that inscribes itself into the repetition. Since plan and execution are simultaneous in nature, nature cannot be conscious of itself, whereas if the human mind tries to repeat the *natura naturans*, there arises difference, which triggers reflecting acts and arouses the mind to consciousness of itself. This indicates the ordinary idealistic interplay between mind and nature. Being initially nature's otherness, the mind eventually detects its own possibilities in the mirror of nature that turns out to be the mind's unconscious. *Natura naturans* therefore entails making nature into mind, and mind into nature—a never-ending process that takes place in the finite mind as the "eternal I AM." This process works like a rudimentary Hegelianism, though Hegel would not have invoked the imagination for it.[37] For Coleridge, however, the imagination is of prime importance because the mind cannot become conscious of itself of its own accord. Consciousness needs something else that in itself has to be groundless so that it will not define the mind according to its own terms.

The to-ing and fro-ing between mind and nature, with the mind being revealed as the interior of nature and nature being revealed as the unconscious mind, shows "primary imagination" at work. It always solidifies into a product when the play movement issues into an image, for only through images can the mind ascertain that it is a repetition of the *natura naturans*. The image, however, is an offshoot of the oscillation between mind and nature, and consequently arrests the back-and-forth movement. Whenever this happens, the process of self-constitution comes to a standstill, as none of the images issuing from this play movement will ever represent the goal the mind tries to obtain: to be identical to the principle underlying the *natura naturans*.

For this purpose, "secondary imagination" is required; it differs from the "primary imagination" only in matters of degree but is nevertheless distinguishable insofar as its actions apply to the world of objects. It is an "echo" because it decomposes the world of objects and then creates this world anew in such a manner that the hitherto inconceivable structure of consciousness becomes present to the mind. The oscillation through which the imagination unfolds itself takes place between the mind, as it tries to secure its self-constitution, and the data of empirical reality. But when the same oscillation once again comes to a standstill in images, "secondary imagination" models them differently. On the higher plane, mind and nature were made to reflect each other, whereas here the necessary precondition for form is decomposition. The more specific the achievements demanded of the imagination, the more clearly it reveals itself to be a destructive force. Because of their awareness of its potential, the Romantics were able to channel the destructive aspect of the imagination.

Although imagination is not to be defined in its own terms, or in those of the subject or of the context within which it becomes operative, it must nevertheless be something that precedes both the activating stimulant, the functions exercised, and the impact made, because all of these depend on a presupposed entity that they qualify. How is this entity to be described, if it cannot be the sum of qualities or predicates?

The hallmark of all three faculties activated by the subject is the back-and-forth movement: there is oscillation between mind and nature (primary imagination), between decomposition and recomposition (secondary imagination), and between combination and separation (fancy). This is a basic movement of play that, however, is not to be equated with imagination proper, or with its qualifications and predications; nor does it originate from the activating agent or from the context; instead, it presents the three imaginative faculties in action. Elsewhere in his work, Coleridge comments directly on the particularity of activated imagination: "As soon as it is fixed on one image, it becomes understanding; but while it is unfixed and wavering between them, attaching itself permanently to none, it is imagination ... The grandest efforts of poetry are where the imagination is called forth, not to produce a distinct form, but a strong working of the mind, still offering what is still repelled, and again creating what is again rejected."[38]

"Wavering" is, however, a special kind of oscillation: Instead of being an unstable, and hence fluctuating, connection between poles, it destabilizes the poles themselves. Hence imagination in action does not congeal into any form; rather, its manifestation as back and forth exposes to change everything that is encompassed by the "wavering." This includes the world of objects as well as the self-constituting subject. "Wavering" as the self-presentation of the imagination indicates the presence of the activated imagination as a movement of play. The characteristics of this movement are what Coleridge calls offering and repelling, creating and rejecting, which then allow an ever-increasing differentiation of the interplay between subject and faculties, faculties and context, and finally groundless faculties and attributed predications. The play is constantly threatened by the ambivalence that underlies all oscillation, for the never-ending process is in conflict with the need for a result. Consequently Coleridge goes on repelling what is offered and re-creating what is rejected, so that imagination attains its presence through play. He knows that the "power of poetry is, by a single word perhaps, *to instil that energy into the mind, which compels the imagination to produce the picture.*" This sentence forms part of his criticism of certain contemporary poets whose work is highly pictorial, "where all is so dutchified, if I may use the word, by the most minute touches, that the reader naturally asks why words, and not painting, are used?"[39] The picture is always a product of the imagination, and so cannot be imagination itself. What Coleridge termed "wavering" is grasping the imagination at a moment when it turns into a product, or, better still, when it turns into a generative matrix.

To become manifest, imagination requires an external stimulant that, in turn, will be drawn into the play it has triggered. As the faculty is groundless, it cannot shape the subject, and as the subject has no immediate access to its ground, it needs the activation of its imaginative faculties in order to appear before itself. "The other position," says Coleridge, "namely, I AM, cannot so properly be intitled a prejudice. It is groundless indeed; but then in the very idea it precludes all ground, and separated from the immediate consciousness loses its whole sense and import. It is groundless; but only because it is itself the ground of all other certainty."[40] It is therefore only logical that the relation between the groundless faculty and the groundless subject, "a subject which becomes a subject by the act of constructing itself objectively to itself,"[41] should occur as a movement of play that, as "wavering," lacks structure.

Self-constitution implies that, at the beginning of this activity, the subject has neither knowledge nor consciousness of itself. I. A. Richards therefore rightly stresses that "Coleridge's theory of knowing treats knowing as a kind of making, *i.e.* the bringing into being of what is known."[42] Clearly, then, there can be no precise preconception as to what the subject is aiming at in the course of its self-constitution. It follows that whatever the subject needs to constitute itself may also overwhelm it. Indeed, this might be an additional reason why one faculty splits itself into several, because the subject controls its self-constitution through different contexts within which it activates the faculties in order to make itself present to itself. These contexts in turn not only channel the faculties but also motivate them in their various ways. In *Table Talk*, Coleridge points out that one "may conceive the difference in kind between the Fancy and the Imagination in this way, that if the check of the senses and the reason were withdrawn, the first would become delirium, and the last mania."[43] In this respect one could regard the different contexts as ways through which the subject prevents self-constitution from going out of control.

When the imagination, activated by the subject, becomes operative in the world of objects whose decomposition is to provide the material for new creation, it does not have a free hand but will inevitably be patterned by the context concerned. But since the subject as the activating agent is itself groundless, it, too, will be affected by these patternings. Initially it seemed that the subject only needed to tap its faculty in order to make itself present to itself; in the course of such a process, however, the subject experiences continual modifications. If the imagination appeared at the beginning to be a potential that could be manipulated for whatever purpose, it turns out, when pricked into action, to be a force that may manipulate its manipulator.

This occurs because every form of intentionality, including that of the "conscious will," is of limited range, and cannot fully control its aim. As a consequence, when the world of objects is dissipated by the imagination, this dissipation will in turn affect the subject that has created it. During activation, the subject embeds its intentionality in the imagination, which thus becomes active. As an "actant," imagination enables the subject that would like to see itself as its own ground to unfold itself as the endless mirroring of itself. The process is made possible by the asymmetry of the oscillation, which opens up the groundlessness of subject and faculties into an infinite multiplicity of aspects. The movement has to be asymmetrical because the imagination is required to become active, and can succeed in constituting the self only by continually overshooting the stages of the subject during its journey toward itself.

This concept of the imagination has now become a thing of the past, perhaps largely because it was so closely connected to the self-grounding of the subject. Nevertheless, there are several points that remain relevant to our discussion. The imagination is not a self-activating potential, and when it is mobilized by an outside stimulant, it reveals itself as a differentiated play movement described by Coleridge as "wavering." Furthermore, imagination is characterized by a duality; since production is preceded by destruction, the idea of *creatio ex nihilo* is revealed to be pure mythology.

Coleridge still spoke of the imagination as a faculty. Even so, the question arises as to whether the description of it as "groundless" denotes cognitive capitulation in the face of its inaccessibility, or whether it refers to whatever it is that precedes its effects and therefore cannot be identical to them. If it is the latter, then the reference is certainly not to a faculty in the traditional sense of a potential that can be tapped for whatever purposes; instead, the now manifest imagination is revealed as a movement of play that plays with and against the very agent that has mobilized it.

The Imaginary as Act (Sartre)

So long as the imaginary was linked to the subject, it could be regarded as a faculty that, like all the other faculties, appeared to represent the natural equipment of human beings. Even the prevalent concern for the self-constitution of the subject only modified the inherited concept. However, the loss of certainty as regards the ground of the faculties led Coleridge to view the imagination not only as divided but also as an "actant." If the imagination enables the subject to grasp itself as the consciousness of an unconscious nature, this interrelationship reveals cybernetic features, feeding back the subject's 'other' as part of the process of its self-grasping.

The nature of a 'faculty' is bound to change when the agent that activates it changes. Coupling the imagination with the self-constituting subject considerably altered the traditional concept of the faculties; but, finally, the classification of the imagination as a faculty became virtually obsolete when it ceased to be linked to the subject. This was the step taken by Sartre in his early book *L'Imaginaire*. He replaced the imagination as a faculty with a multiple manifestation of the imaginary. For Coleridge, the faculty of the imagination was unknowable. The same holds true for Sartre's imaginary, which can be grasped only in stages that lead from what appears to be the "certain" through the "probable" to what is considered to be a bare outline of "imaginary life"—to use the terms of description that Sartre himself regarded as part of phenomenological psychology.

Phenomenologically, the imaginary must be viewed as an act of consciousness. Sartre therefore begins with a statement that his "book aims to describe the great functions of consciousness to create a world of unrealities or 'imagination', and its noetic correlative, the imaginary."[44] If the imaginary is closely allied to the activities of consciousness, then the categorization of the imagination as a faculty is invalidated. Instead of being an unplumbable attribute of human beings, the imaginary is a mental image that indicates "only the relation of consciousness to the object; in other words, it means a certain manner in which the object makes its appearance to consciousness, or, if one prefers, a certain way in which consciousness presents an object to itself. . . . However, in order to avoid all ambiguity, we must repeat at this point that an image is nothing else than a relationship."[45] The stress laid on the imaginary as being a relation of consciousness to its objects reflects Sartre's phenomenological approach, according to which there is no knowledge of what consciousness is, apart from its relation to objects. The imaginary, then, is a particularly striking form of connection and manifests relations of consciousness to objects as mental images.

To understand the nature of these relations, we must bear in mind that for Sartre perception and ideation embody "the two main irreducible attitudes of consciousness" (p. 138), with the act of perception directing intentions toward a given object, and the act of imagining involving an object that is *being grasped as nothing and being given-as-absent* (p. 209). While perception grasps a given object, the mental image links consciousness to an object that is not given and so has to be supplied. There are two basic forms of such objects; either they are absent or they are nonexistent (see p. 60).

If consciousness is able to posit objects through the act of imagining, it appears "to itself as being creative, but without positing that what it has created is an object" (p. 14). This qualification is important and needs to be kept in mind. Consciousness controls the object posited as a mental image, but it does not have the same control over its own activity in the course of this positing. It is creative insofar as through its act of ideation it produces something that does not exist or does exist elsewhere; in both cases the object is absent (see p. 60) and must be put together in such a way that it takes on almost perceivable qualities. These may range from the illusion of having a perception to having a hallucination, which vividly illustrates how consciousness may lose control of its "creative character," and is thus swallowed up by its own mental images. These images always present their object as *"being given-as-absent"* (p. 209); they can do so only by drawing on memory, knowledge, and given information in order to fashion it. By making the absent present, they bring into being an imaginary object that is *"being grasped as nothing"* (p. 209). The "nothing," of course, refers to the absence or nonexistence of the object, and this makes it quite different from the dissipation of the world of objects that enabled Coleridge's subject to make itself present to itself through a "recreative process."

For Sartre, the negating as a real presence of what can be "seen" in a mental image makes way for the irreal presence of the absent. The presence of a mental image means that, as part of being caught up in it, we are lifted out of the condition that we were in before. The "nothing" inherent in the imaginary object becomes "creative" as it causes an almost total turnabout of our condition, and this turnabout may go so far as to make our present existence unreal.

There is another side to this "nothing" that is fundamental to approaching the imaginary. The mental image as such is not yet the imaginary itself but a mode of consciousness, while consciousness, in turn, is the necessary backdrop against which the imaginary manifests itself.[46] Sartre also takes this "nothing"—which is an integral part of the imaginary object—as a means by which consciousness protects itself from being absorbed by the images it has posited. "Besides, it is because consciousness feels itself but slightly enchained that it posits its object as non-existent. It pretends to see a cat; but since it is aware in spite of all of the origin of the vision, it does not pretend that this correlative exists. Whence this paradox: I really do see something, but what I see *is nothing.* This is the reason why this chained consciousness takes the form of an image: because it does not reach its own end. In the dream the captivity is complete, so the cat is posited as an object."[47] Consciousness is exposed to the danger of being trapped by its projected images because it can exist only as consciousness of something (see pp. 76f., 85). In the act of perception, consciousness can direct itself toward given objects, but in the act of imagining it posits its own object. This means "that the theme is not added to the image but that it is its most intimate structure" (p. 212). Thus consciousness slides into the mental image and becomes an ideating consciousness, which is clearly different from being a perceiving consciousness. It follows that there is no such thing as consciousness in itself, since consciousness can only be consciousness of what it has made conscious.

This whole process can be observed on various levels. Forming a mental image entails capturing the absent or nonexistent through an analogue that feeds on knowledge, memory, experience, information, desire, and so on. But although these sources play an important role, they have no control over the act of imagining, which springs from a thetic consciousness but simultaneously has repercussions on it. This interaction deforms all the material that goes to make up the mental image, because it has to be adapted to the image and therefore simplified both structurally and visually.

The formation of mental images is necessary not only in order to conjure up the absent or nonexistent but also—and indispensably—for acts of comprehension. Sartre contends that all comprehension is accompanied by symbolic schemata that represent those thoughts that are necessary for the mastery of what is to be undersood. These schemata increase in proportion to the difficulty that comprehension encounters, and the knowledge stored in memory has to be actualized accordingly. "Knowledge is in some manner a recollection of ideas. It is empty, it implies past and future understanding but is itself not understanding" (p. 118). The symbolic schemata, however, are present only as "provisional, insufficient, a step to be surpassed" (p. 131), and are discarded if they prove unsuitable for the purpose. They also function as a selective screen, for otherwise thought would be swamped by their recall. The schemata that accompany thought are filters screening out those memories and experiences that are relevant to the matter requiring comprehension. The schemata function as representatives, concretizing the possibilities that thought needs for its acts of comprehension. What they represent is neither thought, nor knowledge, nor memory by itself but, rather, a mixture of them as a means of testing and adjusting thought operations.

Here we have, then, a back-and-forth movement between suitability and unsuitability that enables the imaginary to manifest itself, having been called upon by consciousness. The proliferating change of representatives highlights the presence of the imaginary, insofar as the representative has to be negated whenever it does not tally with the demands of thought. This reversal is a further aspect of the "nothing" as a component of the mental image that is not exclusively confined to indicating the presence of the absent, or the self-protection of consciousness against its possible captivity, but also indicates the negation of what is inevitably posited through the mental image as an appearance accompanying thought. This negation is essential, because no single schema can represent what thought aims at. Indeed, any attempt at comprehension would have to fail if these representatives—which, as symbolic schemata, merely offer possibilities of orientation—already stood for the thing itself. By manifesting itself as a negation of representatives, the imaginary prevents them from representing thought.

Relations can also be reversed, and the mental images called forth by consciousness may begin to affect consciousness itself—as, for example, in dreams and hypnagogic images. When we are daydreaming or half asleep, the attentiveness of consciousness is reduced; it is still present, as is evident from the fleeting configuration of images that come and go, but their sequence is out of control. In such a situation "the fascinated consciousness . . . yields to the blandishments of the moment and forms an absurd synthesis in conferring a *meaning* on its new image which permits the retention of the unity of thinking" (p. 50).

Two things may be learned from this. First, there is evidently no consciousness without imagemaking, for only through imagemaking is consciousness able to fulfill its intention that is concretized to the degree in which its target becomes determinate. As it seeks to open up this target, what is given must be animated by mental images—not least in order to bridge the difference between intention and object.

Second, because there is no overarching reference to regulate the close relationship between intention and mental image, consciousness will be flooded by its images if attention lapses. But since consciousness posits its own images that contain nothing but what has been put into them, consciousness in such situations will become a prisoner of itself (see p. 50). To be caught up in one's images means being in the presence of the absent, whose power increases to the degree in which consciousness is absorbed by these images; these will then triumph over the intentionality that first brought them into being.

In dream, the difference between consciousness and its images is canceled out; according to Sartre, "the dream is the perfect realization of a shut imaginary consciousness, that is, a consciousness for which there is absolutely no exit and towards which no external point of view of any sort is possible (p. 193). Even if, as Husserl suggests, one can dream oneself into a situation "in which I dream myself dreaming, or more clearly, in which I dream that I am dreaming," the dreamed dreams themselves still cannot become perceptible objects from which consciousness could withdraw.[48] For "fantasy," as Husserl contends, is a modification of consciousness that manifests itself—where it is predominant—as a "consciousness of non-actuality" (p. 299). Since actuality "means as much as taking stands" (p. 363), nonactuality is nothing but an "analogue of pure fantasy (and fixes a concept of imagination, insofar as pure imagination expresses the prevention of actuality)" (pp. 363f.).

If consciousness can be thrown out of gear by its posited mental images, this is because, as consciousness of something, it is dependent on what it targets. Since pure consciousness would be either empty or groundless, referential contexts emerge whenever consciousness seeks to grasp itself. We get either referential frameworks that are ego-oriented or that are built on the nonexistence of such a concept.[49] If there is only consciousness of something, then consciousness assumes qualities of its targets, in consequence of which we sometimes have a positing consciousness, sometimes an ideating, perceiving, comprehending, and realizing consciousness. As an ideating consciousness, it posits its own object, which, contrary to a perceiving consciousness, makes it focus on its own product. Once the absent or nonexistent has become present, intentionality is fulfilled, although at this stage the mental image begins to take effect. While perceiving consciousness controls and is controlled by the objects given to it, the impact of the mental image cannot be so restrained. Indeed, any attempt to model the image will simply bring forth other images that will ramify into a flood of unconnected pictures, for the object of the mental image only expresses a connection of consciousness, and its content will change when the connections change. Thus, if a thetic consciousness changes into an ideational one, it tends to become enthralled by the images posited, which, in turn, begin to hold sway over their own source. We then have a consciousness dependent on its own production. Consciousness, on the other hand, is inconceivable without its positing activity, since otherwise "it would have to be conceived as completely engulfed in the existent and without the possibility of grasping anything but the existent."[50] The shrinking of distance between consciousness and its product makes consciousness slide into what it has brought forth.

We may examine the process from two different perspectives, both of which will shed light on how the imaginary is manifested through a positing consciousness. One of these perspectives is described by Sartre himself: Every mental image gives presence to either the absent or the nonexistent, and therefore contains a certain "nothing," because the presence does not eliminate the absence or give existence to the nonexistent but actually maintains the nonbeing of what appears as presence in the mental image. This "nothing" has a certain suction effect that the intentionality of consciousness cannot escape.

Another perspective on the slide of consciousness into its own product is offered by Wittgenstein: "'The image must be more like its object than any picture. For, however like I make the picture to what it is supposed to represent, it can always be the picture of something else as well. But it is essential to the image that it is the image of *this* and of nothing else.' Thus one might come to regard the image as a super-likeness."[51] However similar "the picture is made to what it is supposed to represent," it must contain elements of memory, knowledge, information, and so on drawn from mental stocks that cannot do justice to the particularity of the thing to be conceived. "Super-likeness" thus entails wiping out the representative features of the materials that have enabled the image to assume its shape. And so ideational consciousness loses the grip it had thanks to its stored knowledge, and slides into the image in direct proportion to its loss of representativeness. The "nothing" as a component of the mental image takes on an additional feature: Not only does it indicate that the absent can never come to a real presence but it also shows that given data have to be 'irrealized' for the object of the mental image to become real; otherwise the imaginary object would not be one in its own right but would be a representation of something other than itself.

The idea, then, turns out to be an important junction where consciousness comes to full fruition by luring the imaginary into shape, for consciousness as pure intentionality is empty and the imaginary is unable to posit itself. Sartre's prime concern is not to describe the idea but to understand it as a form that permits the imaginary to be transcendentally reduced for phenomenological purposes. His extensive description of both consciousness and idea is due to the fact that the imaginary can no longer be isolated as a faculty with an existence of its own, independent of consciousness that directs itself to targets in the world. The questions Sartre has to answer are how the imaginary asserts itself through consciousness, and what happens to consciousness when it has to mobilize the imaginary in order to fulfill its intentions. He sees consciousness as always being anchored in the world, the grasping of which governs its intention; consequently, to "posit an image is to construct an object on the fringe of the whole of reality, which means therefore to hold the real at a distance, to free oneself from it, in a word, to deny it."[52] "And if the negation is the unconditioned principle of all imagination, it itself can never be realized except in and by an act of imagination. That which is denied must be imagined" (p. 218). The world is negated in the act of imagining, because all comprehension entails overstepping what is to be comprehended. But in this situation there are no frames of reference for what is to be comprehended, and it is only the act of imagining that opens up the possibility of correlations by means of mental images. Thus the negation of the world is as indispensable for this process as it is ambiguous.

This ambiguity reveals itself in Sartre's wavering over whether consciousness precedes the imaginary or vice versa. If the world has to be negated as a precondition for its comprehension, then the imaginary has no control over consciousness. "Thus the imaginative act is at once *constitutive, isolating* and *annihilating*" (p. 210). This means that consciousness, which is always anchored in situations, can only direct itself toward a particular segment of the given world, which must be isolated by negation and reconstituted for comprehension. What, then, triggers the negating impulse? Is it the imaginary, working directly through consciousness? Or is it a realizing consciousness that, by fulfilling its intention, has changed to an ideational consciousness? Sartre seems at times to opt for the second of these, because for him every positing "of the imaginary will be accompanied by a collapsing of the world" (p. 218). What is unmistakable, however, is that the imaginary can negate only by way of consciousness, because before taking on such a function it is neither knowable or cognizable; it could manifest itself only through consciousness, and would make consciousness itself appear as if it were the negating agent. This being so, negation becomes the salience of the imaginary in the mirror of consciousness. But this might also be taken to mean that the imaginary must enlist the aid of consciousness if it is to make any kind of appearance. In this case negation would be less a precondition for conceiving the world for the purpose of comprehension than a matter of the imaginary being the "other" of consciousness—an "other" that can make itself present in consciousness only as negation.

This option also appears to play a role in Sartre's thinking. Toward the end of his book he says, "So imagination, far from appearing as an accidental characteristic of consciousness, turns out to be an essential and transcendental condition of consciousness" (p. 219). If this is so, negation becomes extremely ambiguous. As a transcendental condition of consciousness the imaginary—by way of the ideating consciousness— "uses the world as the negated foundation" (p. 218). But it can also negate the ideating consciousness, as it does in hypnagogic images and dreams, where "the imaginary world occurs as a world without freedom" (pp. 198f.). If the imaginary, even though initially patterned by the intentionality of consciousness, can negate both the world and the ideating consciousness, the question arises whether negation is an inherent quality of the imaginary or only its manifestation as conditioned by consciousness. Since the imaginary, though given in evidential experience, is not knowable, one can focus only on its manifestations. With the imaginary negating in order to promote operations of consciousness, the resultant ambiguity of the negation is unmistakable: On the one hand, the imaginary presents itself as "*something* which is nothingness in relation to the world, and in relation to which the world is nothing" (p. 217); on the other hand, it fascinates consciousness to the point of captivity. Moreover, as we have already seen, a "nothing" may reveal itself insofar as the absent or nonexistent is present in the mental image but is negated in its real presence, and such distinctions are impossible without an ideational consciousness. The latter channels the imaginary, which it has aroused, and also becomes a backdrop against which the activated imaginary reveals itself to be too ambiguous for consciousness to grasp. Thus negation by the imaginary, once it enters consciousness, splits into various modes of "nothing," and these in turn show the imaginary to be a modification of consciousness.

To a certain degree this might amount to a conceptual definition of the imaginary. "Fantasy," says Husserl, "is through and through modification, and it cannot contain anything other than modification."[53] Every modification is characterized by the fact that "in itself is contained the reference to another consciousness of which it is called modification, a consciousness that is not really contained in it and yet can be grasped for a suitably directed reflection."[54] For fantasy, one should add, has no objects of its own; instead, it manifests itself in consciousness by altering the latter's relation to objects through changing a realizing consciousness into an ideating one. Consciousness needs the imaginary in order to give presence to the nongiven absent, and in the act of imagining, consciousness itself undergoes a modification that inscribes itself into intentionality by splitting it into various modes of positing, perceiving, ideating, and realizing. Thus, when Sartre calls the imaginary the transcendental condition of consciousness, this is not because the imaginary actually constitutes consciousness but because, by modifying stances, it makes consciousness operative. Conversely, consciousness is not without influence on the imaginary, because modification presupposes something to be modified, and the latter in turn is bound to affect the modifying operations. The range of modification extends from the negated world to the imprisonment of consciousness through its images in dreams. So long as the imaginary manifests itself as an act negating the world, it remains under the control of a consciousness that has, however, been modified into an ideational consciousness. But when the images take over, consciousness is modified to nonactuality. These are the two extremes of the imaginary as manifested in consciousness.

Regardless of how the relationship is articulated, modification is what tilts the balance between consciousness and the imaginary. Indeed, the imaginary is present in all the tilting operations that direct attitudes of consciousness. Modification does not bring about irrevocable changes but takes place when consciousness slides into what it has posited, or when attitudes of consciousness are tilted, in movements that articulate various forms of negation and are peculiarly double-edged. They are products, and yet at the same time they are the unstoppable dynamism that produces the products, which in their turn cannot halt the double movement. Products are tailored to meet specific requirements, and these do not disappear completely when consciousness—as in dreams—becomes enthralled by its images. But the sliding and tilting movements are infinite in their scope.

Since this play movement is not without structure, it differs from what Coleridge called "wavering." We have seen that the imaginary, as a mental image posited by consciousness, may take effect as a negation of reality or as a modification of consciousness. This gives rise to an interacting relationship that makes it impossible to understand consciousness or the imaginary in isolation. Thetic consciousness that posits the imaginary as mental imagery will slide into its images because it participates in its own processes of production. Thus consciousness that is anchored in the world will be driven beyond the world by what it has posited. Illusions, dreams, daydreams, and hallucinations show how consciousness may be overwhelmed by the effects of its productions. Thetic consciousness then changes into a backdrop, permitting its own incipient helplessness to be registered. While the imaginary is posited by consciousness as the mental image, its effect tends to split, paralyze, and imprison consciousness. During the act of positing, consciousness slides into the mental image. This, in turn, tilts thetic consciousness into different stances, so that it may change into a realizing, perceiving, or ideating consciousness.

As consciousness is bound to participate in its production, even thetic consciousness is nothing but one of the stances into which consciousness is tilted. In consequence, it is as impossible to talk of *the* consciousness as it is of *the* imaginary in itself. Instead, the ensuing play movement of back and forth operative between consciousness and the imaginary makes them interpenetrate to such a degree that tilting and sliding play against one another. Thetic consciousness slides into the idea posited and thus is tilted into kaleidoscopically changing stances that indicate the presence of the imaginary in terms of consciousness. If an imaginary activated by consciousness manifests itself as a play structure by making its activating agent slide into its product and continually tilt the attitudes of consciousness, then its unfathomableness is translated into an endlessness of gaming.

Since in play everything is ready for tilting, playing is not predetermined but, rather, arises out of a basic indeterminacy. As the to-and-fro movement is patterned, sliding and tilting reveal that form has been imposed on the imaginary—a form, however, that also molds the manner in which consciousness is played. The result is the close interrelation between consciousness and the imaginary in a connection whose continual sliding and tilting are unpredictable because play inscribes into it the unpredictability of what first makes the gaming possible.

The Radical Imaginary (Castoriadis)

As long as the imagination was considered to be a faculty, it remained linked to the subject and, as with Coleridge, served the finite mind as a means of ascertaining itself in the mirror of Nature as *natura naturans*. And as long as the imaginary was considered to be a component of the mental image, it remained linked to consciousness, providing a transcendental condition for changing intentions (negating the world, modifying consciousness). Subject and consciousness activate the imagination/imaginary, and in their turn become the media for its different manifestations. It would seem, then, that any cognitive approach to the imaginary must always link it with something else in order to make it palpable. If it were not for the evidence of experience, one might take the imaginary for a postulate explaining the properties of the mental image and the homology between subject and Nature, whereas both of these serve as the setting in which the imaginary makes its appearance. But if these versions of the imaginary have become increasingly obsolete, how *is* it to be grasped?

Until the end of the eighteenth century, while the notion of faculty remained unquestioned, the workings of the imagination presented little difficulty even if interpretations differed. The imagination was defined according to its functions, which were often mistaken for its ontological foundation; in other words, it was continually equated with the purposes underlying it. This basic flaw undermined the faculty concept, the traditional form of which became obsolete the moment the potential itself came under closer scrutiny. But the less apt this conceptual framework was found to be, the more difficult it apparently became to find a replacement. Furthermore, the increasing emancipation of the imaginary from epistemological classifications proved to be proportionate to its growing importance. So long as it was conceived in terms of faculty psychology, this initially inferior faculty was bound to work its way upward: For Hume and Kant it became, respectively, mysterious and incomprehensible, not least because the other faculties had an ever greater need for the imagination.

From its humble beginnings, the imaginary embarked on an unforeseeable career, advancing to a kind of *materia prima* in such spheres as psychoanalysis, anthropology, and, in recent times, social theory. Concepts like Ur-fantasy or the primordial *état imaginaire*, which play a role in present-day discussion, show that the imaginary is on the way to becoming a be-all and end-all. But such concepts contain a flaw, though not the same one that undermined the faculty concept. The imagination as a faculty became mysterious toward the end of the eighteenth century because its functions clearly could not also be its ground. The problem with Ur-fantasy and the primordial *état imaginaire* is that if they are meant to be ultimates, they are frequently something other than what we may understand by "the imaginary."

This is evident in certain psychoanalytical and anthropological discourses. With Freud, for instance, fantasy is the meeting point for ideas of expectation and fulfillment.[55] Lacan conceives the imaginary as an oscillation between a specular self and the core self that looks at itself in the mirror with fascination and aggression.[56] For Winnicott, the imaginary is a "transitional object" that allows the infant to bridge the gap after separation from the mother.[57] And Gehlen regards the *état imaginaire* as a state of transference, indicative of man's deficient instincts, which he can repair by projecting himself into a featureless future, thus countering a challenging reality by overlaying it with self-projections.[58] Projecting entails transposing oneself into something other, and incorporating it into oneself to such a degree that one can cope with the rift between deficient instincts and the pressure of the external world.

In all the above-mentioned forms of discourse, fantasy as an all-encompassing generative matrix—no matter how it is understood—turns out to be the infrastructure of self-fashioning. The question arises, however, whether it is responsible for making itself into a meeting point, an oscillation, a transitional object, or a self-projection. In other words, is fantasy independent, as was thought in the eighteenth century—even if this independence was attributed only to poetic imagination—or has it become an ultimate because the infrastructure of self-fashioning is now the center of interest? Whichever it may be, this supposedly independent fantasy can be thought of only in terms of play that unfolds as meeting point, oscillation, and so on. Even the trial movements triggered by the transitional object are those of play. In all the cases described above, some kind of core self sets the game in motion so that, in the process of continually drawing and lifting boundaries, it can play its way into the formation of itself. What is certain, however, is that fantasy as *materia prima* eludes the cognitive grasp, not solely because there can be no transcendental stance from which an ultimate may be conceptualized but also because it is logically impossible for something determinate to arise out of something that is in itself also determinate.

This is the problem Castoriadis tries to deal with through his concept of the radical imaginary as the unfathomable precondition for the institutionalization of society. The imaginary, for Castoriadis,

> has nothing to do with the representations currently circulating under this heading. In particular, it has nothing to do with that which is

presented as 'imaginary' by certain currents in psychoanalysis: namely, the 'specular' which is obviously only an image *of* and a reflected image, in other words a *reflection,* and in yet other words a byproduct of Platonic ontology *(eidolon)* even if those who speak of it are unaware of its origin. The imaginary does not come from the image in the mirror or from the gaze of the other. Instead, the 'mirror' itself and its possibility, and the other as mirror, are the works of the imaginary, which is creation *ex nihilo.* Those who speak of 'imaginary', understanding by this the 'specular', the reflection of the 'fictive', do no more than repeat, usually without realizing it, the affirmation which has for all time chained them to the underground of the famous cave: it is necessary that this world be an image *of* something. The imaginary of which I am speaking is not an image *of.* It is the unceasing and essentially *undetermined* (social-historical and psychical) creation of figures/forms/images, on the basis of which alone there can ever be a question *of* 'something'. What we call 'reality' and 'rationality' are its works.[59]

Castoriadis intends to separate himself from Lacan and current psychoanalytical trends, for with them, as elsewhere, a decision has already been made about what the imaginary actually is; instead of producing an *eidos,* the imaginary in current discourse figures only as its unreal double. But if the imaginary precedes its form, then it cannot, in contrast to the traditional view of it, coincide with its function. This gives rise to a second point in Castoriadis's program: "We are challenging the functionalist view, in particular, because of the gap it presents just where its attention should be focused: what are the 'real needs' of a society, the needs institutions are there merely to serve? Is it not obvious that, once we leave the company of higher apes, human groups provide themselves with needs that are not simply biological? The functionalist view can realize its programme only if it supplies itself with a criterion for the 'reality' of the needs of society. Where will it find this criterion?"[60]

The Romantic subject and thetic consciousness as activating instances of the imaginary have here been replaced by the institutionalization of society. Castoriadis's departure from subjectivity to society is strikingly linked to a global view of the imaginary. By releasing the imaginary from the faculty concept, Sartre had revealed the wide range of actions of which it was capable; now, not only the subject but also society are "made" into what they are, first and foremost by the imaginary. For social institutions have to be set up, and no matter how important individual goals may be for giving guidelines, goals are not in themselves institutionalizing acts. If the imaginary were subordinate to such goals, functioning only to achieve them, then its role in establishing social institutions would be merely technical and inferior. The inherent inability of a functionalist approach to provide a blanket explanation for the emergence of social institutions leaves an empty space, which is now to be occupied by the imaginary. Castoriadis emphasizes this:

> The ancient views on the 'divine' origin of institutions were, under their mythical cloak, much truer. When Sophocles spoke of divine laws that were stronger and more lasting than those made by human hands (and here, as if by chance, this concerns the precise case of the prohibition of incest, which Oedipus has violated), he pointed to a source of the institution beyond the lucid consciousness of men as legislators. This same truth underlies the myth of the Law given to Moses by God—by a *pater absconditus,* by an invisible unnameable. Beyond the conscious activity of institutionalization, institutions have drawn their source from the *social imaginary.* (p. 131)

Nowadays, however, myth can no longer be considered the primordial foundation of social institutions, since historically observable change would demand that such an "Ur-foundation" should continually be recast. As for Castoriadis, change is an integral element of society, the imaginary replaces myth as the foundation, not only in order to emphasize the fact that society is a product but also in order to make the actual stages of this production available to analysis. As something that makes social self-change possible, the radical imaginary is an ultimate that needs society as a medium for its appearance, just as society needs it in order to become institutionalized.

This may at first appear to create a multitude of problems, for if myth is replaced by the radical imaginary, the latter, even though it is described in different terms, seems basically no different from an Ur-foundation. This apparent similarity, however, helps Castoriadis to bring out the difference between his ideas on social institutionalization and traditional social theory. He argues that being cannot arise out of being, regardless of whether an assumed first being is the divine law, Ur-horde, social contract, or economic factor. In contrast to such an originary being, which is presupposed in many social theories, Castoriadis stresses that myth as a primordial foundation represents something categorically different for the process of social institutionalization, since the societies that emerged from it were not mythical. What distinguishes current social theories from those positing myth as their origin is the fact that they are conceived in terms of an "identitary logic" (see esp. p. 341), meaning that whatever is, arises out of or is brought back to an underlying originary being. In this respect, even the demiurge is not a creator, since all he does is repeat and imitate an already predetermined *eidos,* and hence an intelligible form (see pp. 197f.). But since creation is to be viewed neither as transition nor as "clearing" (Heidegger's term), "a profound questioning of the received significations of being as determinacy and of logic as determination" (p. 174) is required.

Such determinacy must be disavowed, because what is, could always be different, while a presupposed primordial being can go on developing into forms of being only through modes of becoming and disappearing. Such rhythms articulate a plan that underlies them; they exclude interruptions, violations, production, and construction in equal measure, so that, according to Castoriadis, "we once again see that what has been termed 'ontological difference', the distinction between the question of being and the question of beings, is impossible to maintain or, to say the same thing another way, simply exposes the limit of inherited thought" (p. 182). As long as the "ontological difference" is upheld, not only creation appears to be inconceivable; so does the self-generation of society that arises out of the coexistence of the manifold. Therefore Castoriadis switches his terms of reference when drawing a conclusion from the dismissal of the "ontological difference." Instead of terms from inherited ontology, he outlines his basic premise in those of semiotics: "The main reason is that, in the case of the imaginary, the signified to which the signifier refers is almost impossible to grasp as such, and, by definition, its 'mode of being' is a mode of non-being" (p. 141).

This seems like a Romantic idea echoing one of Schelling's basic convictions: "The ground is, against that for which it is the ground, not existent."[61] But Castoriadis is not speaking of the radical imaginary as a ground; his semiotic terminology is aimed at another figure of thought. The signifier refers to a signified whose essence is "non-being," because there is no code nor convention that would allow the signified to be defined. The signifier as a determinate sign in fact signalizes the boundaries of definability, thereby problematizing that "hyper-category of determinacy" which "always equates being and determinacy, thus highlighting a basic tendency in Western thought."[62] This does not imply, however, that the imaginary is indeterminate, as such a qualification would entail subjecting it to the principles of "identitary logic"; it is, rather, the "other" of determinacy—and hence the potential transformation of determinacy. The "non-being" of the imaginary is therefore not the ground of being either; instead it is unfolded by way of projection, violation, and change, so that any determinacy must always be something brought about. As determinacy is only a product, it can again be done away with, which could not happen if determinacy were a form of being, whose becoming and fading expressed nothing but changes of Being itself.

How can we get to know the imaginary, if its "non-being" entails not the cause but the otherness of what there is? "The radical imaginary exists as the social-historical and as psyche/soma. As social-historical, it is an open stream of the anonymous collective; as psyche/soma it is representative/affective/intentional flux."[63] These two contexts, though closely intertwined, cannot be reduced to one another; they manifest the presence of the imaginary, which establishes both psychogenesis and sociogenesis, though never in such a way that they can be ultimately determined, let alone perfected. For whatever arises as an institution remains subordinate to what it has arisen from—namely, transformation by otherness. In order to clarify this, Castoriadis replaces the "hyper-category of determinacy" by the term "magma," which he describes as "the mode of being of what gives itself before the identitary or ensemblist logic is imposed" (p. 343).

> Let us try then, by means of an accumulation of contradictory metaphors, to give an intuitive description of what we mean by magma (the best intuitive support the reader can present to himself is to think of 'all the significations of the English language' or 'all the representations of his life'). We have to think of a multiplicity which is not one in the received sense of the term but which we mark out as such, and which is not a multiplicity in the sense that we could actually or virtually enumerate what it 'contains' but in which we could mark out in each case terms which are not absolutely jumbled together. Or, we might think of an indefinite number of terms, which may possibly change, assembled together by an optionally transitive pre-relation (referral); or of the holding-together of distinct-indistinct components of a manifold; or, again, of an indefinitely blurred bundle of conjunctive fabrics, made up of different cloths and yet homoge-

neous, everywhere studded with virtual and evanescent singularities. (p. 344)

Magma is a basic metaphor for the determinate in the state of its being changed; the 'other' of the determinate causes its constitution, decay, and rejection—in short, its whole range of potential transformation. Although the notion of magma is meant to exemplify the workings of both identitary and ensemblistic logic, which intervene in what there is in order to shape determinate significations, the coexistence of determinacy and otherness could also be taken as a possible answer to an old philosophical question: Why is many? The answer would be: Because the imaginary inscribes itself into everything present as its transition to otherness; it can do this because all forms of being are posited by operations of *legein* and *teukhein*: "*Legein* is the ensemblist-ensemblizing dimension of social representing/saying, just as *teukein* [sic] (assembling-adjusting-making-constructing) is the ensemblist-ensemblizing dimension of social doing" (p. 238). Whatever is posited becomes a being through its determinacy. Consequently, the imaginary is not the 'other' in an ontological sense but becomes the 'other' only through *legein* and *teukhein* operations, whose resultant imaginary significations proceed neither from what is nor from the operations themselves.

Furthermore, the radical imaginary is not of itself active but must be activated, as we have already seen from the fact that it has been conceptualized as a faculty and as an act of imagining. In the former it was the subject, and in the latter it was consciousness that set things in motion, though with the result that the imaginary became an active agent itself, working back on the subject to change it, or putting consciousness under the spell of its own projected images. The imaginary is always present in the magma as the 'other' of the determinate, and is transported into meaning by *legein* and *teukhein;* the imaginary can then take the determinacy that has been imposed on it and again plunge it into the stream of change. Thus the mobilizing impulse is different from the imaginary, although the radical imaginary can take on its fluid gestalt only through the "social-historical" or the "psychical," a gestalt that, in relation to society, solidifies into "imaginary significations"; in relation to the psyche, it becomes a "Vorstellung," which as "representation (*Vorstellung*) is not re-presentation (*Vertretung*); it is not there for something else or in place of something else, to re-present it a second time" (p. 329).

Such ideas are different from the mental images that Sartre described as the setting for the manifestations of the imaginary, although Castoriadis does not dispute that the idea is a mode of giving presence to the absent. But because he universalizes the imaginary, thereby coming into close proximity to the Romantics, elucidation is necessary. Coleridge had not discussed the modes through which the infinite mind was repeated in the finite through the imagination, but this is not the only reason why the very process, according to Castoriadis, has to be questioned; even more important is the need to expose the imagination as a power of unification. "It is this desire, master of all desires, of total unification, of the abolition of difference and of distance, manifested above all as being unaware of difference and distance, which, in the field of the unconscious, arranges all the representations that emerge in the direction of its own lines of force. If the unconscious is unaware of time and contradiction, this is also because, crouched in the darkest part of this cave, the monster of unifying madness reigns there as lord and master" (p. 298). The Romantic impetus for universalizing the imagination as the unifying faculty has become partial, and for Castoriadis Romantic ideality shrinks to a mere oceanic dedifferentiation, characteristic of the primary process.

Castoriadis's notion of the imaginary as otherness is also different from current psychoanalytical concepts of the other. If the unconscious, as conceived by Lacan, is the discourse of the other in one's own self, then this other is characterized by a relatively high degree of determinacy, which is inconsistent with what Castoriadis claims: the imaginary as otherness of the determinate.

In this respect the imaginary as entertained by Castoriadis can be marked off from both Romanticism and psychoanalysis. But now the question arises: How does it manifest itself within the psyche?

The sole unfulfillable (and for this reason indestructible) desire for the psyche is the one which aims, not at what could never be presented in the real, but at what could never be given, as such, in *representation*—that is to say, in psychical reality. What is missing and will always be missing is the unrepresentable element of an initial 'state', that which is before separation and differentiation, a proto-representation which the psyche is no longer capable of producing, which has always served as a magnet for the psychical field as the presentification of an indissociable unity of figure, meaning and pleasure. This initial desire is radically irreducible not because *what* it aims at does not find in reality an object that embodies it, or in language words that state it, but because it cannot find in the psyche itself an image in which to depict itself. Once the psyche has suffered the break up of its monadic 'state' imposed upon it by the 'object', the other and its own body, it is forever thrown off-centre in relation to itself, oriented in terms of that which it is no longer, which is no longer and can no longer be. *The psyche is its own lost object.*[64]

What mobilizes the imaginary is quite different from the efforts of the Romantic subject to repeat Nature in itself, although here, too, certain demarcations are maintained in relation to a psychoanalytical self-fashioning. Mobilizing the imaginary means using images in order to try to produce what from the very beginning has been lost to the psyche. Such images do not bring back into the present the absent that must have existed in a past of time or space; nor are they those of the nonexistent, for what they seek to invoke must not have such a status; they do not "represent" anything, and so they are imaginings by means of which the psyche turns itself into a stage for its own phantasms. This form of psychogenesis mirrors the entelechy of the radical imaginary. The psyche "creates" itself, not according to any given plan but from the desire to overcome the primordial experience of separation through images of something prior to it. For what "exists there refers back to what does not exist there, or to what calls for it; but it does not call for it under the auspices of a determined and formulable rule."[65] As a result, the psyche is free to gratify its desire, but the gratification itself can never achieve its aim. Through its imaginings, the psyche is set to reach beyond itself and back to its beginnings, which have not been withheld from it by an alien power but by the very fact that the "initial state" prior to separation is irretrievable. In the image the psyche therefore refers to something outside itself, even though it is attempting to have itself prior to all separation and thus be with itself. If it were to succeed, the image would have to disappear, since it is targeted on something that is not present. Trying to make an unreachable beyond into one's own and yet, through the image, always having to refer to something external makes for a contradictory phantasm: it is a mania for success that always devalues the success it strives for.

In the image, the desire of the psyche to have itself by taking possession of its beginning interferes with the necessity of directing itself toward something outside itself. This countermove gives rise to a ceaseless flow of images, through which the radical imaginary translates itself into the actual imaginary. It highlights the interplay between the inaccessible beginning and the constant superimposition of imagery, out of which arises a feedback loop, incessantly differentiating the image-producing capability by means of what is unattainable. Instead of remaining self-related, the counteraction prevalent in the image drives the psyche into drawing and lifting boundaries of itself. This counteraction is not yet the radical imaginary but the point at which the imaginary as "an inexhaustible supply of otherness, and as an irreducible challenge to every established signification" (p. 371) is shifted into psychogenesis.

Psychogenesis differs from sociogenesis in that once the psyche enters into society, the "creation" of the individual is brought about by the intervention of other human beings. Determinacy is imposed on the psyche; as an offshoot of *teukhein*, determinacy indicates the mode according to which the imaginary is channeled into production.

> The 'end', 'result', 'product' in view of which the means, tool, instrument or act is posited or simply is, does not exist 'effectively' at the moment when this positing is made. It exists as an *aim*, an intention, and this intention can exist socially only as an *eidos*, form or type, an instituted figure representing that which is, possibly, going to exist. The 'product' has to exist in and through the actual social imaginary before it can and in order to be 'real'. The counterpart in the individual is the imagination as the representation of that which, possibly, will be, in other words, the power-to-posit as capable-of-being that which is not. (pp. 263f.)

If *teukhein* and *legein*, as organization and designation, represent operations of identitary and ensemblistic logic, then they establish signs that posit imaginary significations. "On the register of the 'external' or 'internal' perceived (real), the distinct physical existence of the signifier and the signified is immediate: no one would confuse the word 'tree' with a real tree, the words 'anger' or 'sadness' with the corresponding effects" (p. 141). But it is quite different with words like *reification* or *God*, which have a constitutive signification for society. Here the signified referred to by the signifier is clearly of a different type, not least because an analogue is not to be formed in accordance with perception. Similarly, if the alienation of the industrial worker is referred to in terms of his being an animal or a commodity, images of animals or pieces of merchandise do not enter our heads. In any case, the relation between sign and object—even when the context is regulated by a shared code—still embodies something that defies ideation, for what, exactly, does it mean to equate a linguistic sign with an existing object? The question itself recalls the whole myth of Adamitic, realistic naming. The word *tree* may bring about an image semivisual and semisemantic, but with words like *God* and *reification* the imagistic quality of the ideas evaporates into indistinctness. "God is perhaps, for each of the faithful, an 'image'—which can even be a 'precise' representation— but God, as an imaginary social signification, is neither the 'sum', nor the 'common part', nor the 'average' of these images; it is rather their condition of possibility and what makes these images images 'of God'" (p. 143). Therefore imaginary significations are those for which there is no specific code-governed signified, so that the signifier points to an empty space, allowing for a nonbeing to be posited as a signified.

In this respect, imaginary significations are very closely related to the images of the psyche, which seeks to have its own beginning and so produces a ceaseless flow of images with which the inconceivable interferes, thereby making the psyche "a *forming*" (p. 283) of itself. In being the sequent images of itself, it is separated once and for all from its beginning; it can create its all-encompassing possession of itself only by varying its phantasms. This also means that the psyche has itself only in and through imaginary significations, which—because they are imaginary—drive it into self-transformation. Psychogenesis therefore has no teleology but is a constant shifting into otherness.

Imaginary significations pin down the nonbeing and thus establish society exactly as they do with the phantasms of the psyche. Although Castoriadis says that the social-historical and the psychical cannot be reduced to one another, they do unfold under similar conditions. The psyche undergoes its sociogenesis to the social institution of the individual by way of the *teukhein* of the other, and in the same way *legein* and *teukhein* fix imaginary significations in order to establish the being of society as well as that of individuals. But institutionalization is a pragmatic operation, not in itself deducible from institutions and therefore able to recast them. The imaginary signification achieves two things: it institutes society, and it makes society into a possibility of its own self-transformation. This contraflow results from the nature of imaginary signification. To his own question "What is a signification?" Castoriadis answers:

We can describe it only as an indefinite skein of interminable *referrals* to *something other* than (than what would appear to be stated directly). These other things can be both significations and non-significations— that to which significations relate or refer. The lexicon of the significa- tions of a language does not revolve around itself, is not closed in upon itself, as has flatly been stated . . . A signification is nothing 'in itself', it is only a gigantic loan—and yet it has to be *this* particular loan; it is, one might say, entirely outside of itself—but it is *this sig- nification* that is outside of itself. (pp. 243f.)

Meaning, then, cannot be adequately defined either through words or through use. The lexical level offers a code-regulated definition, but codes do not belong directly to words; they are "ensemblistic" forma- tions that enable language to become a code in the first place (see p. 238). For Castoriadis, meaning is not a quantity, it is magma, and this qualitative difference is already apparent from the very fact that a word can have meaning only if it is equally capable of assuming another meaning or of referring to others. This takes us far beyond the defini- tion of meaning resulting from its use, and if we keep in mind what Bakhtin said about the dialogic character of words that, having tra- versed many contexts, ring out as the constant hubbub of cross talk,[66] we shall not be far from the mark by speaking of meaning in itself as a "non-signification." Each meaning consolidates itself through what it excludes, and whatever is said, adumbrates something that is not meant. The more a meaning tends to figure something, however, the less important is what it designates, and its reference begins to shift away from denotation toward connotation. What is to be figured can only be imagined, and its conceivability orients itself by what is being said in order to grasp the adumbrations. A meaning that primarily figures something not only has to borrow from other meanings but also "means one thing, at the same time means *another*, and yet at the same time does not cease to mean the first thing."[67] This interplay between what is said and not meant, meant and not said, serves to shape the figuration.

Imaginary significations are those that privilege figuration. The code-regulated relationship of signifier and signified is outstripped, because imaginary significations are devoid of any reference to the world of objects; instead, as signifiers they are instructions for bringing about what they figure.

It therefore is necessary to establish what imaginary significations are meant to designate, for they provide the foundation of a society, whose self-image they in turn embody. Social life has no original content of its own that is independent of imaginary significations and their resultant institutions. The structure of a society grows out of its imaginary significations, although these are of a strangely hybrid nature: on the one hand, they are posited, being underpinned by facets selected from different realms of figuration, and on the other hand, they tend to overshoot any such pinpointing because they do not correspond to tangible objects.

Institutionalized meaning is not unaffected by this hybrid quality, for it can always be shifted or even replaced by new imaginary significations that bring to bear a different context of figurations. This is why Castoriadis uses the expression "social-historical," a combination of terms which is meant to show that society and history are not two separate entities, but that history takes place as a surfacing of new social configurations whose 'being' consists in their self-transformation. The "traditional schemes of coexistence" are therefore no longer apt, and "so history cannot be thought of within any of the traditional frameworks of succession. For what is given in and through history is not the determined sequence of the determined but the emergence of radical otherness, immanent creation, non-trivial novelty."[68] All these phenomena embody themselves in imaginary signification "as a 'coherent deformation' of the system of subjects, objects and their relations; as the curvature specific to every social space; as the invisible cement holding together this endless collection of real, rational and symbolic odds and ends that constitute every society, and as the principle that selects and shapes the bits and pieces that will be accepted there. Imaginary social significations—at any rate, those that are truly primary—*denote* nothing at all, and they *connote* just about everything" (p. 143). And precisely because they do not denote an existing world of objects, the things they connote lack determinacy, and such a lack cannot ultimately disguise the fact that their 'being' is a mere positing which can be undone or replaced by something else. It must be borne in mind, however, that the radical imaginary would have to remain virtual, and hence unknowable, if it could not take on an existence through systems of symbols such as that of language. This is why imaginary significations are only an actual imaginary that does not denote but, by means of connotation, creates what it speaks of.

A trace of the radical imaginary, however, always remains inscribed in such symbolic forms, insofar as imaginary significations are not geared to anything given and instead bring about what they point to. For this reason the imaginary needs the symbolic, since, having "*no flesh of its own,* it borrows its substance from something else, it is the investment of phantasy, the ascription of value, the autonomization of elements that in themselves do not stem from the imaginary: the limited rationality of the understanding and the symbolical" (p. 159). The symbolic, in turn, is dependent on the imaginary, because as a representation it cannot coincide with what it is meant to figure.

The radical imaginary as an ultimate manifests itself differently in the psyche and in society: in the latter it is the "interminable referral to something other" as enacted by imaginary significations, and in the former it is the contraflow of images of the unimaginable and irrecoverable. Although the radical imaginary institutionalizes psychogenesis, sociogenesis, and society, it does not 'exist' next to psyche or society, and these, in turn, are not given independently of the imaginary. Therefore the imaginary cannot be described as *materia prima* or Ur-fantasy, not because its status would be lower in comparison with these traditional terms but because the undisputed equality of its universalization is not to be thought of as a being with an existence of its own, independent of its manifestations. *Materia prima* and Ur-fantasy have always been conceived of as unconditionally given, like a Platonic idea, although they would scarcely have found a place in the Platonic firmament of ideas. As the foundation of what is, they would even have to be the origins of the *eide,* though without giving the slightest indication of how or why all forms of being have emerged from such a presupposed originary being.

The radical imaginary has inherited something from that all-embracing foundational nature of *materia prima* and Ur-fantasy, but only insofar as it is "the perpetual orientation of otherness" (p. 369) of the psyche and of society. Both exist only through the imaginary, while the imaginary can be manifested only through them. There are no longer any preconditions here, and so the radical imaginary differs fundamentally from the *materia prima* that was viewed as something substantial, and from Ur-fantasy, both of which functioned as the causal producer of being and were evidently still in a position to activate themselves.

Castoriadis's replacement of the "hyper-category of *determinacy*" (p. 341) by the radical imaginary seems highly plausible, "since being means being-determined, being one, being the same, being the same for all, being common" (p. 330). Nevertheless, one has to ask what is meant by the term *creation* that he so frequently uses. Basically, creation is an institutionalizing act, which does not emerge from a presupposed originary being, since the forms of its embodiment in psyche and society are perpetually exposed to disintegration and reorganization. An originary being could not be its own undoing. Nevertheless, the question of how such processes of institutionalization come into being poses itself. Some elucidation is necessary if the concept of *creation* is not to be relegated into an *asylum ignorantiae*.

With its two discernible propellants for activating the imaginary, Castoriadis's theory highlights the creative character of institutionalization. Psychogenesis arises out of the unfulfillable desire to enter into the inconceivable before all separation and differentiation, and *legein* and *teukhein* work on the primary level of what is given by Nature. Between the psyche's irredeemable loss of itself and the biologically given Nature the creative work of imaginary institutionalization takes place. These two extremes function as driving forces that arouse the radical imaginary, which unfolds as a play movement on all levels and makes the levels themselves play against one another.

The imaginary is at its most radical in the domain of the psyche that, being its own lost object, triggers a countervailing movement between its images, which are meant to recover the inconceivable beginnings and their continual cancellation by what is irretrievable. This counteraction is basically one of play. There is the goal-oriented movement toward regaining what has been lost, which one might call instrumental, and there is free play, manifesting itself in the perpetual invalidation of such an attempt. This back-and-forth movement indicates that the psyche "has" itself through continually overshooting the target aimed at by the instrumental movement. The oscillation between the two is a radical contraflow, with free play and instrumental play acting against each other. Since there is no access for the psyche to its beginnings, the frustration of its desire causes it continually to move beyond its images, and since it exists only as an interplay of images (see p. 354), it is able to maintain itself through the contraflow as its own self-transformation. Every image is but a phantasm that, as the product of a play movement, contains both the unfulfillable desire and the invalidation of all attempts at fulfillment. As free and instrumental play tend to cancel one another out, each phantasm reflects an institutionalizing act and its undoing as the hallmark of creation.

Through the intrusion of the 'other', the psyche experiences its sociogenesis, which equally results from a movement of play. What penetrates into the psyche is repulsed if not destroyed, and this very reaction is already an imprinting of the other on the psyche that gives rise to the socially institutionalized individual. This is where free play becomes destructive; instead of overshooting itself by invalidating its own imagery, the psyche wants to reject the other. In doing so, it sets up the other as its opponent, so that it finds itself being played against. When free play serves to trigger instrumental play, the sociogenesis of the psyche is initiated.

There are even more intricate manifestations of the imaginary on the level of social imaginary significations that, as we have seen, can only be described "as an indefinite skein of interminable *referrals* to *something other* than (than what would appear to be stated directly). These other things can be both significations and non-significations— that to which significations relate or refer" (p. 243). Once again we encounter the basic play movement of back and forth, but here the oscillation is not the same radical contraflow that is to be observed in the domain of the psyche. For a signifier that does not point to a given object—like God, alienation, or the economic factor—tends to disperse what it is meant to figure by constantly borrowing references from other significations, so that in the final analysis the 'floating signifier' itself is turned into a signified.

Whenever something is figured, each meaning must mean more than it says, and therefore what the saying designates has to be down-graded in order to make the figuring appear as if it were designating something. This exchange takes place through a movement of play that issues into configurations, all of which, however, are basically pro-grammed to change because they arise out of the contraflow of saying and meaning. This oscillation not only facilitates imaginary significa-tions but actually conditions their establishment insofar as free play overshoots designation, and instrumental play makes the figuration appear as a designation of something not given. Imaginary significa-tions result from the interrelation of counteracting play movements, and since this contraflow does not disappear in the synchronization, imaginary significations are by their very nature exposed to change.

Something similar can be observed on the level of *legein* and *teuk-hein*. "The instrumental institution of *legein* is the institution of the identitary-ensemblist conditions for social representing/saying. The instrumental institution of *teukhein* is the institution of the identitary-ensemblist conditions for social doing. The two institutions mutually imply one another, they intrinsically inhere in one another, and each is impossible without the other" (p. 370). This means no less than that *legein* and *teukhein* are linked together in the continuous oscillation, even if here the play movement reveals itself to be one of reciprocal implication. The contraflow disappears as each movement complements the other, and this allows the trial runs enabling *legein/teukhein* to function. Since both of them operate by working on the primary level of what is given by Nature, they are "primordial institutions instrumental for every institution (which does not imply any temporal or logical anteriority)" (p. 238).

Castoriadis argues that whatever "is" between the inconceivable beginning of the psyche and dependence on the naturally given, has its being through the imaginary, which—if we carry the argument a little further—reveals itself as a form of play. This play unfolds as a variation of contraflows, which are radical in psychogenesis and sociogenesis, and synchronous and complementary in the social-historical. As this playing never ends, its results—the phantasms of the psyche, the socially instituted individual, the configurations of imaginary significations, and the identitary/ensemblist organizations of *legein* and *teukhein*—can always be undone.

The various types of oscillation that we have observed on these different levels show that even the basic play movement of back and forth has a structure. The structure is essential, because something has to be gained, and it will vary in accordance with the desire of the psyche, with social imaginary significations, or selective grouping and reshuffling of *legein/teukhein*. All of these, however, are somehow related, so that the contraflow of images, the interchange of denotation and connotation in the self-referential signifier, and the reciprocal implications of *legein/teukhein* are not yet in themselves games but open the way for various types of interplay that permit us to grasp what Castoriadis calls social creations. Creation, then, is neither a *creatio ex nihilo* nor the re-creation of what has already been created; it is the self-transformation of the institutionalized.

The radical imaginary is therefore present as perpetual playing. It is activated through the irretrievable loss of the psyche as well as the need to master the biologically existing Nature, so that the different play movements, as distinguished by psyche and society, initiate interplay with the other. The radical contraflow of the psyche is reversed in sociogenesis: The 'other' breaks through the defenses and, on the level of social imaginary significations, turns saying and meaning against one another, until finally with *legein/teukhein* the basic condition of play, the mutual precondition of the partners, is established. The individual play movements are an actual imaginary that, by becoming activating agents initiating interplay between the various levels, again diversify the structure of the imaginary. The resultant differences reveal themselves in the particular institutions, but what they all have in common is play; and this never ends because psyche and society cannot 'be' without their respective 'others'. This could mean not only that psyche-soma and the social-historical interact because psyche-soma is mortal and, therefore, can perpetuate itself only through social institutions but also that play grants an illusory deferral of death. It may be for this reason that the radical imaginary is present as perpetual playing.

The degree to which the radical imaginary manifests itself as play can be gauged from the fact that transformation is the hallmark of all playing. The basic play movement of back and forth will vary according to the nature of the game but will always be instrumental in the attainment of something determinate. The imaginary realizes itself through play as the continual changing of what is being played. This change is also marked by endlessness, but the latter is merely a quality of change; or, rather, change is the paradigmatic characteristic of the endlessness of play. In each game, endlessness is integrated with change, and this is why play, as the mode through which the imaginary manifests itself, renders everything possible.

Thus play is not the thing itself, which in our present context means the social institution. It is true that play disappears in what it has brought forth, but all results of play are exposed to their reversal, and consequently social institutions do not finally solidify into reifications but, emerging from play, are at one and the same time the result and the transformation.

Interplay between the Fictive and the Imaginary

In spite of the different conceptualizations to which the imaginary has been subjected as *faculty, act,* or *radical imaginary,* there are certain features they have in common. The imaginary is not a self-activating potential but has to be brought into play from outside itself, be it by the subject (Coleridge), by consciousness (Sartre), or by the psyche or the social-historical (Castoriadis), a list that by no means exhausts the potential stimulants. It follows that the imaginary has no intentionality of its own but has intentions imposed on it by the demands of its activator. And precisely because it is without intentionality, it appears to be open to all intentions that will always be tied to what they trigger, so that something will "happen" to the activator. Thus the imaginary can never be identical to its intention-led mobilization (otherwise it would constitute the intentional activation of itself). Instead, the imaginary discloses itself in interplay with its different activators. This interplay is identical neither to the intentions nor to the imaginary gestalt that it brings about, although this gestalt could not come into being without the intention-led mobilization of the imaginary. The play movement that arises from this purpose-oriented activation is also the area in which the imaginary interacts in all its different ways with its activators. Consequently, play may be seen as a product of activation as well as the condition for the productivity brought about by the interaction it stimulates. It is this dual process that gives the imaginary its presence.

To say, however, that the imaginary manifests itself as play is to employ discursive language which may distract us from the fact that it can never be perceived, let alone defined as a "whole" or as whatever it is. Designating the imaginary as play entails making a cognitive statement, but this cannot be taken as an ontological foundation of the imaginary. For to understand something in terms of something else involves grasping it only through its aspects and not as a totality. Play would appear to be a prominent aspect of the manifested imaginary that can take on a variety of functions by way of its manifestations but can never by pinned to any one of them. Every statement about the function of play is *eo ipso* a philosophical one, and there is no shortage of philosophies of play. But the philosophical statement seeks to define the function of play, while the basic to-and-fro play movement within which the imaginary bodies itself forth can never be defined a priori through any particular functions.

In the paradigms we have discussed, the imaginary unfolds itself as play but cannot be thematized as such, because whether it is faculty, act, or radical imaginary, it always remains tied to prevailing exigencies: Play as oscillation leads to the self-constitution of the subject; play as sliding and tilting leads to changes in attitudes of consciousness;

play as contraflow splits the psyche off from itself and drives it into otherness; and play as figuration regulates the self-transformation of society. All these different movements are asymmetrical, often with multiple fields of reference that make transitoriness into the hallmark of playing, not least because these changing forms of to and fro are not an end in themselves but serve to fulfill particular purposes. These may be the mind's internalization of Nature, the kaleidoscopic sliding and tilting of conscious attitudes, psychogenesis, or changes in society. Once the purpose is fulfilled, play ends, appearing retrospectively, in relation to the results achieved, as a transitory phase of extreme latency. Such latency of continually differentiating play movements, triggered by various agents that mobilize the imaginary, makes play into a matrix for production.

Since the transitory nature of play in the ordinary world is geared to goals to be achieved, a philosophy of play needs to postulate purposes if it is to grasp the character of the transitory. This is most commonly done through the attribution of a symbolic quality[69]—in other words, by establishing preconceived correlations that, in effect, dissipate rather than capture the transitory nature of play. Because of this drawback, rather than adopting a philosophy of play in the conventional sense in order to do justice to the transitoriness, it is necessary to turn to the variety of games themselves. Only these disclose the surprising proliferations—the fecundity—of the transitory in all its forms. And although the games lead to a result, which primarily indicates that they are over, as long as they last, they are animated by the transitory nature of play.

Since the mobilization of the imaginary discloses itself as play, the paradigms we have discussed reveal how the activating agent utilizes the basic to-and-fro play movement for its own purposes. And since how play is to develop depends on the activating agent, the potential of the play's transitory character will be given freer rein where pragmatic purposes are less in evidence. In this respect, the fictive component of literature is bound to mobilize the imaginary in a different manner, for it has far less of the pragmatic orientation required by the subject, by thetic consciousness, or by the social-historical, all of which channel the imaginary in quite specific directions. The increase in play variations, proportionate to the decrease in pragmatic purposes, also distinguishes the fictive from all philosophies of play that try to equate the transitory movement with postulated symbols. The fictive is not to be understood as a definition of play but functions, rather, as a means of making the imaginary accessible to experience outside its pragmatic function, without allowing it to swamp the mind in the manner of dream or hallucinations.

What distinguishes the fictive from the activators we have discussed so far is its doubling structure. The classic example of this doubling is—as we have seen—pastoralism, which, by linking an artificial, deliberately concocted world with a socio-historical one, epitomizes doubling as the hallmark of literary fictionality. The structural formula of the coexistence of two mutually exclusive sign systems, which we derived from this example, is attributable to the fact that one and the same text possesses what Friedrich Schlegel (in a different context) called "two centra,"[70] whereby "the single indivisible work is actually, in a certain sense, something twofold and double."[71] For the early Romantic poets, this doubling characterized the work of art, whose basic structure had found its first paradigmatic self-presentation in pastoralism. Ever since Virgil the unmistakable tendency to make art itself the subject matter of pastoral poetry prevailed, and the doubling of two worlds was an archetypal blueprint for such a presentation. This basic feature was not merely maintained but constantly elaborated in pastoral literature, so that the "two centra," which Schlegel later pinpointed as fundamental to all great literature, proved to be a generative matrix for all art. "The theory of the two centra, or the constitutive duality of a work, can be viewed as an ideal rendering of reflexivity in its essence, namely as dual play between two poles of reflexivity."[72] Thus pastoralism may be taken as a metatext of literary fictionality. Our concern in this regard has therefore been less to interpret pastoral poetry than to extrapolate a basic structure that is a generative matrix. It is worth stressing again that literary fictionality is not the work itself but is what makes the work possible.

In pastoralism, the interaction and counteraction between two worlds mark the extremes to which the structural formula can be unfolded, but the two centra of literary fictionality can also be found in less divergent forms of the coexistence of what is nonidentical or even incompatible. This is a constitutive feature of the work to encompass what has been separated by difference. The coexistence of mutually exclusive worlds makes each of them into a signifier that cannot be fulfilled through what it signifies. Neither the artificial nor the historical world is significant in itself; rather, each signifier is at best the signified of the other signifier. But the pastoral world cannot be said to signify the historical, or vice versa. Consequently, the convention-governed link between signifier and signified no longer holds. Instead, the signifiers "read" each other in the sense that the artificial world is seen through the eyes of the sociohistorical, and the latter through the eyes of the artificial. Such mutual readings draw attention to the signs as signs, not least since these no longer designate a signified, let alone give presence to it, but indicate the cancellation of any preestablished correlation between signs. Thus the referentiality of the sign begins to fade, as neither the artificial nor the sociohistorical world can fulfill itself through what it represents. Neither of them is significant enough to dispense with the other, in consequence of which they no longer refer to anything pregiven.

The reciprocal "reading" of signifiers, then, issues into an iterative movement between two mutually exclusive sign systems. The iteration arises partly from the polarization of the two worlds, and partly from the fact that the artifical world is not confined to denoting pastoral life and the sociohistorical one does not solely denote a pregiven world outside the text. Reading therefore may unfold itself into a variety of activities: It deciphers a palimpsest, projects a meaning, uncovers the hidden, disputes the given, and imagines the possible, to name but a few possibilities for the mutual "reading" of signifiers. Such an iterative movement reintroduces into what is present whatever the present has excluded. The mutually exclusive worlds thus trigger a reciprocal "readibility," in the course of which a simultaneity of the present and the absent comes about. The iteration tends to create an illusion of completeness, not because it embraces everything but because the reciprocal "reading" of signifiers is serial in character and is limited only by the intention underlying the work.

Pastoralism, with the overstepping of borders and the iterative interweaving of two worlds, offers the most striking paradigm of the structural formula of literary fictionality, but the doubling structure is by no means limited to this literary system, which has already spilled over into other genres. What pastoralism presents as an image is inherent as a function in the different acts of fictionalizing. The acts themselves bring forth the two worlds in a doubling that in every text opens up a play space within which the coexistence of the mutually exclusive can be acted out.

The act of selection creates room for play insofar as it makes inroads into extratextual fields of reference and, by disrupting them, creates an eventful disorder. In consequence, both structure and semantics of these fields are subject to certain deformations, and their respective constituents are differently weighted according to the various deletions and supplementations. Each one is reshuffled in the text and takes on a new form, a form that nevertheless includes, and indeed depends on, the very function this field has within the structure of the given world.

This function now becomes virtual and provides the background against which the operation of restructuring may stand out in relief, featuring the intention underlying the "coherent deformation." In addition, the act of selection splits each field of reference, since the chosen elements can take on their significance only through the exclusion of other elements—this being the precondition for the eventful disorder, the resolution of which demands the assembly of a new meaning. The ensuing tension indicates that the world which has been overstepped is still present in the text.

The act of selection also invades other texts, thus bringing about intertextuality. The clustering of texts adds to the complexity of the play space, for the allusions and quotations take on new dimensions in relation to both their old and their new contexts. Since both old and new always remain potentially present, there is a coexistence of different discourses that reveal their respective contexts as a play of alternating fade-ins and fade-outs. Whatever the relationship may be, two different types of discourse are always present, and their simultaneity triggers a mutual revealing and concealing of their respective contextual references. From this interplay there emerges semantic instability, which is exacerbated by the fact that the two sets of discourse are also contexts for each other, so that each in turn is constantly switching from background to foreground. The one discourse becomes the theme viewed from the standpoint of the other, and vice versa. This iterative movement enables old meanings to become material for new; it opens up long-established borders, and allows excluded meanings to enter and challenge the meanings that had excluded them. The more a text accumulates other texts, the more thoroughgoing will be the doubling process induced by the act of selection. The text itself becomes a kind of junction where other texts, norms, and values meet and work upon each other; as a point of intersection, its core is virtual, and only when actualized by the potential recipient does it explode into its plurivocity.

The doubling manifests itself as a play space in which all the different discourses come together to form the matrix that enables the text to end up with a potentially infinite variety of relations to its surroundings.

The structure pinpointed in the act of selection also underlies the act of combination. Here the boundaries that are crossed are intratextual, ranging from lexical meanings to the constellation of characters, but overstepping should not be mistaken for an act of transcending. Rather, the various clusters, whether they be words with outstripped meanings or semantic enclosures exceeded or infringed by the characters, are inseparably linked; they inscribe themselves into one another, every word becomes dialogic, and every semantic field is doubled by another. Through this double-voiced discourse every utterance carries something else in its wake, and once again the act of combination unfolds a play space in which the presence is always doubled by the absent, frequently redistributing the weight by making the present totally subservient to the absent: What is said ceases to mean itself, so that what is not said can thus gain presence. For there is no third dimension in the text to determine precisely what is to be related to what; instead, the textual segments and the encapsulated items are related through the different influences they have upon each other. Every textual segment bears with it traces of things outside itself, and the more significant the segments, the more manifold the traces. Since each trace marks both difference and interaction between segments, the act of combination opens up the play potential of each segment.

Finally, the self-disclosure of literary fictionality brings about a peculiar act of doubling. This takes place on two different levels: that of the attitude to be imposed on the reader, and that of what the text is meant to represent. Because the literary text invokes conventional signs to establish itself as a 'staged discourse' that places the textual world under the sign of the 'as-if', readers know that they must bracket off their natural attitudes toward what they are reading. But this does not and cannot mean forgetting or transcending those natural attitudes, which cannot be abandoned. Instead, they figure as a virtualized background, which as a latent instance of comparison, or at least as a testing ground, is essential if the textual world is to be digested. Thus the bracketing-off process splits the reader's attitude into one that is simultaneously natural and artificial. The natural attitude loses its validity, so that the new one may develop, but the new one would not achieve stability if it could not be played off against the old one.

The signals of fictionality also bracket off the world of the text, simultaneously indicating that it *is* to be viewed as if it were a world, a world, however, that has no empirical existence. Consequently, there is a difference between the actual world and the world from which it is bracketed off, for the textual world takes its shape from the deformation of the referential fields of the text through selection and combination, which then relate the encapsulated elements and open them out into their potential multiplicity. This difference signals the presence in the text of two worlds, of which the textual does not mean what it says and the empirical becomes a metaphor. This simultaneous presence of the two is caused by each of them making the other unreal: the textual world loses its function of designation, and the empirical world loses its objectivity.

Fictionalizing acts, then, may be distinguished from each other through the nature of their doubling, which produces different areas of play. Selection opens up one area between fields of reference and their distortion in the text; combination opens up another between interacting textual segments; and the 'as-if' opens up another between an empirical world and its transposition into a metaphor for what remains unsaid. The doubling structure of these fictionalizing acts creates the area of play by holding on to everything that has been overstepped, thus making it a partner in the game of countermoves. Each overstepping multiplies the difference that constitutes the play area. "Whatever may be the ontological-metaphysical status of difference, and its incarnation as 'writing' (Derrida) or something similar . . . differences do not . . . condition a system; they specify and extend its possibilities of self-conditioning."[73] Difference is therefore no longer a matter merely of distinctions; as an empty space it operates both as a divider and as a stimulus for the linking of what has been divided. These simultaneous countermovements take place as a continual referring of the separated elements to one another; thus difference never disappears through link-ups, and the iteration never ceases. Since the countermovements are initiated by the overstepping acts of fictionalizing, the intratextual difference ensuing from such overstepping does not indicate deferral of origins but constitutes a structure that enables the text to play itself out beyond the boundaries of its own individual world.

Although the doubling structure opens up a play space, it is not yet—in spite of the iterative movement triggered between what has been doubled—a fully fledged game. Because it exceeds what is, fictionalizing is imbued with an intention that can never totally control what it aims at. For this reason, though it has form, the fictive depends on the imaginary in order to bring to full fruition what it has targeted. Simultaneously, the fictive appears to present ideal conditions for activating the imaginary, in that its doubling structure allows the imaginary to unfold itself as play unimpaired by the prevailing pragmatic orientations of the paradigms we have discussed.

By opening up play spaces, the fictive compels the imaginary to take on a form while at the same time acting as the medium for its manifestation. Because the play spaces resulting from boundary-crossing are comparatively empty, the fictive has to activate the imaginary, since the fulfillment of intentions requires imaginings. For intentionality cannot itself bring forth what it targets. Imposing form, therefore, entails determining what is otherwise indeterminate, and such an attempt becomes successful to the degree in which an indeterminable imaginary is shaped by differentiated contexts. Fictionalizing acts are ideally suited to such a task, and the question arises as to whether the fictive in literature is not bound to divide itself into such acts if it is to provide the basis for the molding of something that by its nature is featureless. This would then constitute the first repercussion of the imaginary on the medium of its manifestation, in which case the fictive would only be an overarching term for the fictionalizing acts into which the imaginary splits its activator. But what is meant by compelling the imaginary to take on form, especially if the fictive needs the imaginary in order to give itself adequate realization?

Fictionalizing opens up a horizon of possibilities in relation to what is; to this extent it remains linked to realities. But while realities are concrete, the possibilities remain abstract, for they result from boundary-crossing and thus cannot be fashioned by what they have exceeded. The horizon of possibilities adumbrated by boundary-crossing inevitably modifies the reality that has been overstepped. Modification, however, is—to refer to Husserl again—the central quality of fantasy: "Fantasy is modification through and through and it cannot contain anything other than modification."[74] For fantasy, defying definition, is to be grasped only through its effects; consequently, whenever it is released, what is, cannot remain the same. This is why Husserl also maintained, as pointed out earlier, that fantasy is characterized by "arbitrariness," and "so ideally it distinguishes itself by its absolute self-will" (p. 535). But fictionalizing acts compel fantasy to take on form so that the possibilities they open up can be made conceivable. This imposing of form has a twofold effect: (1) it makes the diversified boundary-crossing concrete; (2) it simultaneously turns into a medium for the imaginary. Whenever the latter is given shape by an intentional act of consciousness, the realities that fictionalizing has overstepped are rendered nonactual, so that the modification exercised by the imaginary manifests itself as "a consciousness of non-actuality" (p. 299). This means no less than that the imaginary, lured into presence by acts of fictionalization, becomes a nullifying act. In this form the "modification" now begins to unfold, and it cannot do without the world referred to if it is to spotlight what now has lost its status of reality. Here, then, we can see the first moves in the game: The nullified world stands opposite an initially empty horizon of possibilities. What generally happens then is that the individual fictionalizing acts differentiate this "consciousness of non-actuality"; and in this way, compelled to take on form, the imaginary manifests itself.

The act of selection cancels out the original organization of the realities that recur in the text. These, as we have already noted, appear in eventful disorder, or "coherent deformation."[75] This applies generally to the structure, function, and semantics of the systems referred to. The cancellation may vary in degree. It will be all the more marked in proportion to the number of systems incorporated, and it is further intensified by the fact that it can even penetrate as far as the language system that makes up the text itself. Striking examples of this are nonsense poetry, Dada, and *Finnegans Wake*. According to Sartre, "The gliding of the world into the heart of nothingness ... can happen only through the positing of *something* which is nothingness in relation to the world, and in relation to which the world is nothing. By this we evidently define the structure of the imagination. It is the appearance of the imaginary before consciousness which permits the grasping of the process of turning the world into nothingness as its essential condition and its primary structure."[76]

The structure, function, and semantics of referential realities recur in the text in their nullified state, and this reveals a particular impact of the imaginary as modification. Fictionalizing itself cannot be cancellation, for then the overstepping process we have described would become one of mere transcending: former realities would be left behind, and fictionalizing would be reduced to an act of removal that would make those abandoned realities irrelevant. The overstepped realities, however, remain present in the text, albeit in their state of nullification, and they condition whatever has motivated their invalidation, so that the play space opened up by fictionalizing acquires its tangibility. What has been validated becomes past, and the motivation for such a change becomes the new present. Again, this is something that can only be imagined, and this imagining is not possible without recourse to the invalidated reality.

It is the same, mutatis mutandis, with all the fictionalizing acts. Combination oversteps the encapsulated items from external fields of reference, the linguistic designations, the relations between characters, textual schemata, and semantic enclosures. But since all of these remain present, they mirror one another, and whatever they have denoted or represented becomes latent—not nullified but derestricted. Derestriction entails modifying, not canceling, convention-governed meanings and significations that can now be opened up to new and manifold applications. Designation and representation, though relegated to latency, nevertheless remain present and function as a backdrop for making otherness capable of being both developed and conceived.

While selection unfolds the imaginary as counterplay between past and present, combination sets off the given against otherness. The play space of selection takes shape as a horizon of possibilities against the background of realities made nonactual; the play space of combination takes shape as the otherness of the given. And here we have the precondition for all new possibilities: They are not extrapolated from the given, but they play it away.

Another change in the imaginary occurs when the modifications it engenders are governed by the as-if proviso. For fiction's self-disclosure signals that the world of the text is not really a world, but for particular purposes has to be taken as if it were. This means that the textual world loses its reality in order to render conceivable that for which, in the sense of Vaihinger's "As-if," it represents only the "impossible" or "unreal" point of comparison. This form of doubling shapes the mobilized imaginary in such a way that the 'derealized' textual world turns into a guide for the "perceptive fantasy,"[77] which will permit something nonexistent to be visualized as a reality. It is said that Philostratus, when asked whether Greek artists had been to heaven and seen the gods there, replied: "Imagination made them, and she is a better artist than imitation; for where the one carves only what she has seen, the other carves what she has not seen."[78]

Through self-disclosure, feigning becomes an ideal medium for the imaginary to appear, which in this form makes the invisible conceivable in a process that would not be possible if fictionalizing did not channel the imaginary by setting up necessary and sufficient conditions. For the imaginary as such cannot invent anything, as indicated by the traditional invocation to the Muses when invention became necessary. The Muses embody the intentional structure that must be imposed on fantasy from outside if fantasy is to be unfolded.[79] Freud maintained that the "'creative' imagination, indeed, is quite incapable of *inventing* anything; it can only combine components that are strange to one another."[80] The imaginary therefore needs a medium, not only in order to become manifest but also in order to execute what the medium wants the imaginary to perform by imbuing it with intentionality. Hence the imaginary cannot coincide with its medium. On the other hand, one could no longer speak of a medium if the imaginary were not subjected to certain tasks by the fictive that has spurred it into action. For the "imagination," in Caillois's words, awaits the moment when it can "come to the surface: to a certain degree, the moment of its coagulation . . . Its way of life generally as well as particular, individual external qualities, can work on the imagination like an inoculation, with positive reactions; thus it is set in motion."[81]

The fictionalizing acts embody this "inoculation," and their intentionality channels the unfolding of the imaginary in the text. Their common feature of boundary-crossing becomes diversified by their respective operations. In each instance, what has been overstepped is subjected to different qualifications: selection cancels out the organization of referential realities, combination relegates denotation and representation to latency, and self-disclosure makes the textual world unreal. In each case something determinate is canceled, pushed into latency, or derealized in order to release the possibilities inherent in the given. Selection works on referential realities, whose relegation to the past adumbrates the motivation of such a shift. Combination works on convention-governed functions of denotation and representation, whose reduction to latency permits new relations as otherness. Self-disclosure, finally, sets itself apart from such realities, and through its 'as-if' turns the textual world emerging from selection and combination into pure possibility. This embodies a radical alternative to the referential world of the text insofar as it cannot be extrapolated from the latter's reality, and may therefore stand as a model for the production of

new worlds. For possibility is an analogue for conditioning conceivability; where there is a possibility, there is a conceivable reality. This,
however, seems to contradict the tried and trusted relationship between
reality and possibility, whereby we believe that possibilities can exist
only in relation to realities, and not vice versa. For possibilities, we
argue, do not precede realities. But if realities are in themselves constructs, then they cannot have proceeded from themselves. The interplay between the fictive and the imaginary therefore shows that the
referential realities of the text, having proceeded from possibilities,
revert to possibilities in order to allow (and condition) the emergence
of other worlds.

How is this emergence of possibilities to be conceived, and what
could it possibly mean? First of all, it must be acknowledged that the
imaginary—even when compelled to take on form—can never by fully
grasped, and so in itself is a kind of "nothingness." This unsubstan-
tiality manifests itself starkly in the fictionalizing acts as cancellation,
derestriction, and irrealization, which in turn indicate that these nullifying operations are doubled by an impulse to replace what has been
invalidated. This means no less than that the fictive unfolds the imaginary as a dual countering of simultaneous decomposing and enabling.
"Dual countering" (*Gegenwendigkeit*) is a term introduced by Heidegger
in his discussion of the origin of the artwork, and it is pertinent here
only insofar as the rift that constitutes the dual countering emerges as
the ineluctable condition for enabling by decomposing. "The conflict is
not a rift (*Riss*) as a mere cleft is ripped open; rather it is an intimacy
with which opponents belong to each other."[82] Without this dual
countering, the imaginary would remain hidden from view, but by
unfolding itself in such a way it bears witness to the fact that nullification and enabling go hand in hand.

The extent to which the fictive "splits" the imaginary into such a
dual countering is the extent to which it remains, in its turn, dependent
on the imaginary. For as boundary-crossing, fictionality is an act of
pure consciousness whose intentionality is punctured by indetermina-
cies, and therefore it can maintain only the general direction toward its
target. Thus the fictionalizing act provides a frame for what is to be
captured, but the intention of the act does not provide a concrete picture to fill the frame. At best, it provides an empty idea that requires
substantiation. Without the imaginary, the fictive would remain an
empty form of consciousness, but without the fictive, the imaginary

would not be able to appear as a dual countering. Insofar as the fictive is a medium, it unleashes the imaginary as the simultaneity of decomposing and enabling—without, however, being in control of what is acted out in this dual countering. This is one basic reason why the motivation underlying the nullifying operations reveals itself in a multiplicity of possibilities. When the doubling structure of the fictive predominates in this interplay, the absent is overshadowed by the present, the reverse side of phenomena comes to the fore, denotation and representation expand into polysemy, and irreality becomes an illusion of perception. When the dual countering of the imaginary gains the upper hand, the doubling structure is deformed into duality, ambivalence, and duplicity, and this in turn leads to an unmanageable expansion of differentiated possibilities.

These possibilities, then, take on their shape by way of nullifying realities, which can be nullified simply because they are themselves realized possibilities. The interplay between the fictive and the imaginary can therefore be seen as the enactment of this process of destruction and enabling, which finds its paradigmatic form in literature, because the fictive is able to unfold the imaginary as counterplay when freed from all the pragmatic burdens of the empirical world.

Why do we need such a staging? First of all, in order to highlight the fact that reality is not to be conceived as a limitation of the possible, not least because possibilities cannot be extrapolated from what is. They can, of course, become a horizon to realities, but whenever this happens, the latter will not stay the same. If, then, there are no a priori distinctions between the real and the possible and, indeed, if possibilities precede their realizations, one is bound to ask where they actually come from. Following Leibniz, Globus suggests that "World models are produced without benefit of copies of the world or instructions from the world; they are created formatively. . . . The actual world is produced from this plenum of possibilia, selected by input and intention . . . *Possibility is implicate existence.* Actuality depends on a process of unfolding enfolded order to explicate existence."[83] This implies that human beings are the "plenum" of their possibilities. But if this were so, and human beings bore all their possibilities within themselves, they could not be identical to any of them but would always be left dangling between them. This in turn would mean that they could never become present to themselves because, as the originators of their own possibilities, they would always precede them. But if human beings are not identical to their possibilities, the plenum of these cannot be something purely given; it could be conceivable only as a continual process of emergence, and only in this way could there be any distinction between the possibilities. For without distinguishing between them, one could not talk of a plenum.

In this context, the interplay between the fictive and the imaginary takes on profound anthropological implications. If human beings can step out of themselves only by means of a constant self-unfolding, their possibilities evidently cannot possess a pregiven shape, for this would mean imposing preexisting patterns on the unfolding. But if the shapes of and the distinctions between possibilities are not pregiven, they must be acquired, and since they cannot be extrapolated from realities, it follows that they can be acquired only through realities being, as it were, played away. This once more means that human beings, as the unfolding of themselves, can never be fully present to themselves, because at any one stage they possess themselves only in the possibility realized, and that is what they are not: one limited possibility of themselves. Therefore continual self-unfolding has to be sustained by playing out the plenum of possibilities through a constant alternation of composing and decomposing fabricated worlds. As there is no way to grasp how this alternation operates, the playing out can be enacted only in its potentially innumerable variations in order for it to be perceived as it happens. This, in turn, is brought about by the fictive mobilizing the imaginary as a dual countering, which issues in each of its manifested instances into another shape. Enactment, then, may be considered a transcendental condition, allowing perceptibility of something intangible and simultaneously providing an experience of something that is unknowable.

Such an enactment can only be played; its inception is the boundary-crossing of fictionalizing, which allows referential realities as well as other writings to recur in the text; these, even if they appear to be mere reproductions, always recur with a difference, giving rise to a back-and-forth movement between what is in the text and the reality that is being referred to. The same applies to the imaginary, which the fictive mobilizes into a dual countering, and which evolves as cancellation and production, derestriction and combination, irrealization and conceptualization, incorporating all the text's referential realities into the resultant to and fro. This play movement is not dialectic by nature, nor does it develop teleologically, nor is it an inherent quality of what it brings into play.

If we examine how the word 'play' is used and concentrate on its so-called metaphorical senses, we find talk of the play of light, the play of the waves, the play of gears or parts of machinery, the interplay of limbs, the play of forces, the play of gnats, even a play on words. In each case what is intended is to-and-fro movement that is not tied to any goal that would bring it to an end ... The movement of playing has no goal that brings it to an end; rather, it renews itself in constant repetition. The movement backward and forward is obviously so central to the definition of play that it makes no difference who or what performs this movement. The movement of play as such has, as it were, no substrate. It is the game that is played—it is irrelevant whether or not there is a subject who plays it. The play is the occurrence of the movement as such. Thus we speak of the play of colors and do not mean only that one color plays against another, but that there is one process or sight displaying a changing variety of colors.[84]

Since "the movement of play as such has ... no substrate," the play movement bears within itself its own unfathomableness that invites penetration. The resultant dynamism is not without structure, though it is not exclusively based on either the boundary-crossing of the fictionalizing acts or the dual countering to which the imaginary has been unfolded.

The intentionality underlying fictionalizing is comparatively determinate when it seeks to cancel what it has overstepped, although it will aim in the direction of a still indeterminate target. In other words, fictionalizing is free play. It oversteps what is, and turns in the direction of what is not. Free play, however, would draw the fictionalizing act into a transcending movement that would make us forget what it has turned away from. Yet the fictionalizing act keeps in play what has been overstepped in order to expose it to becoming something other than itself. Thus free play is tied to another form of play whose aim is to bring to light the motivation for the overstepping. Fictionalizing opens up a difference that can no longer be eradicated by consciousness, because there can be no knowledge as yet of what intentionality targets; consequently, difference is revealed by way of the countervailing movements of free and instrumental play. This back and forth does not allow free play to reach beyond what it leaves behind, but it also prevents instrumental play from fulfilling itself, for this play movement "dreams of deciphering a truth or an origin which escapes play and the order of the sign."[85] And so free play has to play against endings, while instrumental play works against its own being played away. This play of difference, although triggered by fictionalizing, can no longer be controlled by it; it can only be acted out.

It would seem at first that overstepping favors free play, whereas the imaginability of constitutive conditions goes together with instrumental play. In fact, however, fictionalizing retains the presence of the worlds overstepped as fully as the dual countering of the imaginary—with its cancellations, derestrictions, and irrealizations—appears to be free play. But the very interaction between the fictive and the imaginary becomes palpable in this play movement when free and instrumental play enter into a relationship, ultimately playing with and against each other. *Play arises out of the coexistence of the fictive and the imaginary.* The boundary-crossing reveals the irrepressible tendency of free play to distance itself from what is, even though this detachment holds fast to the referential worlds that allow free play to become tangible. From this arises the irrepressible tendency of instrumental play to use the discarded reality as a precondition for imagining possible motives for its cancellation. The fictive and the imaginary merge, each in itself incapable of fulfilling any function but together setting in motion a play movement that will enable both to take effect. Becoming effective implies playing out what is inherent in an interrelationship that defies conceptualization because there is no ultimate determining frame of reference. Energizing this playing is the drive to overcome basic deficiencies that mark both the fictive and the imaginary. What the fictive targets is as yet empty and thus requires filling; and what characterizes the imaginary is its featurelessness, which thus requires form for its unfolding.

Excursus: Beckett's *Imagination Dead Imagine* and Fantasy Literature

The countermovement of free and instrumental play derives from the interrelationship between the fictive and the imaginary, and the nature of the movement will be considerably influenced by which of the elements is dominant. Fantasy literature and science fiction are extreme instances of a cognitive coagulation of the imaginary. Without the intentional acts of fictionalizing, the imaginary takes neither shape nor effect, but it can be brought under the control of the fictive to such a degree that the modifications it causes become the exclusive subject matter.

This is particularly the case with fantasy literature, in which the imaginary appears to be total modification. In fantasy literature, reality is completely nullified, and fantasy parades in the "garments" of that nullified reality. Irwin maintains that to "make nonfact appear as fact, is essential to fantasy."[86] If the modes of depiction used to represent realities serve to endow fantasy with a sense of reality, whatever might jeopardize this illusion must be strictly avoided: "In successful fantasy all is clarity and certainty, as far as presentation goes" (p. 55). In order to achieve this clarity by lending verisimilitude to the unbelievable, recourse to rhetoric appears to be indispensable: ". . . from the outset a fantasy is governed by the requirements and devices of rhetoric, much more than of art" (p. 58). It is rhetoric that takes on the task of convincing the reader that nonfacts are facts (see p. 60). This is relevant to our discussion insofar as rhetoric entails the intentionality of a consciousness through which fantasy is tailored to a specific application; and again it follows that fantasy is not a self-activating force. But how can something that goes against all known facts demand and achieve credibility? Through its narrative realization, brought about by means of rhetoric, fantasy reaches full fruition when it entails "human involvement" (p. 64). This makes it possible for fantasy to stage as 'fact' something that obviously runs counter to empirical facts. Such literature maps out the parameters of what in a historically given situation has to be highlighted, and it acts as a divining rod in the search for historical needs. But this means that fantasy as pure modification remains subjugated to pragmatic use, which indicates the predominance of the fictive; the latter makes fantasy into reality, and reality into the territory conquered by fantasy.

Although Irwin was dealing only with a certain type of fantasy literature, here as elsewhere fantasy is to a great extent subsumed under cognitive constraints. This also applies when fantasy is concerned with more than just the rhetorical plausibility of its impossibilities—in other words, when its aim is subversion. "Fantasy re-combines and inverts the real, but it does not escape it: it exists in a parasitical or symbiotic relation to the real. The fantastic cannot exist independently of that 'real' world which it seems to find so frustratingly finite . . . The actual world is constantly present in fantasy, by negation . . . fantasy is what

could not have happened; i.e. what *cannot* happen, what *cannot* exist . . .
the negative subjunctivity, the *cannot* or *could not*, constitutes in fact the
chief pleasure of fantasy."[87] This description makes clear the negating
character of fantasy, but only insofar as the pleasure of seeing the inex-
pressible side of a culture expressed ultimately meets a compensatory
need. For instance, fantasy often ties up the mimetic with the mirac-
ulous in order to exhibit what has been lost in a technologically oriented civilization. This very goal makes it necessary to set up the fantastic in cognitive trappings, not least because its true significance as a
contribution toward overcoming deficiencies has to be communicated
according to the prevailing codes in civilized societies.

     In regard to the ossification of the imaginary in fantasy literature—
which is often light literature and rarely inspires a second reading,
since the imaginary is manipulated according to prevailing needs—it is
well worth noting Caillois's observations expressed in his book *Der
Krake. Versuch über die Logik des Imaginativen:*

> If a mystery can stir, if the unusual can grip, if poetry is possible, then
> perhaps this is because of the complex, confusing correspondences
> into which the unity of cosmos has disintegrated. Everything that
> reminds us of this unity calls forth within our feelings agreement and
> good will, an *ab initio* approving echo and longing for unanimity . . .
> Many philosophers have blithely defined the real and the rational. I
> am convinced that another, equally daring action, so long as it was
> based on and would inspire many very precise investigations, could
> discover the network of established analogy and hidden links that
> constitute the logic of the imaginative.[88]

What Caillois describes in his book is a fantastic infiltration by the
tentacled, suckered kraken in which he sees at work a logic of the
imaginative. For him the imaginary is neither a faculty nor *materia
prima* nor Ur-fantasy but a continual regaining of what human beings
have never lost. Thus the imaginary remains a blank that constantly
invites fillings, but then empties itself again when cognitive constraints
thematize the imaginary in accordance with the conventions of perception psychology, as happens in fantasy literature. The imaginary is therefore set up under conditions that are alien to itself. Caillois reverses the
perspective when he records what happens to the activators that mobilize the imaginary into its protean multiplicity of shapes and features.
Instead of taming the imaginary for specific purposes—which are
especially evident in science fiction—the imaginary manifests itself as

an inundation of cognition. This flood of bizarre shapes that explode into countless images indicates the helplessness of cognition, and gives free rein and visible expression to the imaginary. For the mysterious features projected onto the kraken spotlight a consciousness under the spell of its images. If there is a "logic of the imaginative," it consists predominantly in the suspension of a focusing consciousness, whose traces are to be found only in the bizarre fantasies that overwhelm it.

Ossification and inundation mark the extreme manifestations of the imaginary in its associations with conscious activity. It solidifies where it is thematized, and it overflows when consciousness loses control. There are, of course, intermediate positions as well, but the question arises as to whether other categories are conceivable, that is, whether the imaginary 'as itself' could become visible before being set up or before it has taken effect. In our present context, Beckett's *Imagination Dead Imagine* supplies a possible answer to this question. Imagining that imagination is dead would mean directing an imaginative act toward its source. An act becomes an act through the impetus of intentionality, and this element of consciousness is also present in Beckett's injunction. But now the imaginative act is to incorporate the obliteration of what constitutes it. The conscious component can do no more than point the way, and its influence will be clipped, since what has to be imagined is the self-removal of the act of imagining. Consciousness must be neutralized, because otherwise the imaginary, whether as ossification or as inundation, will once again be manipulated for whatever purpose. Consciousness must, so to speak, be ligated if the imagination is to be viewed prior to all activity. This can be done only if the imagination is imagined dead, because otherwise it is present only in its effects. Being dead therefore means being separated from its manifestations, so that it would be nonsense to give it any other substance than its own nonbeing. But if this nonbeing is called "dead," there must be a consciousness present in order to conceive of the nonmanifested imagination as no longer being. For consciousness, which Sartre maintains always activates the imaginary, will, in relation to an imaginary that is itself, have lost its partner, as it were, so that such an autonomous imaginary will then, from the viewpoint of consciousness, embody a no-longer-being.

At the same time the presence of a consciousness is necessary because without it a preactivated imaginary can have no presence of its own. This is evident from the fact that in Beckett's text the imagining of

a dead imagination takes place in what seems to be a space at one time
in a rotunda and at another in what may be a skull.[89] In his *Allgemeine
Psychopathologie* Jaspers points out that nearly all processes of consciousness are represented through spatial metaphors, [90] a fact that also
characterizes fictionality as an offshoot of consciousness. For ranging
from topographical to semantic enclosures, fictionality continually sets
up areas that must be overstepped in order to open up other areas. In
Beckett's text, even though consciousness no longer awakens the imaginary into activity, the presentation of the autonomous imaginary still
takes place through modes of consciousness. But concrete areas are
now present only in a state of ceaseless disappearance: "Islands, waters,
azure, verdure, one glimpse and vanished, endlessly, omit."[91] This vanishing of space into a generally vague sort of rotunda is accompanied by
an abundance of imperatives, through which the narrating voice calls
for entrance into or withdrawal from the white vault. "No way in, go in,
measure" (p. 7). What the voice has been excluded from is to be mea-
sured! "Go back out, move back, the little fabric vanishes, ascend, it
vanishes, all white in the whiteness, descend, go back in" (p. 8). The
imperative can do no more than give an intentional directive, and since
nothing can be gained from it, all that remains is to wait: "Wait, more or
less long, light and heat come back, all grows white and hot together"
(pp. 8f.).

These double movements denote a revocation that reveals two
things. First, imagination has to be activated in order to become tangible. The intentionality manifested in the imperatives is the minimal
impetus necessary for the imaginary to be unleashed. We have already
seen this process in various guises from Coleridge through literary
fictionality. Second, if the imaginary becomes present in its manifestation, what is it that is present? The imaginary, or the form of its utilization? If we are to go on speaking of the imaginary, then the intentionality must incorporate its own negation; the unfolding of the
imaginary must always entail the revocation of the impulses that have
activated it. This is necessary because the round space always displays
the imaginary under conditions imposed by consciousness, which
remains indispensable, since the imaginary has to be translated. But
consciousness must not do more than provide the space for the imaginary, because otherwise the latter would turn into a gestalt of its own
activation. And so the conscious element in the process of display must

be minimized as far as possible in order to reduce the influence of the medium.

What is left when the imaginary is isolated as itself, and does not appear in the form of its utilization? Beckett describes it as follows:

> More or less long, for there may intervene, experience shows, between end of fall and beginning of rise, pauses of varying length, from the fraction of the second to what would have seemed, in other times, other places, an eternity. Same remark for the other pause, between end of rise and beginning of fall. The extremes, as long as they last, are perfectly stable . . . It is possible too, experience shows, for rise and fall to stop short at any point and mark a pause, more or less long, before resuming, or reversing, the rise now fall, the fall rise, these in their turn to be completed, or to stop short and mark a pause, more or less long." (pp. 9f.)

Consciousness provides space for the imaginary, and in this there is a temporal movement of rise and fall. If consciousness can no longer grasp the rotunda it has set up, it releases the imaginary into a time structure whose central element is the pause, which alone gives stability to the extremes. The extremes of the rotunda are heat and cold, white and black, and these are both kept apart and interwoven by the pause. Precisely because the pause does not take on its shape through the extremes, but actually conditions their opposition as well as their merging, in relation to these extremes it remains a nothing: "Light and heat remain linked as though supplied by the same source of which still no trace" (p. 11).

What makes this nothing so incomprehensible is that it obliterates the extremes only in order to set them up again. The double movement of nullification and production is at least glanced at here even if it is not yet given situational application. For the pause can do no more than indicate the interweaving of fall and rise, the erasing and fixing of contours, and the fading out of spatial differences. The pause is not yet given presence through a medium that would endow it with set usages. And so in his exposé of the pause, Beckett turns to experience. For consciousness could understand the pause only as an unfathomable difference, defying a conceptual grasp. This, however, would not constitute a self-presentation of the imaginary. Even though it may activate the imaginary, consciousness cannot subsume it. On the other hand, experience teaches us that the imaginary exists. The quality of this experience includes its eluding knowability because of its evidential nature, which renders knowability superfluous.

On the ground of the rotunda, curved in a semicircle, lie a human couple. Beckett chose the word "ground" (p. 7), and not "bottom," and in view of his extreme sensitivity to language, we may assume that the choice was not by chance. Apparently frozen to lifelessness, the white couple merge with the white ground. "Sweat and mirror notwithstanding they might well pass for inanimate but for the left eyes which at incalculable intervals suddenly open wide and gaze in unblinking exposure long beyond what is humanly possible ... Never the two gazes together except once, when the beginning of one overlapped the end of the other, for about ten seconds" (pp. 12f.). The pause articulates the rhythm of animated lifelessness, which makes the extreme of heat and cold, black and white seem comparatively moderate. The extremes have little effect on the couple; they seem to lie, as it were, outside them. "Leave them there, sweating and icy, there is better elsewhere. No, life ends and no, there is nothing elsewhere, and no question now of ever finding again that white speck lost in whiteness" (p. 14). Since the white speck is lost in whiteness, it articulates that whiteness as well as articulating what no longer exists anywhere else. Present in the helplessness of comprehension is the experience that the imaginary is pure lifelessness that contains all life, though this life can never be completely, but only partially, realized under conditions imposed by something else. Beckett's text shows the gap between consciousness and the imaginary; indeed, it is possible to talk of them as being different only because of the gap, since here we have an observing consciousness at work, practicing its intentionality as a constant revocation in order to prevent the imaginary from taking on a presence through exercise. However, without such a self-restraining consciousness, the imaginary would remain sealed within itself.

Imagination Dead Imagine may depict the imaginary in the state of its awakening. The pause and the white speck lost in whiteness are the metonymies of the conscious mind for the imaginary, which can present itself to consciousness only through discontinuity by playing away its possible imaginability, as can be seen from the constantly varying pause between the extremes or from the white speck in animated lifelessness. It remains open whether a self-restraining consciousness views the gap between itself and the imaginary as a pause and as a speck disappearing into its surroundings, and projects it onto the imaginary in order to give shape to the latter's otherness, or whether the imaginary in its autonomous state is epitomized by the duality of negating emptiness and pure creativeness. This openness makes Beckett's text aesthetic, because the alternatives merge seamlessly into one another, with consciousness standing before its own helplessness, and the imaginary appearing as the projected emptiness of consciousness.

Imagination Dead Imagine takes on additional relevance if we consider it against the background of the increasingly popular genre of fantasy literature. Beckett's text also offers conscious access to the imaginary as seen in the frameworks of faculty psychology, the act, the radical imaginary, and the fictive. In all these cases, the imaginary presents itself as the ever-changing gestalt of its own manifestations. The more dominant the intended application, the more the imaginary will be subjected to the control of conscious processing. Although the fictionalizing acts impose their own doubleness on the imaginary because their overstepping nature makes them into empty forms of consciousness, they also set it free for the dual countering of nullifying and enabling.

In fantasy literature, however, the imaginary is reified by being thematized according to what it is considered to be. Therefore it is turned into a tangible object that—in spite of the monotonous variations common to many such texts—consists in the factual existence of the nonreal. At the same time, however, readers cannot be left in doubt of the fact that they are being confronted by an impossibility in the garb of an illusory reality. Because this strange doublethink has to be maintained throughout the reading, despite our awareness of the unreality we have to be drawn fully into the story. Such involvement is made possible by the fantasy's being wrapped in apparent reality. Simultaneously, if we are to be conscious of the alienation we are meant to undergo, we must also remain conscious of the reality suppressed by the fantastic. For fantasy negates reality only in order to give real clothing to the unreal. In this way, readers are induced to accept things that go against all expectations and credibility, although, of course, these unrealities must always retain an adequate degree of plausibility. This doubling mirrors the manifestation of fantasy under the cognitive dominance of the fictive. But since fantasy is reified by being thematized, and since it constitutes the reality of the impossible, it brings about a latent split in the reader's consciousness.

In the context of this split, we may discern two different types of fantasy literature. One uses rhetoric and psychology[92] to give the reader a homeopathic dose of the split in order that it may be sustained, and the other always incorporates "a break in the acknowledged order, an irruption of the inadmissible within the changeless everyday legality,"[93] so that the reader is plunged into a state of "*hesitation.*"[94] In the first case, the split is to be concealed, and in the second it is to be played out.[95] What is revealing is that even when fantasy is reified, it appears as a dual countering, bearing witness to the fact that it has been activated by the fictive. The popularity of fantasy literature suggests that this splitting of consciousness corresponds to some basic human requirement. Being something else within one's consciousness without giving up what one thinks oneself to be—this turns out to be a human need that literature uncovers by meeting it in a striking variety of ways, including the extreme form of fantasy literature.

Beckett, by contrast, depicts a consciousness that has suspended its own intentionality, with the result that the imaginary can no longer be fashioned by a particular application. Consequently, what is thematized is not the imaginary but the gap between consciousness and the imaginary. This gap can be experienced through endless cognitive efforts to bridge it. A consciousness that blocks itself off, and an imaginary that can only run in circles—these are the last remnants of a game in which we no longer know whether it is ending or beginning. These remnants are nothing more than a dynamic emptiness that also imposes itself on language; only language that consumes itself can give articulation to the imaginary.

Chapter Five

Text Play

The Play of Map and Territory

The contraflow of free and instrumental play does not necessarily aim at a result but is an integral part of particular games in which there is to be a settlement one way or the other. If such a play movement is transposed into language, it will begin to reorganize basic linguistic functions, as in the splitting of the signifier as the smallest, though most universal, of 'language games'. Rather than removing the difference within such gaming, the contraflow develops it into possibilities of play that, in the cases of cancellation and production, derestriction and combination, irrealization and conceptualization, pluralize the difference. As Gregory Bateson has pointed out in another context: "[it is] a difference which makes a difference."[1]

In ordinary language use, the signifier and the signified—though correlated by conventions—are distinguished by a difference, and when the signifier is bracketed off from its denotative use by the 'as-if', it undergoes further differentiation. One result of the separation from the basic function of denotation is that all subsequent linguistic actions no longer denote what they would have denoted if they still stood for convention-governed denotation. Instead, the linguistic sign is now freed for unpremeditated uses. In evolutionary terms something similar occurs in the games played by animals: "Not only does the playful nip not denote what would be denoted by the bite for which it stands, but, in addition, the bite itself is fictional. Not only do the playing animals not quite mean what they are saying but, also, they are usually communicating about something which does not exist" (p. 182). The signifier is fictionalized—both in the animals' game and in the text—because denotation is laid to rest and what is said is not meant. In the resultant play space, the split signifier signals that this is play. What is no longer valid is clear, but what is to be achieved by the invalidation remains open and can therefore only be played out.

Rather than removing the semiotic difference between signifier and signified, splitting the signifier doubles that difference and, in consequence, allows the signifier to be used in other ways. If it no longer means what it denotes, then no longer meaning what it denotes becomes itself a denotation, bringing into existence something that does not yet exist. The suspended denotative function adumbrates the conditions under which the not-yet-existing may be conceived, and here the imaginary begins to develop its dual countering. By removing something, it makes something else possible.

In characterizing play, Bateson borrowed from Korzybski (see p. 180) the term "map-territory relation." The relation of language to what it denotes resembles that of a map to the territory it charts. All language signs are thus illustrative abstractions of what their denotations are related to. If the fictionalized signifier imposes play conditions on this relationship, extensive changes will result. The split signifier must now support the whole map-territory relationship. Its denotation no longer being its meaning, it no longer refers to a territory but does remain a map insofar as the suspended denotation means something, even if its meaning can only be adumbrated negatively. A reversal of the map-territory relationship has taken place. Instead of a map denoting a territory, the suspended denotation becomes the map, enabling at least the contours of a territory to emerge. The territory will coincide with the map because it has no existence outside this designation. At the same time, however, it remains distinct from the map, because it is a product of the split signifier and not the signifier itself.

This is a paradox that Bateson attempts to explain by referring to other phenomena such as dreams, daydreams, and primary and secondary processes, which are also permeated by differences, and then distinguishing between them and the play difference. When we are awake, the difference between signifier and signified is generally maintained, but in dreams and daydreams it often vanishes completely, leaving the dreamer totally immersed in images. Bateson concludes "that play marks . . . the crucial step in the discovery of map-territory relations. In primary process, map and territory are equated; in secondary process, they can be discriminated. In play, they are both equated and discriminated" (p. 185). The difference is eliminated insofar as the fictionalized signifier is map and territory at the same time. The difference is maintained insofar as the signifier supplies the condition under which a territory has to be imagined for a map. The paradox of a difference that is simultaneously removed and preserved arises from the fact that the signifier stands under the proviso of the 'as-if'; it has been uncoupled from its conventional code, which therefore no longer determines the denotation of the signifier.

This is still not enough to make it into a floating signifier, but it does set free all the implications that it bears within itself and that have remained virtual throughout its code-governed applications. The new denotation generated by the canceling of denotation can now take on presence by way of the newly released implications, which suggest the possible contours of the hitherto uncharted territory. The split signifier turns into play, swinging to and fro between its code-governed determinacy and a signified to be brought forth. As a map it delineates an imagined territory that, like all ideas, can consist only of what has been put into it. This content is provided by the now liberated implications of the signifier, which is no longer bound by its code-governed function. The signifier appears to coincide with what it generates, yet the product emerging from the free-floating implications also remains different from the signifier. From the diversification of the liberated implications comes the potential variability of the imagined territory, whose contours are not predetermined but can only be shaded in with various nuances by means of play. Play replaces the conventional code; in other words, it becomes the code of the split signifier, which thus points the way to different kinds of reading.

In this process the signifier participates in a metacommunication, because the production of what it signifies can be stabilized only through the way in which it comes into being. For there is no transcendental condition that can facilitate the charting of something that does not yet exist. Only play allows for metacommunication of what happens in linguistic action, because this is primarily a performance which ends with the achievement of its aims. Consequently, the performance has to be staged, if language is to be used to talk about language. The language game of the split signifier therefore takes place as the performance of a linguistic action and, at the same time, as the staging of that action. Hence the need to separate the signifier from the signified, so that whatever is inherent in the denotation can be played out. In this way the performance becomes its own subject matter. Literary texts can therefore speak about the manner of communication, and indeed this is necessary because they deal with something that is not given but has to be brought forth.

The Tilting Game of Imitation and Symbolization

The play of the split signifier can obviously be acted out in different ways, as it takes the place of the canceled, transcendental signified. The simultaneous, permanent identity and difference between map and territory can result at one moment in a structure of double meaning, at another in one of the palimpsest—with the signified shining through the nonmeaning—and at another in oceanic dedifferentiation of denotation, so that the unspeakable may be spoken, with the aid of the disappearing vestiges of denotation. Such a scale also begins to sketch the variable interrelationships between the fictive and the imaginary, together with the changing shapes of the territory that is to be imagined.

The play may consolidate itself into specific figures of speech and rhetorical tropes that sometimes say more than they mean, and sometimes say something different from what is meant; in any case, the repertoire of rhetoric allows the split signifier to take specific forms geared to the intended achievement.[2] The reversal of map and territory that results from this split is an important step in the continuing development of communication, which is thereby enabled to exhibit its workings. For if the sign remained irrevocably bound to a transcendental signified, "Life would then be an endless interchange of stylized messages, a game with rigid rules, unrelieved by change or humor."[3]

The question now arises whether the manner of play will reveal general structures such as those that may be discerned in the play of the split signifier. It is necessary to spot the moves, since only through these does play manifest itself. By contrast, asking what, exactly, play is, tends to make it disappear, since such questions only try to make play represent something other than itself. But if we take play as arising out of the interpenetration of the fictive and the imaginary—which means seeing the doubling structure of the fictive as a medium for the unfolding of the imaginary as a dual countering—then such play cannot be traced back to a base outside itself. Because giving it a base would mean removing difference, since the manner of play can be manifested only by distinguishing between the possibilities of play. However, such differentiation is not the variability of the existing, pregiven difference that deconstruction has called deferral of origins. Instead, differentiation here means the multiplication of differences ("a difference which makes a difference"), so that play unfolds as a continual specification of itself.

The interplay between the fictive and the imaginary turns the basic play movement of back and forth into a contraflow between free and instrumental playing that—when drawn into language—inverts the semiotic difference; similarly, on the level of relations between text and empirical world, the play movement is a contraflow between imitation and symbolization.

To clarify this, we might remind ourselves of two anthropological preconditions for such play that finds its paradigmatic manifestation in the literary text. Remarkably, two very divergent ideas concerning the manner of play—those of Jean Piaget and Friedrich Georg Jünger—converge in their central argument. Their premises differ in that Piaget develops his theory of play from child psychology, whereas for Jünger psychological motivations for play are "heillos" (hopeless), and so his creed is "In order to avoid the mishmash of such hypotheses, let us steer well clear of all psychological derivations of play."[4] In view of such diametrically opposed approaches, the similarities become all the more striking. Jünger gears his concept of play to what he calls "Ahmung," which means assuming an attitude of imitation that comprises both "involvement in and execution of imitation" (p. 48), but which turns into play only when it represents "something not present, something missing" (p. 57). "The characteristic feature of such games marked by both involved and executed imitation [*vorahmend-nachahmende Spiele*] is that in playful manner they reproduce behavior which is not play. A movement which is not play becomes play" (p. 51). This, for Jünger, is a "characteristic feature of all games" (p. 57), and in spite of his contempt for psychological premises, he takes as his example a girl playing with her doll (see, e.g., pp. 59, 192f.).

For Piaget, too, imitation is a central precondition for play. It bridges the gap between the self and reality brought about by a quasi-Kantian schema allowing the self to adapt itself to reality. But in contrast with Kant, Piaget's schemata are not considered to be an indispensable a priori of cognition; they are more like Winnicott's "transitional objects,"[5] by means of which the infant fills the intermediate area between its

mother and a gradually perceivable external world. While these schemata accommodate the self to reality, at the same time they embody the
beginnings of symbolizations, which here, as elsewhere, serve to repair
a deficiency. The more smoothly the schemata of adaptation function,
the more swiftly occurs "what might be called a 'ritualisation' of the
schemas, which, no longer in their adaptive context, are as it were
imitated or 'played' plastically."[6] This is remarkably similar to Jünger's
"involvement in and execution of imitation [*Vorahmung und Nachah-
mung*]," which also gives rise to play.

But for Piaget, imitation is initially a precondition for adaptation,
and so he asks, "how can we explain the fact that imitation and play,
from being antithetic at first, can become complementary?" (p. 103).
His answer is "We must first point out that no schema is ever, once and
for all, adaptive, imitative or ludic, even when its initial function has
made it tend in one of these three directions. Therefore an imitative
schema can as easily become ludic as can an adaptive schema. Moreover, it must be remembered that every schema always includes both
assimilation and accommodation, since each of these two processes is
essentially inseparable from the other. It is therefore only their ratio
which determines the adaptive, imitative or ludic character of the
schema" (p. 103). Therefore "play is seen to be the function of assimilation extended beyond the limits of adaptation" (p. 95), with the result
that every schema is dual in character, and the duality allows for playing out what is inherent in it. Assimilation simply reverses the direction of aim; instead of adaptation to realities, it is now realities that are
adapted.

The more the accommodating role of the schema stabilizes the
relation to reality, the more this primary imitation becomes a limitation, so that the assimilative component gains the upper hand in order
to undo the growing restrictions. Since for this purpose there are no
guiding references, let alone norms, the assimilative application of the
schema can take place only as a play of trial movements. The schema
still bears the imprint of imitation, but this no longer relates to a world
of objects; instead, it serves to assimilate things that lie beyond the
reach of the self. "We can therefore say that if adapted activity and
thought constitute an equilibrium between assimilation and accommodation, play begins as soon as there is predominance of assimilation" (p. 150). This reversal indicates multiple ways of mastering the
difference between self and reality: Accommodation entails the self

adapting to reality; assimilation is the other way round. The very fact that the symbolizing component of the schema can achieve an appropriation of reality is due to the nature of the symbol, which Blumenberg has described as "indifference to the presence of that which [the symbol] indicates is to be imagined ... It may be that the capacity of the symbol has arisen out of the incapacity of depiction, as Freud suspected; or from magic with its technical need to treat whatever splinter of reality it likes and thereby have reality itself—and as a whole—at its disposal ... What is decisive is that this elementary means of relating to the world facilitates a departure from perception and visualization, and hence a free mode of access to the non-present."[7]

However, as Piaget remarks, the

> appearance of symbolism ... is the crucial point in all the interpretations of the ludic function. Why is it that play becomes symbolic, instead of continuing to be mere sensory-motor exercise or intellectual experiment, and why should the enjoyment of movement, or activity for the fun of activity, which constitute a kind of practical make-believe, be completed at a given moment by imaginative make-believe? The reason is that among the attributes of assimilation for assimilation's sake is that of distortion, and therefore to the extent to which it is dissociated from immediate accommodation it is a source of symbolic make-believe.[8]

Piaget's terminology aside, this observation is relevant to our present discussion because ontogeny confirms that play becomes play in the first place through the interaction of the fictive and the imaginary. As a trial run, play is only "a kind of practical make-believe" that indicates no more than an overstepping and therefore needs "imaginative make-believe" in order to be made into 'real' play. "Imaginative make-believe" brings about the "distortion" of what has been overstepped, which means that only when accommodation—understood as imitation—has been nullified can play that aims to assimilate what has been concealed by adaptation be set in motion.

Thus imitation undergoes a change of status: What it has been is now committed to memory, and though its function is laid to rest, its form is recalled, guiding the appropriation of what is beyond the reach of the self. Instead of imitating the empirical world, the assimilative use of the schema entails absorption of the inaccessible. Piaget tries to explain this very process by having recourse to the idea of the image:

As we have seen, the image is interiorised imitation, *i.e.,* the positive
of accommodation, which is the negative of the imitated object. The
image is therefore a schema which has already been accommodated
and is now used in present assimilations, which are also interiorised,
as "signifier" for these "signified." The image is therefore a differentiated signifier, more so than the index since it is detached from the
perceived object, but less so than the sign, since it is still imitation of
the object, and therefore is a 'motivated' sign, as distinct from verbal
signs which are "arbitrary."[9]

The same doubling of application is characteristic of the schemata
in the literary text. From the start, it is more than just a signifier; semi-
otically it might be called a supersign, whose structure is determined
by its use. There is no text that does not contain a discernible number
of inherited schemata—a fact Gombrich has shown to apply to nonver-
bal art as well. The schemata of the literary texts generally do not
imitate a given empirical world of objects; instead they reproduce affective attitudes, memories, knowledge, mental and perceptual dispositions, and so on, whose amalgamation, however, is not brought about
for its own sake. It goes without saying that the affective and cognitive
dispositions that are called upon during this process comprise data
drawn from the external world, and these are incorporated into the
schema, supplying it with its components of accommodation. But in
literature such an imitation always serves the assimilative function,
whose aim is so to symbolize the absent, the unavailable, the ungraspable that they may become accessible.

Cassirer says that it is one of humankind's original achievements
to reinterpret "the external 'impression' as 'expression' of the internal
. . . and in this way to substitute for something strange and inaccessible
something other and graspable by the senses."[10] If that is so, then symbolic forms will often tend to merge with what they stand for, even
though as representatives they must remain definitively separate from
it. It is therefore not surprising that particularly successful symbolizations are taken for imitations, since this would seem to guarantee that
what is made present (though can never be reached) by the symbol
may be understood as a reality. The more openly the schema reveals its
symbolic nature, the more closely will that which is presented appear
as an enactment designed not to coincide with what is meant to be
made conceivable. A contrary impression arises when successful sym-

bolization works as if it really were an imitation, for then an intangible state of affairs is endowed with a seemingly objective gestalt.

But once again this is, in Piaget's sense, a process of assimilation, highlighting the appropriation of something beyond our reach under conditions that characterize ourselves. It follows that without imitation the symbolic application of the schema would remain empty, and without symbolic application the imitation would remain directionless. This duality of the schema can become functional only as play, for only the groundlessness of play can bring about the constant interchange between imitation and symbolization without removing their difference. The schema unfolds itself as play insofar as the distribution of imitative and symbolic application is constantly changing, since each depends on the other. The intangible cannot be imitated, and its symbolization requires concretization, which again cannot be derived from intangibility.

Thus the schema turns into what might be called a tilting game. It suspends the validity of accommodation, whose form is utilized in order to assimilate the inaccessible. The component of accommodation no longer serves principally to imitate but instead must enable something to be visualized that by its very nature is unseeable. Theoretically there are no limits to this tilting game; it is driven by its own dynamism, in which imitation no longer functions as accommodation, and the intangible appears as something imitated. The basic movement of free and instrumental play takes on a specific form insofar as the characteristic features of the two countermovements are negated: Imitation is no longer what it used to be, and the inaccessible becomes perceptible. As the components of the schema overturn each other in the course of the gaming, what has to be assimilated springs to life. But this is not, as is commonly supposed, the product of successful imitation; it comes from the assimilative application of the imitative component, which enables the invisible to be visualized. Lifelikeness such as we find in the characters of novels and plays is the result of the tilting game. These characters are not imitated people; they are schemata whose imitative component serves to make conceivable what they symbolize. Lifelikeness is not, then, to be equated with imitation or with symbolization. Like the tilting game that produces it, it cannot be traced back to any base.

The tilting game is also relevant for the formation of literary tradition. The schemata of historically distant texts often seem like imitations of once given situations. Yet they cannot be imitations because schemata are always characterized by their tilting between accommodation and assimilation. The impression that these historically distant texts are imitations arises from the schema's assimilative component, which gives vivid presence to a past that can never be recovered. What is unavailable cannot be imitated.

The case of one poet's supposedly imitating another, for example, Virgil's "imitating" Homer, proves this point. Imitated schemata—as in the classical tradition especially—are not mere reproductions but serve to symbolize something that did not lie in the orbit of the original forms and is now used to give shape to something intangible. It is not the schema that is imitated; instead, the imitation is turned into a component of accommodation in order to assimilate whatever has to be tackled. Tradition, therefore, grows less from what is handed down through the generations than from the constant reshuffling of what is inherited, and the observable interchange between the accommodative and the assimilative component of the schema allows such recasting to be pinpointed. Tradition, then, plays the tilting game of imitation and symbolization in different ways. And the manner of such play endows tradition with its physiognomy, not least because there is no transcendental stance from which tradition may be judged.[11]

In the final analysis, the continuation of what is called tradition develops from the interplay between the fictive and the imaginary. The repeated schema is overstepped and thus opened up again to be filled in a manner that is inevitably alien to its previous function, thereby revealing that what appeared to be successful imitation is in fact the work of symbolization. As the tilting game is an offshoot of the interpenetration of the fictive and the imaginary, the symbolization of the previous text can become a component of accommodation in the subsequent text in order to endow a new symbolization with a tangible shape.

It may well be that there is no such thing as progress in art and literature, but the game of imitation and symbolization always raises barriers, and every success widens accessibility in its own way.[12] For the inaccessible varies historically, determined as it is by human interests of the time, and the tilting game of imitation and symbolization is able to master all situations because it can be played in any number of ways. This is one reason why literature to a large extent always arises out of literature.[13] It is not some sort of retreat into the ivory tower that motivates this apparently incestuous relationship between literature and literature; rather, successful visualizations of the invisible are taken over in order that their symbolizations may be used to chart new areas of the ungraspable.

If we take the schema to be a supersign, its tilting game brings to full fruition the inversion of map and territory that results from the split signifier. For tilting means releasing the imitative component from its objective reference in order to use it to visualize what is being symbolized. But tilting also means that symbolization loses its representative function, so that it may use the imitative component to make conceivable something that is either incapable of objectification or nonexistent. Tilting itself, however, even though it is observable as a process, remains an empty space within this game that, since it has no substratum, causes the ceaseless reciprocal overturning of imitation and symbolization without ever removing their difference. The latter is marked by a striking duality: It separates imitation and symbolization, and at the same time it has each of them constantly changing into something else; it also remains present as a trace when imitation and symbolization have been played into their respective changes of function.

Games in the Text

The play of map and territory and the tilting game of the schema both result from interaction between free and instrumental play. The split signifier and the interchanging functions of imitation and symbolization give concrete form to the contraflow of the play, though at the price of limitations laid down by language. For the intentional character of language works against the endlessness of play. But even if such a movement is made the object of language games—as was attempted, for instance, by Dadaism—the endlessness of play cannot be maintained, since the text itself is limited. This does not mean, however, that play itself is ended. Instead, the endlessness of play has to be conveyed by playing through specific possibilities, and this is done by means of games. The games structure the contraflow of free and instrumental play, just as the latter unfolds itself in the games as the playing out of possibilities. For this process the split signifier and the tilting game of the schema provide the linguistic framework whose flexibility enables it to be used for all kinds of games.

Games in the text always pit free and instrumental play against each other. At the same time, they vary the manner in which the split signifier and the tilting game of the schema are applied, depending on whether the text is to play primarily against its referential world, or to play its assembled positions out beyond itself, or to win possible worlds, or to play with the expectations of potential readers. Each individual game uses the basic contraflow of play in its own particular way, and play remains dynamic even beyond its pragmatic specifications insofar as the different games of the text continue to be played against each other.

The multiplicity of games has engendered an intensified endeavor to categorize gaming—not least because play can best be grasped by way of its structures. Since the late 1940s there has been a proliferation of classifications, which have arisen partly in direct opposition to Huizinga, who so globalized contest that for him it figured as the one and only game extant, not least because he considered it to be the origin of culture.[14] There is often a similar tendency to privilege a single game even when the existence of other games is explicitly recognized. Friedrich Georg Jünger, for instance, distinguishes games of chance, skill, and imitation but leaves no doubt that there is an inherent hierarchy of significance. He wants to shift the emphasis, and so it appears that he is directly opposing Huizinga when he says that the "game arises out of imitation, not out of contest. If there is no imitation, there will be neither game nor contest."[15] Roger Caillois, despite his admiration for Huizinga, is even more explicit. By reducing everything to contest, he claims Huizinga "deliberately omits, as obvious, the description and classification of games themselves, since they all respond to the same needs and reflect, without qualification, the same psychological attitude. His work is not a study of games, but an inquiry into the creative quality of the play principle in the domain of culture, and more precisely, of the spirit that rules certain kinds of games—those which are competitive."[16] Caillois then offers his own classification of games, and although his categories are not related to the text but are seen as an attempt at "laying the foundations for a sociology *derived from* games,"[17] they are of direct relevance to our own discussion.

Caillois distinguishes four categories of games: *agōn, alea, mimicry,* and *ilinx. Agōn* is contest, and has the characteristics attributed to it by Huizinga: It is "a combat in which equality of chances is artifically created, in order that the adversaries should confront each other under ideal conditions, susceptible of giving precise and incontestable value to the winner's triumph" (p. 14). *Alea* is a type of game which "in contrast to *agōn* ... [is] based on a decision independent of the player, an outcome over which he has no control and in which winning is the result of fate rather than triumphing over an adversary" (p. 17). *Mimicry* entails "the temporary acceptance, if not of an illusion (indeed this last word means nothing less than beginning a game: *in-lusio*), then at least of a closed, conventional, and, in certain respects, imaginary universe. Play can consist not only of deploying actions or submitting to one's fate in an imaginary milieu, but of becoming an illusory character oneself, and of so behaving. One is thus confronted with a diverse series of manifestations, the common element of which is that the subject makes believe or makes others believe that he is someone other than himself. He forgets, disguises, or temporarily sheds his personality in order to feign another" (p. 19). And *ilinx*, the "last kind of game includes those which are based on the pursuit of vertigo and which consist of an attempt to momentarily destroy the stability of perception and inflict a kind of voluptuous panic upon an otherwise lucid mind. In all cases, it is a question of surrendering to a kind of spasm, seizure, or shock which destroys reality with sovereign brusqueness" (p. 23).

These four categories need to be rethought if they are to be viewed as games in the text. This is simple enough, since games always express attitudes that are not manifested in rigid forms but take on their individuality only through interactive relationships. Caillois himself draws attention to this correspondence between game and attitude:

> It should be recalled that these distinctive attitudes are four in number: the desire to win by one's merit in regulated competition (*agōn*), the submission of one's will in favor of anxious and passive anticipation of where the wheel will stop (*alea*), the desire to assume a strange personality (*mimicry*), and, finally, the pursuit of vertigo (*ilinx*). In *agōn*, the player relies only upon himself and his utmost efforts; in *alea*, he counts on everything except himself, submitting to the powers that elude him; in *mimicry*, he imagines that he is someone else, and he invents an imaginary universe; in *ilinx*, he gratifies the desire to temporarily destroy his bodily equilibrium, escape the tyranny of his ordinary perception, and provoke the abdication of conscience.[18]

These attitudes incorporate anthropological dispositions, which in each of the different games are enacted as prototypes. The attitudes concerned unfold their multifarious features when, by being acted out, they permit a form of self-experience that is freed from the constraints of consciousness. This is what makes games enjoyable, for they break all the bounds of everyday pragmatic needs that otherwise hold our attitudes in check. Play, then, stages anthropological dispositions that, because they can never be disclosed in their entirety, can assume presence only through a range of their different aspects; the text stages the games themselves, and these must interplay among themselves in order to prevent the text—which by its very nature is limited—from playing the end of play.

We shall now take a separate look at each of the textual games through which, in different ways, the contraflow of free and instrumental play is structured. The conditioning of this structure arises out of the basic constituents of play, which is an offshoot of the interpenetration of the fictive and the imaginary.

Agōn is undoubtedly one of the basic games, even if it is not the be-all and end-all that Huizinga—and occasionally Bloom[19]—consider it to be. The contraflow of play is manifested as strife, or even a rift, through which referential realities are antagonistically arranged and intratextual positions are antithetically arranged, so that the textual world clashes with the reader's expectations. *Agōn* has a double effect: On the one hand, it consolidates the opposing norms, values, feelings, thoughts, opinions, and so on into positions; on the other, it initiates the surmounting of what has congealed into positions through the conflict. Thus *agōn* entails both consolidation and undermining of what has been consolidated. Strife and rift can therefore set denotation to play against figuration in the split signifier, and they can set the imitative component against the symbolizing component of the schema. But precisely at this point it becomes evident that the strife and rift of *agōn* either demand resolution or aim at all-embracing unification. Consequently, the interplay of denotation and figuration, as well as that of imitation and symbolization, must have its efficacy tested in order to reveal what lies behind strife and rift. *Agōn* has to be played toward a result that will overcome the antagonisms that have become palpable in the course of the confrontation. If the decision is given in the text itself, the latter will all too often become trivial, showing that *agōn* has been used to justify a pregiven intention, instead of playing out all the implications of the antagonistically arranged positions. The more the rift dominates the strife, the more irreconcilable the adversaries will be, so that finally it will not be a matter of winning or losing but of visualizing the gap itself.

Alea in the text is not, of course, a game of chance in the normal sense, although it is still a necessary game insofar as it endows the inevitable restrictedness of the text with an element of the unforeseeable. This is bound to happen anyway, since every game begins with a move whose consequences can never be totally foreseen. And since every game has to develop, "fundamental to the dynamism of play is the element of 'surprise', 'adventure', and 'inspiration'.[20] Free play triumphs over instrumental play, but no matter how drastically the former rejects the latter, instrumental play will still be a necessary foil in order to prepare for the unexpected, as the pragmatically oriented movements begin to break down. Instead of compressing referential realities into antagonistically arranged positions, *alea* breaks open the semantic networks formed by the referential worlds and also by the recurrence of other texts. In this respect, *alea* plays against *agōn,* whose antithetical arrangement reduces the element of chance, whereas *alea* explodes everything within the text into an unpredictable structuring of its semantics. If *agōn* aims to overcome the difference that arises out of antagonistically arranged positions, *alea* aims to intensify it, thereby making it into a rift that cannot be overcome, and reducing all play to mere chance.

This is of special significance for intertextuality. *Alea* is certainly not the only game of intertextuality, but without the generator of chance, there could not be the rich variety of combinations that permeates the interweaving of texts. By giving free semantic range to all the broken correlations, *alea* unfolds this variety in ways that make intertextuality a game of almost unrestricted semantic dissemination.

In this context, it is worth noting the observation of Eigen and Winkler, who in describing the game of evolution remark: "In the work of art the strict conception of evolution, based on optimal functionality, is abandoned. The playful character of the contingent is given greater emphasis ... But just as evolution is the result of chance and necessity, the creation of the work of art is also subject to strict criteria of mental evaluation—or, as Theodor W. Adorno says: 'Where art does nothing but play, there is nothing left of expression.'"[21] For then everything is, so to speak, played away, even if there have to be certain pregiven conditions whose removal is the prerequisite for the game of chance.

Agōn thrives on overcoming difference and *alea* on making it absolute, whereas *mimicry* aims to make difference disappear. But since what has to be removed is what actually constitutes *mimicry*, the process becomes a game—primarily one of transmogrification but also one of illusion. In the text this means making the denotative function of the split signifier as strong as the imitative component of the schema. Denotation and imitation thus dominate this game, although they can never degenerate into mere copying, because the split signifier and the tilting game of the schema both stand under the proviso of the 'as-if'. Since that proviso cannot be eliminated, play that is *mimicry*, or the forgetting of difference, is only a refinement of illusion.

The same is true when the illusion is broken. Then the mimicking of reality is punctured and the text reveals what it cannot be—reality—though it presents this very reality that it has mimicked for observation. If the broken illusion makes transparent what it pretended to be, the seemingly eradicated difference reasserts itself, and illusion as deception tilts into illusion as a means of grasping what has been imitated. Apart from this one vestige, the component of free play is laid to rest in *mimicry* by that of instrumental play. Imitation is all that can be played, for what is to be mimicked is given and lies outside the game. *Mimicry* is therefore a counter to *alea*, which shows the text neither as pretended reality nor as a mirror image of something given, but as the setting for the unpredictable.

The final category, *ilinx*, is difficult to apply to the text in Caillois's sense of vertigo, but it may be viewed as a game of subversion whose "vertiginous" element consists in the carnivalization of all the positions assembled in the text. In his study of games, Buytendijk says that "Vertigo is essentially a cancellation of being, a self-losing, self-surrendering, not as in sleep, but in order to experience oneself in an existence that is not bound in by one's own person."[22] There is clearly an anarchic tendency in *ilinx*, and this not only liberates what has been suppressed; it also reintegrates what has been excluded. Thus it allows the absent to play against the present, and in everything that is present it opens a difference that makes whatever has been excluded fight back against the representative claims of what excluded it. Whatever is present is as if mirrored from its reverse side. *Ilinx* may therefore be seen as a game in which free play is at its most expansive. But for all its efforts to reach beyond what is, free play remains bound to what it overshoots, because it can never quite extinguish the undercurrents and overtones of instrumental play. Precisely for this reason, *ilinx* remains a game, since otherwise it would eliminate itself or would never be able to issue into a form.

In the text these different games rarely occur in isolation; they generally mix, and their respective combinations can be understood as a textual game. With regard to literature, then, *agōn, alea, mimicry,* and *ilinx* are not games but the constitutive elements of a game. *Agōn* is called into play when conflicts predominate, *alea* when chance is the necessary driving force, *mimicry* when mimicking and deception come to the fore, and *ilinx* when games are to be reversed or subverted. One can even judge texts by which of the individual game forms is made strong or weak in the interplay. Generally it is unlikely that any of the games will be totally excluded from the constitution of the textual play; instead, there are different degrees of balance and domination.

The combination of games is due not least to the fact that each contains elements of the others. *Agōn,* for instance, cannot exist without chance, deception, or subversion. What gives each type its concrete individuality is the dominance of the single determining factor. The text game may well be the only paradigm of games that amalgamate.

What this means may best be illustrated by particular combinations. If the text links *agōn* and *ilinx*—which may play both with and against each other—possible results on the scale of combinations might be as follows. With *ilinx* dominant, the conflict of norms, values, feelings, and whatever else is incorporated into the textual repertoire will become illusory; in consequence, the opposing positions will seem like a past world that has been left behind. If *agōn* dominates, then *ilinx* will bring about differentiation between the antagonistically arranged norms, values, and such that can withstand the challenge to their legitimacy only through a differentiated defense of their validity. If *alea* is combined with *mimicry* and *alea* has the upper hand, there will be illusion-breaking at one moment and discontinuity of events at another; the supposed equation between text and world will appear as a mirror image of the latter or a deception practiced by the former. If *mimicry* gains the upper hand, there will be proliferating variations in transformation and disguise. One could continue indefinitely to exemplify further possible combinations of text game, each of which provides guidelines as to how each game of the text is to be played and to what end.

The combination of games can also be played against ingrained expectations. *Agōn* and *alea* are the two types that are geared primarily to the alternative of winning or losing. From the Middle Ages to the late eighteenth century, *agōn* was not only a strategy of play but, with the vast number of contests, tournaments, competitions, and other types of confrontation, it became a theme in itself and formed the basic structure of the plot in narrative. Here interest was focused more on winning than on losing. And it is this expectation that enables postmodern literature, for example, to play *agōn* with the emphasis on losing, or at least on the continual postponement of a result. Instead of thematizing *agōn, alea* expands the possibility of antagonistically arranged positions to such a degree that all the traditions of Western culture are dispersed in a welter of unforeseeable conflicts. But in this way *agōn* in turn foregrounds contingency as the constitutive condition of *alea.* If *alea* plays *agōn* to lose, and *agōn* plays *alea* to highlight contingency, the resultant game—frequently played in postmodern literature—can be broken off only by the physical limitations of the book.

With such counterplay, *agōn* and *alea* give up their respective result-oriented natures and come closer to games, such as *mimicry* and *ilinx,* that do not set out to achieve decisions. For transmogrification and carnivalization are potentially endless. This is why in older literature the Fool—the *ilinx* player par excellence—is always given a limited extraterritoriality within the existing social hierarchy, which generally tends to be dominated by the game of *agōn.* This still creates a balance between the endlessness and the finality of play—two countervailing tendencies that may be viewed both from a historical and from a systematic point of view.

Historically, if endlessness outplays finality, it can be observed doing so only within a limited framework; consequently, older literature favored *agōn* as the structure of the plot. But the more peripheral the finality of the game, the more emancipated transmogrification (*mimicry*) and carnivalization (*ilinx*) become, whereas previously they had been rigidly channeled by masks and prevailing rituals.

Systematically, if endlessness outplays finality, play will begin to present itself. And this in turn ultimately reveals something else: "If Being or essence or pure presence is to be construed as that which grounds, centers, and presumably ends the play of play, then we must accept that such grounding concepts are arbitrary and false to the very sense of play. Play *never* stops playing, and there is no substratum of Being to which it refers. It is ungrounded, for there is no sense in which we can conceive of the end of play, in which we can dream of its end in the pure understanding of Being."[23] What becomes present in the game is exposed to perpetuation and becomes what is played with, for play always plays with what has been achieved by playing. Postmodern texts make such play observable.

Because of their forms, games must inevitably be limited; in contrast with play, they are designed for endings. The result ends play. The textual game works against this tendency, for limitation and endlessness are set in relationship to one another. Limitation is necessary in order to give each individual game its form; derestriction is also necessary because play cannot be identical with what it leads to. Therefore the text game is one in which limitation and endlessness can be played to an equal degree. The weighting of this relationship will initially vary in proportion to the number of games combined, and then in accordance with the hierarchy of those games. It will tend to take on seriality to the extent to which the duality of each game is played out within the amalgamation of games; that is, if there is a simultaneous playing of *agōn* as losing, winning, or drawing; *alea* as aid, surprise, and immobilization; *mimicry* as deception, imitation, and transmogrification; and *ilinx* as subversion, chaos, and the recurrence of what has been excluded. Since our concern here is only to name paradigms of play—which are certainly to be supplemented by others—it will suffice to say that for the text game there is a series of possible combinations that enable limitation and endlessness to unfold in an integrated and integrating process.

Through its inlaid seriality, the text game separates itself from all result-oriented games, especially mathematical, strategic, and economic ones, as well as those of chance and skill, all of which are designed to remove existing play spaces. In contrast, the text game, by working against such a loss, enables the games to be played against each other. *Agōn* can oppose other games, *alea* can function as a change of strategy, *mimicry* can expose games as disguises, and *ilinx* can bring uncontrollability to the amalgamation of games.

It is equally possible, however, to play the games in the text itself, so that—in total contrast to result-oriented games—there will emerge the potential endlessness of the playing of each individual game. When, for example, Uncle Toby in *Tristram Shandy* repeats the campaigns of the War of the Spanish Succession on his bowling green, he plays *agōn* as *mimicry*, with *agōn* constituting the content of the game and *mimicry* being Toby's self-transformation into a strategist fighting the battles of the War of the Spanish Succession all over again. Walter, on the other hand, plays *agōn* against reality, which he wants to force to comply with his philosophy, with the result that his fight against what is unpredictable gives rise to the production of chance and contingency. Walter's typically indefatigable playing of *agōn* against *alea* does not just play away any prospect of winning; it also leads to the player himself being played by what he had intended to eliminate. If *alea* takes control of the agonistic attitude, then the unpredictability of the outcome will become permanent. This means that no matter what form of play the characters may make the content of their games, they will always be played by what they play. For all the limitations of the individual games, their possibilities of play remain inexhaustible, and the endlessness will bring out the limitations of the player. Such a text, making games the object of play, stages the opposition of limitation and endlessness, and shows that this game is not ended by itself but by its player.[24]

Since the text game allows free combination of counteracting games, the question arises whether there are regulative factors underlying the interplay. For play turns into games when rules are introduced. This also applies to the game of evolution as outlined by Eigen and Winkler, which obviously has a degree of regulatory flexibility known in game theory as conservative and dissipative rules.[25] "Conservative forces freeze chance and continually create forms and patterns. Dynamic states of order arise from the temporal synchronization of physical and chemical processes with a constant dissipation of energy. The order of life builds up on the 'conservative' as on the 'dissipative' principle."[26] The text game differs from this alternation quite simply because it is not homeostatic, being concerned neither with the conservation of an organism nor with evolution in the phylogenetic sense. Centering and dissipating do, however, play a regulatory role in individual games—as can be seen from the combination of *agōn* and *ilinx* as extremes on the scale—but the text game itself does not aim at achieving a balance. *Agōn* is guided by conservative rules—the original balance between positions is destroyed, so that a new balance has to be attained; *ilinx* takes on everything that is present, and throws it into dissipation. Only in rare instances will the text game—most notably in didactic literature—unfold as an alternation of conservative and dissipative rules, for its course is far more likely to be a decentering of whatever begins to consolidate itself.[27]

For all the dissimilarities between the game of the text and that of natural evolution, they do resemble each other in their underlying orderliness. This is not due to any normative regulations existing independently of the game or determined beforehand; rather, it unfolds out of the game itself and at the same time structures it. While the game of law and chance characterizes evolution, human games allow for a diversification of their patternings, if only because there are so many different ways of structuring time.[28] Since there are these categorical differences between games, whose regularity develops in accordance with a particular intention that guides playing, the text game as a combination of counteracting games will issue forth into further specifications of conservative and dissipative rules.

The principle underlying the centering and dissipating develops in the text game as regulatory and aleatory rules. The regulatory rule arises out of the fact that *agōn, alea, mimicry* and *ilinx* owe their respective forms to constitutive conditions that make the games distinguishable from one another. Such basic conditions predetermine the range according to which each of these single games can be played. This applies even when the games play with or against one another, since their individual patterning is sustained in spite of the reversals they may suffer in their mutual counteraction.

If the regulatory rule is basically prescriptive concerning what is to be observed in each individual game, the aleatory rule unfolds the game by setting free the inherent possibilities of playing. Insofar as it is a rule, it also indicates that not everything is possible, not least because it prestructures what is possible. Its constraints are less the form of the games that are determined by the regulatory rules than the amalgamation of games, the encapsulated referential worlds, and the inherited schemata and conventions that recur in the text. Every move in every game—even those which set games against each other—is governed by the need to achieve something, so that inevitably the possibilities of playing become increasingly narrowed. Play movements are designed to block the opponent's intentions, thereby opening up new possibilities for one's own play. They will be all the more effective, the less confined they are to merely blocking, although the countermove will develop out of the situation it seeks to block. Counterplay constantly gives rise to new possibilities that are not arbitrary, since the blocking of a move conditions the possibility that is now to be unfolded. This is the point at which the variations of playing become aleatory. Ever new possibilities are played out against what is to be overcome, and these cannot be extrapolated, let alone derived, from what they oppose, though they are nevertheless conditioned by it. Thus the aleatory rule structures the variations of gaming. The possibilities generated in playing are unforeseeable, yet they are not a free-for-all, because they are confined to what the regulatory rules of each game permit and are tied to what has to be outplayed.

This is true of all the game levels that we have discussed so far in relation to the text. The basic back-and-forth movement is aleatory, with free play turning away from what instrumental play intends to achieve; the aleatory rule thus epitomizes the continual deferral of origin, leaving open even the question of whether the origin has ever been lost. The game of map and territory that is produced by the split signifier is also governed by the aleatory, which unties the implications of the signifier in order to let these implications build ever new imaginable territories as signifieds. Similarly, the tilting game of the schema turns imitation into a means for appropriation, unfolding accommodation as assimilation of the unavailable.

Finally, the text game turns *agōn, alea, mimicry,* and *ilinx* into roles that, like all roles, are characterized by an ineradicable duality. For roles always embody something that is to be achieved through them. But at the same time they are not able to exercise complete control over what they mean to present. Therefore roles have adumbrations no longer to be encompassed by the fulfillment of their intent. In the text game, these allusive adumbrations may turn into possibilities that may actually play against the roles themselves. The aleatory then organizes these adumbrated possibilities in such a way that *agōn* plays the uncontrollability of winning and losing, *alea* plays chance decisions exploding into a welter of possible alternatives, *mimicry* plays the transparence of the transmogrification sought for, and *ilinx* plays the intentions underlying the subversion. In this respect, the aleatory rule varies what can no longer be controlled by the respective regulatory rules governing the individual roles within the text game. It remains dependent, however, on its pregiven points, and indeed cannot undermine these because, in doing so, it would eliminate itself, for its function is to prestructure what the regulatory rule cannot master.

It is therefore no coincidence that the aleatory rule is so prominent in the work of art. By making the uncontrollable adumbrations of the game forms evolve into a seriality of its variations, it provides a precondition for experiencing whatever makes a particular work unique—a uniqueness that is endangered by the representativeness basic to depiction. What is unique, however, cannot be representative, and thus its unrepresentability can be made apparent only by the aleatory. Representativeness demands a degree of generalization, and in the text this is supplied by the regulatory rule; uniqueness, which is essential to every literary depiction that lays claim to the status of art, can be brought forth only through the aleatory rule. But art must be representative, too, and if uniqueness is what endows each work with its particular fascination, this is because its individuality offers a vivid idea of how to conceive of overarching general concerns. Thus the mutual permeation of the singular and the representative takes its shape through the interplay of regulatory and aleatory rules. Only by drawing out into the open what can no longer be controlled by the regulatory rule, and by unfolding it in all its variability, can overarching general concerns become present in the transfiguration of singularities.

So long as games are to be acted out and played into one another, the aleatory rule serves to disclose the singular variations contained in the text game. But it is also possible for the games themselves to serve the unfolding of the aleatory. When this happens, the forms of the game concerned will be made to clash in playful action. The individual games still remain discernible, but now contest, unpredictability, disguise, and subversion serve to produce unforeseeable turns and are designed to create surprises through what is brought out both in and by them. Their regulatory structures are dispensed with, although they will still form the backdrop against which the turbulence of the developing text game can assume salience. The text game will gain a certain degree of precision from the still discernible forms of the games. Hermetic texts reveal this sort of turbulent dynamism, whose fascination consists in one's desire to discover the 'rules' that govern such a game. The more of these one discovers, the more varied play will become, since in one's search for the aleatory the latter will continually be shifting its own boundaries.

Indeed, it is quite possible for the tilting game of the schema and that of the split signifier to be taken up into the game of the aleatory. In Beckett's characters, for instance, the imitative component of the schema shrinks to such a degree that their conceivability as human beings fades almost completely. And if one wished to take this fading as something to be symbolically appropriated, there is no longer any imitative component available to give shape to what is to be imagined. Thus the tilting game in the service of the aleatory generates an enigma that bears the inscription of its impenetrability. The relation between imitation and symbolization, stabilized by expectations, is suspended; and instead of an aleatory playing of the tilting game, the imitative component conditions its own abolition, while the component of symbolization invalidates all suggested ideas. Through this counterplay, the components of the schema develop the aleatory itself into a game.

Something similar occurs with the signifier in *Finnegans Wake*. The contamination of signifiers strips each one of its convention-governed designations, with the result that as a "map" such contaminated signifiers point to a "territory" that never consolidates itself. One of the effects is to make any transcendental signified and the reciprocal reading of signifiers appear as manifestations of an obsolescent semiotics. Here the aleatory plays out the boundaries of the conceivable.

The aleatory can also become a game in the text, because it is a rule without a code. Since its workings have to be discovered, the game involves finding the underlying structure. Reference points in this search are the agonistic, unpredictable, illusory, and carnivalizing components that prestructure the game of the aleatory, a game that is released from its otherwise expected function of organizing the text game as a combination of its multiple games. Such a game of the aleatory appears to be set on actualizing the plenum of possibilities, although the latter can never come into presence as such. Possibilities take a discernible shape not least by what they sacrifice. Playing losses against what is present is the driving force behind the aleatory, which by giving presence to what has been excluded creates new losses that sustain the game. What is lost is stamped with the features of the present possibility that remains present as a trace in the possibilities that follow it. This is also true of the sequence of ideas. Two ideas are never present simultaneously, but one is always replaced by another when the content has to be modified. While the aleatory is the propellant for this transformation, the range of possibilities can hardly be conceived as a pregiven plenum but as one that ceaselessly comes into being. The game of the aleatory structures this endlessness.

On the various levels of play that we have discussed, a variety of relationships indicate that the fictive and the imaginary not only constitute play but are simultaneously its basic components. This interplay assumes a degree of balance in the contraflow of free and instrumental play, for the boundary-crossing of the fictive links free play to what has been overstepped, just as the dual countering of the imaginary relates instrumental play to the underlying motivation that is responsible for nullifying the overstepped. The basic play movement assumes different shapes in the games of the text, or the individual games of the text arise out of the prevailing asymmetries of free and instrumental play. In *agōn,* free play is confined to unfolding a conflict; it serves to establish opposition. In *mimicry* it seeks to achieve an illusory similarity; it serves to undo difference. In *alea,* free play is totally unchained; it serves to abolish all pregiven intentions. In *ilinx* free play is a ceaseless undermining; it serves to exceed all constraints.

In this respect, the games in the text embody different types of interaction between the fictive and the imaginary. In *agōn* and *mimicry,* the fictive appears to dominate by both stressing (*agōn*) and disguising (*mimicry*) its doubling structure so that the dual countering of the imaginary has to work under constraints. In *alea* and *ilinx,* the imaginary appears to dominate by both freeing its dual countering from constraints (*alea*) and giving it free rein (*ilinx*) so that the doubling structure of the fictive is present only as a disappearing trace.

In play, the fictive and the imaginary take on ideal manifestations, since they come into a kind of pure focus, independently of their practical functions in the worlds of discourse. But this also means that play is the only setting in which the fictive and the imaginary can be separated from each other without having to posit any transcendental stance for such a distinction. Play allows this for two reasons: the two can unfold themselves only through interplay, and gaming itself actually springs from their interplay. The fictive and the imaginary produce their own context of description, for they are as groundless as the play through which they are manifested. Through play they provide a context for each other, since what is groundless can assume tangibility only by being contextually assessed. Without play, it would not be possible to talk properly about them, because their groundlessness could be compensated only by a transcendental definition, which would imply predetermining exactly what the fictive and the imaginary are; nor can they be defined ontologically, because they change whatever is defined. Although the fictive gives cognitive guidance to the imaginary, in so doing it unleashes the imaginary as something uncontrollable. If it were not for this uncontrollability, there could not be play, for play proceeds by changing whatever is in play.

It follows that the text as play is the transformation of its own positions. In the basic play movement, when free and instrumental play invert one another, everything encompassed by their interconnection is available for transformation into something else. The word as a split signifier indicates the lexical meaning as being absent in order to give presence to an indexical meaning that is not in the dictionary. In the schema, imitation is stripped of its nature in order to make conceivable what cannot give presence to itself. The games of the text subject all positions to different permutations: *agōn* organizes them as conflict, *alea* disperses them into unpredictability, *mimicry* doubles them through disguises, and *ilinx* constantly overturns them into something other than themselves. And finally, in the text game, the individual games derestrict each other, unveiling the transformative tendency to bring to the fore whatever has been hidden by determinacy.

Since this result is not possible at a single stroke, whatever enters into play must be acted out on a multiplicity of levels. Only in this way can determinacy, which cannot reveal what it hides, be exposed to change. Such overturnings require different forms of play, because any overarching frame of reference would determine beforehand what was to emerge from playing out the determinate. The same danger of teleological foreshortening occurs if the text is limited to the playing of a single game. For this reason, play becomes all-encompassing through the basic contraflow, the split signifier, the tilting game of the schema, the games of the text, and again the games against games as played in the text game. The text plays the transformation of the world that it has drawn into itself, and it allows this process to become present as a sequence of phases. In such a game positions are represented only to the extent that they uncover what they exclude, thereby reflecting the limitations of determinacy that reveals itself as a pragmatically conditioned necessity. The game makes the text into a mirror world in which nothing can escape its doubling, and this mirror world is distinctive because it simultaneously reflects the empirical world in unforeseen refractions and embodies a break with the very world it reflects. It is "'opened up' in our direction, disclosed to the observer, yet at no point does it lead over to the real world, and is not like the real room behind a window. One cannot 'get into' the mirror world, one cannot enter it, it is 'inaccessible'—but one can look into it; it grants us a 'view', and is as it were only the 'window' through which we look in."[29] If it is only one's gaze that can penetrate through to the mirror world, the reader will never be able to play the game of transformation to the full, not least because what is acted out there will be played to an end in reading the text. Only by stopping the game is it possible to appropriate what refuses access. But this also means that in playing the text, the reader cannot escape being played by the text.

Playing and Being Played

In Bateson's words, reading resembles "life—a game whose purpose is to discover the rules, which rules are always changing and always undiscoverable."[30] This also applies to the play structure of the text, in that its rules are not marked, let alone revealed. In his attempt to systematize the inherent regularity of speech acts, Searle distinguishes between regulative and constitutive rules, which he attempts to distinguish in the following way: "As a start, we might say that the regulative rules regulate antecedently or independently existing forms of behavior; for example, many rules of etiquette regulate inter-personal relationships which exist independently of the rules. But constitutive rules do not merely regulate, they create or define new forms of behavior. The rules of football or chess, for example, do not merely regulate playing football or chess, but as it were they create the very possibility of playing such games."[31]

Constitutive rules permit a certain range of combinations while also establishing a code of possible play. Such a code is present in the text game only as a trace, insofar as conventions and the games of the text impose certain restrictions on combination without actually producing the text game itself. They simply denote that not everything is possible, and this restriction of choice does not lay down conditions for combination or point toward what decisions are to be taken. Since these rules limit the text game without producing it, they are regulatory but not prescriptive. They do no more than set the aleatory in motion, and the aleatory rule differs from the regulatory in that it has no code of its own. For reading, this means that, exactly as Bateson says, the aleatory rule has to be "discovered" and is constantly changing. But only by playing the text in accordance with the aleatory rule (while simultaneously trying to discover it) can the reader adequately engage in the text game. Since the lack of predetermined guidelines for the aleatory rule prevents any engagement from being definitive, the reader remains on the threshold of that inaccessibility which Fink calls the "mirror world" of the game. It remains inaccessible, for it is only an imaginary setting that one would like to endow with reality because it can be viewed. The aleatory element of the text game thus entails the reader's own disposition becoming the code that governs the aleatory rule. "This view," writes Lotman in a different context, "forces us to pay far greater attention to the history of the way texts have been received in the reader's consciousness. Each new code of consciousness brings out new semantic layers in the text."[32]

If each realization of the text is guided by the reader's code, the aleatory rule also functions as a means of identifying that code, for the latter is revealed through what it allows to be realized. And like all rules, the aleatory can be violated. The violation of prescriptive rules will bring forth sanctions: that of regulatory rules leads to failure of whatever should have come into being; that of the aleatory unmasks the supposedly discovered combination as something trivial. The effects again may be due to different causes. Incompetence may prevent the reader from realizing the possibilities released by the restrictions of the regulatory rules, or the reader's code may be projected onto the combination to such a degree that the latter appears identical to the former.

The text game is never merely a performance that the reader attends because of an attraction to the inaccessibility of this "mirror world"; it is a game that the reader must play in an individual way. While the text plays the changeability of what has been brought into play, the reader can join in the game of transformations only to the extent that it will permit a result. For change seems to imply an aim that, in the case of reading, will not receive confirmation from the text itself. The result is therefore only a supplement. It differs from the possible intention of the text game because it may be taken for the meaning of the text. By contrast, the text game can only be the enabling matrix for producing such supplements, for meaning cannot arise out of meaning. The supplements are such because they add to the games something that in itself is not play, even if it does appear to round off the game. The supplements are also substitutes because they are meant to help the reader cross the threshold into the inaccessible "mirror world," thereby bridging all the differences between the games of the text in an effort to master the text game, which unfolds as an event. A substitute, however, is always different from what it was meant to replace, and as such a difference can never be eliminated. Instead of finding a definitive strategy for eliminating differences, the reader always has options for participating in the text game.

Initially, the reader might be enticed by the predominant game in the text, but the playing of this game will be hindered by the fact that generally each individual game only embodies a role within the text game. As a result, in principle playing has to take place on two different levels, especially since the individual game is disproportionately more concrete than the interplay between the games. The more intensively the text game develops, the less of a solo part will be played by each individual role, although the reader can come into play only by way of these roles. Consequently, reading always converges on alternatives: either it is very selective, which means excluding possibilities of play, or it opens itself up to the various counteractions directed at the role initially assumed.

It is largely up to the reader to select the particular game components that enable the text game to be played in an individual way. Thanks to its aleatory layout, the text game never prescribes precisely how it is to be played, so that the result sought can be brought about in different ways. Since the resultant supplement will therefore always be individual in character, the text can be played in many different ways. Nevertheless, it is possible to discern categories of such supplements that will reveal how the reader comes closest to the text game when the awareness of being played by the text grows.

As a prelude to differentiating between these categories, it is important to bear in mind that no matter how one interprets the rules of the text game, they must be seen only as guides to communication; they do not make communication possible. All we perceive in reading are distinctive written signs that mark a digital division, and this as such does not constitute communication. The latter arises only when a digital order merges into an analog coherence. The terms *digital* and *analog* were introduced by Wilden in his description of communication, and he considers this pair of concepts to be "as important for art, literature, and music as it is for economics, psychoanalysis, psychotherapy, anthropology, and human communication theory in general."[33] *Digital* is every denotation and marking of differences, and so "digitalization is always necessary when certain boundaries are to be crossed" (p. 159). *Analog* is all relating and condensing of coherence so that "we can say . . . that digital distinctions introduce GAPS into continuums . . . whereas analog differences, such as presence and absence, FILL continuums" (p. 186). Wilden also asserts that "The amorphous domain of play provides a sort of bridge to conceptualize the digitalization of the analog" (p. 173).

If we look back on the play structure of the text, we can see quite clearly how digital distinctions turn into analog coherencies. Free and instrumental play are mainly digital with regard both to the exceeding of what is given and to the recourse that such a movement has to its possible ground. The latter is then the gap to be filled by ideas in such a way that the digital division engenders a picture of analog coherence. The split signifier increases the scope of this gap-filling.[34] Digital denotation cancels itself out yet gives shape to the resultant idea. In the tilting game of the schema, digital distinction is narrowed to the inversion of imitation and symbolization, thereby opening up multiple conceivability of the imperceptible. "Digital thought is analytic and two-valued; analog thought is dialectical and many-valued."[35]

However, the "perceptive imagination" of the nongiven remains under the guidance of distinct patterns of perception. In the games of the text there is only the digital marking of what plays there, whereas gaming goes on as the continual modification of whatever is in play that brings about the changing conceivability of the possible. But since not everything is possible, the digital trace simultaneously sets in motion and restricts the combination of ideas. Finally, the text game appears as a kind of ultimate opening up of the boundary marked by the interplay of games themselves; but here, too, a proliferating conceivability is permeated by traces of digital minimalization: The world conceived is only a possible one, which on the one hand is different from those worlds out of whose material it has been fashioned and on the other hand delineates salient features for a reality to be imagined.

Without such divisions ideation would remain oceanic; without the ideation the markings would remain empty. "The analog is pregnant with MEANING whereas the digital domain of SIGNIFICATION is, relatively speaking, somewhat barren."[36] Digital distinctions and analog coherences constitute communication, which comes about through ideational fillings of prestructured gaps. The digital markers are distinct, whereas the ideation triggered by them is basically blurred in a way that allows potentially multifarious ideas to be formed. As this communication between text and reader can occur only by way of ideation, the digital score of the text can be played in a variety of ways.

One predominant way of playing the text is the search for meaning as a game that ends when meaning has been found. In view of such anticipation, all forms of play, from the to-and-fro through the split signifier and the tilting game of the schema to the aleatory interplay of the games in the text, are subjected to semantics as an overarching frame of reference. What can be identified in the text appears as the representative of something other than itself. This is so even though the text game unfolds the transformation of its components, whose representative quality is acted upon, if not played away altogether. Indeed, the fact that the discovered meaning itself is won as an offshoot of gaming—without having any particular location in the text—bears witness to the fact that *winning* here is not a mere metaphor, for it is a result obtainable only within the given parameters of the particular text game.

In this mode of playing, the aleatory rule remains governed by the reader's code, which, because it is not part of the text, inevitably brings the game to a standstill. The code itself can involve several things. In the first place, a semantic orientation of reading will be led by the need for, and indeed the necessity of, understanding, which raises the question of whether this quest for comprehension is an end in itself. The code can also involve the reader's desire to appropriate the experience of the play in such a way that whatever happens must be semanticized. But the code can also indicate a defensive impulse that looks for meaning as a rampart against the intrusion of the unfamiliar. Whatever particular form it takes, the semantic orientation is an intervention into a game of transformation that stabilizes itself in proportion to what it excludes. This probably will not bother the reader, but since meaning in whichever shade is "won" by way of the aleatory rule, it is shaped to a large extent by what has not been realized and, indeed, has been excluded. Thus the meaning arrived at begins to function as a diagnosis for a semantically oriented reader's code, as it sets up the meaning found against the backdrop of the losses it has produced.

The situation is different when the text is played as a mode of gaining experience. Then one has to expose oneself to the game. Instead of letting our own code govern the aleatory rule, we let the code be played away by what it can no longer govern. Our own norms and values are put at stake in order to summon up precisely what the semantic operation cannot cover. Such an approach is undoubtedly closer to the text game, whose transformations become effective through the suspension of our own norms and values. But in terms of gaining experience, the transformations are ultimately added to our own store of knowledge, exhausting the transformational capacity of the text game that cannot be repeated as a new experience.

A text can also be approached from the standpoint of the pleasure one hopes to derive from reading it. Traditionally, aesthetic enjoyment was always the yardstick in classical poetics for measuring the encounter with the work of art. For H. R. Jauss, the quintessence of aesthetic experience is "self-enjoyment in the enjoyment of something other".[37] This pleasure springs from the activation of our faculties in the Kantian sense, and the extraordinary demands of the text game can undoubtedly heighten it. This is especially true when the text keeps its rules of play hidden, so that their discovery can become a game in itself. If this leads to a one-sided application of the cognitive faculties, the pleasure will increase when the rules found challenge the sensory and emotive faculties. Such an activation leads to the readers' playing themselves, and this can turn into "self-enjoyment" when the unaccustomed occupation of the faculties leads to our becoming present to ourselves. Unlike the gaining of experience, this game is long-lasting; gaining experience means tilting one's own code, whereas activating faculties creates a self-presence that, even if to a certain degree it comes to rest, may turn out to be less of a result than a suspenseful attention to oneself. For in this process, because the self is not tilted, the activation of faculties retains a latent awareness of the transformation wrought by the text game. Such an activation makes the reader into a player allowed to watch himself or herself playing a role. To be caught up in a role and yet at the same time to be outside it is a form of doubling, through which the transformations of the text game translate themselves into the reader's reaction as shaped by the exercise of the faculties.

There is one more approach—to be distinguished from those outlined so far—which Roland Barthes called "the pleasure of the text." This embodies the most intensive absorption of the reader in the text game. For Barthes, there are

> two systems of reading: one goes straight to the articulations of the anecdote, it considers the extent of the text, ignores the play of language ... the other reading skips nothing; it weighs, it sticks to the text, it reads, so to speak, with application and transport, grasps at every point in the text the asyndeton which cuts the various languages—and not the anecdote: it is not (logical) extension that captivates it, the winnowing out of truths, but the layering of significance; as in the children's game of topping hands, the excitement comes not from a processive haste but from a kind of vertical din (the verticality of language and of its destruction); it is at the moment when each

(different) hand skips over the next (and not one *after* the other) that the hole, the gap, is created and carries off the subject of the game—the subject of the text. Now paradoxically . . . this second, *applied* reading . . . is the one suited to the modern text, the limit-text. Read slowly, read *all* of a novel by Zola, and the book will drop from your hands; read fast, in snatches, some modern text, and it becomes opaque, inaccessible to your pleasure: you want something to happen and nothing does, for *what happens to the language does not happen to the discourse:* what 'happens,' what 'goes away,' the seam of the two edges, the interstice of bliss, occurs in the volume of the languages, in the uttering, not in the sequence of utterances: not to devour, to gobble, but to graze, to browse scrupulously, to rediscover—in order to read today's writers—the leisure of bygone readings: to be *aristocratic* readers.[38]

There are two aspects that are central to this "pleasure of the text":
1. The "duplicity" that is "the site of a loss, the seam, the cut, the deflation, the *dissolve*"[39] presents itself as the ineradicable difference that constitutes play and cannot be done away with by whatever form in which it is acted out.
2. Instead, the subject is swept into this split, which itself is "the subject of the text" insofar as everything that is played in the text emerges from it.

In the to-and-fro the split does not allow free play to untie itself from what it has discarded, or instrumental play to turn back into origins; in the split signifier, denotation is not allowed to uncouple itself from figuration; in the schema, appropriation cannot be separated from adaptation; in the games even a beaten opponent cannot be gotten rid of; and in the text game, the combinability of games cannot be undone. The split is negativity, which brings about play by pulling the ground from beneath everything that has been made determinate. This is why in such reading the subject always slips into an in-between position where it is possible to play out what the rift has opened up. We bring ourselves into play by putting ourselves at stake; we slide into the text, which keeps us so busy that our efforts to discover meaning, to gain experience, or to activate our faculties fall victim to "dissolving." For if the game of the text is a "mirror world" that ultimately we cannot enter, then we must extinguish ourselves as a reference in order to cross its threshold. Disregarding oneself in such an activity is what makes one into Barthes's "*aristocratic* reader," but this does not mean an elite reader. It is a matter here of giving up habits that the reader has hitherto taken for granted, but such renunciations are generally not elitist. And so the "pleasure of the text" is to be gained not on conditions laid down by the reading subject but on those of the text. The advantage of this is that the pleasure does not disappear in its momentariness, as would happen if it were exclusively that of the subject.[40] Instead, it lets itself be drawn out, because the split continually delivers possibilities, in the playing of which the reading subject can lose himself or herself. In contrast to the ways of appropriation in reading that bring the game to an end, "pleasure of the text" awards endless renewal as its prize for the subject's self-forgetting. Thus if all pleasure longs for "eternity,"[41] that of the text appears to grant what remains unobtainable in ordinary life.

"Pleasure of the text" and "supplement" therefore drift apart into distinguishable alternatives. What is possible may be disquieting, yet it simultaneously discloses that any longed-for certitude is a substitute. While the constitutive difference of play inhibits all attempts to remove it, because play as the generation of infinite possibilities is basically groundless, "pleasure of the text" allows the reading subject to slide into its own groundlessness.

If such an experience of the self is pleasurable, this is because it permits a condition prior to all becoming. It is also pleasurable because such a state engulfs the self that can neither distance nor relate itself to it, thus making the reading subject collapse into the "subject of the text."[42]

Chapter Six

Epilogue

Mimesis and Performance

The text game proceeds as a transformation of its referential worlds, which gives rise to something that cannot be deduced from these worlds. It follows that none of these worlds can be the object of representation, that the text is in no way confined to being the representation of something given. In any case, there can be no representation without performance, and the source of performance is always different from what is to be represented. If representation means mimesis, it always presupposes something that is to be presented in an act of depiction, and so the question arises whether the state of affairs to be depicted has an existence of its own, independent of the representation. So long as representation was equated with mimesis, the answer was generally affirmative. In view of the fact that traditional poetics handed down this tacit knowledge through the centuries, it would certainly be inappropriate simply to replace the idea of mimesis with that of performance, especially since the Aristotelian tradition provides "recipes" for the manufacturing of art which at least indicate that representation is unthinkable without performance.

Our concern here is not to reexamine the Aristotelian tradition, though it is important to remember why Aristotle's view of mimesis as the imitation of something given solidified into a basic premise of Western poetics. From the start, representation as mimesis was an ambivalent concept whose wavering duality has still not totally disappeared. One must keep in mind Plato's devaluation of mimesis in order to appreciate the impact of the repairs Aristotle undertook. For Plato, imitation denoted the deficiency of the phenomenal world as compared with the intelligible one, for imitation meant *not* being the idea imitated. In *Timaeus*, the incline between idea and copy is at its sharpest, with the Demiurge taken to be not a Creator but a kind of craftsman in order to explain the "embarrassment" of how a world of phenomena could come into existence in the first place.

Artistotle responded to this situation. For him, art consisted

> in 'completing on the one hand and imitating (the naturally given) on the other'. The dual definition is closely tied to the ambivalence of the concept of 'Nature' as producer (*natura naturans*) and as product (*natura naturata*). It is, however, easy to see that the element of 'imitation' is the overarching component, for art takes up what Nature appears to have left incomplete, and while conforming to what is prefigured by Nature, starts out from the entelechy of the naturally given and brings it out into the open. Art's 'substituting' for Nature is of such a degree that Artistotle can say: whoever builds a house only does precisely what Nature *would do* if it let houses 'grow,' so to speak. Art and Nature are isomorphic in structure: the basic immanent features of one sphere can be substituted by those of the other. There is justification, therefore, for the Aristotelian definition being foreshortened to the formula 'ars imitatur naturam,' as Aristotle himself uses it.[1]

For Plato, the inferiority of imitation was evident from the fact that the Demiurge could only imitate the pregiven pattern of the universal design; Aristotle's revaluation of mimesis was based on his view that the eternity of ideas became the eternity of the world. Thus the exemplarity of ideas gave way to a correspondence between idea and appearance, which bodied forth the completeness of the cosmos and consequently embraced all possibilities. For the possible is only what, according to its constitutive *morphē*, is already real or at least potentially real. Art becomes the *technē*, laying bare the entelechy through imitation. Therefore the artist achieves only what Nature is capable of achieving, and mimesis, with its inherent repetition, is to be seen only as the completion of an as yet uncompleted state. The artist has skills but not the ability to design, let alone to create, the world itself.

> When Aristotle says it is the artist's business to imitate the things of Nature as they *ought to be,* this does not entail reference to some norm that transcends these objects, but it means 'extrapolation' from the process of becoming to the aim of becoming ... In order that Art should not rest content with the factual *state* of being, but should

focus on the *aim of becoming* which is formatively at work in that state ... the generative side of the concept of Nature is essential for mimesis, but only because after and despite the removal of ideas, something like 'ideality' is still needed in order to understand what determines the human being in his work, and above all in his work of art. (p. 73)

This element of "ideality" makes it clear that, in spite of the isomorphic structure, Nature and mimesis are not identical, and the reason for this is that human work—which Art is meant to justify—differs from that of Nature. Even though the artist's *technē* repeats a state of being in the work produced, this repetition, despite the fact that it may complete what Nature has left incomplete, is meant to cope with the awkward question posed by Plato: Why, in view of the world's eternity, does human work exist at all? Thus mimesis has a dual reference: as imitation of Nature it performs what is performed in Nature; but this does not happen for Nature's sake—it is for the sake of humankind. Nature does not need mimesis, and even if *technē* were the perfect extrapolation of Nature's principle of production, it would still be an extrapolation that differs from Nature. If Nature itself produced this *technē*, such doubling would be redundant, since Nature always bears the inherent possibility of its own completion as reality. It does not need the artist's *technē* in order to achieve what it is.

Technē simply brings the constitutive *morphē* out into the open and tries to complete what Nature has left incomplete, though this incompleteness is such only in human eyes. *Technē* does not, therefore, repair Nature—it is not necessary to do so—but, by imitating a pregiven object, objectifies that object. The imitation of natural things as they ought to be then presents itself as "the factually *not yet* arrived-at *goal of becoming*" (p. 73). This means that, although nothing is added to Nature which is not already present in it as a possibility, the extrapolation achieved by *technē* and the objectification of what has been copied constitute performative activities that, in turn, cannot be copies of given objects. For extrapolation and objectification are not given in Nature. If they were, imitation of Nature would be superfluous, whereas in fact *technē* achieves something that is not altogether without importance for Nature itself: as everything real and everything possible, Nature cannot present all her possibilities as things already realized (if they were realized, they would no longer be possibilities).

Extrapolation and objectification therefore have the dual function of imitating Nature and at the same time relating human beings to Nature. This also explains the multiplicity of works, which would not exist if there were a *morphē* underlying this relationship in Nature herself, unless there were one single work that presented such a *morphē* so completely that by comparison all other works would be nothing but an exhibition of failure. The many works are different objectifications of what is imitated, whereby objectification produces the visibility of what ought to be, in the sense that it brings out the ideality of what is being copied. In the classical concept of mimesis, this performative element is certainly minimized, but without the process of objectification mimesis would be unthinkable. Performance remained subservient to mimesis as long as the human being was considered to be firmly embedded in the order of the cosmos, and as long as the Christian-Neoplatonic world picture provided the hierarchical arrangement for everything in the sublunary realm. Under these conditions, performance relates only to the translatability of what is, as always becomes necessary when differences are to be bridged.

Historically, the relation between mimesis and performance changed when the closure of the inherited world order waned; this had repercussions on the wavering concept of mimesis insofar as an increasingly diversified world had to be coped with rather than imitated. Instead of rendering visible what eternal Nature already contained between its genesis and its telos, mimesis in a now open-ended world had to address itself to the whys and the wherefores of imitation. Performance therefore had to accomplish considerably more than mere transpositions that had, nevertheless, been essential to classical mimesis. This does not mean that mimesis disappeared, but a gradual shift of balance was bound to occur when an open-ended world had to be represented or when reality was considered as no longer given but as continually realizing itself. The problems posed by such a change of condition are evident from prominent current theories of representation to which the concept of mimesis remains central. This brings out something already observable in Aristotle: although indispensable, performance remains a blank that is an unexplored constituent of the notion of mimesis, because production cannot be derived from imitation.

Gombrich sharply repudiated the suggestion that the ideas he developed in his *Art and Illusion* constitute a theory of response but not, as he himself believed, a theory of representation.[2] In *Art and Illusion* he quotes a passage from Philostratus's life of the Pythagorean philosopher

Apollonius of Tyana, "who probed much more deeply into the nature of mimesis than Plato or Aristotle."[3] The following dialogue takes place between Apollonius and Damis, his disciple:

"Tell me, Damis, is there such a thing as painting?" "Of course," says Damis. "And what does this art consist of?" "Well," says Damis, "in the mixing of colours." "And why do they do that?" "For the sake of imitation, to get a likeness of a dog or a horse or a man, a ship, or anything else under the sun." "Then," Apollonius asks again, "painting is imitation, mimesis?" "Well, what else?" answers the stooge. "If it did not do that it would just be a ridiculous playing about with colours." "Yes," says his mentor, "but what about the things we see in the sky when the clouds are drifting, the centaurs and stag antelopes and wolves and horses? Are they also works of imitation? Is God a painter who uses his leisure hours to amuse himself in that way?" No, the two agree, these cloud shapes have no meaning in themselves, they arise by pure chance; it is we who by nature are prone to imitation and articulate these clouds. "But does this not mean," probes Apollonius, "that the art of imitation is twofold? One aspect of it is the use of hands and mind in producing imitations, another aspect the producing of likenesses with the mind alone?" The mind of the beholder also has its share in the imitation. Even a picture in monochrome, or a bronze relief, strikes us as a resemblance—we see it as form and expression. "Even if we drew one of these Indians with white chalk," Apollonius concludes, "he would seem black, for there would be his flat nose and stiff curly locks and prominent jaw . . . to make the picture black for all who can use their eyes. And for this reason I should say that those who look at works of painting and drawing must have the imitative faculty and that no one could understand the painted horse or bull unless he knew what such creatures are like." (pp. 154f.)

This is no longer a question of uncovering the *morphē,* or even of completing what Nature has left incomplete. Instead, the focus is upon the procedural implications of mimesis; the Aristotelian *technē* itself becomes the object under discussion. Forms, it appears, are not so much constitutive conditions of Nature as images remembered by the artist, who projects these onto what is given in such a way that the beholder also sees Nature in a manner intended by the artist. Thus even the colors that have to be mixed in order to produce natural phenomena refer to the forms stored in the mind, and the imitation of these forms has this mixture at its disposal.

It seems that the Aristotelian *morphē* has emigrated out of Nature and into the artist's mind, for what is imitated is not Nature but the forms that have settled in the painter's memory, allowing Nature to be, as it were, opened up. This represents a far-reaching change of reference for mimesis, and it derives from a change in the understanding of Nature. Seeing Nature *as* something means that, in contrast to the traditional view of it, it has become open-ended. What now needs to be visualized is not what "ought to be" but the actual accessibility of Nature. It has to be made conformable to a repertoire of schemata and patterns that are shared by both the artist and the beholder of the artwork. Such patternings are no longer characterized by the quality of the *morphē*. Instead, they form an open-ended series, so that what is to be imitated is not objects so much as conditions of perception; by this means, natural phenomena can be viewed in the manner intended by the artist. For even the simple act of perception teaches us that we can never see objects as a whole but only *as* "something." This is clear from the passage quoted, where even a monochrome picture is seen "as form and expression." It follows that imitation of a given object as such is quite impossible, since the observer will always see the object *as* something different. In order to avoid this, what has to be imitated is forms of perception, which will allow us to see natural phenomena in the same way, even if the conditions imitated are not the object of mimesis intended by the picture. For what is to be illustrated is not the memory of forms, while what *is* to be imitated cannot be copied without imitating conditions of perception. Consequently, imitated Nature is present only as an ideated object, even if one is constantly under the illusion that Nature itself is present. This may also be a reason why even in antiquity mimesis was sometimes viewed as a pretense of a genuine object, as can be seen from Zeuxis's painted grapes, which the birds are supposed to have pecked at.

Aristotle's conception of mimesis certainly contained a trace of performance, with the necessary objectification of what *technē* had to achieve as the imitation of given objects, but performance begins to become more prominent when *technē* itself has to be explored. For the imitation of forms stored in the mind serves to instrumentalize conditions of perception through which the represented object emerges as if it were its given state. Of course the forms are not simply projected onto Nature. They function instead as basic guidelines for the imitation of Nature, which unfolds itself under the proviso that these forms are to be taken as if they were constituents of Nature itself, because Nature increasingly needs to be explored and translated into human terms.

A shift has occurred in the notion of mimesis, in that its reference is no longer the Aristotelian cosmos but—more and more—perception. Thus the Apollonius example fits in perfectly with Gombrich's adherence to the concept of imitation, though this is to be thought of principally as a performative act. Gombrich's classic formula is ". . . 'making comes before matching.' Before the artist ever wanted to match the sights of the visible world he wanted to create things in their own right. Nor is this true only of some mythical past . . . the matching process itself proceeds through the stages of 'schema and correction.' Every artist has to know and construct a schema before he can adjust it to the needs of portrayal" (p. 99). The schemata precede the external world, which through the artist's perception imposes itself as a correction on these prefigurements. It is the latter that guide the vision of the visible world; the eye gains its information from the schema and not from the entelechy of Nature, with the result that we can perceive what the inherited schema or contrivance was unable to reveal. The portrayal of the visible therefore takes place as a series of performative acts. The objectification that, in Aristotle's notion of mimesis, embodied a subservient component because it related to something that had always been philosophically known, now turns as a fully fledged performative activity into a basic constituent of mimesis. It does so to the degree that perception as a reference can no longer lay the slightest claim to knowing or being able to know the Nature that is to be imitated.

Performance has to compensate for what the classical concept of mimesis lost when both its connection to a closed world order and its intimate relation to the dignified object of representation were broken off. How, then, are we to conceive of this performance, if "making comes before matching," as exhibited by the "correction" made to the "schema," which in turn only embodies a precondition for perception? If this process is to be regarded as the representation of perceivable objects, imitation is realized in a graduated sequence of transpositions that ultimately, through the beholder's share in bringing representation to full fruition, leads to an illusion of perception. The question arises whether such a process is the imitation of an object at all, or whether in fact it is nothing but a matter of producing the illusion of an object. In the final analysis, the very same process was also operative in classical mimesis, though it remained obscured through the connection of imitation to the ancient cosmos, and consequently could come to light only after this correlation of mimesis had disappeared.

If the illusion of the object is brought about by "making and matching" and is "performed" through "correcting" the inherited schema, then we must consider how these different operations act and interact. The schema is a construct, and even though it bears the inscription of a previous correction, it functions only as an aid to perception when it is handed down. The correction to be inserted cannot therefore be deduced from the schema itself but derives from the painter's observation. Thus the schema provides a dual reference: it prestructures the visible world and, in doing so, adumbrates what is no longer covered by it. To make the observation visible means recasting the schema in order to accommodate what the painter intends to represent. How does this work?

The joints in this graduated process are mainly gaps, although Gombrich, in analyzing his examples, always draws attention to interaction. Interaction, however, arises out of the basic play movement of to and fro that goes on between making and matching, just as it does between schema and correction. Thus an element of play—though in a rather undifferentiated form—inserts itself into the concept of imitation, for only when making and matching, when schema and correction play with or against each other does the illusory object emerge. It appears like an object because the beholder of the picture grasps it as if it were something perceived. The tangibility of the painting derives from these operations, with the schema adapting to conditions of perception in order to allow its reshuffling by correction in such a way that the world envisioned by the painter seems like an object. It remains a striking fact in the history of mimesis that at the very moment when Aristotelian *technē* was supposed to be explained, the notion of performance took the stage, and so ultimately mimesis itself produced the object of its imitation.

"This representative illusion," writes Paul Ricoeur "allegedly stems from the impossible claim of uniting the interiority of a mental image in the mind and the exteriority of something real that would govern from outside the play of the mental scene within a single entity or 'representation.'"[4] For Ricoeur this is also the reason why mimesis came under mounting pressure. "Representation, accordingly, it is said, should be denounced as the reduplication of presence, as the re-presenting of presence. My project will be to try to extricate representation from the impasse to which it has been relegated, to return it to its field of play, without, however, in any way weakening the critique I have just mentioned" (p. 15).

Since reinforcing mimesis against its own illusionism as well as against deconstructive criticism means "emigrating from the closure of representation" (p. 15), Ricoeur intends to treat mimesis as a process "which I shall playfully yet seriously call *mimesis*1, *mimesis*2, and *mimesis*3" (p. 17). Obviously mimesis needs something to imitate, and here he refers to "Aristotle's key expression which says that the poem is the imitation of action" (p. 18). Mimesis therefore presupposes a generally accepted preconception of what an action is; this action is then transplanted into a text and finally realized by the reader. "Indeed, it is the reader—or rather the act of reading—that, in the final analysis, is the unique operator of the unceasing passage from *mimesis*1 to *mimesis*3 through *mimesis*2. That is, from a prefigured world to a transfigured world through the mediation of a configured world" (p. 28).

These three stages structurally resemble Gombrich's concept of mimesis, which describes representation as a sequence of phases, from the painter's inherited schemata through the picture to the beholder's share. The only difference arises from the fact that Gombrich relates mimesis to the visible world, while Ricoeur relates it to action. This could mean that adherence to the concept of mimesis leads to a truncation of the scope of what is to be imitated. For a perceivable world is infinitely more comprehensive than an action, let alone an Aristotelian *morphē*. Both changes and specifications in regard to the object of imitation are intimately geared to the aim of mimesis, which, after the vanishing of its erstwhile cosmic correlation, allows only for partial conceptualizations. Understanding imitation as a process is like "democratizing" mimesis, with the reader pulling the switches that will lead each phase of the process to its completion. It is therefore only logical that Ricoeur should end his reflections by raising the question of the reference that guides such imitation: "Can we keep the classical concept of reference ... for speaking about the transfiguring action of *mimesis*? Not if we take it in the sense of descriptive reference. But yes if we admit that *mimesis*3 splits open descriptive reference and suggests that we forge the notion of a non-descriptive referential dimension. In that case, we must dare to form the paradoxical idea of a productive form of reference ... *Mimesis,* in this sense, is ahead of our concepts of reference, the real, and truth. It thus engenders a need as yet unfilled to think more" (pp. 29–31).

If mimesis produces its own reference, it becomes transcendental to anything pregiven. It now determines what an action is, the original preconception of which is transfigured through the configurative form of the text into the discovery of its polysemy. The pregiven then functions only as a starting point for disclosing what had been concealed in the preconception, and for reaching agreement that we have all set out from the *same* starting point. Gombrich still conceived of perception as the reference for mimesis, but for mimesis as a process reference must be continually diversified, so that the resulting dynamism will produce a referentiality that will allow action as such to become present. This is logical, insofar as the purpose of mimesis can no longer hark back to historically guaranteed certainties, and so ultimately mimesis turns into the producer of its own reference. This also means that it cannot become self-referential if it is to avoid falling into a state of self-contradiction, for mimesis implies a relation between the given and the imitation, and this would disappear if mimesis became its own object. But mimesis that produces its own referentiality (which, however, eludes description) "is an action about action" (p. 28). This similarity to the given, though, serves to represent the process itself, which means no less than that mimesis now becomes the representative of performance.

What mimesis has to accomplish is twofold: it must extrapolate the reference from the figuration of the imitated action in order to make the figurations themselves tangible. This process may be designated by the hermeneutic term *mediation*,[5] though this also forms the *asylum ignorantiae* in hermeneutics. The change brought about by mimesis from prefiguration (preconception) through configuration (text) to transfiguration (reader) articulates the phases of a process but not the points of transition. These remain empty. Indeed, they have to be empty since the change of status of the figuration can be conceived—if at all—only in terms of play, as the shifts in these refashioned figurations are not predetermined and thus are to be acted out by a to-and-fro movement in order to come to full fruition. Play also occurs between the changing figurations and the reference extrapolated from them, for the reference is not a pregiven; it can come about only cybernetically. The reference arises from the feedforward of the status change of figurations, and these in turn are guided by the feedback of the developing reference. This performative interplay unfolds a graduated process that has to be finalized by the act of reading.

The more one analyzes mimesis as a process, the more inescapably one is confronted by the performative character of representation. Only the pregiven binds performance mimetically, though at times even the pregiven appears to have been produced by performance. From this point only one small step is necessary to turn performance against mimesis itself. In Adorno's *Aesthetic Theory*, this step is taken, although it is of interest here only insofar as it will allow us to locate the relevance of the text game. "Jettisoning the idea of imitation from aesthetics would be just as wrong as accepting it uncritically. Art objectifies the mimetic impulse, preserving and negating it at the same time. Imitation of objects is a pernicious spin-off of this dialectic of objectification. Objectified reality is the correlate of objectified mimesis . . . Thus mimesis surrenders to objectification, hoping in vain to close the gap between the object and objectified consciousness. By wanting to be like the objective other, the imitative work of art becomes unlike that other."[6] This is "subversive mimesis,"[7] through which the work of art puts itself on a level with Nature in order to oppose it. Although for Adorno art is still tied to the beautiful in Nature—and this classical thread is in all of *Aesthetic Theory*—through "duplication in art, the appearing quality in nature loses its being-in-itself on which appreciation of nature feeds."[8] "The being-in-itself of art is not an imitation of something real but an anticipation of a being-in-itself yet to come, of an unknown that will determine itself through the subject. Works of art state that there is an in-itself, but they do not spell out what it is . . . art aims at realizing the articulation of the non-human by human means" (pp. 114f.).

This is the basic theme that undergoes almost endless variations in *Aesthetic Theory* and may be epitomized by the statement that the "driving force" of art "may not have been naturalistic imitation at all but protest against reification" (p. 449). "In every work of art something appears that does not exist" (p. 121), but "just because something appears, it must be possible to imbue it with being" (p. 122). Consequently, the appearance is not a copy of something but, as an "apparition" (p. 124), constitutes the momentary trace of what is not. This must be built into the imagistic character of the appearance, and so the work of art, when drawn into language, can avoid reifying the nonbeing only by destroying its own "imagery" (p. 125). It is a matter here of wiping out the illusion—inherent in the appearance—that what is pretended by the appearance actually exists, as a result of which the work of art incorporates the break with Nature into itself. For only by specific negation can the work of art demonstrate that it is the sole governor or the nonbeing in the midst of what is. The break with the objective world is present as a rift in the work of art. "Like riddles, works of art are divided in themselves, being at once determinate and indeterminate" (p. 181). The rift indicates that the performative character of representation can unfold itself only by destroying the "imagery" produced. In the rift, if we may take up Ricoeur's argument, the work of art possesses its reference, which makes the rift appear to be the source of performance. If the latter is uncoupled from mimesis, the mimetic becomes a cover for what shines through the rift as the nonbeing, and consequently must continually be played away in order that the disguise may remain apparent.

Thus the rift becomes a sign of what by nature is irreconcilable: the being and the nonbeing. But it is precisely in order to give presence to this irreconcilability that the work of art has to produce the semblance of reconciliation, though on condition that it also unmasks the semblance itself as such. For this purpose, both irreconcilability and the nonbeing—each of them naturally absent—require a particular form that, instead of determining them, must give presence to their intangibility. For without such a presence, neither of them would be accessible either to consciousness or to experience. This 'present absence' is brought about by aesthetic semblance, which on the one hand produces the illusory presence of what is not, and on the other hand clearly remains transparent as what it is, so that the nonbeing cannot become being. Consequently, semblance reveals itself as a form of mediation between consciousness and what is withheld from consciousness. As a medium it brings about—under conditions of comprehension that are pertinent both for consciousness and for experience—a presence of something that, if it came to *real* presence, would no longer be the presence of the absent. Therefore semblance must always bear the inscription of being inauthentic, because what it mirrors forth can gain presence only as something absent if semblance reveals itself as a transparent illusion.

This distinguishes aesthetic semblance from Schiller's "beautiful semblance" and from Hegel's "sensuous appearance of the idea." The beautiful semblance always presupposes a reality on which it depends but which it was meant to transcend. The sensual appearance of the idea presupposes the existence of truth, with an inseparable unity between its abstract notion and its tangible manifestation; thus "the Idea is not only true but beautiful."[9]

As a transparent illusion, aesthetic semblance remains permeated by the rift that—in Adorno's sense—reveals the being and the nonbeing as partners in irreconcilability. Even though aesthetic semblance indicates irreconcilability as the hallmark of the real, it nevertheless has to cancel the inherent duplication in all representation in order to highlight what eludes mimesis. As there is no overarching reference in Adorno's theory for such an interaction, a play movement is bound to ensue, in which the performative quality of the artwork—no longer subservient to the representation of what is—begins to play against mimesis. This happens agonistically when the work of art sees itself being dominated by a process of "the assimilation of the self to an other,"[10] though it will always oppose such an assimilation (see, e.g., pp. 293f.) in order to undo the inherent reification when the artwork becomes that other. It happens as masking (*mimicry*) when imitation of the beautiful in Nature has to be wrested from the being-in-itself in order to let it parade in the trappings of the "imagery." And it happens carnivalistically when the "imagery" is to be destroyed (see p. 125) in order to prevent what is promised from being confounded with the appearance of its imagistic presentation.

If performance gains the upper hand in this gaming, it is because something by nature nonappearing has to be made present through appearance, and this intangible something, being incapable of objectification, can never be a model for imitation. But even mimesis, in its traditional understanding, can come to full fruition only through performance, for simply giving presence to given objects entails their modification. Performance will increase, the more indeterminate the reference of representation becomes, and when there is talk today of the "end of representation,"[11] one has to ask whether it is meant to describe only a historical condition, or the inadequacy of the concept of representation when it comes to grasping what happens in art and literature.

The difference between the pregiven and imitation—pertinent to all theories of representation—widens into a rift when performance[12] becomes predominant in view of the intangibilities the artwork is supposed to cope with. Difference in mimesis theories always remained a blank that—because it separated the pregiven from imitation—could not be equated with what it had distinguished; the rift, on the other hand, unleashes the contraflow of incompatibles and manifests itself as the basic impulse for the to and fro of gaming, in the development of which nothing will stay the same.

Thus difference does not appear as such, and has no presence of its own. But owing to the distinctions marked, it allows positions to consolidate and enter into relationships with one another, not least because they consist of different signs and establish different referential systems in the text. Difference, therefore, triggers a dual operation: in marking distinctions it sets off impulses for its own removal, though these impulses issue not from difference itself but from what it has made different. Thus duality is maintained, unfolding the distinguished positions into a changing multiplicity of their various possible relationships. Difference becomes operative insofar as the attempt to overplay it issues into a potentially unending play movement. Consequently, positions in the text are no longer present exclusively as representatives of their respective referential system, but also as changing aspects and relations, by means of which the game once again forces difference into the positions themselves. These positions are thereby developed as a continual switching between present and absent aspects. During this process, the game brings to the fore what had been obscured by the representative character of the various positions, and what emerges will in turn have retroactive effect on representation. Play becomes a mode of discovery but is itself changed by what it has set in motion; consequently, in the text game the play-forms themselves switch kaleidoscopically between what they are and what is eclipsed by their being.

Representation, then, brings about the reciprocal permeation of what is separated by such doublings, and since these doublings are brought about by play, it is play that forms the infrastructure of representation, for the latter is a figuration of what play reveals as the binding together of the incompatible. Figuration is neither the image of an imitated object nor pure invention; it is based on givens to which, however, something happens in the game. Although the game is not grounded in any one specific position of the text (which it would then have to represent), it is nevertheless not without structure. This is ensured by the text game, both through its form and through the manner in which it is played. Figuration therefore comprises all the given factors of every position in the text, together with their reciprocal overplaying, as a result of which representation as performance takes on the character of an event.

If representation is performance directed by play, the question arises of how one is to describe the figuration thus produced. What is pregiven to representation is processed, and thus cannot be a constitutive condition of figuration. As the product of this play-engendered processing, figuration has no tangible property of its own, although this is not to say that it is pure fantasy. In the Husserlian sense of the term it might be described as a phantasm: "The p h a n t a s m shows itself as nonpresent, and resists the presumption that it should be taken for present; from the first it carries with it the character of irreality, and has primarily the function of standing for something else. Only indirect reflection lends it an acquired presence."[13] The phantasm has no substance, even though it has form that makes it the bearer of what it cannot be itself. Consequently it is neither copy nor hallucination, even if it seems to eliminate the doublings wrought by play. But if representation is to be seen as the bridging of what difference has separated, one must ask whether it is really possible to eliminate difference. If representation does indeed spring from the removal of difference, which occurs only in playful possibilities, representation eliminates something that, by its very nature, is not grounded in any form of being. Representation cannot hide this fact but will, rather, incorporate it, which is why the figuration that it produces is a phantasm. The phantasm is marked by the duality of simultaneously being present and not being taken for present; it is simultaneously something and not itself. It becomes the medium for the appearance of what is not.

The phantasm evinces the resistance that difference puts up against being mediated, so that what is revealed in the figuration is deprived of any authenticity. But while difference relegates representational figuration to phantasm, it needs this phantasm in order to manifest itself. How else could difference, as nonbeing, establish itself in what is?

This process conditions reception, or, conversely, the operations of reception show that figuration as a product of representation is a phantasm. If representation relates to a state of affairs that has no tangible property of its own, then figuration must condition the production of an ideated object, which gains its salience by semanticizing what has been figured; the phantasm, then, is given a pragmatic something that it cannot be, because it is the appearance of something that is not, and partly by symbol and analogy, which help one another to restore an obviously ungraspable representativeness to the phantasm. But this means that reception is concerned with discovering an object that is nonperceivable, even if habit assumes that it is there. While difference is incorporated into the phantasm's very status, the semanticizing impulse operative in reception—however it may manifest itself in each individual case—is based on its removal. But if the semanticizing of representation springs from removal of difference, then difference itself cannot already be semantic, for semantics does not arise out of semantics. For this very reason, the performative nature of representation repeats itself in the performative act of ideation. It is this repetition, triggered by representation as figuration, that secures the transfer between the literary text and the reader's consciousness.

Now difference seems to have been bridged, and the game is finished. But since the game can be played all over again by the same recipient, the gestalt of the reader's reception will turn out to be merely partial and hence open once again to difference. For through its phantasmic appearance in result-oriented reception, what is not engenders proliferating iterations.

Staging as an Anthropological Category

If representation is phantasmic figuration, it becomes a means of staging that gives appearance to something that by nature is intangible. This applies above all to the decentered position of human beings, who are but do not "have" themselves. However, even such a split does not seem to be a well-established feature of the human condition merely to be taken up by literature. For if human beings cannot become present to themselves, this does not necessarily mean that they are driven to "have" themselves. Indeed, the insurmountable distance between "being" and "having" oneself is one of the discoveries of literature, highlighted by its explorations of the space between. This discovery would be gambled away if literature were to follow lines of thought pertaining to the pragmatics of human life, in which unavailabilities are generally done away with by hard-and-fast definitions. Instead of doing so, however, and thereby eliminating the space between, literature makes itself into a setting in which that very space launches into multifarious patternings. The staged unavailability of human beings is manifested in a welter of unforeseeable conflicts, which can become tangible only by running the whole gamut of play. Such play is endowed with endlessness, because staging allows the otherwise impossible state that one can experience one's own inability to have oneself. This again becomes conceivable through a trace of inauthenticity that remains inherent in the removal of unavailability, so that staging becomes truthful because it dispenses with the compensatory character of the images presented. For what is staged is the appearance of something that cannot become present. Since every appearance, however, is imbued with an element of determinacy—otherwise it could not appear—it inevitably pales into areas of indeterminacy, which on the one hand point to what eludes the grasp and on the other hand stimulate the desire to lure into presence what has been excluded.

Staging in literature makes conceivable the extraordinary plasticity of human beings, who, precisely because they do not seem to have a determinable nature, can expand into an almost unlimited range of culture-bound patternings. The impossibility of being present to ourselves becomes our possibility to play ourselves out to a fullness that knows no bounds, because no matter how vast the range, none of the possibilities will "make us tick." From this we may infer a lead as to the purpose of literary staging. If the plasticity of human nature allows, through its multiple culture-bound patternings, limitless human self-cultivation, literature becomes a panorama of what is possible, because it is not hedged in either by the limitations or by the considerations that determine the institutionalized organizations within which human life otherwise takes its course. To monitor changing manifestations of self-fashioning, and yet not coincide with any of them, makes the interminable staging of ourselves appear as the postponement of the end.

The need for staging does not arise solely out of the decentered position of the human being. Just as inaccessible to us are the cardinal points of our existence—the beginning and the end—although their inaccessibility is not something that literature has to discover. They have always been present as sources of disquiet—not least because their very certainty defies experience. Since ungraspable certainties, especially of so fundamental a nature, are evidently unbearable, we ceaselessly try to make them as tangible as possible.

This is equally borne out by the countless myths that counterbalance impenetrable beginnings with imagery and by the many religions that transform inevitable endings. In myth, no distinction is made between the contingency of the beginning and its mastery through the stories narrating its origin; similarly, in religions the impermeability of the end is not considered to be a pregiven that the promise is meant to transmogrify. Etiological myths *are* the beginning and prophecies *are* the end. But it is different with staging, which always bears the inscription that whatever it pictures can offer only a glimpse of the inaccessible. This does not exclude the possibility that staging may also provide answers, but whenever this happens, literature turns into Utopian fantasy, reifying the semblance of make-believe, whose emerging meagerness denotes that now the mode itself has become the object.

The more definitive the version of beginning and end offered by myth or religion, the more evanescent appears what happens between them: the multifariousness of human life. This will then seem to be no more than the fulfillment of something predetermined and ritually secured, for what has long been decided upon must not be altered by the vicissitudes of life. Therefore literary staging does not aim primarily at capturing beginning and end in stories or pictures; instead, it seeks to unfold what has been fenced in by the cardinal mysteries. As boundaries of life, beginning and end can equally mobilize life's unforeseeable multifariousness, which then emerges as if it could offer us access to the inaccessible, without ever enabling us to chart it definitively. Since we cannot recover our lost beginning and cannot survive beyond our inevitable end, the reenactment of life in literature entails "genuine repetition"—a repetition that is "recollected forward"[14] in order to make the inaccessible areas of life appear as the immediacy of its diversity. Play as the infrastructure of representation then becomes the driving force behind the phantasmic figurations of staged life.

Since the ever-expanding range of life defies completion, there is no final limit to what is possible. But it appears that we still want access to this infinity of possibilities, and such access is provided by staging. Precisely because it does not provide answers to what eludes knowledge or experience, staging allows us to conceive what the empirical life appears to be—a continual emerging and collapsing of features and patterns that, in the final analysis, only figure life's inexhaustibility. Staging thus becomes a mode that functions to its maximum effect when knowledge and experience as ways of opening up the world come to the limits of their efficacy. It relates to states of affairs that can never have full presence, for empirical life as such is as closed to knowledge as it is to experience. Staging inscribes this inaccessibility into all its exemplifications, allowing it to permeate the whole range of patternings that appear to give presence to what can never be present. Staging therefore cannot be an epistemological category, but it is an anthropological mode that can claim a status equal to that of knowledge and experience insofar as it allows us to conceive what knowledge and experience cannot penetrate.

This need for staging should not be taken to mean that staging is primarily a process of completion. Simply "having" life in literature cannot be compensation or completion, let alone a mirror reflection that—when taken seriously—could only reproduce what is. The inaccessible also varies from one case to another, and thus is not to be mistaken for a kind of hidden or unfathomable substance that would qualify what remains evanescent. For not being accessible to oneself is something different from the unknowable and inexperienceable range of empirical life. The kaleidoscopically shifting inaccessibilities as well as the reenactments of life in literature are triggered by what is, and staging is not meant to eliminate this, as it would if it aimed at completion or compensation. Instead, staging gives rise to simulacra of the inaccessible, which equally cast the latter in changing patterns and, as pictures, fantasize hidden regions.

Strikingly, a similar situation is to be observed even when human beings are in full possession of what is or of what they are in. This applies to all evidential experiences of life, which, characterized by instantaneous certainty, embody the exact opposite of inaccessibility. Evidential experiences are in the nature of an epiphany.

Love is probably the most intense of these experiences, and it is also the most central topic of literary staging. It is far from being excluded from experience, but it is excluded from knowledge, because there is no knowledge of what evidential experience actually is, or because evidence seems to make all knowledge redundant. Evidential experiences evince indubitability, which obviously tempts us to start asking questions. Is this simply because we would like knowledge of what is guaranteed by other certainties? This would give special priority to the thirst for knowledge, in particular since the staging of evidential experiences does not seek to repair the deficiencies of knowledge. In a different context, Jerome Bruner writes: "For the object of understanding human events is to sense the alternativeness of human possibility. And so there will be no end of interpretations."[15] If so, then the staging of evidential experiences is concerned with laying out alternatives for instantaneous certainty. Such a display, however, would seem to be without limits, since with evidential experience one cannot separate the matter experienced from the appearance. This makes the alternatives endlessly proliferating, as is proved by staged love in literature. Evidential experience is almost like an assault; it happens to us, and we are inside it. But the experience awakens in us a desire to look at what has happened to us, and this is when the evidence explodes into alternatives. The alternatives cannot make themselves independent; they remain linked to the evidential experience to which we want to gain access. But this means that instantaneous certainties trigger the need for staging in exactly the same way as the cardinal mysteries. Now, however, we can see the decentered position of the human being in a somewhat different light. Not being present to oneself is now only one of the spurs to staging, and in the visualization of certainty it springs from the opposite impulse of wishing to face oneself. However, if certainty cannot be understood as compensation for unavailabilities, this asymmetry reflects a craving for alternatives, even to those experiences which provide immediate certainty.

Since evidential experiences are generally affective, their staging springs from the endeavor to master the impact of affectability.[16] This brings another alternative into view. Evidential experiences teach us that consciousness cannot adequately cover human experiences;[17] this may even explain why we have experiences of evidential certainty. Staging then entails giving them form, but this form can only be a simulacrum that highlights the inadequacy of form when it comes to providing appearance for such an experience, which far exceeds the capacity of consciousness.

In the final analysis, all alternatives to evidential experiences are simulacra that feign objectivity without concealing their insubstantial character. This holds not only for alternatives to evidential experiences but also for highlighting what it is to be in the midst of life, as well as for the enactment of the decentered position of the human being. What defies grasping can only be lured into appearance as a possibility that can never coincide with what it is a possibility of. Therefore the simulacrum exhibits the denial of its apparent representation in order to show that every appearance is a faked mode of access to what cannot become present. Unlike the picture, which does not merely reproduce but also, in reproducing, can redeem what craves for presence, the simulacrum is a product of sophisticated invention that reveals the artificiality of endowing a phantasmic figuration with form. One of the reasons the simulacrum as a contrivance for staging does not degenerate into arbitrariness is the infrastructure of presentation, which is play. This infrastructure regulates the degree of contrivance required by the simulacrum, which, because it is invented, can be abandoned again, although then the negated and obsolete contrivances will imprint themselves on those that follow, imbuing the changing requirements of staging with traces of history.

Staging must always be preceded by something to which it has to give appearance. This something can never be completely covered by the staging, because otherwise staging would become its own enactment. In other words, every staging lives on what it is not. For everything that materializes in it stands in the service of something absent, which, although given presence through something else that is present, cannot be present itself. Staging is thus the absolute form of doubling, not least because it always retains awareness that this doubling is ineradicable.

What enables staging to make such a presentation is its inherent separation between the mode and the something that is to be given appearance. Since this ineradicable division is always present, unlike the symbol, for example, staging prevents the inaccessible from being occupied. It does give form to the inaccessible, but it preserves the status of the latter by revealing itself as a simulacrum. This dual character gives rise not only to its fascination, as it reveals impenetrable worlds, but also to its potency, since it can give such vivid presence to intangible states of affairs that these appear to the conscious mind as if they were an object of perception. What can never become present, and what eludes cognition and knowledge and is beyond experience, can enter consciousness only through representation, for consciousness has no barrier against the perceptible and no defense against the imaginable. Consequently, ideas can be brought forth in consciousness from an as yet unknown state of affairs, indicating that the presence of the latter does not depend on any preceding experience. Something similar may be said of the dream. Here, too, the dream thoughts are staged as they push something through into consciousness that is not identical to themselves. This applies irrespective of whether the dream event is to be seen as a recurrence of the repressed (Freud) or as the "formative" creation of a world (Globus). Only what has been staged as representation, in the dream and in literature, has the chance to penetrate into consciousness, so that it can gain an ideated presence in the mind without being affected by the pragmatic course of life in which human beings are ordinarily involved.

Staging can be regarded as an institution of human self-exegesis that, precisely because of its general lack of consequences, is able constantly to expand the play space that it needs. Pre-Aristotelian, archaic representation, as Gehlen has shown, aimed at stabilizing the external world. If anything at all was imitated then, it was not in order to copy what was there but to "detach from the irrational welter of givens the life-supporting items,"[18] so that what was selected from the realm of space and time could be kept and made to last. For Gehlen this is "one of the anthropological roots of art" (p. 55) that by representation achieves "storage of life-supporting items" (p. 54) "for one's own ability to endure living vis-à-vis the precariousness and exposure of being human."[19] If representation aims to keep what has been selected, so that the items detached from the irrational welter of givens can be preserved, this accumulation will help not only to stabilize the external world but also to give it voice. And this means that as far as stabilizing the external world is concerned, it becomes, in Sir Richard Paget's terms, a "holophrase"[20] that is eventually broken into variable combinations of its individual units when the "stabilization of the external world" begins to speak.

This archaic structure of representation is also inherent in staging, except that the phantasmic figurations no longer serve to stabilize the external world but are concerned with what is withheld, unavailable, and inaccessible. Consequently, staging is always a simulacrum that does not even pretend to be copying anything pregiven. For it feigns to be a form of something that defies shaping, and it shatters all conceptions of the human being as a monad, subject, self, or transcendental ego—not least because the simulacrum always bears the inscription that what it is forming is unformable. In other words, the simulacrum reveals the human being as a fractured "holophrase" that shows the self-presence of human beings as something permanently lost. It follows that there could be no staging, if historical definitions of human beings actually were their "nature," for it is their undefinability that provides the source for staging. Never being finally present to ourselves is the mechanism that allows us to keep changing in the mirror of our possibilities. As a result, being one's own other does not mean being one's own opposite, and self and otherness as conceptualizations of the human being are nothing but transcendental postulates, indicating at best a historical situation out of which they have arisen.

Yet even if we understood ourselves as the plenum of our possibilities, the question of what could bring about the unfolding of these possibilities would arise. If it were interaction with our empirical environment, then the latter would act as a filter, converting the plenum to a store of eventualities. For such a process, staging could only supply a kind of training ground, whereas it tends to be a kind of institution that undermines all institutionalizations by exhibiting what both institutionalizing acts and definitions have to exclude in view of the stability they are meant to provide. Instead of being the plenum of our possibilities, we can step out of what we are, because abandoning, losing, or playing away what we appear to be will open us up to other possibilities. If we are our own otherness, then, staging is a mode of exhibition in which such a disposition comes to full fruition. Ontogenesis provides corroborative evidence for this situation, since human beings, from early infancy onward, experience changing patternings of themselves that never issue into a final determinacy of what they are. And the need for staging testifies to the fact that the patternings we undergo release the impulse to subvert these patternings by bodying forth our own otherness in the mirror of possibilities. Ultimately, this may even be the root from which aesthetic pleasure springs. Staging is the indefatigable attempt to confront ourselves with ourselves, which can be done only by playing ourselves. It allows us, by means of simulacra, to lure into shape the fleetingness of the possible and to monitor the continual unfolding of ourselves into possible otherness. We are shifted into ourselves, though this transposition does not make us coincide with what we are able to observe; it simply opens up to us the perceptibility of such self-transposing. The fact that only by being staged can human beings be linked with and present to themselves elevates staging to an alternative that runs counter to all available definitions of humankind.

The need for staging is marked by a duality that defies cognitive unraveling. On the one hand, staging allows us—at least in our fantasy—to lead an ecstatic life by stepping out of what we are caught up in, in order to open up for ourselves what we are otherwise barred from. On the other hand, staging reflects us as the ever-fractured "holophrase," so that we constantly speak to ourselves through the possibilities of our otherness in a speaking that is a form of stabilization. Both apply, and both can occur simultaneously. Precisely because cognitive discourse cannot capture the duality adequately, we have literature.

Notes

CHAPTER ONE
Fictionalizing Acts

1. See Odo Marquard, "Kunst als Antifiktion—Versuch über den Weg der Wirklichkeit ins Fiktive," in *Funktionen des Fiktiven* (Poetik und Hermeneutik 10), ed. Dieter Henrich and Wolfgang Iser (Munich, 1983), pp. 35–54.

2. For our present purpose, *real* should be understood as referring to the empirical world, which is a 'given' for the literary text and generally provides the text's multiple fields of reference. These may be thought systems, social systems, and world pictures as well as other texts with their own specific organization or interpretation of reality. *Reality,* then, is the variety of discourses relevant to the author's approach to the world through the text.

3. By *fictive* here is meant an intentional *act,* which has all the qualities pertaining to an event and thus relieves the definition of fiction from the burden of making the customary ontological statements regarding what fiction is. The time-honored definition of fiction as an unreality, as lies, and deceit usually serves as a contrast to something else (so-called reality), and this tends to obscure rather than illuminate the special quality of the fictional.

4. I have introduced the term *imaginary* as a comparatively neutral concept that has not yet been permeated by traditional associations. Terms such as *imagination* or *fantasy* would be unsuitable, as they carry far too many known associations and are frequently defined as human faculties comparable with and distinguishable from other faculties. The term *fantasy,* for example, meant something quite different in German idealism from what it meant in psychoanalysis, and in the latter field Freud and Lacan had quite different notions of it. As far as the literary text is concerned, the imaginary is not to be viewed as a human faculty; our concern is with its modes of manifestation and operation, so that the word is indicative of a program rather than a definition. We must find out how the imaginary functions, approaching it by way of describable effects, and this we shall attempt to do by examining the connection between the fictive and the imaginary.

305

5. Edmund Husserl, *Phantasie, Bildbewusstsein, Erinnerung* (*Gesammelte Werke* XXIII), ed. Eduard Marbach (The Hague, 1980), p. 535.

6. See Nelson Goodman, *Ways of Worldmaking* (Hassocks, U.K., 1978), pp. 10–17, 101–2.

7. This is the term used by D. W. Winnicott, *Playing and Reality* (London, 1971), pp. 11–14.

8. T. S. Eliot, *Collected Poems 1909–1935* (London, 1954), pp. 13f.

9. See Jurij M. Lotman, *The Structure of the Artistic Text* (Michigan Slavic Contributions 7), trans. Ronald Vroon (Ann Arbor, 1977), pp. 240ff.

10. See Goodman, *Ways of Worldmaking*, p. 102.

11. Jonathan Culler, *Structuralist Poetics: Structuralism, Linguistics, and the Study of Literature* (Ithaca, N.Y., 1975), p. 261.

12. Ibid.

13. Lotman, *Structure*, p. 234.

14. See Karlheinz Stierle, "Die Identität des Gedichts. Hölderlin als Paradigma," in *Identität* (Poetik und Hermeneutik 8), ed. Odo Marquard and Karlheinz Stierle (Munich, 1979), pp. 505–52, as well as the response, Wolfgang Iser, "Figurationen des lyrischen Subjekts," ibid., pp. 746–49, which attempts to elaborate on Stierle's thesis.

15. Johannes Anderegg, *Literaturwissenschaftliche Stiltheorie* (Kleine Vandenhoeck-Reihe 1429) (Göttingen, 1977), p. 93. The concept of relating is equally central to Anderegg's theory of style.

16. Goodman, *Ways of Worldmaking*, p. 93.

17. See ibid., pp. 29–33, 102–7.

18. For a more detailed discussion of the interplay between the fictive and the imaginary, see chapter 4, sec. "Interplay Between the Fictive and the Imaginary."

19. See Rainer Warning, "Der inszenierte Diskurs. Bemerkungen zur pragmatischen Relation der Fiktion," in *Funktionen des Fiktiven* (Poetik und Hermeneutik 10), ed. Dieter Henrich and Wolfgang Iser (Munich, 1982), pp. 183–206.

20. See, among others, Arnold Gehlen, *Urmensch und Spätkultur. Philosophische Ergebnisse und Aussagen* (Frankfurt am Main, 1975), pp. 205–16.

21. See Henry Fielding, *The History of Tom Jones,* (Everyman's Library 2) (London, 1957), pp. 307–11. Floyd Merrell, *Pararealities: The Nature of Our Fictions and How We Know Them* (Purdue University Monographs in Romance Languages 12) (Amsterdam, 1983), pp. 25f., offers the following analysis of such a situation:

> Consider a frightened young boy in the movie theater. At a particular point in the action when a monster suddenly appears on the screen, suppose the boy abruptly contorts his face, grips the arm of his seat more tightly, and lets out a scream. This appears to be an *automatic physiological response*. It seems that the boy's *subjective self* is somehow part of the fictional construct on the screen in such a way that there is a direct linkage between the sense data reaching him and his inner imaginary world—the conceived/perceived fiction. The fictional world is all make-believe, of course, and the young man is even tacitly aware of the fact. Yet he appears, at the instant when he screams, to be imagining himself 'inside' the fictional construct and, since that construct is part of his

sense data from 'outside,' he projects it *into* his 'real world' experiences. Consequently, it becomes *as if* his oscillations between fiction and 'real world' were, so to speak, 'short circuited' such that he remained for a split second exclusively 'inside' the fictional frame: it became his one and only "real world."

22. Hans Vaihinger, *The Philosophy of 'As if'. A System of the Theoretical, Practical and Religious Fictions of Mankind*, trans. C. K. Ogden (New York, 1952), p. 258. (First published in England 1924.) Immediately subsequent citations are in text.

23. See Hans Vaihinger, *Die Philosophie des Als Ob: System der theoretischen, praktischen und religiösen Fiktionen der Menscheit auf Grund eines idealistischen Positivismus*, 8th ed. (Leipzig, 1922), p. 589. This passage is not in the English translation.

24. See Jean-Paul Sartre, *The Psychology of Imagination* (London, 1972), p. 223, from which I have taken the example of the actor. Sartre ends this part of his argument with the statement "It is not the character who becomes real in the actor, it is the actor who *becomes unreal* in his character."

25. Hans Hörmann, *Meinen und Verstehen. Grundzüge einer psychologischen Semantik* (Frankfurt am Main, 1976), pp. 187, 192–96, 198, 207, 241, 253, 403f., 410f., 500.

26. See ibid., p. 210.

27. See Goodman, *Ways of Worldmaking*, pp. 102ff.

28. Winnicott, *Playing and Reality*, pp. 1–25, develops a psychoanalytical view of the 'transitional object', which becomes of prime importance when the child is being weaned and has to build bridges to its perceptual environment. Then 'transitional objects' have to be conceived of.

> From birth, therefore, the human being is concerned with the problem of the relationship between what is objectively perceived and what is subjectively conceived of, and in the solution of this problem there is no health for the human being who has not been started off well enough by the mother. *The intermediate area to which I am referring is the area that is allowed to the infant between primary creativity and objective perception based on reality-testing.* The transitional phenomena represent the early stages of the use of illusion, without which there is no meaning for the human being in the idea of a relationship with an object that is perceived by others as external to that being ... The transitional object and the transitional phenomena start each human being off with what will always be important for them, i.e. a neutral area of experience which will not be challenged. *Of the transitional object it can be said that it is a matter of agreement between us and the baby that we will never ask the question: 'Did you conceive of this or was it presented to you from without?'* The important point is that no decision on this point is expected. The question is not to be formulated ... This intermediate area of experience, unchallenged in respect of its belonging to inner or external (shared) reality, constitutes the greater part of the infant's experience, and throughout life is retained in the intense experiencing that belongs to the arts and to religion and to imaginative living, and to creative scientific work. (pp. 11–14)

CHAPTER TWO

Renaissance Pastoralism as a Paradigm of Literary Fictionality

1. Siegfried J. Schmidt, "Ist 'Fiktionalität' eine linguistische oder eine texttheore-tische Kategorie?" in *Textsorten. Differenzierungskriterien aus linguistischer Sicht*, ed. Elisabeth Gülich and Wolfgang Raible (Frankfurt am Main, 1972), p. 64. Rudolf Haller, "Friedlands Sterne oder Facta und Ficta," *Erkenntnis* 19 (1983): 163, writes about the problem of truth as follows: "This situation seems paradoxical: the fictional assumption leads to true statements, even though the assumption may be contrary to fact. What is contrary to fact also leads to true statements, and so truth cannot serve in all cases as a touchstone to help us distinguish fact from fiction."

2. In order to grasp fictionality, we are bound to go back to paradigmatic dis-courses in which it is of prime concern. This is necessary for two reasons. First, the contrast between fiction and reality tells us relatively little about fiction and nothing at all about their relationship, which our tacit knowledge assumes to be one of opposition. Second, the various current definitions of fiction are based on frames of reference that presume to know or decree what fiction *is*. For instance, John Searle sets fiction in the context of speech-act theory, laying down the rather peculiar premise that "the concept of literature is a different concept from that of fiction" ("The Logical Status of Fictional Discourse," *New Literary History* 6 [1975]: 320), though when he wishes to illustrate what fiction is, he again has recourse to literature. Ultimately, he says that it is the partners in the speech act who must distinguish between fiction and literature: "Roughly speaking, whether or not a work is literature is for the readers to decide, whether or not it is fiction is for the author to decide" (ibid.).

Quite apart from the fact that the borders are fluid, this leaves it up to individual attitudes to determine what is and what is not fiction, and although attitude is un-doubtedly an important factor, it is by no means the only one and requires addi-tional components for establishing a definition of fiction. Searle demonstrates his main thesis, using as an example Iris Murdoch—an author whose work must surely count as literature: "Miss Murdoch is engaging in a nondeceptive pseudoperfor-mance which constitutes pretending to recount to us a series of events. So my first conclusion is this: the author of a work of fiction pretends to perform a series of illocutionary acts, normally of the representative type" (p. 325). Consequently, "What they do rather is enable the speaker to use words with their literal meanings without undertaking the commitments that are normally required by those mean-ings" (p. 326). The author's use of words is therefore a violation of the "sincerity rule" (cf. John R. Searle, *Speech Acts* [Cambridge, 1969], pp. 63, 66f.), and so instead of the necessary "bonding" (cf. J. L. Austin, *How to Do Things with Words*, ed. J. O. Urmson [Cambridge, Mass., 1962], p. 10—*"our word is our bond"*), the fictional speech act releases itself from basic obligations, thereby making speech into pretense.

Austin has already called the literary speech act parasitic, because its use of language is no longer linked to the attitude that the words seem to express (ibid., pp. 22, 24). Literature or fiction—is it the one or the other?—becomes total pretense when Iris Murdoch creates her characters: "One of the conditions on [sic] the suc-cessful performance of the speech act of reference is that there must exist an object that the speaker is referring to. Thus by pretending to refer she pretends that there is an object to be referred to. To the extent that we share in the pretense, we will also pretend that there is a lieutenant named Andrew Chase-White living in Dublin in 1916" (Searle, "Logical Status," p. 330).

Searle's terminology is not necessarily meant to downgrade fiction, although it reflects a highly traditional view that was prevalent in the critique of fictions. The more rigid the frames of reference within which fiction is to be assessed, the less convincing the distinctions offered, especially those long ago discarded by the affirmative view of fiction. And so when Searle ends his reflection on fiction by asking "why bother?" ("Logical Status," p. 332), this is because there is no theory that could explain the mechanism underlying the need for a "pretended illocution" to fulfill a real illocutionary intention (ibid.). This seems like a strange form of doubling: through pretense a justified use of language is to be produced, which will bring forth something that is in keeping with the basic requirements of a performative speech act and yet violates the "sincerity rule."

Since Searle's fictional speech act doubles a serious illocution with a pretended one in an as yet unexplained manner, fiction in terms of an analytically oriented semantic theory once more assumes the character of something deficient. Gottfried Gabriel, *Fiktion und Wahrheit. Eine semantische Theorie der Literatur* (Stuttgart, 1975), p. 28, defines it as follows: "*'fictional speech' is what we may call that non-assertive speech which has no claim to possible referentiality or fulfillment.*"

Such definitions not only are reductionist but also must operate with negative terminology in order to point out their lack of any correspondence between the fictive and the postulated reference. Even if no value judgment is actually intended, the result will be hierarchical distinctions that, in the framework of a semantic theory, will make the fictive seem peripheral. For assertive speech fulfills its claims to truth and adequacy by the very substantiation it provides. .

But if fictional speech is without reference, this may also mean that it oversteps the referentiality necessary for a semantic theory. This would lead to two possible conclusions: either the fictive falls victim to a critique of fiction, as was commonly the case in early epistemology, or the fictive brings out the limitations of what it sets itself apart from.

Neither Gabriel nor Searle opts for such an alternative. Instead, they both shift the problem into literature, which from a speech-act standpoint appears to be pretense, and from the standpoint of a semantic theory cannot fulfill its statements' claims to truth by itself, so that "fictional literature's claims to truth must be fulfilled by the reader" (Gabriel, *Fiktion und Wahrheit*, p. 97). "At this point semantics crosses over into communications theory, which establishes and determines on what grounds sanctions or conventions favor certain intentions and forms of reception. Reception is not to be underestimated" (ibid., p. 30). And so the fictive operates along the borderlines, allows different systems to switch over to one another, and in the communication process appears once more to remove the asymmetry between author and reader. Thus fictionality retains its characteristic quality even when it becomes a deficient *boundary-crossing* in the context of semantic theory, and a parasitic *doubling* in the context of speech-act theory.

C. G. Prado, *Making Believe. Philosophical Reflections on Fiction* (Westport, Conn.,

1984), convincingly attacks all attempts to define fiction by way of the various theories of referentiality. His argument sets out "to undermine the very sharp distinction philosophers draw between fact and fiction" (p. 16).

Thomas G. Pavel, "Ontological Issues in Poetics: Speech Acts and Fictional Worlds," *Journal of Aesthetics and Art Criticism* 40 (1981): 167–78, convincingly dismisses the "Searle-Gabriel variety" (p. 168) of theory: "the distinction between 'serious' and 'pretended' acts is based on a set of idealized assumptions about our collective behavior . . . It must nevertheless be noted that, like every idealization, this stand brings along priorities and preferences, and tends to marginalize the phenomena which don't fit the framework. Like most conventionalist approaches, the speech act theory takes for granted the existence and stability of conventions, neglecting the dynamism and their establishment and their inherent fluidity" (p. 172). "The writer as an individual, the authorial voice, the implied author, the narrator, reliable or not, the voices of the characters, distinct from one another or more or less mixed together, make spurious any attempt to comment on fiction as if it had one well-individuated originator" (p. 171). Inge Crosman Wimmers, *Poetics of Reading. Approaches to the Novel* (Princeton, 1988), pp. 12ff., also rejects Searle's "pretended speech acts" as a highly inapposite means of describing fictional discourse.

Since definitions of fiction lead only to the establishment of what fiction cannot be within each frame of reference, we must seek out manifestations of its use in order to ascertain its function and its nature. Pastoralism provides a vivid perception of fictionality, whereas philosophical discourse highlights the shifting functions of fiction.

A decisive factor in the choice of these two forms of discourse was their historical sequence. Pastoral literature is an iconological patterning of fictionality whose pictorial presentation remained widespread almost to the end of the seventeenth century. Such a vivid self-presentation of fictionality eventually gave way to a more functional structure of doubling as constitutive for literature, and this is paralleled by the fading impact of the long-lived pastoral world. With this iconology changing into a basic literary structure, philosophical discourse began to thematize fiction, which had previously existed as a matter of fact but had not been conceptualized. If initially it was a target for denunciation, because as an unrecognized deception it seemed to threaten self-preservation, the very motif was later to become central to the affirmation of fiction. Hans Vaihinger, *The Philosophy of 'As if'. A System of Theoretical, Practical and Religious Fictions of Mankind*, trans. C. K. Ogden (New York, 1952), p. 170, put the case as follows: "We must not, however, always suppose that the purpose of logical thinking is knowledge. Its primary object is a practical one, since the logical function is an instrument for self-preservation. Knowledge is a secondary purpose and, to a certain extent, only a by-product, the primary aim being the practical attainment of communication and action." If self-preservation conditions both denunciation and affirmation of fiction, then clearly the switch reflects a radical change in attitude toward the fulfillment of one and the same purpose. Critique of fiction entails unmasking the schemata of representation as long as they pretend to be identical with what they represent; affirmation, on the other hand, means acting upon what is cognitively inaccessible.

This historical reversal of attitudes reflects various trends: a revitalized epistemological skepticism for which all aids to cognition must be fictional, though one can live with such a situation, and an awareness that worlds are only made, and so remain open to restructuring. If fiction lends itself to such contrary usage, it equally epitomizes human limitations and extensions.

3. See Gabriel, *Fiktion und Wahrheit*, p. 28. F. E. Sparshott, "Truth in Fiction," *Journal of Aesthetics and Art Criticism* 26 (1967): 1–7, offers a more differentiated assessment than Gabriel's of the situation concerning fiction and truth in relation to the real world, to memory, and to the imagination. This discussion has been continued in a series of closely argued articles and essays that expose the limitations of all semantic references in dealing with the relation between fiction and truth. Particularly relevant are Steven L. Ross, "Fictional Descriptions," *Philosophy of Literature* 6 (1982): 119–32; Kendall L. Walton, "Fiction, Fiction-Making, and the Styles of Fictionality," *Philosophy and Literature* 7 (1983): 78–88; and Martha Nussbaum, "Fictions of the Soul," ibid., pp. 145–61. As regards literature and language, the problem of truth in fiction has been developed in two systematic studies: L. B. Cebik, *Fictional Narrative and Truth: An Epistemic Analysis* (Lanham, Md., 1984); and Michael Riffaterre, *Fictional Truth* (Baltimore, 1990). Riffaterre, p. xiii, is right to stress that the "solution of the truth-in-fiction paradox evidently lies in redefining referentiality." This makes semantic references—such as Gabriel has suggested—into what at best may be regarded as a special case.

4. See Johannes Anderegg, *Fiktion und Kommunikation. Ein Beitrag zur Theorie der Prosa* (Göttingen, 1973); and Aleida Assmann, *Die Legitimität der Fiktion. Ein Beitrag zur Geschichte der literarischen Kommunikation* (Theorie und Geschichte der Literatur und der Schönen Künste 55) (Munich, 1980), esp. pp. 11ff., 71.

5. Manfred Fuhrmann, "Gattungskonstitution durch Leserwahl am Beispiel der Bukolik," p. 16 (manuscript).

6. Ibid., p. 20.

7. Reinhold Merkelbach, "(Der Wettgesang der Hirten)," *Rheinisches Museum für Philologie* n.f. 99 (1956): 102, 106. Immediately subsequent citations are in text.

8. Michael Erler, "Streitgesang und Streitgespräch bei Theokrit und Platon," *Würzburger Jahrbücher für die Altertumswissenschaft* n.f. 12 (1986): 78. For this reference I am grateful to my colleague Wolfgang Rösler.

9. See *The Poems of Theocritus*, trans. Anna Rist (Chapel Hill, N.C., 1978), p. 73.

10. Bruno Snell, *The Discovery of the Mind. The Greek Origins of European Thought*, trans. T. G. Rosenmeyer (Oxford, 1953), p. 301.

11. Ernst A. Schmidt, *Poetische Reflexion. Vergils Bukolik* (Munich, 1972), pp. 184f. In "Arkadien: Abendland und Antike," *Antike und Abendland* 21 (1975): 36–57, Schmidt gives a critical survey of the various phases of how Arcadia has been conceived; he also argues against Snell's ideas in detail.

12. Snell, *Discovery of the Mind*, p. 269.

13. Ibid., pp. 277, 286.

14. Thomas G. Rosenmeyer, *The Green Cabinet. Theocritus and the European Pastoral Lyric* (Berkeley, 1973), p. 214. From then on, the two worlds of pastoral poetry are variously constituted, so that their respective organizations reflect changing historical interests, which are expressed in the relation between the artificial and

312 Notes to Pages 29–37

empirical worlds; see, among others, Helen Cooper, *Pastoral. Medieval into Renaissance* (Ipswich, U.K., 1977), pp. 2, 5, 6ff.; Sukanta Chaudhuri, *Renaissance Pastoral and Its English Development* (Oxford, 1988), pp. 1, 25, 185; Shelag Hunter, *Victorian Idyllic Fiction. Pastoral Strategies* (London, 1984), p. 6.

15. See Bernd Effe, *Die Genesis einer literarischen Gattung: Die Bukolik* (Konstanzer Universitätsreden 95) (Konstanz, 1977), p. 19. For the ideas expressed in this paragraph, I am indebted to a seminar on European bucolics given jointly with my colleague Bernd Effe.

16. Paul Alpers, *The Singer of the Eclogues: A Study of Virgilian Pastoral* (Berkeley, 1979), pp. 103, 107.

17. Snell, *Discovery of the Mind*, p. 268.

18. Paul Alpers, "What Is Pastoral?" *Critical Inquiry* 8 (1982): 442.

19. Schmidt, *Poetische Reflexion*, p. 111; Viktor Pöschl, *Die Hirtendichtung Virgils* (Heidelberg, 1964), discusses in detail the artistic features of Virgil's *Eclogues*. On the mirror-image effect of the *Eclogues*, see esp. p. 73.

20. Carla Copenhaven, "The Domestication of Animals and the Invention of Concepts: Pastoral Forms and Representation as Paradigms of Fictionality in Literature," pp. 20ff. (manuscript), has convincingly detailed these distinctions in her dissertation project (University of California, Irvine). I am indebted to her for certain details.

21. Alpers, *Singer of the Eclogues*, pp. 21ff. I have used Alpers's translation.

22. See Copenhaven, "Domestication of Animals," pp. 28ff.

23. Jacques Derrida, *Of Grammatology*, trans. Gayatri Chakravorty Spivak (Baltimore, 1976), pp. 292, 299.

24. Ibid., p. 299.

25. For the necessary delimitation, see Schmidt, *Poetische Reflexion*, pp. 17, 103, 105. Winfried Wehle, "Arkadien. Eine Kunstwelt," in *Die Pluralität der Welten. Aspekte der Renaissance in der Romania* (Romanistisches Kolloquium 4), ed. Wolf-Dieter Stempel and Karlheinz Stierle (Munich, 1987), pp. 137–65, gives a very convincing account of the peculiar artistic nature of Renaissance pastoralism. This is based on the fictional character of Arcadia, which "as an intermediate realm . . . corresponds precisely to the fictive" (p. 158).

26. Samuel Johnson, *The Rambler*, III (Yale ed. of the *Works*), ed. W. J. Bate and Albrecht B. Strauss (New Haven, 1969), p. 199.

27. Rosenmeyer, *The Green Cabinet*, p. 280.

28. George Puttenham, *The Arte of English Poesie* (English Linguistics 1500–1800), ed. R. C. Alston (Menston, U.K., 1968), pp. 30f.

29. Edmund Spenser, *The Minor Poems*, I (variorum ed.), ed. Charles Grosvenor Osgood et al. (Baltimore, 1943), p. 10.

30. Ibid., pp. 10f.

31. Michel Foucault, *The Order of Things* (New York, 1970), p. 42.

32. On this controversial question see, among others, Agnes Duncan Kuersteiner, "E. K. Is Spenser," *PMLA* 50 (1935): 140–55; D. T. Starnes, "Spenser and E. K.," *Studies in Philology* 39 (1942): 181–200; Robert W. Mitchner, "Spenser and E. K.: An Answer," *Studies in Philology* 42 (1945): 183–90. See also Spenser, *Minor Poems*, I, pp. 645–50, where there is a summary of the whole discussion.

33. Konrad Krautter, *Die Renaissance der Bukolik in der lateinischen Literatur des XIV. Jahrhunderts: Von Dante bis Petrarca* (Theorie und Geschichte der Literatur und der Schönen Künste 65) (Munich, 1983), p. 103; Cooper's *Pastoral* remains essential reading for the transition between the medieval tradition and the Renaissance.

34. Spenser, *Minor Poems,* I, p. 45; Renato Poggioli, *The Oaten Flute. Essays on Pastoral Poetry and the Pastoral Ideal* (Cambridge, Mass., 1975), gives a revealing account of Spenser's relation to himself in the pastoral guise of Colin Clout.

35. Spenser, *Minor Poems,* I, p. 16; as regards the different worlds that Colin Clout represents, see Chaudhuri, *Renaissance Pastoral,* p. 185.

36. Spenser, *Minor Poems,* I, p. 18.

37. For details, see Wolfgang Iser, "Spenser's Arcadia: The Interrelation Between Fiction and History," in his *Prospecting: From Reader Response to Literary Anthropology* (Baltimore, 1989), pp. 73–97.

38. Schmidt, *Poetische Reflexion,* p. 160, rightly observes that "the frequent identification of bucolics with the Golden Age is only of interest as documenting the historical reception of later pastoral poetry." For details of such a history of reception, see Cooper, *Pastoral,* p. 6. Laurence Lerner, "The Pastoral World—Arcadia and the Golden Age," in *The Pastoral Mode. A Casebook,* ed. Bryan Loughrey (London, 1984), p. 154, links the pastoral yearning for the Golden Age to Freud's concept of illusion: "Pastoral is the poetry of illusion: the Golden Age is the historiography of wish-fulfillment." Harry Levin, *The Myth of the Golden Age in the Renaissance* (Bloomington, Ind., 1969), is informative and perceptive on this subject. Karl Veit, *Studien zur Geschichte des Topos der Goldenen Zeit von der Antike bis zum 18. Jahrhundert* (diss.) (Cologne, 1961), argues against Curtius's idea of commonplaces. He tries to do away with the conception of the Golden Age as a topos altogether and considers it instead as "a schema of thinking" (pp. 14f.) that realizes itself in continually shifting forms of reception (on pastoralism, see esp. pp. 133–54).

39. Cf. Thomas Lodge, *Rosalynde. Euphues Golden Legacie* (*Works,* I) (New York, 1963), and Shakespeare's adaptation of Lodge in *As You Like It.*

40. See Iacopo Sannazaro, *Opere,* ed. Enrico Carrara (Turin, 1952), p. 113.

41. See ibid., p. 50.

42. Hellmuth Petriconi, "Das neue Arkadien," in *Europäische Bukolik und Georgik,* ed. Klaus Garber (Darmstadt, 1976), pp. 184f. William J. Kennedy, *Jacopo Sannazaro and the Uses of Pastoral* (Hanover, 1983), pp. 103f., describes the kind of audience to which *Arcadia* addresses itself.

43. See Sannazaro, *Opere,* pp. 101–6; the different relationships to the Golden Age to be found in *Arcadia* are very convincingly shown by Wehle in "Arkadien."

44. See Sannazaro, *Opere,* pp. 89f.

45. See ibid., pp. 96, 118. Kennedy, *Jacopo Sannazaro,* p. 135, argues that these interwoven perspectives are ultimately canceled out: "By choosing to return to the city . . . the speaker in fact reverses pastoral values." In Sannazaro, however, these values are based on the very fact that each illuminates the other. Wehle, "Arkadien," p. 153, is therefore right to stress that "if there is a kind of plot in this somewhat plotless work, then it is the text's development as a growing awareness of its fictionality."

46. See Sannazaro, *Opere,* pp. 202f.

47. Sören Kierkegaard, *Repetition*, trans. Howard V. Hong and Edna H. Hong (Princeton, 1983), p. 131.

48. See Sannazaro, *Opere*, p. 198.

49. See ibid., pp. 194–201, esp. 199. Wehle, "Arkadien," p. 160, summarizes his study of Sannazaro as follows: "Arcadia deliberately thematizes an emerging awareness of fictionality."

50. For details see Reinhold R. Grimm, "Arcadia und Utopia. Interferenzen im neuzeitlichen Hirtenroman," pp. 4f., 9f., 13f., 15f., 20 (manuscript).

51. Sannazaro, *Opere*, p. 219.

52. Grimm, "Arcadia und Utopia," p. 26.

53. See George of Montemayor's *Diana and Gil Polo's Enamoured Diana*, trans. Bartholomew Young, ed. Judith M. Kennedy (Oxford, 1968), pp. 12f., 24–28. Immediately subsequent citations are in text.

54. What that implies has been discussed in a wider context by Paul Ricoeur, *Freud and Philosophy. An Essay on Interpretation*, trans. Denis Savage (New Haven, 1970), and *The Rule of Metaphor. Multidisciplinary Studies of the Creation of Meaning and Language*, trans. Robert Czerni et al., 2nd ed. (Toronto, 1981); and Hans Blumenberg, *Work on Myth*, trans. R. M. Wallace (Cambridge, Mass., 1988).

55. See Montemayor, *Diana*, pp. 159ff.

56. See ibid., p. 158.

57. Miguel de Cervantes Saavedra, *Obras completas*, ed. Angel Valbuena Prat (Madrid, 1967), p. 1001.

58. Gregory Bateson, *Steps to an Ecology of the Mind* (New York, 1972), p. 315.

59. Sir Philip Sidney, *Arcadia*, ed. Maurice Evans (Harmondsworth, U.K., 1977), pp. 73f.

60. See Friedrich Brie, *Sidneys Arcadia. Eine Studie zur englischen Renaissance* (Strassburg, 1918), pp. 185ff., which contains information that is still relevant; see also Walter R. Davis and Richard Lanham, *Sidney's Arcadia* (New Haven, 1965), pp. 47, 90f., 336, 386ff., 394.

61. See Longus, *Daphnis and Chloe* (Loeb Classical Library), trans. George Thornley and J. M. Edmonds (Cambridge, Mass., 1962), pp. 9, 27ff., 47ff., 151, 165; in relation to Sannazaro, see Kennedy, *Jacopo Sannazaro*, p. 96.

62. Sidney, *Arcadia*, pp. 274f.

63. For the concept of "minus prijom" (an expected device deliberately omitted), see Jurij Lotman, *The Structure of the Artistic Text* (Michigan Slavic Contributions 7), trans. Ronald Vroon (Ann Arbor, 1977), pp. 95ff., 139, 183.

64. Sidney, *Arcadia*, pp. 624f. Immediately subsequent citations are in text.

65. The down-to-earth Philanax—despite all his inherited power—is equally dismissive of oracles and fantasy. He finds "these kinds of sooth-sayings . . . to be nothing but fancy, wherein there must either be vanity or infallibleness, and so either not to be respected, or not to be prevented." Ibid., p. 80.

66. See Sannazaro, *Opere*, p. 194; for the historically changing connotations of dream and sleep, see Fritz Schalk, *Exempla romanischer Wortgeschichte* (Frankfurt am Main, 1966), pp. 295–337.

67. The English translator of *Diana*, Bartholomew Young, maintains that the

pastoral disguises conceal persons of high rank "that not many yeeres agoe lived in the Court of Spaine." Montemayor, *Diana*, p. 5.

68. The author leads a peripheral existence in the guise of Philisides; see Sidney, *Arcadia*, pp. 419–29, esp. 426. Davis and Lanham, *Sidney's Arcadia*, pp. 112f., go into details concerning this disguise.

69. Ricoeur, *Freud and Philosophy*, p. 15.

70. Sigmund Freud, *Interpretation of Dreams*, II (*Standard Edition of the Complete Psychological Works*, V), trans. and ed. James Strachey, Anna Freud, et al. (London, 1981), p. 615.

71. Ricoeur, *Freud and Philosophy*, p. 499.

72. Ibid., p. 500.

73. Sidney, *Arcadia*, p. 136.

74. Ibid., p. 824.

75. Ricoeur, *Freud and Philosophy*, p. 522.

76. Derrida, *Grammatology*, p. 245.

77. Sidney, *Arcadia*, p. 129.

78. See ibid., pp. 684–90.

79. Anton Ehrenzweig, *The Hidden Order of Art. A Study in the Psychology of Artistic Imagination* (Berkeley, 1971), p. 120.

80. Ibid., pp. 121, 177.

81. Cornelius Castoriadis, *The Imaginary Institutions of Society*, trans. Kathleen Blamey (Cambridge, 1987), p. 135. The implications of this in concrete historical situations are shown in Karlheiz Stierle's essay "Die Modernität der französischen Klassik. Negative Anthropologie und funktionaler Stil," in *Französische Klassik. Theorie—Literatur—Malerei*, ed. Fritz Nies and Karlheinz Stierle (Munich, 1985), pp. 81–133.

82. Ehrenzweig, *Hidden Order of Art*, p. 174. For a detailed discussion see Anton Ehrenzweig, "The Undifferentiated Matrix of Artistic Imagination," in *Psychoanalytic Study of Society*, III, ed. Warner Muensterberger et al. (New York, 1964), pp. 373–98.

83. Thomas J. Roberts, *When Is Something Fiction?* (Carbondale, Ill., 1972), p. 103, 105.

84. Cf. Gregory Bateson, *Mind and Nature. A Necessary Unity* (London, 1979), pp. 69f., 73, 61–64, 81–83.

85. Friedrich Nietzsche, *Morgenröte* (*Werke*, I), 8th ed., ed. Karl Schlechta (Munich, 1977), p. 1172.

86. Helmuth Plessner, "Soziale Rolle und menschliche Natur," in *Gesammelte Schriften*, X, ed. Günter Dux et al. (Frankfurt am Main, 1985), p. 235.

87. For details see Gabriele Schwab, *Entgrenzungen und Entgrenzungsmythen. Zur Subjektivität im modernen Roman* (Stuttgart, 1987), pp. 35–61.

88. Helmuth Plessner, "Zur Anthropologie des Schauspielers," in *Gesammelte Schriften*, VII, ed. Günter Dux et al. (Frankfurt am Main, 1982), p. 410.

89. For details see Dieter Henrich, "Selbstbewußtsein. Kritische Einleitung in eine Theorie," in *Hermeneutik und Dialektik* (*Festschrift Gadamer*, I), (Tübingen, 1970), pp. 257–84. See also Henrich's *Selbstverhältnisse* (Stuttgart, 1982), pp. 83–130; and *Fluchtlinien. Philosophische Essays* (Frankfurt am Main, 1982), pp. 99–178.

90. For details see Renate Lachmann, "Doppelgängerei," in *Individualität* (Poetik und Hermeneutik 13), ed. Manfred Frank and Anselm Haverkamp (Munich, 1988), pp. 421–39, and other essays in the same volume. On the doubling of the unconscious there are pertinent observations in Elisabeth Lenk, *Die unbewußte Gesellschaft* (Munich, 1983), pp. 31, 33, 39, 85, 92.

91. Franz Rosenzweig, *The Star of Redemption,* trans. William W. Hallo, 2nd ed. (New York, 1971), p. 20.

92. See Michail Bachtin (Mikhail Bakhtin), *Die Ästhetik des Wortes,* trans. Rainer Grübel and Sabine Reese (Frankfurt am Main, 1979), p. 68; see also Renate Lachmann, "Vorwort" to Michail Bachtin (Mikhail Bakhtin), *Rabelais und seine Welt. Volkskultur als Gegenkultur,* trans. Gabriele Leupold (Frankfurt am Main, 1987), p. 40, who gives a detailed interpretation of this concept. The ego stepping across to the other is not, however, what is meant in our present context. Ecstasy as being outside oneself is here seen as a form of doubling, with our simultaneous retention of and departure from what we are. I use Bakhtin's phrase, but with implications that differ substantially from his. In *Art and Answerability. Early Philosophical Essays by M. M. Bakhtin,* trans. Vadim Liapunow, ed. Michael Holquist and Vadim Liapunow, (Austin, Tex., 1990), p. 14, the Bakhtinian term *vnenakhodimost* is translated as "position *outside*," and specified in a footnote, p. 255, as indicating "the state of being situated outside the bounds of . . . ."

93. S. LaBerge, *Lucid Dreaming* (Los Angeles, 1985), p. 6.

94. Gordon Globus, *Dream Life, Wake Life. The Human Condition Through Dreams* (Albany, N.Y., 1987), p. 89.

95. Hans-Georg Gadamer, *Truth and Method,* 2nd ed., trans. rev. Joel Weinsheimer and Donald G. Marshall (New York, 1989), p. 126.

96. Globus, *Dream Life,* p. 56.

97. Ibid., p. 57.

98. Plessner, "Soziale Rolle," p. 240. Along the same lines is the thesis advanced by Gernot Böhme, *Anthropologie in pragmatischer Hinsicht. Darmstädter Vorlesungen* (Frankfurt am Main, 1985), p. 233: "Being human only takes on an appearance in particular cultural form."

CHAPTER THREE
Fiction Thematized in Philosophical Discourse

1. See Aristotle, *Problems,* I (Loeb Classical Library), trans. W. S. Hett (Cambridge, Mass., 1961), p. 367; cited in Frank Kermode, *The Sense of an Ending. Studies in the Theory of Fiction* (New York, 1967), p. 4.

2. Kermode, *Sense of an Ending,* p. 4. Immediately subsequent citations are in text.

3. See L. Festinger, Henry W. Riecken, and Stanley Schachter, *When Prophecy Fails. A Social and Psychological Study of a Modern Group That Predicted the Destruction of the World* (New York, 1964), pp. 9, 11ff., 16f., 23, 25ff., 208f., 214f., 227ff.

4. Kermode, *Sense of an Ending,* pp. 35f. Zulfikar Ghose, *The Fiction of Reality* (London, 1983), p. 75, expresses a similar view: "We create fictions because we do not know what happens after death. In short, we try to improve upon the fictions

created by philosophy and religion which ascribe portentous meanings to life and assume for existence a significance which is entirely hypothetical."

5. See Kermode, *Sense of an Ending*, p. 18.

6. Regarding this problem, see Hans Blumenberg, *Work on Myth*, trans. Robert M. Wallace (Cambridge, Mass., 1988).

7. Hans Blumenberg, *The Legitimacy of the Modern Age*, trans. Robert M. Wallace, 4th ed. (Cambridge, Mass., 1991), p. 340.

8. Francis Bacon, *The Great Instauration* (*The Works*, IV), ed. James Spedding et al. (London 1860), p. 7.

9. Ibid., p. 18.

10. See Hans Blumenberg, *Lebenszeit und Weltzeit*, (Frankfurt am Main, 1986), p. 29.

11. Bacon, *Great Instauration*, p. 26.

12. Blumenberg, *Legitimacy*, pp. 364f.

13. Francis Bacon, *The New Organon; or, The True Directions Concerning the Interpretation of Nature* (*The Works*, IV), ed. James Spedding et al. (London, 1860), p. 193.

14. "But by far the greatest hindrance and aberration of the human understanding proceeds from the dulness, incompetency, and deceptions of the senses; in that things which strike the sense outweigh things which do not immediately strike it, though they may be more important. Hence it is that speculation commonly ceases where sight ceases; insomuch that of things invisible there is little or no observation. Hence all the working of the spirits inclosed in tangible bodies lies hid and unobserved of men. So also all the more subtle changes of form in the parts of coarser substances (which they commonly call alteration, though it is in truth local motion through exceedingly small spaces) is in like manner unobserved. And yet unless these two things just mentioned be searched out and brought to light, nothing great can be achieved in nature, as far as the production of works is concerned. So again the essential nature of our common air, and of all bodies less dense than air (which are very many), is almost unknown. For the sense by itself is a thing infirm and erring; neither can instruments for enlarging or sharpening the senses do much; but all the truer kind of interpretation of nature is effected by instances and experiments fit and apposite; wherein the sense decides touching the experiment only, and the experiment touching the point in nature and the thing itself." Bacon, *New Organon*, p. 58.

15. Manfred Fuhrmann, "Die Fiktion im römischen Recht," in *Funktionen des Fiktiven* (Poetik und Hermeneutik 10), ed. Dieter Henrich and Wolfgang Iser (Munich, 1983), pp. 413f. Whether one can otherwise talk of different concepts of fiction in antiquity is a matter of interpretation; see Wolfgang Rösler, "Die Entdeckung der Fiktionalität in der Antike," *Poetica* 12 (1980): 283–319.

16. Quintilian, *Institutio oratoria*, V.10.95–96 (Loeb Classical Library), trans. H. E. Butler (London, 1921), II, pp. 253ff.; see also Kathy Eden, *Poetic and Legal Fiction in the Aristotelian Tradition* (Princeton, 1986), pp. 47f.

17. Bacon, *Great Instauration*, p. 27.

18. See Jürgen Mittelstraß, *Neuzeit und Aufklärung. Studien zur Entstehung der neuzeitlichen Wissenschaft und Philosophie* (Berlin, 1970), p. 353.

19. Bacon, *New Organon*, p. 53. Immediately subsequent citations are in text.

20. Thomas Aquinas, *Summa theologiae* (Biblioteca de Autores Cristianos), 3rd ed. (Madrid, 1961), 1a, q. 34, a. 3.

21. Bacon, *New Organon*, p. 61. Immediately subsequent citations are in text.

22. Owen Barfield, *Saving the Appearances. A Study in Idolatry* (New York, n.d.), p. 62.

23. See Bacon, *New Organon*, pp. 58, 61, 66, 108f. See also Francis Bacon, *Of the Dignity and Advancement of Learning* (*The Works*, IV), ed. James Spedding et al. (London, 1860), p. 315.

24. Bacon, *New Organon*, p. 114.

25. Bacon, *Great Instauration*, p. 19.

26. See Blumenberg, *Lebenszeit und Weltzeit*, p. 29.

27. Bacon, *Great Instauration*, pp. 24f. Immediately subsequent citations are in text.

28. Bacon, *New Organon*, p. 51. Immediately subsequent citations are in text.

29. See Bacon, *Great Instauration*, p. 13.

30. Bacon, *New Organon*, pp. 121f. Immediately subsequent citations are in text.

31. Bacon, *Great Instauration*, p. 12.

32. Ibid., p. 24.

33. Bacon, *New Organon*, p. 58.

34. See ibid., p. 246, where Bacon calls his intended dissection of Nature logic and not philosophy.

35. *Bentham's Theory of Fiction*, ed. C. K. Ogden (Paterson, N.J., 1959), p. xix.

36. John Locke, *An Essay Concerning Human Understanding*, ed. Peter H. Nidditch (Oxford, 1975), p. 373. Immediately subsequent citations are in text.

37. See David Hume, *A Treatise of Human Nature*, ed. L. A. Selby-Bigge (Oxford, 1968), pp. 216, 220ff., 254, 259, 493.

38. *Bentham's Theory of Fiction*, p. 118; see also Owen Barfield, "Poetic Diction and Legal Fiction," in *Essays Presented to Charles Williams*, 5th ed. (Oxford, 1978), pp. 106–27.

39. *Bentham's Theory of Fiction*, p. 118. Immediately subsequent citations are in text.

40. Bacon, *Dignity and Advancement of Learning*, p. 292.

41. Locke, *Essay*, p. 374.

42. Bacon, *Dignity and Advancement of Learning*, p. 315.

43. *Bentham's Theory of Fiction*, p. 10. Immediately subsequent citations are in text.

44. Ibid., p. 51. Salomon Maimon, *Philosophisches Wörterbuch, oder Beleuchtung der wichtigsten Gegenstände der Philosophie, in alphabetischer Ordnung*, 1 (Berlin, 1791); *Gesammelte Werke*, III, ed. Valerio Verra (Hildesheim, 1970), pp. 60–73, has already stressed the close link between fiction and imagination and elaborated on it in a detailed discussion.

45. See *Bentham's Theory of Fiction*, p. 16. Immediately subsequent citations are in text.

46. *Bentham's Theory of Fiction*, pp. 41f. "Thelematic" is derived from "the Greek, *thelema*, will." According to the *Dictionary of Philosophy*, ed. Dagobert D. Runes

(New York, 1983), p. 332, thelematology is "the doctrine of the nature and phenomenology of the will," whereas the noun "thelematism" is the "equivalent of voluntarism, employed in German, scarcely, if at all, in English."

47. *Bentham's Theory of Fiction*, p. xxxiv. Immediately subsequent citations are in text.

48. See Locke, *Essay*, pp. 372ff.

49. Hans Vaihinger, *Die Philosophie des Als Ob. System der theoretischen, praktischen und religiösen Fiktionen der Menschheit auf Grund eines idealistischen Positivismus*, 8th ed. (Leipzig, 1922), pp. 354-57, maintains that Bentham was not concerned with fictions but only with hypotheses. Vaihinger refers, however, only to "legal and political method" and seems not to have been sufficiently familiar with Bentham's theory of fiction. C. K. Ogden, in *Bentham's Theory of Fiction*, p. xxxii, thinks that Vaihinger—unlike Bentham—underestimated the importance of language for fiction. But even if this is true, he could not have added anything to what Bentham had already explained about the basis of fiction in language.

50. Vaihinger, *Philosophie des Als Ob*, p. xx.

51. Ogden, in *Bentham's Theory of Fiction*, p. cxlviii.

52. Hans Vaihinger, *The Philosophy of 'As if'. A System of the Theoretical, Practical and Religious Fictions of Mankind*, trans. C. K. Ogden (New York, 1952), p. 169.

53. Cf. *Bentham's Theory of Fiction*, pp. xxff., xxvi.

54. Vaihinger, *Philosophy*, p. 105. Immediately subsequent citations are in text.

55. See Max Scheler, *Die Wissensformen und die Gesellschaft* (*Gesammelte Werke*, VIII), ed. Maria Scheler, 2nd ed. (Berne, 1960), pp. 282-358.

56. Vaihinger, *Philosophy*, p. 132. Immediately subsequent citations are in text.

57. Michael Polanyi, *The Tacit Dimension* (Garden City, N.Y., 1966), p. 21. Immediately subsequent citations are in text.

58. Floyd Merrell, *Pararealities: The Nature of Our Fictions and How We Know Them* (Purdue University Monographs in Romance Languages 12) (Amsterdam, 1983), p. 60.

59. Christian von Ehrenfels, "Ueber 'Gestaltqualitäten,'" *Vierteljahrsschrift für wissenschaftliche Philosophie* 14 (1890): 249-92.

60. See Wolfgang Köhler, *Gestalt Psychology. An Introduction to New Concepts in Modern Psychology* (Toronto, 1965), pp. 60f., 105, 119, 163, 167. Concerning the continuation of his experiments, see Wolfgang Köhler, *The Task of Gestalt Psychology* (Princeton, 1969), pp. 95-132.

61. See M. von Senden, *Space and Sight* (London, 1960).

62. See Gilbert Ryle, *The Concept of Mind* (Harmondsworth, U.K., 1963), pp. 17ff., 21, 23, 28, 32f., 35, 49, 56, 59, 62, 81, 110, 149, 154, 212, 300.

63. See Edmund Husserl, *Philosophie der Arithmetik* (*Gesammelte Werke*, XII), ed. Lothar Eley (The Hague, 1970), pp. 203-10. For an interpretation of this concept see Aron Gurwitsch, *The Field of Consciousness* (Duquesne Studies, Psychological Series 2), 2nd ed. (Pittsburgh, 1964), pp. 71-84. See also Rudolf zur Lippe, *Sinnenbewußtsein. Grundlegung einer anthropologischen Ästhetik* (Rowohlts Encyclopädie 423) (Reinbek, 1987), pp. 328f., who points out the significance of this within the natural sciences; Sir David Eccles calls the quality of the gestalt "dynamic engrams" (p. 329).

64. See Ernst Cassirer, *The Philosophy of Symbolic Forms*, III, trans. Ralph Manheim, 9th ed. (New Haven, 1973), pp. 19, 21f., 39f., 101, 133f., 149, 162, 179ff., 271, 305ff., 324f.

65. Hans Driesch, *Ordnungslehre. Ein System des nichtmetaphysischen Teiles der Philosophie* (Jena, 1923), p. 27.

66. Vaihinger, *Philosophy*, p. 73.

67. Vaihinger, *Philosophie*, p. 447.

68. Arnold Gehlen, *Zur Theorie der Setzung und des setzungshaften Wissens bei Driesch* (*Philosophische Schriften*, I), ed. Lothar Samson (Frankfurt am Main, 1978), p. 35.

69. See, among others, Vaihinger, *Philosophy*, pp. 19, 21, 38, 54.

70. Ibid., p. xli.

71. Vaihinger, *Philosophie*, p. 296.

72. Locke, *Essay*, p. 49.

73. See ibid., pp. 56ff.

74. See Hans Barth, *Wahrheit und Ideologie*, 2nd ed. (Erlenbach, Switzerland, 1961), pp. 13f. Immediately subsequent citations are in text.

75. Christian Enzensberger, *Literatur und Interesse. Eine politische Ästhetik mit zwei Beispielen aus der englischen Literatur*, I (Munich, 1977), p. 31.

76. Vaihinger, *Philosophy*, p. 39.

77. Barth, *Wahrheit*, p. 19.

78. Vaihinger, *Philosophy*, p. 167.

79. Ibid., p. 257.

80. Vaihinger, *Philosophie*, p. 581.

81. Vaihinger, *Philosophy*, p. 258.

82. Vaihinger, *Philosophie*, p. 591.

83. Ibid., pp. 587f.

84. Ibid., p. 589. On the 'as if' for the "attainment of purposes for thinking," see also Elisabeth Plessen, *Fakten und Erfindungen* (Munich, 1971), pp. 23f.

85. Vaihinger, *Philosophie*, p. 82.

86. Vaihinger, *Philosophy*, p. 53.

87. Vaihinger, *Philosophie*, p. 315. Immediately subsequent citations are in text.

88. Vaihinger, *Philosophy*, p. 91.

89. See also Merrell, *Pararealities*, p. 86.

90. Vaihinger, *Philosophy*, p. 104.

91. Ibid., p. 101.

92. Vaihinger, *Philosophie*, p. 185.

93. Vaihinger, *Philosophy*, p. 100.

94. Dieter Henrich, "Versuch über Fiktion und Wahrheit," in *Funktionen des Fiktiven* (Poetik und Hermeneutik 10), ed. Dieter Henrich and Wolfgang Iser (Munich, 1983), p. 516. See also Ernst Adickes, *Kant und die Als-Ob-Philosophie* (Stuttgart, 1927), pp. 100–133.

95. Vaihinger, *Philosophie*, p. xv.

96. Nelson Goodman, *Ways of Worldmaking* (Hassocks, U.K., 1978), p. x. Immediately subsequent citations are in text.

97. Hilary Putnam, "Reflections on Goodman's *Ways of Worldmaking*," *Journal of Philosophy* 76 (1979): 611.

98. Goodman, *Worldmaking*, p. 1.

99. See also Thomas G. Pavel, "'Possible Worlds' in Literary Semantics," *Journal of Aesthetics and Art Criticism* 34 (1975): 165–76, who stresses the fact that possible worlds of literature, even if they cannot be determined through actual worlds, nevertheless *are* worlds: "So, we are faced with a literary work which contains some propositions possible *de re* and some propositions impossible *de re* with respect to the actual world and a reader who, although he can do so, makes no distinction between those two types of propositions" (p. 174).

100. See Doreen Maitre, *Literature and Possible Worlds* (London, 1983), though her very generalized descriptions offer little in the way of the necessary differentiation. Nicholas Wolterstorff, *Works and Worlds of Art* (Oxford, 1980), is very informative about this type of classification. Interesting distinctions are to be found in Félix Martínez-Bonati, "Towards a Formal Ontology of Fictional Worlds," *Philosophy and Literature* 7 (1983): 182–95. A very useful survey of the whole problem is offered by Jonathan Hart, "A Comparative Pluralism: The Heterogeneity of Methods and the Case of Fictional Worlds," *Canadian Review of Comparative Literature* 15 (1988): 320–45.

101. Goodman, *Worldmaking*, p. 5; see also Putnam, "Reflections," p. 603.

102. Goodman, *Worldmaking*, pp. 6, 96. Immediately subsequent citations are in text.

103. See *Bentham's Theory of Fiction*, pp. 116f.

104. See Goodman, *Worldmaking*, pp. 96f.

105. Such a concept of fiction still retains something of the erstwhile criticism of fiction as deception, though the deception is accompanied by fiction's self-disclosure. The As-if remains a hybrid insofar as during processing it pretends to be something that is then withdrawn as a consciously false idea by what has been processed. The ultimate emergence of something that is not false is seen by Vaihinger himself as "the secret of all fictions" (*Philosophy*, p. 104) in the attainment of the goal.

106. Jerome Bruner, *Actual Minds, Possible Worlds* (Cambridge, Mass., 1986), pp. 64f.

107. See Goodman, *Worldmaking*, pp. 7–17. Nelson Goodman, *Of Mind and Other Matters* (Cambridge, Mass., 1984), pp. 16f., describes the nature of such differentiations in the style almost of a manifesto:

> Sharply contrasting with universalism is what I call *differentialism*. Here the various linguistic and nonlinguistic symbol systems that must be processed in the exercise of various skills are distinguished from and related to one another according to what promise to be significant features. The resultant partial and tentative systematization of skills both is tested by and puts to test the observations made in the clinic and the laboratory. The serviceability of the theoretical framework may be corroborated or challenged by the data; and the data may sometimes be given illuminating reinterpretation in the light of the theory. One looks not for universal characteristics but for significant differences—and then

looks for anatomical and neural correlates. No claim is made that the distinguishing features noted are the only—or the only important—ones or that symbol systems of certain kinds could not be learned as first systems. But some of the differences among symbol systems—for example, that between 'digital' linguistic and 'analog' nonlinguistic systems— are such that the differences in type of mechanism appropriate for processing systems of these differing kinds are readily envisaged and sought. This form of difference is quite unlike that suggested by Aleida Assmann, "Fiktion als Differenz," *Poetica* 21 (1989): 239–60. Although she also refers to constructivism, she sets out to demonstrate that the concept of fiction "throughout its long history has been linked to very different opposite numbers. It has always been defined as a difference to something else, and this 'something else' has varied considerably in kind" (p. 240).

108. Goodman, *Worldmaking*, p. 96. Immediately subsequent citations are in text.

109. Goodman, *Mind*, p. 125; Thomas Pavel, "The Borders of Fiction," *Poetics Today* 4 (1983): 83–88, offers a similar argument. The question of how to conceive of fiction as outlined by Goodman nevertheless remains. Does it mean that fictions elude qualification, or does it imply that fictions are a version of zero in the sense of Frege, who develops "the concept 'not identical with itself'" and defines it as follows: "[0] is the number which belongs to the concept 'not identical with itself'." If one were to equate Frege's number [0] with fiction, its apparent contradiction of not being identical with itself sets it off from the versions of world. "All that can be demanded of a concept from the point of view of logic and with an eye to rigour of proof is only that the limits to its application should be sharp, that we should be able to decide definitely about every object whether it falls under that concept or not. But this demand is completely satisfied by concepts which, like 'not identical with itself', contain a contradiction; for of every object we know that it does not fall under any such concept" (Gottlob Frege, *The Foundations of Arithmetic. A Logico-Mathematical Enquiry into the Concept of Number*, trans. J. L. Austin, 2nd ed. [Oxford 1959], p. 87e). Thus, in terms of logic, fiction as zero would be a contradiction, and one would have then to ask what makes a contradiction operative.

110. Goodman, *Mind*, p. 126. Immediately subsequent citations are in text.

111. See ibid., p. 68; and Goodman, *Worldmaking*, pp. 7–17.

112. Goodman, *Mind*, pp. 150, 200.

113. Goodman, *Worldmaking*, p. 70.

114. This procedure is structurally similar to that of John Dewey, *Art as Experience* (New York, 1934). If experience is to be dealt with in the framework of pragmatism, it can be done only by means of a distinct experience like that of art, since pragmatism, like constructivism, precludes any transcendental standpoint.

115. Goodman, *Worldmaking*, p. 102.

116. Ibid., p. 32.

117. Charles Altieri, *Act and Quality. A Theory of Literary Meaning and Humanistic Understanding* (Amherst, Mass., 1981), p. 279, is therefore right to point out that Goodman's concept of exemplification, unlike the iconic sign, permits one to describe the connections between works of art and their contexts.

118. Goodman, *Worldmaking*, pp. 67f.
119. Goodman, *Mind*, p. 60.
120. Ibid., p. 64.
121. Goodman, *Worldmaking*, p. 137.
122. Ibid., pp. 104f.
123. See Goodman, *Mind*, pp. 124, 136f.
124. Goodman, *Worldmaking*, p. 106.
125. See, among others, Goodman, *Mind*, p. 199.
126. See Dieter Henrich, "Kunstphilosophie und Kunstpraxis. Ein Interview," *Kunstforum* 100 (1989): 175ff., who offers a critical perspective on this question.
127. Putnam, "Reflections," p. 615.
128. Bruner, *Actual Minds*, p. 104.
129. Concerning variations on the nature of substitution, see J. Baudrillard, *Der symbolische Tausch und der Tod*, trans. Gerd Bergfleth et al. (Munich, 1982), pp. 77–130; and Renate Lachmann, *Gedächtnis und Literatur* (Frankfurt am Main, 1990), pp. 13–50, who sheds a good deal of light on the deep-lying links between mnemonics and simulacra. See also Friedrich Kittler, "Fiktion und Simulation," in *Philosophien der neuen Technologie*, ed. Ars Electronica (Berlin, 1989), pp. 57–79.
130. Vaihinger, *Philosophy*, p. 82.

CHAPTER FOUR

The Imaginary

1. See also Hans Robert Jauss, "Das Vollkommene als Faszinosum des Imaginären," in *Funktionen des Fiktiven* (Poetik und Hermeneutik 10), ed. Dieter Henrich and Wolfgang Iser (Munich, 1983), pp. 443–61.
2. See Friedrich Nietzsche, *Werke*, II, ed. Karl Schlechta, 8th ed. (Munich, 1977), p. 995.
3. Rolf Vogt et al., "Experimentelle Rorschach-Untersuchung zur 'pensée opératoire,'" *Psyche* 33 (1979): 834.
4. See Adam Smith, *The Theory of Moral Sentiments* (Glasgow ed. of *Works and Correspondence*, 1), ed. D. D. Raphael and A. L. Macfie (Oxford, 1976, pp. 12, 22, 75, 317.
5. This is how James Engell, *The Creative Imagination: Enlightenment to Romanticism* (Cambridge, Mass., 1981), p. 55, summarizes Hume's view of the imagination. In his essay "Of Tragedy" Hume writes: "To confirm this reasoning, we may observe, that if the movements of the imagination be not predominent above those of the passion, a contrary effect follows; and the former being now subordinate, is converted into the latter, and still further increases the pain and affliction of the sufferer" (David Hume, *Essays, Moral, Political and Literary* [Oxford, 1963], p. 228). For Hume's concept of the passions, see Ralph Cohen, "The Transformation of Passion: A Study of Hume's Theories of Tragedy," *Philological Quarterly* 41 (1962): 450–64, which offers a most illuminating insight.
6. In "Tag- und Jahreshefte (1805)," in *Autobiographische Schriften*, II (Hamburger Ausgabe 10), 7th ed. (Munich, 1981), p. 490, Goethe writes:
> Then it became truly apparent how necessary it is in education not to eliminate the imagination but to regulate it, and through the timely

introduction of noble images to give it pleasure in the beautiful and a need for excellence. What use is it to control sensuality, to refine understanding and to ensure the supremacy of reason: the imagination lurks as the mightiest foe; by nature it has an irresistible urge toward the absurd, which even in educated people is a powerful force and, in opposition to all culture, brings to the fore the innate brutality of grotesquerie-loving savages in the midst of the most respectable worlds.

7. Zachary Mayne, *Two Dissertations Concerning Sense and the Imagination* (London, 1728; repr. New York, 1976), p. 74.

8. Thomas Hobbes, *Elements of Philosophy* (*The English Works*, I), ed. Sir William Molesworth (London, 1839; repr. Aalen, Germany, 1962), p. 396; *Leviathan* (*The English Works* III), p. 5.

9. See John Locke, *an Essay Concerning Human Understanding*, ed. Peter Nidditch (Oxford, 1975), p. 164: ". . . the Mind . . . can, by its own power, put together those *Ideas* it has, and *make new complex ones*, which it never received so united." Immediately subsequent citations appear in text.

10. Thomas McFarland, *Originality and Imagination* (Baltimore, 1985), p. 184.

11. See David Hume, *The Philosophical Works*, IV, ed. Thomas Green and Thomas H. Grose (London, 1882; repr. Aalen, Germany, 1964), p. 164.

12. Engell, *Creative Imagination*, p. 39.

13. See ibid., p. 52.

14. David Hume, *A Treatise of Human Nature*, ed. L. A. Selby-Bigge (Oxford, 1968), p. 24. See also Mary Warnock, *Imagination* (Berkeley, 1978), pp. 35–41.

15. Johann Gottfried von Herder, *Ideen zur Philosophie der Geschichte der Menschheit* (*Sämtliche Werke*, XII), ed. Bernhard Suphan (Berlin, 1887), pp. 307f., writes: "In general, fantasy remains the least explored and perhaps the least explorable of all human spiritual powers: for it is linked to the whole structure of the body, particularly to the brain and the nerves, as is shown by so many wondrous diseases, and so it seems to be not only the ligament and the foundation of all our finer spiritual power, but also the knot that binds spirit and body together—a kind of blossoming flower of our whole sensual organization for the further use of our thinking faculties."

16. Johann Gottlieb Fichte, *Gesamtausgabe* II, 1, ed. Reinhard Lauth et al. (Stuttgart, 1962), p. 308.

17. Ibid., I, 2, pp. 368f., and I, 3, p. 213.

18. Samuel Johnson, *A Dictionary of the English Language*, I (London, 1755; repr. Hildesheim, 1968).

19. Lord James Burnett Monboddo, *Of the Origin and Progress of Language*, I (Edinburgh, 1773; repr. Hildesheim, 1974), p. 165.

20. See Locke, *Essay*, pp. 372ff., esp. 374.

21. See Johann Nicolas Tetens, *Philosophische Versuche über die menschliche Natur und ihre Entwicklung*, I (Leipzig, 1777; repr. Hildesheim, 1979), p. 116. Immediately subsequent citations appear in text.

22. On the importance of Tetens for the late-eighteenth-century view of the imagination, as well as for Kant's expectations regarding the publication of Tetens's work, see McFarland, *Originality and Imagination*, p. 101; Engell, *Creative Imagination*, pp. 119ff.

23. Tetens, *Philosophische Versuche*, I, p. 154. Immediately subsequent citations appear in text.

24. Dugald Stewart, *Elements of the Philosophy of the Human Mind*, I (*Collected Works*, II), ed. Sir William Hamilton (Edinburgh, 1854), p. 467.

25. Thomas Brown, *Lectures on the Philosophy of the Human Mind*, II (Edinburgh, 1820), pp. 389f.

26. P. F. Strawson, "Imagination and Perception," in *Experience and Theory*, ed. Lawrence Foster and J. W. Swanson (Amherst, Mass., 1970), p. 43.

27. Warnock, *Imagination*, p. 192.

28. Opinions differ as to whose ideas most influenced Coleridge. McFarland, *Originality and Imagination*, pp. 100–119, thinks Tetens was the source of Coleridge's threefold division and reinforces his argument on the basis of Hartley Coleridge's corrections of the manuscript; see esp. pp. 99 f. Warnock, *Imagination*, p. 94, thinks that the central distinctions within the faculty were taken from Schelling. Although McFarland's argument is the more convincing, it makes no difference either way for our present discussion.

29. S. T. Coleridge, *Biographia Literaria*, I, ed. J. Shawcross (Oxford, 1958), p. 64. Immediately subsequent citations appear in text.

30. S. T. Coleridge, *The Friend*, II, ed. Henry Nelson Coleridge (London, 1863), p. 242.

31. F. W. J. Schelling, *Grundlegung der positiven Philosophie*, ed. H. Fuhrmans (Turin, 1972), p. 440.

32. Coleridge, *The Friend*, pp. 242f.

33. Coleridge, *Biographia Literaria*, I, p. 199.

34. Ibid., p. 202. The extent to which this view of the imagination still holds sway can be seen from Gaston Bachelard, *On Poetic Imagination and Reverie*, trans. Colette Gaudin (Indianapolis, 1971), p. 19: "Imagination is always considered to be the faculty of *forming* images. But it is rather the faculty of *deforming* the images offered by perception, of freeing ourselves from the immediate images; it is especially the faculty of *changing* images. If there is not a changing of images, an unexpected union of images, there is no imagination, no *imaginative action*." The way in which Romantic ideas proliferate and extend into modern literature has been brilliantly illuminated in John Paul Riquelme, *Harmony of Dissonances. T. S. Eliot, Romanticism, and Imagination* (Baltimore, 1991); see esp. pp. 92–109, where he gives an in-depth analysis of how Coleridge's ideas of fancy and imagination have been recast by Eliot.

35. See Coleridge, *Biographia Literaria*, I, pp. 18–94. Luiz Costa Lima, *Control of the Imaginary. Reason and Imagination in Modern Times* (Theory and History of Literature 50), trans. Ronald W. Sousa (Minneapolis, 1988), pp. 54–120, offers an illuminating historical and systematic account of the close connections between imagination and subjectivity.

36. Coleridge, *Biographia Literaria*, II, pp. 257f.

37. G. W. F. Hegel *Aesthetics. Lectures on Fine Art*, I, trans. T. M. Knox (Oxford, 1975), p. 574, accords a rather subordinate role to the imagination:

> As we saw at the outset, the Christian religion, unlike the oriental and
> Greek gods, has not grown up, either in content or form, on the ground of

imagination. Now while imagination [in the East] creates the meaning from its own resources in order to [try, though in vain, to] bring about the unification of the true inner with its perfect shape, and while it does actually bring about this linkage in classical art, we find on the contrary in the Christian religion the mundane particularity of appearance, just as it is immediately from the start, accepted as one factor in the Ideal, and the heart is satisfied in the familiarity and contingency of the external, without making any demand for beauty. But nevertheless man is at first only implicitly and potentially reconciled with God; all are indeed called to felicity, but few are chosen; and the man to whose heart the kingdom alike of heaven and this world remains a 'beyond' must in the spirit renounce the world and his selfish presence therein. His point of departure is infinitely far away; and to make what is at first merely sacrificed into an affirmative 'here' for him, i.e. to bring about the positive discovery and willing of himself in his present world, which elsewhere is the *beginning*—this endeavour is but the *conclusion* of the development of romantic art and is the last thing which man reaches by plumbing his own depths and concentrating his whole experience into a single point.

  38. S. T. Coleridge, *Shakespearean Criticism*, II, ed. T. M. Raysor (*Everyman's Library*) (London, 1967), p. 103. Coleridge expresses a similar view in *The Notebooks*, I (1794–1804), ed. Kathleen Coburn (London, 1957), pp. 1541f.: "Mix up Truth & Imagination, so that the Imag. may spread its own indefiniteness over that which really happened, & Reality its sense of substance & distinctness to Imagination/For the Soother of Absence—." This idea comes out even more clearly when Coleridge says:

Fancy and Imagination are Oscillations, *this* connecting R. and U.; *that* connecting Sense and Understanding.

lowest	highest
Sense	Reason
Fancy	Imagination
Understanding	Understanding
Understanding	Understanding
Imagination	Fancy
Reason	Sense

(Roberta Florence Brinkley, ed., *Coleridge on the Seventeenth Century* [New York, 1968], p. 694)

On the destructive character of fantasy as a condition of its 'image-making faculty', see Elisabeth Lenk, *Die unbewußte Gesellschaft* (Munich, 1983), p. 60, though she relates this process exclusively to fantasy that "in order to survive as fantasy [must] destroy the collective stereotypes that constrict it." On the structural variety of creative process, see Brewster Ghiselin, ed., *The Creative Process. A Symposium*, 2nd ed. (Berkeley, 1985).

  39. Coleridge, *Shakespearean Criticism*, II, pp. 134f.

  40. Coleridge, *Biographia Literaria*, I, p. 178.

41. Ibid., p. 183.

42. I. A. Richards, *Coleridge on Imagination* (Bloomington, Ind., 1960), p. 49.

43. S. T. Coleridge, *The Table Talk and Omniana* (Oxford, 1917), p. 309.

44. Jean-Paul Sartre, *The Psychology of Imagination* (London, 1972), p. vii. The difficulty of grasping such concepts is made evident by Richard Kearney, *The Wake of Imagination. Ideas of Creativity in Western Culture* (London, 1988), pp. 224–39, who considers Sartre's *L'Imaginaire* as a manifestation of existentialism, and so misses a good deal of its phenomenological side.

45. Sartre, *Psychology,* p. 5. All immediately subsequent citations are in text.

46. See Sartre, *Psychology,* p. 105, where Sartre considers the image as something "intermediate between the concept and the perception."

47. Ibid., p. 55f. All immediately subsequent citations are in text.

48. Edmund Husserl, *Phantasie, Bildbewusstsein, Erinnerung* (Gesammelte Werke, XXIII), ed. Eduard Marbach (The Hague, 1980), p. 184. Immediately subsequent citations are in text.

49. See Dieter Henrich, "Selbstbewußtsein. Kritische Einleitung in eine Theorie," in *Hermeneutik und Dialektik (Festschrift Gadamer,* I) (Tübingen, 1970), pp. 257–84; Manfred Frank, *Die Unhintergehbarkeit von Individualität. Reflexionen über Subjekt, Person und Individuum aus Anlaß ihrer 'postmodernen' Toterklärung* (Frankfurt am Main, 1986).

50. Sartre, *Psychology,* p. 217.

51. Ludwig Wittgenstein, *Philosophical Investigations,* trans. G. E. M. Anscombe (Oxford, 1967), p. 119e.

52. Sartre, *Psychology,* p. 213. Immediately subsequent citations are in text.

53. Husserl, *Phantasie,* p. 268.

54. Ibid., p. lxx.

55. Sigmund Freud, "Creative Writers and Day-Dreaming," in *The Standard Edition of the Complete Psychological Works,* IX, ed. James Strachey et al. (London 1959), pp. 147f., says of this:

> The relation of a phantasy to time is in general very important. We may say that it hovers, as it were, between three times—the three moments of time which our ideation involves. Mental work is linked to some current impression, some provoking occasion in the present which has been able to arouse one of the subject's major wishes. From there it harks back to a memory of an earlier experience (usually an infantile one) in which this wish was fulfilled; and it now creates a situation relating to the future which represents a fulfilment of the wish. What it thus creates is a day-dream or phantasy, which carries about it traces of its origin from the occasion which provoked it and from the memory. Thus past, present and future are strung together, as it were, on the thread of the wish that runs through them.

56. See Jacques Lacan, *Schriften,* I, ed. Norbert Haas (Olten, Switzerland, 1973), pp. 63f., 67, 78.

57. See D. W. Winnicott, *Playing and Reality* (London, 1971), pp. 1–25, esp. 11–14. For a further analysis see Caroline Neubaur, *Übergänge. Spiel und Realität in der Psychoanalyse Donald W. Winnicotts* (Frankfurt am Main, 1987), pp. 94–115;

and Gabriele Schwab, "Die Subjektgenese, das Imaginäre und die poetische Sprache," in *Dialogizität,* ed. Renate Lachmann (Munich, 1982), pp. 63–84. For further diversifications of this problem, see Alfred Schöpf, ed., *Phantasie als anthropologisches Problem* (Würzburg, 1981).

58. See Arnold Gehlen, *Der Mensch. Seine Natur und seine Stellung in der Welt,* 6th ed. (Bonn, 1950), pp. 35, 38, 347f.; see also Wolfgang Iser, "The Aesthetic and the Imaginary," *The States of Theory,* ed. David Carroll (New York, 1989).

59. Cornelius Castoriadis, *The Imaginary Institution of Society,* trans. Kathleen Blamey (Oxford, 1987), p. 3. For Dietmar Kamper, *Zur Soziologie der Imagination* (Munich, 1986), p. 97, "such a vindication, however right it may be in opposing the tradition of reason's self-instituting, with its hostility to fantasy and its slavish adherence to continually providing blueprints for political systems ... [comes] in certain respects too late." Nevertheless, "the 'Irrealis' is of undeniable importance, as it diametrically opposes what reality is officially taken to be." Although Castoriadis did not use the term "Irrealis," the following discussion tries to find out what it might entail and is therefore not intended to provide a critical analysis of Castoriadis's social theory.

60. Castoriadis, *Imaginary Institution,* p. 116. Immediately subsequent citations appear in text.

61. Schelling, *Grundlegung,* p. 440.

62. Johann P. Arnason, *Praxis und Interpretation. Sozialphilosophische Studien* (Frankfurt am Main, 1988), p. 272.

63. Castoriadis, *Imaginary Institution,* p. 369. Immediately subsequent citations appear in text.

64. Castoriadis, *Imaginary Institution,* pp. 296f. Similar observations, though based on very different premises, are to be found in Hans Blumenberg, *Matthäuspassion* (Frankfurt am Main, 1988), p. 301: "It is no coincidence that a quality of *Anamnesis* never ever attained since Platonism recurs almost simultaneously in the theological and the aesthetic fields; it is the unexpected idea that only through 'memory' of what is lost can the full 'reality' of what has been be achieved, 'produced' and authenticated."

65. Castoriadis, *Imaginary Institution,* p. 276. Immediately subsequent citations are in text.

66. See Michail M. Bachtin (Mikhail Bakhtin), *Die Ästhetik des Wortes,* ed. Rainer Grübel (Frankfurt am Main, 1979), pp. 169f., 185.

67. Paul Ricoeur, *Hermeneutik und Strukturalismus: Der Konflikt der Interpretationen,* I, trans. Johannes Rütsche (Munich, 1973), pp. 82f.

68. Castoriadis, *Imaginary Institution,* p. 184. Immediately subsequent citations are in text.

69. The changes in such attributions, and the historical variety of purposes through which play has been defined since the eighteenth century, are dealt with most informatively and thoroughly by Mihai I. Spariosu, *Dionysus Reborn. Play and the Aesthetic Dimension in Modern Philosophical and Scientific Discourse* (Ithaca, N.Y., 1989); an excellent and still pertinent account of play as a philosophical problem and the symbolic nature involved is given by Eugen Fink, *Spiel als Weltsymbol* (Stuttgart, 1960). Daniil Elkonia, *Psychologie des Spiels,* trans. Ruth Kossert (Cologne,

1980), pp. 98–205, offers a detailed survey of game theories that are also relevant for the literary text. The notion of play as advanced by the various philosophies of play is critically reviewed by Ingeborg Heidemann, *Der Begriff des Spiels und das ästhetische Weltbild in der Philosophie der Gegenwart* (Berlin, 1968).

70. See Winfried Menninghaus, *Unendliche Verdoppelung. Die frühromantische Grundlegung der Kunsttheorie im Begriff absoluter Selbstreflexion* (Frankfurt am Main, 1987), pp. 155ff.

71. Quoted in ibid., p. 171. To what extent such a pattern remained constitutive for literature is very convincingly shown by Austin E. Quigley, *The Modern Stage and Other Worlds* (New York, 1985), pp. 37–65, in relation to dramatic literature: "The world of the audience and the world of the play are not radically separable, and neither are the world of the play and the world of the theatre. *Each of these opposing worlds in part constitutes and is in part constituted by the others*" (p. 40).

72. Menninghaus, *Unendliche Verdoppelung*, p. 172. This state of affairs lends itself to a generalization related to an observation, made in a completely different context, by Lew S. Wygotski, *Psychologie der Kunst*, trans. Helmut Barth (Dresden, 1976), pp. 160ff. Commenting on a remark of Shukowski's concerning the poetic fable, he writes: "In the fable of *The Hawks and the Doves* one might seek ... the description of a battle. When one reads it, one can imagine it concerns the Romans and the Germans: there is so much poetry in it!" Consequently, for Wygotski, "If the two levels in the fable, of which we constantly speak, are supported and represented with the full force of the poetic method, i.e. are present not only as a logical but also still more as an affective contradiction, then the experience of the fable-reader is basically an experience of contrasting feelings, which develop with varying strength but always together" (p. 161). A poetic fable, according to Wygotski, can be such only "if the poet develops the contradiction inherent in it, and allows us to dwell actually within the thoughts of this plot, which develops on both levels, and if through the lines and all stylistic effects he can release two stylistically opposed and colored feelings within us, and then destroy them in the dénouement in which the two currents are to a degree short-circuited" (pp. 163f.). "We may say that the affective contradiction evoked by the two levels of the fable is the true psychological basis of our aesthetic reaction" (pp. 164f.).

What is here called the contradiction between two levels in the fable corresponds to the structure of literary fictionality, which manifests itself as a contradiction in the fable—a Simple Form (Jolles's term), that is, a formulaic genre—in order to bring forth emotions that must be shaped in accordance with the individual content of the fable itself. Simple Forms lay greater emphasis on the doubling structure, not least because the reader's emotional store is of a more elementary nature than his or her personal modes of perception and comprehension. Wygotski's insights are relevant to the problem under discussion insofar as a reinforcing of the doubling structure of fictionality as evidenced by Simple Forms strikes home at different dispositions of the reader.

On both the doubling structure and on fictionality as an act, Barbara Herrnstein Smith, *On the Margins of Discourse. The Relation of Literature to Language* (Chicago, 1978), p. 29, writes:

The fictiveness of prose fiction is, of course, commonly acknowledged, but it is more radical than is sometimes supposed. For not only are the characters and events narrated in a novel fictional, and not only is the narrator whose voice relates the events fictional, but most significantly, so also is the entire structure of discourse through which the narration is presented. Indeed, as we all know, many novels such as *War and Peace* allude to quite real persons and events, a consideration that has created theoretical problems for many literary theorists. The essential fictiveness of novels, however, is not to be discovered in the unreality of the characters, objects, and events alluded to, but in the unreality of the *alludings* themselves. In other words, in a novel or tale, it is the *act* of reporting events, the *act* of describing persons and referring to places, that is fictive.

If the allusions are the fictive element, as Ulrich Keller maintains, "the fictive character of poetic texts is to be seen not in the contents, but in the status of poetic speech itself; but this status is not defined merely as the suspension of reference to reality, but as fiction or the imitation of real speech relating to reality" (Ulrich Keller, *Fiktionalität als literaturwissenschaftliche Kategorie* [Heidelberg, 1980], p. 15). Imitation of "natural discourse" may be understood as a kind of score that, when performed, allows the conceivability of what is intended. This, however, would mean that what is intended would not emerge from the act itself, which would consist simply in the staging of language applications whose aims would have to be discovered. If the act entails a repetition of enabling language to be staged, such a process cannot be an end in itself. Why, then, do such acts exist, and why are they necessary?

Staging always contains a process of doubling, of which Barbara H. Smith says:
We should . . . acknowledge the fact that part of the effect of a poem, as distinct from a natural utterance, derives from the reader's awareness of the poet standing, as it were, behind the poem as its creator and artificer. This awareness is also commonly reflected in our interpretations, for among the meanings we seek for and infer from a poem are those that, in Aristotelian terms, might be called its *final* causes: that is, the motives or intentions, the governing design, of the poet as an artist, distinct from either a natural speaker or the fictive speaker of a poem. Thus, we can interpret Hamlet's abuse of Ophelia both in terms of a plausible set of human motives projected for Hamlet *and* in terms of a plausible set of artistic motives projected for Shakespeare; and the same sort of double interpretation could be offered for any poem. This double aspect of interpretation reflects a more fundamental doubleness in the nature of poetry, indeed the duplicity of art itself. . . . As we watch the play, the stage recedes and the personal identities of the actors yield to those of the fictions whom they portray, but when, at the final curtain, we clap our hands, it is not Hamlet whom we are applauding, but the performers and the playwright himself. The illusions of art are never *de*lusions. The artwork interests, impresses, and moves us both as a thing represented and as the *representing* itself: as the actions and passions of Prince Hamlet, and as the achievement of William Shakespeare, as the speech of men—and as the poet's fictions. (*Margins of Discourse*, pp. 39f.)

Doubling and duplicity here entail the simultaneity of something significant and its adequate actualization. Doubling means that there are processes in which different things can no longer be kept apart. The result is an illusion that sets out not to deceive but to involve. The doubling, however, is ultimately to be traced back to that of author and work, or work and performance. Nevertheless, Barbara H. Smith may have been one of the first critics to realize that the act and the doubling are components of fictionality, although in her attempt to set fiction apart from its stock-in-trade definitions, she once more linked its modality to the imitation of speech.

Floyd Merrell, *Pararealities. The Nature of Our Fictions and How We Know Them* (Purdue University Monographs in Romance Language 12) (Amsterdam, 1983), offers a different approach to fiction. His concept is derived from the interaction between fiction and reality: ". . . when we talk *about* a fictional text, there is no need to use the fictional operator, since we merely talk *about* the text *as if* true *in* that fictional world. In this sense it is also tacitly acknowledged that the 'real world' constituting the background against which the fiction is perceived ordinarily remains implicit, yet it is omnipresent . . . *To Conceive/Perceive-Imagine a Fiction Is to Oscillate between What the 'Real World' Is and What It Is Not*" (p. 23). Thus fiction is fictive because it bears within itself an implied negation of the real world. It is important to note that Merrell does not see this negation as a mere contradiction, which would necessitate a transcendental standpoint from which to define fiction and/or reality. Instead, the relatedness between the two gives rise to an oscillation of reciprocal differentiation between the negating and the negated. "And, this 'pulsating' back and forth occurs so quickly that like the discontinuous frames of the film which pass through the projector at such a rapid rate that they appear to be a continuum, we are not aware *that* our conceptual/perceptual-imaginary focus constantly undergoes alteration. Consequently, what is tacitly experienced as a continuum is in reality a discontinuity between complementary frames. Hence *simultaneity of frames is only apparent*" (p. 24).

All fictions, then, entail the (ordinarily tacit) establishment of a continuum between two wholes which would otherwise be at least partly
incompatible . . . It has been suggested often that aesthetic value stems
from a 'tension,' whether existing in a metaphor or in an entire artistic
construct, between what would ordinarily be two incompatibles. Perhaps
such 'tension'-between-discontinuous-incompatibles-made-continuous-
by-consciousness can adequately account for the attraction fictions hold
for us, whether artistic or scientific constructs, jokes or puns, myths or
parables. While conceiving/perceiving-imagining fictions, we oscillate
between one frame and the other, but, naturally unaware of this oscillation, we sense simultaneity where temporal seriality is actually the case,
and, non-consciously, we sense the necessary 'tension' between incompatibles. What is 'tension,' but the result of an imbalance? And what is
imbalance, but the product of something at one pole of a system which is
in part or in whole *not* at the other? Without 'tension' there can be no
movement, either in the inorganic or the organic universe. (p. 60)

As Merrell tries to define fiction first and foremost by setting it apart from a real world, literary fiction is for him at best only a special case. He says of his study that "By and large, it continues the line of inquiry initiated by Hans Vaihinger's *Philosophy of 'As If'* " (p. vii). Hence Merrell, like Vaihinger, starts out with a pregiven real world, so that the oscillation between the two "frames" can ultimately produce only apparent simultaneity. But as the formulations show, it is apparent only in the recipient's activities of comprehension: He or she perceives the separate as a continuum, even if one must say that a condition of this perceptual deception lies in the fact that "fictions and the/a 'real world' cannot be categorically separated, for they are *interdependent*" (p. 56). If, despite their interdependence, fiction and the real world are ultimately "incompatible" (p. 56), this difference, as far as literary fictionality is concerned, is inscribed into the text itself. Thus the simultaneity of mutually exclusive "frames" can no longer be equated with the perceptual deception of the recipient but constitutes a basic condition of the text itself. Since Merrell views the interdependence of incompatibles as the way in which the "frames" of real world and fiction are given in the ordinary world of our day-to-day living, literary fictionality enacts these mutually exclusive frames and thus exhibits a state of ecstasy in relation to that ordinary world. For in the constitution of the literary text itself, two mutually exclusive worlds are made copresent in a way that ceases merely to indicate a deception in the recipient's attitude.

Merrell's concern was to find out what makes fictions knowable—a concern that again links him to Vaihinger. He was therefore preoccupied with delimitations that, in all cases, entail holding a real world *in mente:*

> The barrier between a fictional frame and the "real world" is not air-tight for the reason that, with respect to relatively sophisticated and relatively complex fictions, it is usually tacitly implied. However, imagine what it would be like if there were absolutely no awareness, tacit or otherwise, *of* the boundary . . . One would be exclusively 'inside' the fictional frame. Now, it could not be said, "This fiction has *this* in it, but *not that*," for the boundary separating fiction from nonfiction would not be known. In this light, it follows that when properly reading a fiction *as* fiction with respect to the "real world," there is not *always* conscious awareness exactly of where the boundary exists, for awareness *of* it ordinarily remains tacit—yet somehow we know it without needing consciously to be aware *that* we know it. (pp. 36f.)

Here, too, a boundary—of whatever sort—must be evident between fiction and reality if fiction is to be seen as fiction. What is not discussed, however, is where such boundaries originate. Perhaps ultimately the doubling structure of the fictive may give us an answer. It both marks and crosses boundaries without eliminating them.

73. Niklas Luhmann, *Liebe als Passion*, 3rd ed. (Frankfurt am Main, 1983), p. 107. Paul B. Armstrong, *Conflicting Readings. Variety and Validity in Interpretation* (Chapel Hill, N.C., 1990), pp. 69–75, offers a brilliant analysis of the doubling structure in literature by elucidating the meaning production of metaphor: "The foundation of a metaphor is not a direct thought supporting an indirect one but a failure to fit that provokes a creative response from the reader. When consistency is restored, this is accomplished not by discovering the 'underlying idea' beneath the

literal meaning but by revising and expanding the semantic range of the figurative term. The extrapolation of meaning that creates coherence does not rest on the literal meaning as a support or a carrier but points out the limits of the term's previous stock of meaning in order to enlarge it" (p. 74).

74. Husserl, *Phantasie*, p. 268. Immediately following citations are in text.

75. See Maurice Merleau-Ponty, *Das Auge und der Geist. Philosophische Essays*, trans. H. W. Arndt (Reinbek, 1967), p. 84.

76. Sartre, *Psychology*, p. 217. There is a revealing analysis of negation in art and especially in literary texts by Eckhard Lobsien, *Das literarische Feld. Phänomenologie der Literaturwissenschaft* (Übergänge 20) (Munich, 1988), pp. 196–216.

77. Husserl, *Phantasie*, pp. 506ff.

78. Quoted in Owen Barfield, *Saving the Appearances. A Study in Idolatry* (New York, n.d.), p. 128.

79. First distinctions between the fictive and the imaginary are to be found on the threshold of the modern age in the sixteenth century, though this was primarily an awareness of a difference rather than any firm concept. An outstanding example is to be found in Sir Philip Sidney, *Defence of Poesie* (*Prose Works*, III), ed. Albert Feuillerat (Cambridge, 1962). In view of the masquerade developed by Sidney in his *Arcadia*, it is logical that in his poetics he should clear fiction of the charge of deception, or at least rehabilitate its deceptive nature on the grounds of its possible achievements. Sidney asks "whether the fained Image of Poetrie, or the reguler instruction of Philosophie, hath the more force in teaching?" (p. 15). His answer is clear, for fiction presents "not stories what have bin," but "what should be" (p. 29). For a "picture" is meant to "move" the recipient with what was for the Renaissance the intended purpose of education, and fiction is especially suitable for such a purpose, "since the fained may be tuned to the highest key of passion" (p. 17). Sidney therefore defends the poet against the old and persistent accusation that he is a liar:

> I think truly: that of all writers under the Sunne, the *Poet* is the least lyer
> . . . for the *Poet*, he nothing affirmeth, and therefore never lieth: for as I take it, to lie, is to affirme that to bee true, which is false . . . But the *Poet* as I said before, never affirmeth, the *Poet* never maketh any Circles about your imaginatiõ, to conjure you to beleeve for true, what he writeth; he citeth not authorities of other histories, but evẽ for his entrie, calleth the sweete *Muses* to inspire unto him a good invention. In troth, not laboring to tel you what is, or is not, but what should, or should not be. And therefore though he recount things not true, yet because he telleth them not for true, he lieth not. (pp. 28f.)

All pictures of desirable or necessary ideality must be fictional, because they have no correspondence in re. Indeed, even nature has to be exceeded, if poetry is to succeed by "moving" its readers through its "speaking pictures." "Onely the Poet disdeining to be tied to any such subjectiõ, lifted up with the vigor of his own invention, doth grow in effect into an other nature: in making things either better then nature bringeth foorth, or quite a new, formes such as never were in nature: as the *Heroes, Demigods, Cyclops, Chymeras, Furies*, and such like; so as he goeth hand in hand with nature, not enclosed within the narrow warrant of her gifts, but freely raunging within the Zodiack of his owne wit" (p. 8). If poetry is meant to bring forth something that does not exist in Nature, even though Nature's variety already bears witness to "her uttermost comming" (p. 8)—as it is called in the continuation of the passage quoted—then fictionalizing is quite clearly an overstepping of what is.

However, if it is to become effective, as Sidney emphasizes both here and elsewhere, fiction needs "invention," which comes as a gift from the Muses to the poet. Fictionalizing is therefore an intentional act on the part of the poet, whereas "invention" is a gift from the Muses for which the poet must ask. Fictionalizing alone cannot produce "invention." Since fiction oversteps Nature in order to achieve the ideality of a Muse-inspired "invented picture"—for instance, the perfect Cyrus—the gap between the nonexistent and its recipient must be bridged in such a way that the latter may gain insight into those aspects of his or her conduct that require correction. In modern terms, human modes of perception must be "imitated" to the extent that the recipient may absorb the "picture" so that he or she is actually affected by it. For the purpose of fiction is to improve human conduct, and such a process of correction can only be comparative and never final. Sidney's *Defence*, then, is permeated by the awareness that fiction and invention are two different things that interact in the production of the "speaking picture."

This is set out most clearly when Sidney distinguishes between historiography—characterized by its assertions—and poetry: ". . . and therefore as in historie looking for truth, they may go away full fraught with falshood: So in *Poesie*, looking but for fiction, they shal use the narration but as an imaginative groundplat of a profitable invention" (p. 29). Fiction is therefore not the same as invention but simply marks out the basis for its development. While fiction springs from the intention of the poet, he receives invention as inspiration from outside, for the possibilities of what ought to be, depend on such inspiration, which may be furthered by the intentionality of fiction but cannot be produced by it.

The fact that this distinction occurred at the historical moment when poetry ceased to serve merely as the imitation of an intelligible world and took on the function of influencing the empirical world, suggests that the processing of this empirical world required a welter of possibilities according to which the latter is to be acted upon. As such, fiction is not confined simply to the world of experience, for the gift offered by the Muses also has to be shaped, and the *furor poeticus* required for this represents a dangerous form of madness even within an intelligible world order. From now on, fiction must cooperate with invention, which for its part cannot come to full fruition without fictionalizing. Fiction makes intentionality manifest, for intentions can become visible only through the overstepping of what is. This is why fiction makes no statements about what is, but replaces assertions by the possibilities of what ought to be. However much fiction may overstep Nature and thereby open up a framework of possibilities, it cannot fill this framework with the concrete picture of what ought to be. For this the poet requires inspiration of the Muses, which are external.

Whatever may be our understanding of this exteriority, it cannot be identical to fiction, whose overstepping of Nature would remain empty if it were not filled in by invention. At the same time, invention does not entail the poet being overcome by a *furor poeticus*, for inspiration is, to a large extent, guided. Once again this guidance is brought about by fictionalizing, the intentionality of which adumbrates what ought to be, and also communicates to the recipient what invention has now made into a content of substance. Indeed, the invention itself testifies to the cognitive control of inspiration. Sidney himself said nothing about the interplay between fiction and invention that he regarded as so essential; instead, he relied ultimately on the traditional invocation to the Muses, though these had always been the mythological embodiment of the imaginary. Such recourse to mythology represents both an indication and a concretization of the difference between fiction and invention.

80. Sigmund Freud, "The Dream-Work," in *The Standard Edition of the Complete Psychological Works*, XV, trans. James Strachey et al. (London, 1961), p. 172.

81. Roger Caillois, *Der Krake. Versuch über die Logik des Imaginativen*, trans. Brigitte Weidmann (Munich, 1986), pp. 63, 7. Both Costa Lima, *Control of the Imaginary*, p. 47; and Josué V. Harari, *Scenarios of the Imaginary. Theorizing the French Enlightenment* (Ithaca, N.Y., 1987), p. 61, stress the close connection between fiction and the imaginary. "Obviously, it is fiction that actualizes the imaginary, insofar as any writer or thinker must resort to fiction in order to resolve the paradoxical situations the real imposes on him" (Harari, p. 61).

82. Martin Heidegger, *Poetry, Language, Thought*, trans. Albert Hofstadter (New York, 1975), p. 63.

83. Gordon Globus, *Dream Life, Wake Life. The Human Condition Through Dreams* (Albany, N.Y., 1987), pp. 135f. Globus makes the stimulating suggestion that possibilities are not to be deduced from realities but—going back to Leibniz—precede realities. As a scientist, however, he is not content to remain with the statements of the philosopher but, through an analysis of the human immune system, attempts to show how far this possesses a preprogrammed structure of possibilities that precedes its effectiveness. "Over the entire species, the immune systems generate the set of all possible antibody antiworlds and worlds . . . The monadic immune system utilizes its own resources to create de novo by selective amplification its antiworld and world models. Its core processes are specifying, matching and producing" (pp. 127f.).

84. Hans-Georg Gadamer, *Truth and Method*, trans. and rev. Joel Weinsheimer and Donald G. Marshall, 2nd ed. (New York, 1989), p. 103. Fink, *Spiel als Weltsymbol*, p. 239, calls play a "groundless swinging within itself (into the self)," characterized by its "features of groundlessness." Otherwise, though, there are very clear differences between Gadamer's and Fink's concepts of play. For criticism of Fink, see Hans-Georg Gadamer, *Neuere Philosophie*, II, *Probleme—Gestalten* (*Gesammelte Werke*, IV) (Tübingen, 1987), pp. 95–102. For an assessment of Gadamer's concept of play in this context, see Richard Detsch, "A Non-subjectivist Concept of Play—Gadamer and Heidegger Versus Rilke and Nietzsche," *Philosophy Today* 29 (1985): 156–71.

85. Jacques Derrida, *Writing and Difference*, trans. Alan Bass (Chicago, 1978), p. 292. Eugene Goodheart, "Literature as Game," *Tri-Quarterly* 52 (1981): 144, maintains that "Deconstructive discourse is a game that undoes the game."

86. W. R. Irwin, *The Game of the Impossible* (Urbana, Ill., 1976), p. 9. Immediately subsequent citations are in text.

87. Rosemary Jackson, *Fantasy: The Literature of Subversion* (London, 1981), pp. 20, 22.

88. Caillois, *Der Krake,* p. 142.

89. Samuel Beckett, *Imagination Dead Imagine* (London, 1965), pp. 7f. Typical expectations (though somewhat reductive as regards the text) are described by Richard Kearney, *The Wake of Imagination. Ideas of Creativity in Western Culture* (London, 1988), p. 310: "We are exposed to a text which refuses to satisfy our reader's appetite for representation—a featureless writing which bespeaks the vanishing of all forms of language, an anti-narrative where action is reduced to the technical repetition of an algebraic formula (a, b, c, d)."

90. Karl Jaspers, *Allgemeine Psychopathologie,* 8th ed. (Berlin, 1965), p. 115: "*Pictorially* we imagine consciousness as the *stage* on which individual spiritual phenomena come and go." See also pp. 115 passim, 75, 67ff.

91. Beckett, *Imagination,* p. 7. Immediately subsequent citations are in text.

92. See Irwin, *The Game,* and Jackson, *Fantasy,* who respectively regard rhetoric and psychology as the basis of fantastic literature.

93. Tzvetan Todorov, *The Fantastic. A Structural Approach to a Literary Genre,* trans. Richard Howard (Cleveland, 1973), p. 26, quotes Caillois in support of his thesis. It is difficult, however, to accept his argument in the light of other observations that Caillois makes in *Images, images . . . Essais sur le rôle et les pouvoirs de l'imagination* (Paris, 1966), pp. 19, 26: "La littérature fantastique se situe d'emblée sur le plan de la fiction pure. Elle est d'abord *un jeu* avec la peur. Il est même probablement nécessaire que les écrivains qui mettent en scène les spectres ne croient pas aux larves qu'ils inventent." Stanislaw Lem, *Philosophie des Zufalls. Zu einer empirischen Theorie der Literatur,* II, trans. Friedrich Griese (Frankfurt am Main, 1985), p. 197, makes certain distinctions here: "The impression made by the fantastic is a fleeting, transcient condition, the cause of which lies in the fact that the reader is not sure whether the events which a work describes take place in a natural (rational) or supernatural (irrational) order."

94. Todorov, *The Fantastic,* p. 31.

95. Irwin, *The Game,* p. 55, prefers to exclude this type from fantasy literature: ". . . the writer of fantasy avoids prompting those hesitations, uncertainties, and perceptions of ambiguity that Todorov takes to be essential in the experiencing of *littérature fantastique.*" Lem (*Philosophie,* pp. 196–230), the great practitioner of science fiction, offers a comprehensive critique of Todorov's arguments. For different assessments of science fiction as a branch of fantastic literature, see Teresa de Lauretis et al., *The Technological Imagination: Theories and Fictions* (Madison, Wis., 1980), pp. 135–93.

CHAPTER FIVE
Text Play

1. Gregory Bateson, *Steps to an Ecology of the Mind,* 9th ed. (New York, 1981), p. 315. Immediately subsequent citations are in text.

2. See the detailed evidence assembled and evaluated in Peter Hutchinson, *Games Authors Play* (London, 1983).

3. Bateson, *Steps,* p. 193.

4. Friedrich Georg Jünger, *Die Spiele. Ein Schlüssel zu ihrer Bedeutung* (Frankfurt am Main, 1953), p. 185. Immediately subsequent citations are in text.

5. D. W. Winnicott, *Playing and Reality* (London, 1971), pp. 11-14. On the exploratory nature of play with "transitional objects" and the possibilities they release, see Caroline Neubaur, *Übergänge. Spiel und Realität in der Psychoanalyse* (Frankfurt am Main, 1987), pp. 94-114; a systematic analysis of how Winnicott's concept of play may be applied to literature is in Gabriele Schwab, "Die Subjektgenese, das Imaginäre und die poetische Sprache," in *Dialogizität*, ed. Renate Lachmann (Munich, 1982), pp. 63-84.

6. Jean Piaget, *Play, Dreams and Imitation in Childhood*, trans. C. Gattegno and F. M. Hodgson (London, 1962), p. 93. Immediately subsequent citations are in text.

7. Hans Blumenberg, *Schiffbruch mit Zuschauer. Paradigma einer Daseinsmetapher* (Frankfurt am Main, 1979), pp. 89f.

8. Piaget, *Play, Dreams and Imitation*, pp. 162f.

9. Ibid., p. 163.

10. See Hans Blumenberg, *Wirklichkeiten in denen wir leben* (Stuttgart, 1981), p. 114.

11. This is dealt with historically and systematically in Sanford Budick, "Tradition in the Space of Negativity," in *Languages of the Unsayable. The Play of Negativity in Literature and Literary Theory*, ed. Sanford Budick and Wolfgang Iser (Irvine Studies in the Humanities 3) (New York, 1989), pp. 297-322.

12. On the question of progress in art, Murray Krieger, *Words About Words About Words: Theory, Criticism, and the Literary Text* (Baltimore, 1988), pp. 20-24, gives a balanced and authoritative view.

13. The connection is subtly analyzed in Renate Lachmann, *Gedächtnis und Literatur* (Frankfurt am Main, 1990), pp. 65-87.

14. Johan Huizinga, *Homo Ludens. Vom Ursprung der Kultur im Spiel* (Rowohlts Deutsche Enzyklopädie 21) (Hamburg, 1956), pp. 7, 12, 51, 60, 78, 90f., 118, 126, 167, 185ff. Kostas Axelos, "Planetary Interlude," *Yale French Studies* 41 (1968): 6-18, shows a similar tendency, deriving all games from the primal game of time.

15. Jünger, *Spiele*, p. 193.

16. Roger Caillois, *Man, Play, and Games*, trans. Meyer Barash (Glencoe, Ill., 1958), p. 4. On Caillois's distinctions and their consequences for the concept of play, see Hans Scheuerl, "Spiel—ein menschliches Grundverhalten?" in *Theorien des Spiels*, ed. Hans Scheuerl, 10th ed. (Weinheim, Germany, 1975), p. 207.

17. Caillois, *Man, Play, and Games*, p. 67. Immediately subsequent citations are in text.

18. Caillois, *Man, Play, and Games*, p. 44. A far more detailed account of the basic play attitudes is in Owen Aldis, *Play Fighting* (New York, 1975); see also Heinrich Kutzner, *Erfahrung und Begriff des Spieles. Versuch, den Menschen als spielendes Wesen zu denken* (diss.) (Berlin, 1973); a more comprehensive survey is given by Gustav Bally, *Vom Spielraum der Freiheit. Die Bedeutung des Spiels bei Tier und Mensch*, 2nd ed. (Basel, 1966).

19. See Harold Bloom, *Agon* (New York, 1982), pp. 16-51.

20. F. J. J. Buytendijk, *Wesen und Sinn des Spiels. Das Spielen des Menschen und der Tiere als Erscheinungsform der Lebenstriebe* (Berlin, 1933), p. 114.

21. Manfred Eigen and Ruthild Winkler, *Das Spiel. Naturgesetze steuern den Zufall*, 7th ed. (Munich, 1985), p. 343.

22. Buytendijk, *Wesen und Sinn*, p. 78.

23. James S. Hans, *The Play of the World* (Amherst, Mass., 1981), p. 15.

24. For details, see Wolfgang Iser, *Laurence Sterne's 'Tristram Shandy'* (Landmarks of World Literature) (Cambridge, 1988).

25. See Eigen and Winkler, *Das Spiel*, pp. 87–112; for an assessment of such a "model function" see Gerd-Klaus Kaltenbrunner, "Vorwort," *Im Anfang war das Spiel*, ed. Gerd-Klaus Kaltenbrunner (Munich, 1987), p. 13.

26. Eigen and Winkler, *Das Spiel*, p. 87. For distinctions between strategies of play and the rules that can be derived from them, see Ewald Burger, *Einführung in die Theorie der Spiele*, 2nd ed. (Berlin, 1966).

27. Caillois therefore characterizes his contrasting *ludus* and *paidia* not as "categories of play but ways of playing, they pass into ordinary life as invariable opposites, e.g. the preference for cacophony over a symphony, scribbling over the wise application of the laws of perspective. Their continuous opposition arises from the fact that a concerted enterprise, in which various expendable resources are well utilized, has nothing in common with purely disordered movement for the sake of paroxism" (*Man, Play, and Games*, p. 53). He therefore ranges these modes of play alongside the individual games as the suitable manner in which they are to be played. *Ludus* "disciplines and enriches. It provides an occasion for training and normally leads to the acquisition of a special skill, a particular mastery of the operation of one or another contraption or the discovery of a satisfactory solution to problems of a more conventional type" (*Man, Play, and Games*, p. 29). *Paidia* is an unbridled, all-consuming passion for play, which is most strongly manifested in *mimicry* and *ilinx* but which must be subjected to an increasing control of *ludus* if games are to take on their own particular gestalt. Consequently the regulatory element is not, as play in the processes of nature, based on homeostasis but on refinement of games, in order to represent what they are meant to express. On regulations, see also Ingeborg Heidemann, *Der Begriff des Spiels und das ästhetische Weltbild in der Philosophie der Gegenwart* (Berlin, 1968), pp. 64f.

If the earliest game theory is to be found, according to Arno Borst, *Barbaren, Ketzer und Artisten. Welten des Mittelalters* (Munich, 1988), p. 461, "in a book about *Rithmimachia*, around 1130," these games are characterized by complicated, though strict regulations. "It is . . . a matter of establishing a harmonious configuration of numerals, if possible by capturing something of value to one's opponent, who of course may intervene. It would be cleverer for him, however, to put together a triad as fast as possible, and so pacify his partner" (p. 460). Arno Borst, *Das mittelalterliche Zahlenkampfspiel* (Supplemente zu den *Sitzungsberichte der Heidelberger Akademie der Wissenschaften*, Philosophisch- historische Klasse 5) (Heidelberg, 1986), gives an extremely detailed account of the rigid mathematical rules that govern these games of numerals. Chess, as a related game, is by contrast much freer, so that at the end of the Middle Ages, the application of its rules had become increasingly variable. Borst is inclined to assume that this process of growing flexibility even extended into the strategies of war. Accordingly, the relation between conservative and dissipative rules could also be seen as one of historical evolution. The dissipative—or aleatory—rule tends to take on growing importance both for the interplay of rules and for the rules of play.

28. See Eric Berne, *Games People Play*, 21st ed. (New York, 1983), pp. 16–19, esp. 16; and Adolf Portmann, "Das Spiel als gestaltete Zeit," in *Im Anfang war das Spiel*, ed. Gerd-Klaus Kaltenbrunner (Munich, 1987), pp. 54f., 68. They start from different premises but come to the same conclusion.

29. Eugen Fink, *Spiel als Weltsymbol* (Stuttgart, 1960), p. 99.

30. Bateson, *Steps*, pp. 19f.

31. John Searle, *Speech Acts* (Cambridge, 1969), p. 33.

32. Jurij Lotman, *The Structure of the Artistic Text* (Michigan Slavic Contributions 7), trans. Ronald Vroon (Ann Arbor, 1977), p. 68.

33. Anthony Wilden, *System and Structure. Essays in Communication and Exchange* (London, 1972), p. 190. Immediately subsequent citations are in text.

34. For it is basically "the fate of all sequences of signs or signifiers: what they say cannot be of the same logical type as what they signify, nor of the same type as that to which they refer" (Wilden, *System and Structure*, p. 187). How such play space may be used for the construal of metaphor is shown with many revealing variations in Murray Krieger, *A Reopening of Closure. Organicism Against Itself* (Wellek Library Lectures) (New York, 1989), pp. 57–84, esp. 65f., 70, 73ff.

35. Wilden, *System and Structure*, p. 189.

36. Ibid., p. 163.

37. Hans Robert Jauβ, *Aesthetic Experience and Literary Hermeneutic* (Theory and History of Literature 3), trans. Michael Show (Minneapolis, Minn., 1982), p. 32.

38. Roland Barthes, *The Pleasure of the Text*, trans. Richard Miller (London, 1976), pp. 12f.

39. Ibid., p. 7.

40. See Sören Kierkegaard, *Abschließende unwissenschaftliche Nachschrift zu den philosophischen Brocken*, I (*Gesammelte Werke*, 16. Abt.), trans. Hans Martin Junghans (Düsseldorf, 1957), p. 187.

41. Friedrich Nietzsche, *Also Sprach Zarathustra* (*Werke*, II), 8th ed., ed. Karl Schlechta (Munich, 1977), p. 557.

42. To invoke Barthes as a witness for the absorption of the reader into the text may not do full justice to Barthes's elaborate charting of reader involvement in his careful analysis of Balzac's readerly text *Sarrasine—S/Z. An Essay*, trans. Richard Miller (New York, 1974). The readerly text, as opposed to the writerly, "is a galaxy of signifiers, not a structure of signifieds; it has no beginning; it is reversible; we gain access to it by several entrances, none of which can be authoritatively declared to be the main one; the codes it mobilizes extend *as far as the eye can reach*, they are indeterminable (meaning here is never subject to a principle of determination, unless by throwing dice); the sytems of meaning can take over this absolutely plural text, but their number is never closed, based as it is on the infinity of language" (pp. 5f.). Therefore Barthes calls "any readerly text a classic text" (pp. 4). Yet in further specifying, he simultaneously admits "that any classic (readerly) text is implicitly an art of Replete Literature . . . This Replete Literature, readerly literature, can no longer be written: symbolic plenitude (culminating in romantic art) is the last avatar of our culture" (pp. 200f.). Thus the bliss of the text is forever polarized by the pleasure of the text. Incompatible as such a division may seem, it remains to be questioned whether "our literature is characterized by the pitiless

divorce which the literary institution maintains between the producer of the text and its user, between its owner and its customer, between its author and its reader" (p. 4). If the pleasure of the text, basically dispensed by the modern, "the limit-text," requires "the leisure of bygone readings" for the reader to become an "*aristocratic reader*," such a disposition is not so totally different from the bliss that the readerly text is able to offer.

> *I read a text.* This statement, consonant with the "genius" of the language (subject, verb, complement), is not always true. The more plural the text, the less it is written before I read it; I do not make it undergo a predicative operation, consequent upon its being, an operation known as *reading*, and *I* is not an innocent subject, anterior to the text, one which will subsequently deal with the text as it would an object to dismantle or a site to occupy. This "I" which approaches the text is already itself a plurality of other texts, of codes which are infinite or, more precisely, lost (whose origin is lost) . . . reading is not a parasitical act, the reactive complement of a writing which we endow with all the glamour of creation and anteriority. It is a form of work (which is why it would be better to speak of a lexeological act—even a lexeographical act, since I write my reading), and the method of this work is topological: I am not hidden within the text, I am simply irrecoverable from it: my task is to move, to shift systems whose perspective ends neither at the text nor at the "I." (p. 10)

At this juncture bliss and pleasure shrink to an almost infinitesimal difference. The readerly text makes the reader merge with the text whose network of codes is nevertheless operated by someone who is indistinguishable from the text. If the bliss of the readerly text signals plenitude, the pleasure of the writerly or "limit-text" indicates the collapse of the reader into the "subject of the text." Yet in either instance what the reader is given to do "is a form of work," and in doing it the reader is bound to be subject to transformation.

CHAPTER SIX
Epilogue

1. Hans Blumenberg, *Wirklichkeiten in denen wir leben* (Stuttgart, 1981), pp. 55f. Immediately subsequent citations are in text.

2. See Murray Krieger, "The Ambiguities of Representation and Illusion: An E. H. Gombrich Retrospective," *Critical Inquiry* 11 (1984): 181–94; E. H. Gombrich, "Representation and Misrepresentation," *Critical Inquiry* 11 (1984): pp. 195–201; Murray Krieger, "Optics and Aesthetic Perception: A Rebuttal," *Critical Inquiry* 12 (1985): 502–8.

3. E. H. Gombrich, *Art and Illusion. A Study in the Psychology of Pictorial Representation*, 2nd ed. (London, 1962), p. 154. Immediately subsequent citations are in text.

4. Paul Ricoeur, "Mimesis and Representation," *Annals of Scholarship. Metastudies of the Humanities and Social Sciences* 2 (1981): 15. Immediately subsequent citations are in text.

5. See Ricoeur, "Mimesis and Representation," p. 19: "To use a phrase from Clifford Geertz, human action is always symbolically mediated."

6. Theodor W. Adorno, *Aesthetic Theory*, trans. C. Lenhardt (London, 1984), p. 399.

7. See Michael Cahn, "Subversive Mimesis: T. W. Adorno and the Modern Impasse of Critique," in *Mimesis in Contemporary Thought: An Interdisciplinary Approach*, I, *The Literary and Philosophical Debate*, ed. Mihai Spariosu (Philadelphia, 1984), pp. 27–64.

8. Adorno, *Aesthetic Theory*, p. 100. Immediately subsequent citations are in text.

9. G. W. F. Hegel, *Aesthetics. Lectures on Fine Art*, I, trans. T. M. Knox (Oxford, 1975), p. 111.

10. Adorno, *Aesthetic Theory*, p. 453. Immediately subsequent citations are in text.

11. See Michel Foucault, *The Order of Things. An Archaeology of the Human Sciences* (New York, 1970), pp. 217–49; Jacques Derrida, *Writing and Difference*, trans. Alan Bass (London, 1978), pp. 232–50; and Gabriele Schwab, *Samuel Becketts Endspiel mit der Subjektivität. Entwurf einer Psychoästhetik des modernen Theaters* (Stuttgart, 1981), pp. 4–34, who puts this in a historical and systematic perspective. Ian Hunter, "After Representation: Recent Discussions of the Relation Between Language and Literature," in *Ideological Representation and Power in Social Relations: Literary and Social Theory*, ed. Mike Gane (London, 1989), pp. 167–97, speaks categorically of the end of representation.

12. For the anthropological implications, see Victor Turner, *The Anthropology of Performance* (New York, 1986), esp. pp. 33–71, who details the ethnographic background of performance through narrative paradigms from different cultures; for further reference see Victor Turner, "Are There Universals of Performance?, with an Introduction by Barbara Babcock, 'The Arts and All Things Common: Victor Turner's Literary Anthropology,'" *Comparative Criticism* 9 (1987): 35–58.

13. Edmund Husserl, *Phantasie, Bildbewusstsein, Erinnerung* (*Gesammelte Werke*, XXIII), ed. Eduard Marbach (The Hague, 1980), pp. 80f.

14. Sören Kierkegaard, *Repetition*, trans. Howard V. Hong and Edna H. Hong (Princeton, 1983), p. 131.

15. Jerome Bruner, *Actual Minds, Possible Worlds* (Cambridge, Mass., 1986), p. 53.

16. See Arnold Gehlen, *Urmensch und Spätkultur*, 4th ed. (Frankfurt am Main, 1977), p. 153.

17. See Peter Sloterdijk, *Literatur und Lebenserfahrung. Autobiographien der zwanziger Jahre* (Munich, 1978), p. 12.

18. Gehlen, *Urmensch*, p. 54. Immediately subsequent citations are in text.

19. Gehlen, *Urmensch*, p. 56. Irenäus Eibl-Eibesfeldt, *Der Mensch—das riskierte Wesen. Zur Naturgeschichte menschlicher Unvernunft* (Munich, 1988), pp. 243f., has a similar view, despite his implied criticisms of Gehlen: "For us humans, it is a matter of continuing to keep cultural and biological possibilities of development open for ourselves. The chances for this are unique."

20. Sir Richard Paget, "The Origins of Language with Special Reference to the Paleolithic Age," *Cahiers d'histoire mondiale* 1 (1953/54): 408, 414.

Index of Names

Abelard, 42
Addison, Joseph, 175
Adickes, Ernst, 320
Adorno, Theodor W., 261, 291, 293, 341
Alcmaeon, 88
Aldis, Owen, 337
Alexander, William, 62, 70
Allen, Woody, 156
Alpers, Paul, 29, 31, 312
Alsberg, Paul, xi
Alston, R. C., 312
Altieri, Charles, 322
Anderegg, Johannes, 10, 306, 311
Anscombe, G.E.M., 327
Apollonius of Tyana, 285
Aristotle, 28, 31, 88, 100, 173, 176, 178, 188, 281, 282, 284–90, 302, 316, 317, 330
Armstrong, Paul B., 332
Arnason, Johann P., 328
Arndt, H. W., 333
Assmann, Aleida, 311, 322
Austin, John L., 308, 322
Axelos, Kostas, 337

Babcock, Barbara, 341
Bachelard, Gaston, 325
Bacon, Francis: *New Organon*, 93–115, 164, 165, 166, 317, 318
Bakhtin, Mikhail, 84, 216, 316, 328
Bally, Gustav, 337

Balzac, Honoré de, 339
Barash, Meyer, 337
Barfield, Owen, 318, 333
Barth, Helmuth, 329
Barthes, Roland, 278, 279, 320, 339
Bass, Alan, 335, 341
Bate, W. J., 312
Bateson, Gregory, 57, 247, 248, 273, 314, 315, 336, 338
Baudrillard, Jean, 323
Beckett, Samuel, 238, 241–46, 269, 336
Bentham, Jeremy, 109; *Theory of Fiction*, 110–32, 138, 144, 152–54, 157, 165, 167, 168, 170, 318, 319, 321
Bergfleth, Gerd, 323
Berne, Eric, 338
Blamey, Kathleen, 315, 328
Bloom, Harold, 260, 337
Blumenberg, Hans, 182, 253, 314, 317, 318, 328, 337, 340
Böhme, Gernot, 316
Borst, Arno, 338
Bosch, Hieronymus, 162
Boswell, James, 162
Brie, Friedrich, 314
Brinkley, Roberta F., 326
Brown, Thomas, 179, 180, 325
Bruner, Jerome, 155, 299, 321, 323, 341
Budick, Sanford, 337
Bunyan, John, 114

Compiled by Dr. Monika Reif-Hülser

343

Index of Names 345

Goodman, Nelson, 6–8, 10, 20; *Ways of Worldmaking,* 152–70, 306, 307, 320–23
Goya, Francisco, 162
Green, Thomas, 324
Griese, Friedrich, 336
Grimm, Reinhold R., 314
Grose, Thomas H., 324
Grübel, Rainer, 316, 328
Gülich, Elisabeth, 308
Gurwitch, Aron, 319

Haller, Rudolf, 308
Hallo, William W., 316
Hamilton, William, 325
Hans, James S., 338
Hanson, Norwood, 154
Harari, Josué V., 335
Harris, Marvin, xi
Hart, Jonathan, 321
Hartley, David, 181, 325
Haverkamp, Anselm, 316
Hegel, Georg W. F., 78, 190, 292, 325, 341
Heidegger, Martin, 209, 234, 335
Heidemann, Ingeborg, 329, 338
Heliodor, 59
Henrich, Dieter, 149, 305, 315, 317, 320, 323, 327
Herder, Johann Gottfried von, 175, 324
Hett, W. S., 316
Hobbes, Thomas, 173, 175, 178, 181, 324
Hodgson, M., 337
Hofstadter, Albert, 335
Holquist, Michael, 316
Homer, 256
Hong, Edna H., 314, 341
Hong, Howard V., 314, 341
Hörmann, Hans, 307
Howard, Richard, 336
Huizinga, Johan, 258, 260, 337
Hume, David, 108, 111, 112, 114, 116, 117, 123, 142; *A Treatise of Human Nature,* 173–87, 205, 318, 323, 324
Hunter, Ian, 341
Hunter, Shelag, 312
Husserl, Edmund, 3, 90, 130, 141, 199, 202, 230, 295, 306, 319, 327, 333, 341
Hutchinson, Peter, 336

Irwin, W. R., 239, 335, 336
Iser, Wolfgang, 305, 306, 313, 317, 320, 323, 328, 337, 338

Jackson, Rosemary, 335, 336
Jaspers, Karl, 242, 336
Jauss, Hans Robert, 278, 323, 339
Johnson, Samuel, 34, 175, 176, 312, 324
Jolles, André, 329
Joyce, James, 7
Jünger, Friedrich G., 251, 252, 258, 336
Junghans, Hans Martin, 339

Kaltenbrunner, Gerd-Klaus, 338
Kamper, Dietmar, 328
Kant, Immanuel, 100, 123, 130, 141, 142, 149, 150, 152, 165, 166, 175, 181–83, 205, 251, 278, 320, 324
Kearney, Richard, 327, 336
Keller, Ulrich, 330
Kennedy, Judith M., 314
Kennedy, William J., 313
Kermode, Frank, 88, 89, 316, 317
Kierkegaard, Sören, 50, 314, 339, 341
Kittler, Friedrich, 323
Knox, T. M., 325, 341
Köhler, Oskar, xi, xiii
Köhler, Wolfgang, 140, 319
Korzybski, Alfred, 248
Kosík, Karel, xi
Kossert, Ruth, 328
Krautter, Konrad, 313
Krieger, Murray, 337, 339, 340
Kürsteiner, Agnes D., 312
Kutzner, Heinrich, 337

LaBerge, S., 316
Lacan, Jacques, 81, 172, 206, 207, 212, 305, 327
Lachmann, Renate, 316, 323, 328, 337
Lanham, Richard, 314, 315
Lauretis, Teresa de, 336
Lauth, Reinhard, 324
Leibniz, Gottfried W., 235, 335
Lem, Stanislaw, 336
Lenk, Elisabeth, 316, 326
Lerner, Laurence, 313
Leroi-Gourhan, André, xi

The Fictive and the Imaginary

Designed by Ann Walston

Composed by Connell-Zeko
in Berkeley Oldstyle Medium

Printed by Edwards Brothers, Inc.
on 50-lb. Glatfelter Natural

Made in the USA
Las Vegas, NV
25 January 2023

66256212R00207